Skills Tasks And Results Training

Second Edition

Your hospitality career **STARTs** *here!*

AHLEI
AMERICAN HOTEL & LODGING
EDUCATIONAL INSTITUTE

Disclaimer

ISBN: 978-0-86612-330-3

Printed in the USA

12 13 14 15 16 17 22 21 20 19 18 17

Acknowledgments

We would like to thank the following organizations and people for their contributions to helping this program achieve excellence:

Brenda Chrisman
Deputy Director
Workforce, One-Stop Career Center, Workforce Central Florida

Gene Coulson
Director, Office of Hospitality Education and Training
West Virginia Department of Education

Cheryl Learned
Director of Education
Massachusetts Lodging Association

Linda Tierney
Regional Director of Operations
JHM Hotels

Alan R. Tudor
Vocational Program Administrator
Workforce Development & Distance Learning
Florida Department of Corrections

Harry Gayes, CHI, CHT
Hospitality Instructor

The Legend of the Pineapple

The pineapple has been a symbol of hospitality since the days of the early American colonies. The legend began with the sea captains of New England, who sailed among the Caribbean Islands and returned to the colonies bearing their cargo of fruits, spices, and rum.

According to the legend, the captain would spear a pineapple on a fence post outside his home to let his friends know of his safe return from the sea. The pineapple was an invitation for them to visit, share his food and drink, and listen to tales of his voyage.

As the tradition grew, colonial innkeepers added the pineapple to their signs and advertisements, and bedposts carved in the shape of a pineapple were a common sight at inns across New England. The legend has continued to the present, and frequently one sees the pineapple symbol in hotels and restaurants to signal the presence of hospitality.

—Harry Nobles, Hospitality Consulting
www.nobleshospitalityconsulting.com

Contents

Unit

1

Hospitality Orientation

World of Hospitality

Sections

2

A bustling convention hotel in a big city, a timeshare resort on a sunny beach, a cozy ski lodge, a limited-service property on a busy interstate, a quaint bed-and-breakfast, a fun-filled cruise ship, even an elegant private club—these are just some of the many destinations in the world of lodging.

Whatever your interests and whatever your goals, the lodging industry has a destination and a career to fit your plans. There are more than 200 different careers in hospitality.

For instance:

Do you like interacting with people? Are you detail-oriented? Are you good on the phone? You might enjoy working in a hotel's front office, where you'll impress guests with your ability to deliver great service.

Are you persuasive? Do you like to find out what others want and then find a way to make it happen? You might find a career in sales and marketing, letting people know how terrific your property is, and bringing in new business.

Are you creative in the kitchen? Does everyone turn to you to plan the perfect party? Do you know how to turn ordinary ingredients into a special dish? Maybe a career in food and beverage is down the road for you.

Are you most comfortable with a wrench in your hands? Can you fix mechanical problems? Do you get satisfaction from keeping things running smoothly? A hotel's maintenance and engineering department may be the place for you.

Do you like working with numbers? Are you organized? Do you make careful decisions and manage money well? You might be happiest working in hospitality accounting where you'll keep track of revenue and keep the property within its budget.

Today's lodging industry is looking for people who enjoy variety, challenges, and above all, people. Whatever your interests, there's a lodging career that's just right for you.

1.1   The World of Hospitality

AFTER SUCCESSFULLY COMPLETING THIS SECTION, YOU WILL BE ABLE TO:

♦ Describe the food service industry.

♦ Identify the different types of clubs in the private club industry.

♦ Explain how the meetings industry functions.

♦ Describe the cruise line industry.

♦ Identify spa services and the different types of spas.

What is the **hospitality industry**? There are many different answers to this question. Some view the hospitality industry as comprising four sectors: lodging, food, entertainment, and travel. However, usually the hospitality industry is viewed as mainly lodging and food service businesses.

The U.S. hospitality industry has grown tremendously in recent decades. Some of the reasons for this growth are a generally higher standard of living among Americans, increased leisure time, increased longevity as a result of medical advances, the growth in education, and the greater opportunities available in a rapidly developing society.

The Food Service Industry

Food service is a huge industry. Career opportunities abound throughout the various segments. Compared to other industries, the food service industry offers unmatched opportunities for entrepre-neurship. Restaurant entrepreneurs have followed various paths to success. Some have created entire restaurant chains; others have nourished a single restaurant to perfection.

The restaurant industry runs the gamut from gourmet restaurants to hot dog stands. The restaurant industry is truly an equal opportunity employer. It employs more minority managers than any other industry.

Someone entering the food service field might work for a small, independent operator who runs a fine-dining restaurant, pizza parlor, or ice cream stand. Another career track might begin in the management training program of a large corporation. There are many opportunities in the quick-service field. Airline meals are supplied by in-flight catering operators. Many big banks, insurance companies, and adver-tising agencies have executive dining rooms run by professional food service managers. Contract food companies place future managers in executive or employee dining facilities; in schools, colleges, and universities; and at tourist attractions.

The restaurant industry includes many different types of facilities and markets. Some of the most common segments are:

- Eating and drinking places

- Lodging operations

- Transportation market

- Recreational market

- Business and industry market

- Educational market

- Health care market

- Retail market

- Corrections food service

- Military food service

- Contractors

Club Management

Private clubs are gathering places for members only. They bring together people of like interests. Those interests could be recreational, social, or professional.

There are two basic types of clubs: city clubs and country clubs. **City clubs** can be categorized as athletic, dining, professional, social, or university.

Athletic clubs are often quite large, sometimes occupying entire downtown buildings, and may include lodging and dining facilities as well as gymnasiums, swimming pools, and courts for squash, handball, and racquetball.

Dining clubs are generally found in office buildings. Many of these clubs are open only for lunch.

Social clubs were originally modeled after men's social clubs in England. Although most social clubs do not discriminate on the basis of sex, race, or religion, some try to limit their membership to persons of the same social and economic background.

University clubs are private clubs for university graduates. Some university clubs have dining and meeting rooms, guest-rooms, and extensive libraries and recreational facilities.

The largest type of private club is the **country club**. Country clubs are primarily recreational and social facilities for individuals and families who live nearby. Since country clubs need a great deal of land for their golf course(s) and other facilities, they are usually in suburban or rural locales.

Other kinds of clubs include yacht clubs, fraternal clubs, and military clubs.

Most private clubs are equity clubs or corporate or developer clubs. **Equity clubs** are owned by a group of founder-members and are generally non-profit, since they are formed not for money-making purposes but only for the enjoyment of their members. **Corporate** or **developer clubs** are for-profit clubs owned by individuals or companies that sell memberships in the clubs.

A club's organization depends on whether it is an equity or a corporate or developer club. The **club manager** is the hired professional responsible for guiding all elements of a club's operation.

The bulk of club revenue is derived from club members. These revenues fall into the following classifications:

- Membership dues

- Initiation fees

- Assessments

- Sports activities fees

- Food and beverage sales

Membership dues are the cost to a member for the exclusivity of the club. It is common for city and country clubs to have several different types of member-ships. A city club might have different membership dues for resident, suburban, and nonresident members, reflecting the location of the member's residence in relation to the location of the club. Country clubs tend to use a different type of dues structure, based on use of recreational facilities, a member's age, and other factors. In addition to dues, clubs generally charge initiation fees and, in some cases, special assessments.

Next to dues, food and beverage sales are the major source of club revenue. Other sources of revenue include guestroom sales (for city clubs), visitors' fees, and service charges on food and beverage sales. A club's payroll is its largest expense.

The Meetings Industry

A **meeting** is any group of people who gather together for a specific purpose. A meeting can consist of a few people in a conference room. In contrast, a **convention** might have 100,000 delegates at a major convention center using a dozen or more hotels in a large city.

Meetings are held by associations, corporations, and governments. There are also trade shows or expositions that may be a part of or independent from a meeting or convention.

Four kinds of **trade shows** are:

- Industrial shows
- Wholesale and retail shows
- Professional or scientific exhibitions
- Public or consumer shows

Convention and visitors bureaus are nonprofit organizations that market the des-tinations in which they are located. Governments may play a similar role.

Almost any kind of facility can be used to hold a meeting. Meetings have been held at amusement parks, football stadiums, and castles. However, most meetings are held in hotels and motels. Conference centers, universities, and cruise ships also serve as popular meeting venues.

Meeting planners may hold a variety of job titles within an organization. Few do it full time. Persons who are actively engaged in meeting planning can be found in associations, corporations, governments, and travel agencies. There are also association management companies and independent meeting planners.

Meeting planners are involved in everything from establishing meeting objectives and selecting sites to budgeting, selecting guest speakers, and booking entertainment. The best meeting planners are superb negotiators and diplomats.

Many of the travel and tourism industry careers associated with serving the meetings market are found in hotels. Hotel sales managers and their staffs, convention service managers, and catering managers all play key roles.

Convention and visitors bureaus employ marketing staffs to handle tourism develop-ment and sell their destinations to meeting planners. Tourism departments, which are usually branches of governments, do the same but often on a global scale.

Finally, there is an entire category of professionals who do nothing but design, promote, and manage exhibits and trade shows. Some exhibit design work is done by full-service exhibit houses, some by custom designers. There are also a number of advertising agencies that are skilled in helping their clients design and build exhibits. There are manufacturers who produce off-the-shelf exhibits that come in modular form and can be customized to fit any exhibit situation. All of these firms have career opportunities for people who want to sell, design, and produce exhibits.

Cruise Lines

More than 175 cruise ships call at more than 32 U.S. ports. These ships are floating vacation resorts—some carrying as many as 3,600 passengers and costing $800 million or more. In North America, they generate revenues of $13 billion annually.

Modern cruising was born in the 1960s and 1970s with the formation of Norwegian Caribbean Line, Royal Caribbean Cruise Lines, Princess Cruise Lines, and Carnival Cruise Lines. Carnival focused on the cruise ships themselves as the center of the cruise vacation experience, creating a perception of a fun vacation for the masses.

Cruise lines are divided into four market segments:

- Contemporary/value
- Premium
- Luxury
- Specialty lines

Today's cruise ships are floating vacation resorts, and in some ways they are very similar to hotels in how they are organized. At the top is the **captain**, who is responsible for the ship's operation and the safety of all those onboard. Three people typically report directly to the captain: the chief officer, the chief engineer, and the hotel manager. The hotel manager is in charge of the ship's hotel division and oversees a purser, food and beverage manager, chief housekeeper, cruise director, physician, and sometimes the heads of other departments and concessions. Besides being ultimately responsible for food and beverage services and cabin services, the hotel manager may also be responsible for medical care, entertainment, and shore excursions.

The **purser** is the ship's banker, information officer, human resources director, and complaint handler. The purser is second in command of the hotel division.

The food and beverage manager oversees the assistant food and beverage manager, executive chef, maitre d', bar manager and provision master. Because of safety and sanitation requirements—as well as passenger expectations—food and beverage operations on cruise ships are highly disciplined operations. Beverages are the single largest source of onboard revenue on every major cruise ship.

The chief housekeeper is responsible for the cleaning and general maintenance of all cabins and interior areas of the ship. The housekeeping department also takes care of passenger laundry and dry cleaning, as well as cleaning all cabin linens, table linens, towels, and the crew's uniforms. The busiest day for the housekeeping department is **turnaround day**, when the ship finishes a cruise and starts another.

The **cruise director**'s staff directs all guest activities and includes entertainers, musicians, and children's counselors. They also sell and coordinate shore excursions and prepare the daily activity calendar.

Modern cruise lines pay great attention to medical care. All ships carry at least one physician and a nurse. The physician typically has a state-of-the-art medical center onboard with which to treat patients. A devotion to accessibility makes cruise ships attractive vacations for people with disabilities and older persons.

Cruise ships carefully orchestrate the entire cruise experience. Employees are highly trained and treated with respect. Very little is left to chance. Guest comments are taken seriously and acted upon almost immediately. These methods produce high satisfaction and repeat business.

Spas

The **spa industry** is a rapidly growing segment of hospitality. Traditional mineral and hot spring spas have been around for centuries. The towns with hot springs became popular vacation and holiday destinations.

Today this is still true, but modern spas offer a wide variety of services to help people relax and feel healthier. Modern spas cater to people who want to lose weight, get in shape, relax, or be pampered. Spa services include:

- Body treatment
- Skin care
- Hydrotherapy/water treatment
- Massage therapies
- Body rubs
- Facials
- Esthetic care/treatment
- Medical treatment
- Health, fitness, and wellness
- Herbal treatments
- Mud treatments
- Stone therapy

While the exact definition of a spa is elusive, there are seven general categories, according to the International Spa Association (ISPA). They are:

- **Club spa:** A spa focused on fitness which offers a variety of professional services on a day-use basis.

- **Cruise ship spa:** A spa aboard a cruise ship that offers professional services, fitness and wellness activities, and spa cuisine menu choices.

- **Day spa:** A spa that offers professional services on a day-use basis.

- **Destination spa:** A spa that provides guests with lifestyle improvement and health enhancement through professional services, physical fitness, educational programming, and on-site accommodations. Spa cuisine is served exclusively.

- **Medical spa:** Individuals, solo practices, groups, and institutions comprised of medical and spa professionals who provide health and wellness care while combining spa services and conventional and complementary therapies and treatments.

- **Mineral springs spa:** A spa offering a source of natural mineral, thermal, or seawater used in hydrotherapy treatments.

- **Resort/hotel spa:** A spa that is within a resort or hotel. It provides professional spa services, fitness and wellness activities, and spa cuisine menu choices.

Day spas are the largest segment of the industry with resort hotels coming in second. Spas experienced tremendous growth in the 80s and 90s and by the first decade of the new century were considered as necessary as pools and fitness rooms to upscale lodging properties.

The **spa director** is typically the employee in charge of the spa. Other important positions in a spa are estheticians, massage therapists, stylists, and front desk receptionists.

Apply Your Learning 1.1

Please write all answers on a separate sheet of paper.

1. Which industry employs more minority managers than any other industry?
2. What are five segments of the restaurant industry?
3. What is the difference between an equity club and a developer club?
4. Who is the professional responsible for guiding all elements of a club's operation?
5. What are four types of trade shows?
6. What does a purser on a cruise ship do?
7. What sort of services do spas offer?

1.2   The Lodging Industry

AFTER SUCCESSFULLY COMPLETING THIS SECTION, YOU WILL BE ABLE TO:

♦   Identify what type of guests stay at hotels.

♦   List the different categories hotels are sorted into

♦   Explain how hotels are owned and operated.

Lodging, Tourism, and the Economy

The lodging industry is undergoing many changes. The demand for hotels is affected as the economic fortunes of countries, regions, and cities rise and fall. Each year, companies and hotels change ownership and new companies and brands enter the marketplace.

The lodging industry is a global industry with most of the major hotel companies having properties in multiple countries.

In the lodging industry alone, there are more than 1.8 million employees who are paid $177 billion in wages and salaries. The lodging industry supports another 7.5 million jobs. Exhibit 1 paints a statistical picture of the lodging industry.

Hotel Guests

Lodging properties exist to provide guests with a place to stay—either overnight or for a meeting. They attract many types of guests. Groups of guests with similar characteristics are considered a **market**. Some of the markets for the hotel industry are:

•   Corporate individuals

•   Corporate groups

•   Convention and association groups

•   Leisure travelers

•   Long-term stay/relocation guests

•   Airline-related guests

Exhibit 1
2007 At-a-Glance Statistical Figures:

•   47,135 properties*

•   4,389,443 guestrooms

• $133.4 billion in sales

• $61.93 revenue per available room (RevPAR)

•   63.3% average occupancy rate

* Based on properties with 15 or more rooms

- Government and military travelers

- Regional getaway guests

Exhibit 2 paints a portrait of the "typical" lodging consumer.

Guest mix refers to the variety or mixture of guests who stay at a hotel. For example, a hotel's guest mix might consist of 60 percent individual business travelers, 20 percent group business travelers, and 20 percent leisure travelers. Successful hotels carefully manage group mix.

Hotels have to be careful in how they market the hotel since some kinds of guests do not mix well together. Luxury hotels often control their mix very carefully, only allowing groups on weekends and then setting up special facilities for registration and dining so that the groups won't interfere with the regular guests.

Hotel Categories

Hotels often get put into different **categories** depending on the guests they serve, the size of their facility, ownership, price, location, and other factors.

Categories based on location are usually:

- Downtown/center-city

- Resort

- Suburban

- Highway

- Airport

Downtown hotels are usually full-service facilities. They often have restaurants, a coffee shop, a cocktail lounge, room service, laundry and valet services, a business center, a newsstand and gift shop, and a health club. Most of the guests are business travelers—

Exhibit 2
The Typical Lodging Customer

56% are on vacation

44% are transient business travelers

The typical business room night is generated by a male (65%), age 35–54 (50%), employed in a professional or managerial position (44%), earning an average yearly household income of $85,900. Typically, these guests travel alone (56%), make reservations (90%), and pay $112 per room night.

The typical leisure room night is generated by two adults (42%), ages 35–54 (41%), earning an average yearly household income of $77,102. The typical leisure traveler also travels by auto (77%), makes reservations (86%), and pays $103 per room night.

For a hotel stay, 35 percent of all business travelers spend one night, 26 percent spend two nights, and 39 percent spend three or more nights.

Of leisure travelers, 42 percent spend one night, 30 percent spend two nights, and 28 percent spend three or more nights.

either corporate individuals or convention guests. Generally speaking, downtown hotels have the highest average room rate of all the non-resort hotel categories.

Resort hotels are usually found in places where people like to travel because of its weather, beauty, attractions, or history. They are often found near water or in the mountains. They often have elaborately landscaped grounds with hiking trails, gardens, and extensive sports facilities. Guests are almost always leisure and vacation travelers.

Suburban hotels cropped up as suburbs were built after World War II. Corporations that didn't want to pay high downtown rents, began building where there was more reasonably priced land. Land developers realized there was a need for building new hotels near the suburbs. These hotels often had large space for parking and amenities were more affordable. While suburban hotels are often hard to distinguish from other types of hotels, they usually share the following characteristics:

- They are smaller than downtown hotels. They usually have between 250 to 500 rooms and limited banquet facilities.

- They are usually chain owned and operated.

- Their main revenue source is business, meeting, and convention attendees and individual business travelers.

- They often have excellent restaurants that rely on local residents.

- Many of them have sports and health facilities, including swimming pools.

- They often host weddings, family events, and weekly meetings of major service clubs.

Highway hotels are usually built along major roads. They began as a row of cabins with access to the outside. Now they often offer the same facilities as downtown hotels with a few distinct features. Most feature a large sign that can be seen from the highway and plentiful parking space. The atmosphere is usually informal. They are often away from urban centers and have a lower number of employees per room than suburban or downtown hotels. They have

fewer employees because they generally provide fewer services.

Airport hotels are hotels built near airports. Most of them are affiliated with chains and have high occupancy during the week when there are a lot of business travelers. Airport hotels have to respond to sudden high demand when flights are canceled or weather is bad. Most airport hotel guests stay only a single night.

Another way of categorizing hotels is by the prices they charge and the services they offer. These categories are typically called:

- Limited-service (including economy and budget). **Limited-service** hotels pursue the low-price consumer market. They are sometimes budget properties, though not always. They have lower rates and usually provide only a guestroom, though some also offer limited continental breakfasts.

- Mid-price (including full-service and limited-service). **Mid-price hotels** are attractive to consumers who want something more than the economy/budget segment, but can't afford the first-class hotels. They usually offer some food and beverage services and may also have some other services for guests.

- First-class/Luxury. At the top of the price scale are **first-class** or **luxury hotels**. These hotels offer the best available in service with beautifully decorated rooms. Their guests are usually wealthy leisure travelers or business individuals.

Other property types within the lodging industry include:

- All-suite hotels

- Conference centers

- Vacation ownership
- Condominium hotels
- Seniors housing

Hotel Ownership

Hotels are also broken into categories according to their ownership. There are six ways hotels can be owned and operated:

- Independently owned and operated.
- Independently owned and leased to an operator.
- Owned by a single entity or group that has hired a hotel management company to operate the property.
- Owned and operated by a chain.
- Owned by an independent investor or group and operated by a chain.
- Owned by an individual or group and operated as a franchise of a chain. The franchise holder may be an individual or a management company.

An **independent hotel** is not connected with any established hotel company and is owned by an individual or group of investors. A **management company** contracts with hotel owners to operate their hotels. The management company is usually paid by a combination of fees plus a share of revenue and profit. A **hotel chain** is a group of affiliated hotels.

A **franchise** is the authorization granted by a hotel chain to an individual hotel to use the chain's trademark, operating systems, and reservation system in exchange for a percentage of the hotel's revenue plus certain other fees. A **franchisor** is the party granting the franchise. A **franchisee** is the party granted the franchise.

Apply Your Learning 1.2

Please write all answers on a separate sheet of paper.

1. What is one of the fastest growing industries in the world?
2. What is guest mix?
3. What is the difference between a downtown hotel and a resort hotel?
4. What are the three categories of hotels based on price?
5. What is a group of affiliated hotels?

1.3   Inside a Hotel

AFTER SUCCESSFULLY COMPLETING THIS SECTION, YOU WILL BE ABLE TO:

♦ Describe how a hotel is organized.

♦ Describe the rooms division.

♦ Describe the food and beverage division.

♦ Explain the mission of the marketing division.

♦ Identify the goals of the engineering division.

♦ List the responsibilities of the accounting division.

♦ Explain the functions of the human resources and security divisions.

Hotels are organized into **functional areas** or divisions based on the services the hotel provides. All hotels have a rooms division to manage guestrooms. If the hotel operates a restaurant, it probably has a food and beverage division. Within each division are specialized functions.

Divisions in a hotel are often categorized as revenue centers or cost centers. **Revenue centers** generate income for the hotel through the sale of services or products to guests. **Cost centers**, also known as support centers, do not generate revenue directly. Instead, they support the proper functioning of revenue centers.

Exhibit 1 shows how divisions and departments are separated into revenue and cost centers.

Rooms Division

In most hotels, the **rooms division** is the major division and the central reason for the lodging property to exist. (The exception to this are casino hotels.) Guestroom rentals are almost always the single largest source of revenue for a lodging property. They also generate the most profit.

More information about the rooms division can be found in Chapter 5.

Food and Beverage Division

In a few hotels (most often resorts and convention properties with extensive banquet sales), the **food and beverage division** may produce the same or even more revenue than the rooms division. Whether the division is large or small, though, the food and beverage facilities are important to the reputation and profitability of the hotel. The quality of the food and beverage department may make a difference in whether a guest returns to a property.

More information about the food and beverage division is in Chapter 14.

**Exhibit 1
Revenue and Cost Centers**

Revenue Centers	Cost Centers
Rooms	Marketing
Food and beverage	Engineering
Telecommunications	Accounting
Concessions, rentals, commissions	Human resources
Fitness, recreation facilities	Security

Marketing Division

The mission of a hotel's **marketing division** is to:

- Identify prospective guests for the hotel

- Shape the products and services of the hotel as much as possible to meet the needs of those prospects

- Persuade prospects to become guests

The marketing division keeps rooms occupied at the right price and with the right mix of guests. It accomplishes this by performing many of the following activities:

- Contacting groups and individuals

- Advertising in print and on radio, television, and the Internet

- Creating direct mail and public relations campaigns

- Participating in trade shows

- Visiting travel agents

- Arranging tours

- Participating in community activities that raise awareness of the hotel

Positions in the marketing division include:

- Director of marketing and sales

- Sales manager

- Director of advertising and public relations

- Convention sales manager

- Tour and travel salespeople

- National accounts salespeople

- Group salespeople

Engineering Division

Taking care of the hotel's physical plant and controlling energy costs are the responsibilities of the **engineering division**. The physical upkeep of the building, furniture, fixtures, and equipment is essential to:

- Slow a hotel's physical deterioration

- Preserve the original hotel image

- Keep revenue-producing areas in operation

- Keep the property comfortable

- Keep the property safe

- Create savings by keeping repairs and equipment to a minimum

The engineering department is also responsible for heating and air-conditioning systems, and systems that deliver electricity, steam, and water to the property.

Several types of technicians may be employed: electricians, plumbers, carpenters, painters, refrigeration and air-conditioning engineers, and others. The division is headed by a chief engineer. In small hotels, one all-purpose engineer may perform all engineering functions or subcontract work as needed. In a large hotel, the chief engineer may be called a plant manager.

Accounting Division

A hotel's **accounting division** tracks the business transactions that occur in the hotel. Financial management is perhaps the most appropriate description of what the accounting division does.

The responsibilities of the accounting division include:

- Forecasting and budgeting

- Managing what the hotel owns and what money is due from guests

- Controlling cash

- Controlling costs in all areas of the hotel

- Purchasing, receiving, storing, and issuing operating and capital inventory

- Keeping records, preparing financial statements and daily operating reports, and interpreting these statements and reports for management

To accomplish these tasks, the head of accounting—the controller—relies on a staff of auditors, cashiers, accountants, and other accounting employees.

Human Resources Division

Good managers develop people. The **human resources division** concerns itself with the whole equation of people and productivity—as well as salaries, wages, and benefits. Human resources managers recruit, hire, orient, train, evaluate, motivate, reward, discipline, develop, promote, and communicate with all the employees of the hotel.

Security Division

The security of guests, employees, personal property, and the hotel itself is an overriding concern for today's hotel managers. In the past, most security precautions concentrated on preventing theft from guests and the hotel. However, today such violent crimes as murder and rape and even terrorism have become a problem for hotels.

The head of the **security division** may be called the chief of security. This person usually has an extensive background in law enforcement. In smaller hotels, security may be part of the front office. Those involved in security should have specialized training in civil and criminal law.

Apply Your Learning 1.3

Please write all answers on a separate sheet of paper.

1. What is the difference between a cost center and a revenue center?

2. What is almost always the single largest source of revenue for a property?

3. Why is the food and beverage division important in a hotel?

4. What are two activities that most hotel marketing departments perform?

5. Which division takes care of the hotel's physical plant and controls energy costs?

6. What is the title of the person in charge of accounting?

7. What sort of background does a chief of security usually need?

1.4 Environmentalism

AFTER SUCCESSFULLY COMPLETING THIS SECTION, YOU WILL BE ABLE TO:

♦ List ways in which a property can save energy and water and reduce waste.

♦ Describe the triple benefits properties receive from going green.

♦ Define the concept of "sustainability."

Environmental Issues

Many lodging properties are making an effort to protect the environment. They're creating environmental plans to make the property more environmentally friendly, and save it money through the better use of environmental resources such as energy and water.

In general, a lodging property's environmental plan can focus on the following areas:

• Energy management and conservation. This involves improving energy efficiency, reducing the operating hours of energy-using equipment and machinery, reducing the energy load being supplied to equipment and machinery, recovering and reusing waste energy, and using less costly energy sources.

• Waste management. This takes the form of an aggressive recycling program for solid wastes such as paper, aluminum, and plastics.

• Water management. Focusing both on fresh water and wastewater, water management involves limiting or reducing the amount of fresh water used on a lodging property and properly treating and disposing of wastewater.

• Hazardous substances. Many chemicals are necessary to clean, sanitize, or repair lodging areas. Properties try to reduce the use of hazardous materials or use chemicals that are more environmentally friendly.

There are several ways properties can help the environment. Here are just a few:

• Replacing incandescent lamps with fluorescent lamps results in less energy use and longer life for light bulbs.

• Incorporating a recycling plan into solid waste removal will reap positive environmental results.

• Limiting energy usage during non-peak hours or turning equipment off when not in use will enable the property to conserve energy and save money.

Being environmentally responsible can be a goal of every lodging property, no matter the size. Maintaining a lodging operation that is sensitive to the environment will actually aid in the ultimate goal of satisfying guests.

Triple Bottom Line

Lodging properties have been one of the leaders in the green movement among businesses. Being environmentally conscious—or "green"—has had many benefits to the hospitality industry. They've begun to refer to those benefits as the **triple bottom line.**

The triple bottom line includes:

1. Economic benefits
2. Environmental benefits
3. Social benefits

Economic benefits. Taking actions to green the property has helped properties to be more profitable. Properties have reaped millions of dollars in cost savings. Economic benefits have included:

- Energy savings
- Waste reduction and lower disposal costs
- Eligibility for government incentives
- Reduced labor costs
- Reduced employee absenteeism
- Increased productivity

Environmental benefits. These include saving limited resources. The actions that the hospitality industry takes to conserve water, save energy, reduce waste, and purify the air are making the world a healthier place to live. They reduce pollution and help save natural habitats.

Social benefits. Having green policies makes a property more attractive to its guests and to groups calling for environmental accountability. Social benefits to properties include:

- Creating a sense of pride in the community
- Increasing the morale and health of employees
- Enhancing a property's image
- Providing a competitive edge in the industry
- Establishing the property as an environmental leader
- Creating a deeper level of trust in guests, suppliers, and partners

Sustainability

The concept of **sustainability** is a way of doing business that says a company shouldn't take more than it gives back. It should not sacrifice tomorrow for today's needs.

Properties are looking at six ways to "go green":

- Policy and framework
- Staff training and awareness
- Environmental management
- Purchasing
- People and communities
- Destination protection

Apply Your Learning 1.4

Please write all answers on a separate sheet of paper.

1. List three things hospitality employees can do to help with a property's environmental plan.

2. What is an economic benefit to being a green property?

3. What is an environmental benefit to being a green property?

4. What is a social benefit to being a green property?

5. What does sustainability mean?

Quick Hits

Chapter 1

SECTION 1.1—THE WORLD OF HOSPITALITY

- The hospitality industry can include lodging, food service, entertainment, and travel.

- The restaurant industry includes everything from gourmet restaurants to hot dog stands.

- Private clubs include country clubs and city clubs. City clubs include athletic clubs, dining clubs, social clubs, and university clubs.

- Equity clubs are owned by members and are usually non-profit. Corporate clubs are for-profit and sell memberships.

- The meeting industry includes all the businesses who help put on meetings, conventions, and trade shows. Meeting planners help establish meeting objectives and make sure they are successfully met.

- Cruise line segments include contemporary, premium, luxury, and specialty lines. The captain is in charge of the entire ship.

- The spa industry is rapidly growing and offers a wide variety of services to people who want to relax, get in shape, or be pampered. There are seven general categories of spas.

SECTION 1.2—THE LODGING INDUSTRY

- Groups of guests with similar characteristics are considered a market. Guest mix refers to the variety or mixture of guests who stay at a hotel.

- Hotels are usually categorized by location, price, guests, or ownership.

- Hotel categories based on location include downtown, resort, suburban, highway, and airport.

- Hotel categories based on price are limited service, mid-price, and first class.

- There are six different ways a hotel is categorized by ownership and operation. These run the gamut from independent to management companies to franchises.

SECTION 1.3—INSIDE A HOTEL

- Hotels are organized into functional areas or divisions based on services. These divisions are often categorized as revenue or cost centers.

- The rooms division is the major division of most hotels.

- The food and beverage division can make a difference in whether a guest returns to a hotel.

- The marketing division identifies prospective guests for the hotel, shapes the products and services of the hotel to meet guest needs, and then persuades prospects to become guests.

- The engineering division takes care of the hotel's physical plant and controls energy costs.

- The accounting division tracks the business transactions that occur in the hotel.

- The human resources division manages people and productivity.

- The security division helps protect the security of guests, employees, personal property, and the hotel itself.

SECTION 1.4—ENVIRONMENTALISM

- Hospitality employees have an important role in a lodging property's environmental plan.

- The triple bottom line refers to the economic, environmental, and social benefits to having green policies.

- Sustainability is a concept that means businesses don't take more than they give back.

Guest Service

Sections

Delivering quality service means creating a memorable experience for every guest by:

- Understanding and anticipating each guest's wants and needs
- Meeting and exceeding each guest's wants and needs
- Helping co-workers meet and exceed each guest's wants and needs

If it weren't for guests, there would be no jobs for anyone in the hospitality industry. Guests come to a property for many different reasons. Whatever the reason, guests expect certain things from lodging employees. Guests' expectations and the skills employees need to meet them include the following:

Expectation: Professional Appearance

- Maintain a neat, well-groomed appearance.
- Wear a clean, proper uniform.
- Wear a name tag.

Expectation: Friendliness

- Smile.
- Greet guests and co-workers promptly and happily.
- Look guests and co-workers in the eye.

Expectation: Courtesy

- Give guests and co-workers full attention.
- Treat guests and co-workers with respect.
- Call guests and co-workers by name.

Expectation: Concern

- Imagine how guests and co-workers see a situation.
- Listen with empathy.
- Show sensitivity to guests' and co-workers' feelings.

Expectation: Flexibility

- Treat each guest and co-worker as an individual.
- Welcome each guest as a new opportunity to provide great service.
- Offer creative solutions to meet guests' and co-workers' needs.

2.1   What is Guest Service?

AFTER SUCCESSFULLY COMPLETING THIS SECTION, YOU WILL BE ABLE TO:

♦ Explain the importance of guest service to the hospitality industry.

♦ Define guest service.

♦ Explain why people staying at lodging properties are called guests.

♦ Identify the benefits of guest service.

Guest Service in the Hospitality Industry

The travel and tourism industry is continually growing. As the business of hospitality gets more competitive, providing exceptional guest service has evolved from a competitive advantage to a basic necessity for business survival. Guests don't want to be where they are not appreciated and catered to. Many guests—especially families—spend months saving for and planning their vacations. Once these vacations begin, they want everything to go right. This includes receiving quick and efficient service, with a smile! When great guest service is provided, guest expectations are usually exceeded. The guest service provided, or not provided, can mean the difference between a forgettable or unforgettable lodging experience.

Nearly every employee at a lodging property has opportunities to display guest service. From the reservationist who takes guests' reservations to a bell services attendant who wishes them a fond farewell, everyone in a lodging operation can have an effect on a guest's stay.

Service could be "work done for someone," while guest service could be "any action taken or effort made on the guest's behalf." But based on guest expectations, perhaps the best definition of **guest service** is "meeting any and all guests' needs in the way that they want and expect them to be met."

In hospitality, the consumers who stay at hotels are called **guests** instead of customers, patrons, etc., for a reason. Lodging properties want guests to feel as if they have been invited into someone else's home, treated as though they were special, and provided with all the amenities and services that they would expect at home. The difference is, these guests are paying for this treatment; all the more reason that they should get their money's worth! In fact, they expect more from a lodging property because they usually pay more for a guestroom than for a night's share of their home rent or mortgage payment.

These expectations based on the cost or perceived value of a lodging stay—and the guest service that is expected—is only part of the reason why guest service is so crucial. It isn't hard to see why many lodging properties now consider their employees as part of the product they offer to guests. This "product" must be high quality and worth the cost.

The "Business" of Guests

Guests are at the center of everything lodging employees do at a lodging property. Without guests, there would be no need for the front desk, housekeeping, or room service departments, or even for the property itself. So, guests and their traveling needs are the reason for the hospitality business. Guests are people just like anyone else; they have special needs, wants, expectations, and feelings. Even though guests are individuals with special needs and wants, they have one thing in common: they want good, polite, and swift service. Guests expect at least the comfort, ease, and conveniences they have at home. There's an old saying in the world of hospitality that goes something like this: "If you want to sell what the guest buys, you must see the world through the guest's eyes."

What guests will want to buy is guest service that lasts throughout their stay. This means that the lodging employees that guests interact with in each stage of the guest cycle should show the same level of guest service. Guests don't want to be greeted warmly by a bell services attendant during their arrival stage only to have the room service attendant behave rudely during the occupancy stage. Guests who *don't* receive high quality guest service at a lodging property will likely let others know about it. But guests who receive great guest service are *just as likely* to tell others about it. So, word of mouth can be to a property's advantage or disadvantage depending on their level of guest service.

Benefits of Guest Service

It cannot be stated frequently enough or clearly enough that providing guest service to lodging guests benefits *everyone*. Everyone wins!

Guests arriving, whether they are on a family vacation, a weekend getaway, or business travel, will have specific expectations, concerns, and emotions. By providing quality guest service, lodging employees have the opportunity, the *privilege*, to make the guests' day—and stay—enjoyable and memorable.

The lodging property benefits from having repeat guests, a great reputation, and a full house!

Finally, lodging employees, each individual employee and all of his or her co-workers, have their jobs made easier when all employees practice great guest service. Professional lodging employees practicing great guest service are the best asset a lodging property can have. Often lodging properties reward these employees with compliments, rewards, incentives, great job reviews, and even pay increases.

Apply Your Learning 2.1

Please write all answers on a separate sheet of paper.

1. From a business standpoint, how is guest service now viewed by the lodging industry?

2. List two ways that guest service could be defined.

3. Why are people staying at lodging properties referred to as guests?

4. List the benefits of guest service to the guest, the property, and to lodging employees.

2.2 Exemplary Guest Service

AFTER SUCCESSFULLY COMPLETING THIS SECTION, YOU WILL BE ABLE TO:

♦ Explain the difference between "guest service" and "exemplary guest service."

♦ Describe the importance of "spirit" when providing guest service.

♦ Summarize the importance of viewing guest service from the guest's perspective.

♦ Describe how lodging employees separate their private lives from their work.

Spirit

If guest service were defined simply, such as "work done for guests," or even "providing guests with the services provided by the hotel during their stay," then it would be easy for every lodging employee to perform it. But guest service means so much more. It isn't just what lodging employees do or provide for a guest, it is *how* they do it. A guest who receives extra towels promptly from a room attendant who simply hands them over and walks away will still make use of the extra towels. However, a guest who receives the same towels from a room attendant who says with a smile, "Here are your towels ma'am. Please let us know if we can do anything else for you. Enjoy the rest of your stay," will be left very satisfied. This is the difference between just serving guests and giving them exemplary guest service.

Exemplary means "worthy of imitation; a model of behavior." **Exemplary guest service** is guest service, plus! It is not only giving guests the service they expect, it is giving them service that *exceeds* their expectations. All lodging employees should have the goal of always providing exemplary guest service.

Performing guest service with extra spirit is the key to exemplary guest service. **Spirit** is a lodging employee's positive attitude or feeling of pride; it is a sense of belonging that the employee feels with guests and co-workers. It is the key to the success of the entire hospitality industry. A lodging employee who has the "spirit of hospitality" has a desire to please and satisfy guests by providing them with good memories to take home. A lodging employee's attitude, or spirit, is especially important in the hospitality industry because the guest is paying to have a pleasant experience. The reward for this good attitude and spirit is the respect of co-workers and, more importantly, the positive reactions and responses from guests.

Lodging employees seeking to provide exemplary guest service take their jobs seriously. It requires extra effort, pride in their work and their property, a sense of professionalism, cooperation with co-workers and management, and a desire to learn and improve. In fact, these types of lodging employees consider hospitality, and by extension, guest service a career, not a job.

The Guest's Perspective

Exemplary guest service means that employees are ready at all times to help the guest and to contribute to the enjoyment of the guest's visit. Work done well with the guest in mind is sure to make a good impression. One of the best ways to meet or exceed guest expectations is to see things from the guest's point of view.

Lodging employees should be aware of how they look from the guest's perspective, how their tone of voice sounds, and how the quality of their work appears to others. They should ask themselves, "How does the guest see me?" A big part of working in the hospitality industry is being sensitive to and caring about how employees respond to guests and how they respond in kind.

Guest service should always be measured from the guests' perspective. It is the guest's expectations that count. For instance, lodging employees should never assume that just because they feel they are giving great guest service then it must be so. It is the *guests'* expectations of the quality of the service that count!

What lodging employees say and do are important, but what they don't say and do are equally important. For instance, if a guest looks as though she needs help but the lodging employees do nothing, she will likely form a negative opinion of the property's service.

Being insensitive to the guest's needs or having a bad attitude toward work are two ways in which an employee can give a guest a negative impression of the property. Even one negative experience can seriously alter the guest's impression of the property and memory of the visit.

Lodging Employees are People Too!

Lodging employees are more than just people who perform tasks at work. They are individuals with goals, beliefs, interests, concerns, and so on. These qualities make each lodging employee special.

Sometimes lodging employees' outside interests, family, friends, and activities have little to do with the work they perform. At times, lodging employees' private lives can affect their work because things that happen off the job can make them happy or sad, eager or worried, etc. This can affect the way they treat guests.

It is important that lodging employees keep personal problems from affecting the quality of their work. If they are upset when they get to work, they should take a few minutes to relax, should think before acting or speaking, and should try to stay positive. Successful lodging employees realize that it is up to them to make a guest's stay pleasant. A positive attitude will convey that individual courtesy, respect, and concern that guests truly want and expect.

If lodging employees are secure and comfortable in their jobs, it can and should have a positive, rewarding effect on their lives. A positive approach toward work can make lodging employees' jobs more enjoyable and can affect their life in a positive way. A good attitude, sense of pride in work, and sense of belonging bring job satisfaction.

Apply Your Learning 2.2

Please write all answers on a separate sheet of paper.

1. What is "exemplary guest service?"

2. Define "spirit" as it relates to guest service.

3. List several things required of a lodging employee seeking to provide exemplary guest service.

4. Why is it important to measure guest service from the guest's perspective?

5. What should lodging employees do to help prevent their personal lives from affecting their quality of guest service?

2.3   Guest Service in Action

AFTER SUCCESSFULLY COMPLETING THIS SECTION, YOU WILL BE ABLE TO:

♦ Identify procedures and techniques that lodging employees can use when providing guest service.

♦ Describe ways in which lodging employees can show guests that they care.

♦ Explain the importance of going the extra step when giving guest service.

♦ Describe the special procedures for providing guest service to guests with special needs.

Practicing Guest Service

Lodging employees play a key role in fulfilling the needs, wants, and expectations of guests. Lodging employees are guest service *professionals*. Lodging employees are providers, the people who surround the guest with service. So how is this done? It takes a certain attitude or spirit, and a sense of pride from each lodging employee. There are also techniques for providing guest service. Lodging employees should:

• Give guests immediate and undivided attention

• Greet guests warmly and with a smile

• Listen closely to guests

• Show pride in themselves, their work, and the property

• Use guests' names when possible

• Maintain eye contact when talking with guests

• Take care of guests' needs themselves, when possible

• Make suggestions that will help guests enjoy their stay

• Protect guests' privacy and follow all property security procedures

• Be polite

• Invite guests to return

• Always end a conversation with "Is there anything else I can do for you?" Or, "Let us know if we can do anything else."

• Always look at every situation from the guest's point of view

Whether guests receive good or bad service depends on how lodging employees respond to the guests' needs. Lodging employees should show guests that they:

• Care about the guests' needs

• Are never too busy to attend to guests' needs

• Work together as a team to provide good service

- Do everything they can to keep promises and please guests

Guests who do not receive good service may feel unwelcome and unimportant, and that nobody cares about their needs, wants, or expectations. Sometimes the smallest unprofessional act can have the most serious effect on guests.

Going the Extra Step

Successful lodging employees realize that guest service means doing anything and everything to make sure guests have pleasant, carefree stays. Whenever possible, they put forth extra effort to satisfy guests' needs because they know pleasing guests is a property's top priority. They often meet guests' needs by doing more than is expected. In fact, guest service should always involve doing the unexpected, going the extra step, and giving that extra effort that makes both the employee and the guest feel satisfied. After all, when guests' needs are *more* than satisfied, they are more likely to return to the property and recommend it to their friends.

Serving Guests with Special Needs

All guests are different. Some will want more special attention, such as families with kids, while others, such as business travelers or newlyweds, may be very busy or simply want more privacy. Lodging employees must learn to recognize which guests require more attentive guest service.

There is a special segment of guests that frequently has special needs or requires special attention. These guests include international guests, senior travelers, and guests with disabilities.

International guests

When serving **international guests**, lodging employees:

- Refer to guests by their nationality or as "international guests," not "foreigners."

- Speak at a normal volume level, but slowly and clearly, avoiding slang.

- Address them with courtesy titles (Mr., Ms., etc.) and their last names.

- Inform them of available services such as language services and currency exchange.

Senior travelers

When serving senior travelers, lodging employees:

- Explain small print on registration cards for seniors with poor eyesight.

- Speak clearly and distinctly, especially when on the phone.

- Show consideration for the extra time it may take for older guests to get things done due to physical limitations.

- Offer baggage assistance, if available.

Guests with disabilities

There are some general guidelines for serving guests with disabilities, whether they have visual, hearing, or physical impairments. It should be noted that these guests should always be asked whether assistance is needed before providing it. Different properties may provide such services as barrier-free rooms, wheelchairs, or telecommunication devices for hearing-impaired guests.

When helping guests with disabilities, lodging employees:

- Speak directly to the guest with the disability, not to a companion.

- Show consideration for the extra time it may take for a guest with a disability to say things or get things done. The guest should set the pace.

- Ask guests with disabilities what else can help them (avoid yes or no questions).

Serving guests with hearing impairments

When serving guests with hearing impairments, lodging employees:

- Move to the guest's line of sight first, if possible. If not successful, lodging employees may tap the guest on the shoulder.

- Look directly at the guest and speak clearly, slowly, and expressively at a normal volume level.

- Use written notes to communicate, if necessary.

- Use facial expressions, gestures, and body movements to aid communication.

- Address the guest with the disability and not someone serving as an interpreter for the guest.

Serving guests with visual impairments

When serving guests with visual impairments, lodging employees:

- Identify themselves and their role during the greeting.

- Use specifics such as "left a hundred feet" or "right two yards" when directing a guest with a visual impairment.

- Orient the guest to his or her surroundings by explaining where items are located.

- Separate money into bill denominations before giving it to a guest who is visually impaired.

Apply Your Learning 2.3

Please write all answers on a separate sheet of paper.

1. List six techniques lodging employees should use when providing guest service.

2. List three types of guests who may have special needs.

3. List two tips lodging employees should use when serving international guests.

4. List two tips lodging employees should use when serving senior guests.

5. List two tips lodging employees should use when serving guests with disabilities.

6. What can be done to aid communication when serving a guest with a hearing impairment?

7. How should money be handed to a guest with a visual impairment?

2.4 Handling Guest Complaints

AFTER SUCCESSFULLY COMPLETING THIS SECTION, YOU WILL BE ABLE TO:

♦ Summarize the importance of allowing guests to complain.

♦ Explain the general cautions lodging employees should follow when handling guest complaints.

♦ Identify procedures lodging employees can use when handling guest complaints.

♦ List the types of guest complaints.

♦ Describe procedures properties can use to identify guest complaints.

Handling Guest Complaints

Guest service, unlike an unsatisfactory guestroom or an undercooked meal, cannot be exchanged if the guest is dissatisfied. Guest service is not an object the guests can touch or take with them, it is intangible. When guest service isn't provided, the guest's only option is to complain. No matter how efficient a lodging operation is, at some point a guest may be disappointed or find fault with something or someone.

Guest service can turn a potential negative situation into a positive experience for the guest. Complaints can be avoided, to some extent, if lodging employees try to anticipate guest concerns and plan ways to deal with them as they arise.

Front desk representatives are often the first to learn of guest complaints. They should always be courteous to guests with complaints and do all they can to help them. Perhaps nothing annoys guests more than having their complaints ignored or not taken seriously. Employees should understand that most guests do not enjoy complaining any more than most employees enjoy receiving complaints. Employees should also realize that guests who do not get a chance to complain—or choose not to—often tell their friends, relatives, and co-workers instead. This can harm a lodging property's business.

When it is easy for guests to express their opinions, lodging employees and guests both benefit. Employees learn about possible or actual problems and are given the chance to resolve guest complaints and increase guest satisfaction. When guests have their problems resolved, they feel that the lodging property cares about their needs. From this viewpoint, every complaint is welcome.

Lodging employees should consider the following general cautions when handling guest complaints:

• Guests may be quite angry. Lodging employees should never go alone to a guestroom to respond to a problem.

- Lodging employees should never make a promise that they do not have the authority to keep.

- If a problem cannot be resolved, lodging employees should admit this early on. Honesty is the best policy.

- Some guests complain as part of their nature and may never be satisfied. Lodging employees must learn not to let these guests upset them.

Learning to deal effectively with guests' complaints requires experience. Lodging employees should practice by thinking about how they might resolve some of the property's most common complaints. By anticipating complaints, planning and practicing responses, and receiving helpful feedback, all lodging employees can prepare to deal effectively with guest complaints. When handling complaints, lodging employees are dealing not only with a problem but also with a person. To handle guest complaints correctly, lodging employees should:

- Listen with concern; look at the problem from the guest's point of view.

- Give the guest undivided attention.

- Stay calm; never get angry or defensive.

- Apologize for the problem.

- Offer solutions. Tell the guest what can be done and try to offer options.

- Tell guests the approximate amount of time it will take to resolve the problem.

- Act on the problem.

- Monitor the progress of the corrective action.

- Follow up. Check back to make sure the guest is satisfied once the problem has been resolved.

Types of Complaints

Typically, guest complaints can be divided into four types of problems:

- Mechanical

- Attitudinal

- Guest service-related

- Unusual

Mechanical complaints usually concern problems with temperature control, lighting, electricity, room furnishings, ice machines, vending machines, door keys, plumbing, television sets, elevators, and so forth. Most guest complaints are related to lodging equipment breakdowns. Even an excellent preventive maintenance program cannot completely remove all possible equipment problems.

Attitudinal complaints result from guests who feel rude or tactless lodging employees have insulted them. These guests may have overheard lodging employees arguing or may have had employees complain directly to them. Lodging employees should make sure that guests do not overhear them arguing or complaining. In fact, lodging employees should not argue with or complain to co-workers while at work, if at all. Instead, they should talk calmly with co-workers or tell a supervisor about the problem and handle it in private. This is especially important to maintaining good guest relations.

Guest service-related complaints may concern long waiting times, a lack of help with luggage, untidy rooms, telephone difficulties, wake-up call errors, food or beverage quality problems, or ignored requests for additional supplies or amenities. The busier a lodging property is at a given time, the more likely these types of complaints are to arise.

Unusual complaints may involve the lack of a swimming pool, a lack of transportation, early lounge or restaurant closing times, bad weather, and so on. Lodging employees typically do not have any control over unusual complaints, yet guests often complain to them about such problems. Difficult situations may arise if lodging employees do not expect to receive such complaints.

Identifying Complaints

All guest complaints deserve attention, even though some may seem more important than others. An excited guest who loudly demands immediate attention at the front desk will appreciate a quick response, while a guest who casually mentions a problem may require a different type of response.

One way to improve the overall quality of guest service at a lodging property is to have lodging employees identify common guest complaints. Employees in each department should keep a log of complaints made. If the property is able to identify frequent problems, lodging employees will be more likely to find ways to correct the problems and improve overall service and guest satisfaction.

Another way to identify problems is to study guest comment cards and questionnaires. Many lodging properties use this practice to find out from guests the ways that their visits can be made better. In addition, lodging properties are able to identify specific areas that should be targeted for improvement. Of course, comment cards are not always bad news. Oftentimes guests will single out a particular lodging employee, department, or service, that made their stay more enjoyable. These comment cards or questionnaires may be given out at the front desk, placed in the guestroom, or mailed to guests after they leave.

By examining the number and type of complaints received, lodging properties may learn more about common and less common problems. Lodging employees may handle frequent complaints more effectively and with more courtesy if they are aware of the problems that cause the complaints.

Apply Your Learning 2.4

Please write all answers on a separate sheet of paper.

1. What might happen if an employee ignores a guest's complaint?

2. Why should hotel employees welcome guest complaints?

3. What general cautions should employees note when handling guest complaints?

4. What techniques should employees use when handling guest complaints?

5. Give two examples of a mechanical complaint.

6. What are attitudinal complaints?

7. Give two examples of a service-related complaint.

8. What are unusual complaints that lodging employees may receive?

9. What two procedures can employees follow to identify common guest complaints?

Quick Hits

Chapter 2

SECTION 2.1—WHAT IS GUEST SERVICE?

- Because of the rising competition in the hospitality industry, guest service is now considered a basic necessity for a lodging property to survive.

- Guest service can mean the difference between a guest having a forgettable or unforgettable lodging experience.

- Guest service is best defined as "meeting any and all guests' needs in the way that they want and expect them to be met."

- People who stay at lodging properties are referred to as guests because the properties want the guests to feel as if they have been invited into someone else's home and made to feel at home.

- Guests should receive the same level of service throughout their entire stay, throughout every stage of the guest cycle.

- Benefits of guest service are felt by everyone, the guest, the property, and the lodging employees themselves.

SECTION 2.2—EXEMPLARY GUEST SERVICE

- Exemplary guest service means providing guests with not only the service they expect but exceeding their expectations.

- Lodging employees' spirit is the key to exemplary guest service. It encompasses an employee's positive attitude, feeling of pride and belonging, and desire to please and satisfy guests.

- Exceeding guests' expectations can be made easier by seeing things from the guests' perspective. In fact, because it is the guest's expectations of guest service that count, guest service should always be measured from their point of view, not the lodging employees.

- Things that happen to lodging employees away from work can have an affect on their performance at work. They can avoid this by taking time to relax, thinking before acting or speaking, and trying to stay positive.

SECTION 2.3—GUEST SERVICE IN ACTION

- Lodging employees are guest service professionals who surround guests with great service.

- There are many techniques for providing guest service, including: greeting guests warmly and with a smile, listening closely to guests, making suggestions that will help guests enjoy their stay, and always looking at every situation from the guest's point of view.

- Guest service is important because nearly every act or failure to act on the part of a lodging employee can affect, either positively or negatively, a guest's stay.

- Certain guests may require special needs or services. These guests may include international guests, senior guests, or guests with disabilities.

SECTION 2.4—HANDLING GUEST COMPLAINTS

- All lodging properties will experience some amount of guest complaints. By allowing guests to complain about things they experience while staying at a lodging property, the guest, the property, and the employee all benefit because the problem can then be resolved.

- When handling guest complaints, lodging employees should be cautious of angry guests, making unrealistic promises, maintaining honesty, and never getting upset.

- There are specific procedures that lodging employees can use when handling guest complaints. They include: listening with concern; staying calm, apologizing, and offering solutions, among others.

- Types of complaints include mechanical, attitudinal, guest service-related, and unusual complaints.

- Lodging properties can improve guest service by learning to identify common complaints and being prepared to handle them in advance.

Careers and Professionalism

Sections

Professionalism is the behavior or qualities that mark someone who is excellent in his or her field of work. Professionalism is a spirit, character, or way of pursuing a skill or trade in a dedicated and caring manner. It includes the actions and attitudes that demonstrate that spirit. Professional hospitality employees:

- Know how to do their jobs correctly

- Go the extra mile to get the job done right and always strive to do better

- Strive to meet the company's and the department's goals

In addition, professional hospitality employees are:

- Proud of themselves

- Good team players

- Concerned about themselves, their co-workers, and, of course, the guests

Being a professional requires both the knowledge and skills needed to do the job. It also requires the proper attitude. Hospitality employees who are professionals are respected because of their dependability, their care and attention to detail, and the pride they take in work done well. To always try to do better, hospitality employees must be motivated. To be part of the hospitality team, hospitality employees must understand the importance of teamwork. And to care about themselves and others, employees must have self-esteem and empathy.

3.1 Building a Hospitality Career

AFTER SUCCESSFULLY COMPLETING THIS SECTION, YOU WILL BE ABLE TO:

♦ Describe the advantages and disadvantages to a hospitality career.

♦ Identify the different benefits in working for a large chain and an independent operation.

♦ Describe the opportunities available in food service.

♦ Explain why some people like working in clubs.

♦ Describe the career opportunities in cruise lines.

♦ Identify ways to find a job.

Careers in Hospitality

Why do people go into the hospitality industry? If you were to ask people who have spent their careers in the business what they like most about it, you would get a wide variety of answers. Some of the most popular are:

• The industry offers more career options than most.

• The work is varied.

• There are many opportunities to be creative.

• This is a people business.

• Hospitality jobs are not nine-to-five jobs.

• There are opportunities for long-term career growth.

• There are perks associated with many hospitality jobs.

There are also some aspects of the business that many people don't like:

• Long hours

• Nontraditional schedules

• Pressure

• Low beginning salaries

Lodging Careers

People who choose the lodging industry as a career often do so because they enjoy traveling and living in different places. Hotel management personnel are in great demand, and since most large hotels belong to chains, managers are often offered opportunities to move into new positions in different geographic locations.

The arguments for working for a large chain include:

• Better training

- More opportunities for advancement

- Better benefits

A career with an independent operation also offers some advantages, however:

- More chances to be creative

- More control

- Better learning environments for entrepreneurs

There are numerous entry-level positions in lodging. A short list of those that will be covered in this program are front desk representative, reservationist, PBX operator, bell services attendant, guestroom attendant, maintenance worker, laundry attendant, public space cleaner, concierge, retail cashier, restaurant server, banquet setup employee, banquet server, busperson, room service attendant, and kitchen steward.

Food Service Careers

People who are interested in commercial food service often choose between **independent restaurants** and **chain restaurants**.

At the top of the restaurant spectrum are luxury restaurants, which are mostly owned and operated by independent entrepreneurs. These restaurants are sometimes called **white tablecloth restaurants.**

The top luxury restaurants have a substantial volume and are very sophisticated operations. The best way to the top is to work in a luxury restaurant and learn the ropes. Many of these restaurants are owned by an individual. They are usually sold to an employee or other entrepreneurs who can get financing when the owner retires. Banks and other lending institutions look to see what experience the prospective owner

has before approving loans, so a good track record in management positions at similar restaurants is your best ticket for getting financing.

Chain restaurants recruit most of their managers from hospitality schools. Entry-level jobs for graduates with hospitality degrees are often on the assistant-manager level, with progress to manager, then district manager responsible for a group of restaurants, and then regional manager.

Restaurant chains are the fastest growing part of the restaurant business today. Many of these chains are made up of fast-food restaurants or, as they prefer to be called, quick-service restaurants.

Social catering is another part of the food service industry. Catering businesses are often started by independent entrepreneurs who hire food servers as needed.

Contract food companies are generally hired by organizations whose major business purpose is not food service. Contract food management is somewhat unique because the manager must please two sets of employers—the home office and the client that has contracted for the service. Contract food managers work more regular hours and are under less pressure than restaurant managers. Contract food managers must be highly skilled in professional management techniques and cost control.

Although contract food companies can supply food for schools and hospitals, most of these institutions handle their own food service programs and are part of the **institutional food service** market. Colleges and universities have begun opening table-service restaurants in addition to their traditional cafeterias. Hospital programs are usually administered by a trained dietitian or a professional food service manager working with one. Menus are generally simple and nourishing.

Club Careers

Clubs are very different from other types of hospitality businesses because the "guests"—the club members—are also the owners in many cases. Large clubs have many of the same positions found in hotels and restaurants: a general manager, a food and beverage director, a catering director, and a controller.

Many hospitality managers enjoy working in clubs. First of all, there is a chance to exercise one's own imagination and creativity in such matters as menu selection, party planning, and sporting events. Secondly, you interact with the owners (members) in a more direct way. Moreover, clubs with sports facilities often host celebrity tournaments that bring with them media coverage. This can make the job even more stimulating.

Since the nature of clubs often requires specialized training and knowledge (such as golf, tennis, and marina operations), club managers often come up through the ranks.

Cruise Line Careers

There are opportunities both on shore and at sea within the cruise industry. Shore-side positions include marketing, accounting, provisioning, itinerary planning, and hotel operations. At sea, there are the same kinds of jobs any fine resort has.

Persons who are attracted by travel may enjoy operations jobs at sea but should be prepared to spend a minimum of nine out of every 12 months away from home. Living conditions don't allow for much privacy either, but many like the feeling of having an extended family that occurs on a ship.

Finding a Career

Many hospitality students have a preconceived idea of the job they want in the industry. Their parents, someone they admire, or a family friend may have been in the business and advised them to take a particular position. Or they may have had an enjoyable part-time or summer job in a restaurant or hotel.

In the view of career counselors, however, it is better to keep an open mind. If you don't explore other career possibilities, you might overlook opportunities that could be more appealing in the long run. A sound understanding of your goals and lifestyle, and a thorough knowledge of the companies that might be interested in what you offer, is an important foundation for your career search.

Every job you take should move you closer to your final goal. If you look at jobs as stepping-stones on a **career path** or **career ladder**, there are several questions you should answer before you decide whether a job is right for you:

- What can I learn from this job that will contribute to my career goals?

- What are the long-term opportunities for growth in this company?

- What is this company's reputation among the people I know? Is it a good place to work? Does it deliver on its promises to employees?

- How good is the training program? Will the company really make an effort to educate me?

- What is the starting salary? What about other benefits? Do they add up to a competitive package?

- How do I feel about the location? Will I be living in a place where I can be happy? What about proximity to friends and relatives?

Résumés

To gain experience in the hospitality industry, you will need to prepare a résumé and handle a job interview.

A **résumé** is an advertisement for yourself. Its purpose is to convince the person doing the hiring that he or she should not fill the job without talking to you first. Résumés also introduce you to your prospective employer and provide a brief summary of your educational and employment background.

Résumés for entry-level positions should fit on a single page. Many of the best résumés start with a section called "Summary of Qualifications." The next section is often a direct presentation of your skills and experience that is more specific than the summary. At the bottom of the résumé you should list your education.

Interviews

You should know as much as possible about your prospective employer before you walk in the door for an **interview.** This will make it easier for you to hold a conversation and you will sound more enthusiastic.

The way you are dressed makes a big difference in the way you are perceived. You want to project a professional, responsible image. The interview is not a time to make a bold or unusual fashion statement.

An interview is your opportunity to sell yourself and sell your prospective employer on offering you a job. Always answer questions directly and honestly. If you don't know the answer to something, say so. The best thing you can do is sound positive. You want to be remembered as someone who is enthusiastic, confident, energetic, and dependable. Shape every answer to reinforce those images.

After you leave, you should always write a follow-up thank-you letter. Thank the interviewer for the time he or she spent with you and for considering you for the position. If you were impressed with the company, say so!

If you are offered a job, respond within the time requested. Contact the person making the offer to clarify details if you have additional questions.

Apply Your Learning 3.1

Please write all answers on a separate sheet of paper.

1. What are some of the reasons people begin careers in hospitality?

2. What are the benefits of working for a large chain?

3. What are luxury restaurants owned and operated by independent entrepreneurs called within the trade?

4. Who often starts catering businesses?

5. Why are club careers different from other types of hospitality businesses?

6. What type of shore-side cruise jobs are available?

7. What does a résumé need to do?

8. What do you want to accomplish in an interview?

3.2 Presenting a Professional Image

AFTER SUCCESSFULLY COMPLETING THIS SECTION, YOU WILL BE ABLE TO:

♦ Define what it means to present a professional image in the lodging industry.

♦ Describe the importance of good personal grooming in maintaining a professional image.

♦ Summarize how a pleasant personality affects guests and other employees.

♦ Explain the importance of good posture when assisting guests.

Image represents how others perceive hospitality employees. Image is largely formed by our appearance, personality, and posture. Good grooming, a pleasant person-ality, and attention to posture make profes-sionals stand out in the hospitality industry.

Personal Grooming

Professionals who pay attention to their personal appearance:

• Feel more confident

• Make good impressions on management and co-workers

• Ensure good health and safety in the workplace

• Represent the lodging property well

Even before an employee greets a guest, the guest notices his or her appearance and forms an impression of the employee and the hotel. A well-groomed hospitality employee indicates to the guest that the hotel itself is clean. Three of the most important aspects of personal hygiene are:

Hair

• Keep it tidy, clean, and attractive.

• Keep it away from the face so it doesn't impair vision

• Keep mustaches and beards trimmed, tidy, and clean (some lodging proper-ties may have policies dictating that employees must be clean-shaven)

Personal freshness

• Brush teeth after every meal

• Shower or bathe daily

• Use deodorant daily

• Make sure makeup, if appropriate, is moderate and well blended

- Put on clean undergarments
- Put on a clean, pressed uniform

Hands and fingernails

- Clean underneath fingernails
- Keep fingernails trimmed
- Wash hands before starting a work shift
- Wash hands during a work shift as necessary, especially when handling food
- Wash hands after using the restroom

Looking great makes hospitality employ-ees feel better and function better. It also shows respect for others.

Pleasant Personality

Personality refers to the way a person acts, looks, and thinks. Professional hospitality employees make a point to let their personality show through in their work. When hospitality employees display their pleasant personalities, guests are more likely to feel that:

- They are dealing with a person, not a robot.
- They are seen as individuals—and not as just another guest.
- They are special and important.
- The hospitality employees know what they are doing.

This same pleasant personality is also bestowed on co-workers. In fact, profess-ional hospitality employees treat their co-workers as if they were guests. This will help them treat guests better too. When hospitality employees are patient, their co-workers are less likely to get flustered and to treat guests abruptly. When they are pleasant, co-workers may forget their own problems before those problems affect the way they deal with guests.

In general, professional hospitality employees treat others as they would like to be treated. For example, hospitality employ-ees will often talk briefly with guests to put them at ease. If hospitality employees are shy, they may choose to welcome or compliment the guest with one sincere, original comment, and then begin their job tasks. Either way, this lets guests know that the hospitality employee cares about their experiences at the lodging property.

Good Posture

Good posture, such as the way one stands, sits, and moves, can have a big effect on how guests perceive hospitality employees. For example, when guests check into a hotel, they would rather see a front desk employee who is standing straight, facing them, and smiling as they approach as opposed to one who leans against the wall with his or her arms crossed and yawns as they approach. This simple difference in posture can set the tone, positive or negative, for the guests' entire stay.

Hospitality employees who stand upright with their shoulders back and heads up tell the guest that they are alert, efficient, and ready to provide excellent service. In con-trast, hospitality employees who slouch, look at the ground, and shuffle along indicate that they are bored, lazy, and unconcerned about meeting the guest's needs.

Professional hospitality employees realize that appearance is a form of com-munication. If they have good grooming habits, a pleasant personality, and good posture, they are telling the guests that they are professionals who are prepared to provide excellent guest service. A professional hospitality employee is one whose personality, appearance, and body language all welcome the guest and make him or her feel comfortable and special.

Apply Your Learning 3.2

Please write all answers on a separate sheet of paper.

1. What is professionalism?

2. What makes a hospitality employee a professional?

3. What are four benefits of having a good personal appearance?

4. A well-groomed hospitality employee pays special attention to what three aspects of hygiene?

5. What is personality?

6. How does a hospitality employee's personality affect guest relations?

7. Describe good posture.

3.3 Professionalism on the Job

AFTER SUCCESSFULLY COMPLETING THIS SECTION, YOU WILL BE ABLE TO:

♦ List basic expectations that most lodging employers expect from employees.

♦ Identify standards of professional conduct.

♦ Summarize methods that can be used to get along better with supervisors.

♦ Describe specific workplace expectations such as those related to work schedules, dress regulations, and personal business.

♦ List the benefits that most lodging properties now offer their employees.

Employer Expectations

New employees must quickly learn what is expected on the job as hospitality professionals. These expectations will come from their fellow employees, the guests, and their employers.

No matter the type of hospitality operation, the employer will typically expect the employees to know the following:

• Why the organization exists: that is, its mission.

• Their place in the organization and how they can contribute to making the property a success.

• How to display professional conduct, such as the rules of behavior and standards of conduct.

• The scheduled work hours, breaks, appearance standards, and so forth.

• The type of interpersonal behavior expected, such as how to relate with co-workers and supervisors.

• Safety and security rules and job performance standards.

Most hospitality properties teach these types of professional basics in their new employee orientation training. It is still important for all new hospitality employees to ask questions and watch other employees carefully, especially the person training them.

Professional Conduct

New hospitality employees can quickly learn how to display professionalism. It requires the proper attitude and a desire to learn! New employees should focus on their behavior and attitude to ensure that what they do—and do not do—reflects their interest in being a professional.

Most lodging properties have policies and procedures that guide employee behavior. These policies and procedures are often in a manual that all employees read. Policies state the property's general position on a specific topic. Procedures explain expected actions in detail. Simply stated, these **standards of conduct** outline what employees should and should not do on the job. The standards can form a foundation or template for professional behavior on the job even if the property does not have a formal rule about each of the actions discussed.

While each property has its own list of standards or rules, most share several in common. The following acts are just a few of what may be considered just cause for immediate dismissal:

- Reporting to work under the influence of alchol or illegal drugs.

- Bringing or using alcoholic beverages or illegal drugs on company property during working hours.

- Making false or misleading statements on a job application form.

- Stealing from co-workers, guests, or the property.

- Refusing to perform assigned work.

- Soliciting on company property during working time without permission.

- Carrying or using firearms, fireworks, or any other weapon on the property.

- Starting or encouraging a work slow-down; interfering with work schedules.

- Posting, removing, or tampering with bulletin board notices without permission.

- Willfully defacing or destroying lodging property or another employee's property.

- Sleeping on the job.

- Adding a service charge to a guest bill or an account without the permission of the guest or a supervisor.

There are also a number of acts that lodging properties typically consider worthy of some form of discipline, though not necessarily dismissal. They include:

- Distributing literature in working areas without permission.

- Fighting on the lodging property.

- Failing to report to a supervisor any accident at work.

- Using abusive or threatening language on the lodging property.

- Horseplay or otherwise misbehaving.

- Behaving disrespectfully; failing to give a high degree of service to a guest.

- Taking part in or not reporting activities that could be considered a discredit to the company or its employees.

- Taking property food or beverages from the property without permission.

- Being rude to guests or others.

- Leaving one's job or regular work area during working hours without permission.

- Having unexcused absences or being absent frequently.

- Failing to notify the supervisor when missing work.

- Ignoring the starting and quitting times for shifts and rest periods.

- Performing poor quality work or interfering with the work of others.

- Disobeying safety regulations.

- Failing to maintain productivity standards.

- Using the telephones without permission.

- Parking a personal vehicle in non-designated areas.

- Failing to wear the proper uniform and approved name badge.

- Discussing personal or confidential company matters in public areas where guests could overhear.

On-the-Job Relationships

Most dismissals result from a person's inability to get along with fellow employees and not from a violation of rules. Hospitality is a people business. Getting along with others—supervisors, co-workers, and guests—is one of the most important parts of every job at a lodging property. Guests are the reason for everything employees do in a property. Positive guest relations mean that employees are ready at all times to help guests and to help co-workers help guests.

Getting along with the boss is important to one's job success. When hospitality employees try their best to do a great job, good relationships may develop naturally and be easy to build on. However, no matter how well hospitality employees meet their job responsibilities, sometimes problems may arise. For instance, even if they get along well with their boss, at times they still may feel like:

- Their boss is often too busy to talk with them.

- Their boss does not give them clear directions.

- Their boss seems to pick on them.

When problems like these arise, it's a good idea to get them out in the open. Whether talking will resolve the problem often depends on how the hospitality employee approaches the boss. Some suggestions include:

- *Don't accuse.* If the employee says, "You don't understand my problems," the boss may feel defensive or even angry. It's better to say, "I often feel pressured. Do you think you could give some suggestions for keeping up with all of my job tasks?"

- *Be specific.* Don't say, "You never give me a clear idea of what I'm supposed to do." It's better to say, "I'm confused about part of my duties. I thought you told me to wash the tables at the end of my work shift, but now it seems as if I'm supposed to restock my work station. Did I get something confused?"

- *Don't make problems bigger.* Don't say "You're never around when I need to talk to you. I think you're trying to avoid me." It's better to think about the immediate problem: "I need to talk with you about a couple of things. I tried to catch you Monday after work and Tuesday before my shift. I know you have a lot to do. When is the best time for me to meet with you?"

If hospitality employees believe that it is difficult to get their boss to listen to them, they can try one or more of these tips:

- Schedule a time to talk with the boss when neither is too busy and both can talk in private.

- Make sure information is accurate and complete. Think concerns through carefully.

- Write specific examples to refer to during the meeting to explain the concerns.

- Be brief. Get to the point and make it easy for the boss to respond to the ideas.

- Be aware of voice and body language. Sometimes voice and actions speak louder than words. Try not to sound angry or defensive. Remember, be *professional*.

Sometimes a problem may arise that requires more than a meeting with the boss to resolve. In many lodging properties, people in the human resources department will talk with hospitality employees about any problems they are having with their boss or supervisor.

Workplace Expectations

Some examples of expectations that most lodging properties have of their employees are provided below. Usually, this type of information appears in the employee handbook.

Work Schedule

Lodging properties are open 24 hours a day, seven days a week. As a result, hospitality employees' hours vary depending upon their shift and the time of year so that enough employees will be available at all times.

Absence from Work

All work at a lodging property depends upon teamwork, and when one person is away from the job, everyone else must adjust to balance the work load. This adjustment can be made without much difficulty if a supervisor knows in advance about an absence. So if hospitality employees must be away from their job—even for a few hours—they let their supervisor know. If an emergency arises, they tell their supervisor so arrangements can be made to keep the work flowing with a minimum of interruption and confusion during their absence.

Dress Regulations

Many lodging properties have specific uniforms for specific departments. These uniforms reflect positively on the property. It is important for hospitality employees to wear the correct uniform and to make sure that it is kept clean and neat looking, and in good repair.

Personal Business

Here are a few pointers for hospitality employees to observe carefully:

- If moving, give the department head the new address and telephone number.

- If changing name or marital status, or adding family members, inform the department head.

- Have personal mail sent home—not to the property.

- Keep all information and figures (such as sales, inventory, and payroll figures) confidential.

- Do not accept or encourage personal calls at work—except for emergencies.

Employee Benefits

Only a few decades ago, benefits were almost unheard of. Hospitality employers paid employees a wage or salary and that was all. Today, however, employers face many pressures to provide benefits. Many employers find it necessary to offer benefits to compete effectively with other employers for good, professional employees.

There are many possible benefits a hospitality employer may offer. Some are more common than others. For example, full-time workers often expect some sort of vacation and sick leave benefit. They may also expect to get at least a few holidays off with pay. Many employees also receive some sort of health insurance benefit. A less common benefit might be special discounts to employees staying at affiliated hotels. The benefits an employer chooses to offer depend on several things, including their cost, what competing employers are offering, and the employee's classification. That is, full-time employees are more likely to get benefits than part-time employees.

Apply Your Learning 3.3

Please write all answers on a separate sheet of paper.

1. List four typical employer expectations.

2. List five examples of unprofessional conduct that may warrant immediate dismissal.

3. Give two examples of problems an employee may have with his or her supervisor.

4. What are three suggestions to help employees resolve problems with their supervisors?

5. Why is it important for employees to report an expected absence as soon as possible?

6. Why do many employers offer benefits? Which employees are most likely to receive benefits?

7. What types of benefits are fairly common?

3.4 Hospitality Teamwork

AFTER SUCCESSFULLY COMPLETING THIS SECTION, YOU WILL BE ABLE TO:

♦ Summarize the importance of the hospitality team.

♦ Describe the factors that are important to hospitality teamwork.

♦ Explain the concept of the formal work group.

♦ Describe the differences between formal and informal work groups.

♦ Identify ways in which work groups communicate at lodging properties.

The Hospitality Team

To be successful, a lodging property requires many people working in many different positions, but all working together. Each individual must work as part of a team because the work that he or she does relates very directly to the work done by others.

A reservationist must reserve a room; a front desk representative must assign a room; a room attendant must clean the room; a bell services attendant must take the guest to the room; and so on. Each of these employees relies on the others to be able to do their jobs. All hospitality employees work together to help provide a good experience for the guest. If one employee (team member) does not do his

or her work correctly, it could cause the guest to suffer an unpleasant experience. The guest's bad experience will likely affect the whole team (since the guest is less likely to return and may tell friends about the poor experience).

Hospitality is a people business and the term "people" applies to the employees of the hospitality operation as well as its guests.

Factors Important in Teamwork

It is not hard to recognize that the traits of good teamwork tie in to what is expected of a *professional* hospitality employee.

• *Good attitude*—Attitude is the most important factor necessary for teamwork. Hospitality employees' attitudes toward their jobs, their fellow employees, and the guests visiting the property affects all employees' actions. Often, one's attitude is affected by one's co-workers. For example, if part of a team in which everyone gets along, likes the job and the lodging property, and wants to provide good service, hospitality employees will probably have a good attitude that helps to make the team even stronger. By contrast, if co-workers don't like their jobs, their bosses, or their property, and really don't want to provide quality service to guests, many other employees are likely to share the same attitude.

Teamwork, along with service goals, will suffer. Turnover may be high, and neither the lodging property nor its employees are likely to be successful.

- *Cooperation*—To give good service, hospitality employees must be willing to help each other.

- *Promptness*—When hospitality employees are late to work or are no-shows, it affects other employees. The remaining members of the team must work harder, or goals related to quantity and quality standards will suffer.

- *Loyalty*—Good team members trust and depend on their co-workers and supervisors. At the same time, co-workers and supervisors trust and depend on each team member.

Formal Work Groups

A hospitality property is made up of several groups of employees. At the highest level, all employees of the organization have the same boss: the general manager of the property. However, as work at a lodging property is organized, smaller, formal work groups are established. Therefore, the work force may be divided into divisions such as rooms and food and beverage.

At most lodging properties, especially larger ones, these divisions are too large for just one person to manage effectively. Therefore, they are usually subdivided into departments. For example, a food and beverage division might be divided into food, beverage, and banquet departments. The rooms division might be divided into such departments as front office, housekeeping, and laundry.

These departments can be further divided into work sections. For example, specific floors of a lodging property may be divided into work sections of the housekeeping department. Or specific areas of a kitchen (such as the pantry or bake shop) may be work sections in the food department.

Divisions, departments, and work sections are examples of **formal work groups**. Each has a formal manager or supervisor who coordinates, directs, and controls the work of the group and who is responsible for helping the hospitality employees work together as a team.

Informal Work Groups

Informal work groups develop for many different reasons. When individuals have common interests, backgrounds, and experiences and work close by one another, an informal group will likely develop. Informal groups are not, by definition, good or bad. They might help or hurt the efforts of a lodging property department, division, or work group. Depending on the situation, informal groups might support or oppose management actions.

Every group, including those that are informal, has a leader who affects the behavior of members of the group. Informal leaders are the ones who often set the work pace. They are the hospitality employees to whom co-workers go with their personal and professional problems. Informal leaders communicate easily with employees at all levels of the organization. They may not be the employees with the most experience, but they have earned the respect of others. Informal groups exist to achieve goals set by their own members. Each informal group may have its own set of goals. These goals may have little in common with the goals of other informal groups or with the goals of the organization. For example, the goals of informal groups may be simply to have fun together or to share common interests.

One type of informal group is a **clique.** A clique consists of two or more members of a formal group who have set their own goals. They consider their goals more important than the goals of the formal group. A clique is closely knit and often separate from members of the formal group and other informal groups as well.

Apply Your Learning 3.4

Please write all answers on a separate sheet of paper.

1. Why is teamwork so important in the hospitality industry?

2. What factors are necessary for good teamwork?

3. What are some common formal work groups in a hotel?

4. How are informal work groups different from formal work groups?

5. What is a clique?

3.5 Differences and Diversity

AFTER SUCCESSFULLY COMPLETING THIS SECTION, YOU WILL BE ABLE TO:

♦ Summarize the differences that may exist within a hospitality work force.

♦ Define diversity.

♦ Explain the importance of differences and diversity in the hospitality industry.

♦ Summarize strategies and tips for getting along in a diverse work place.

♦ Describe the importance of diversity awareness.

Understanding Differences

Most lodging property staffs include people from a wide variety of ethnic and racial groups. In some areas of the United States, non-English-speaking employees greatly outnumber those who speak English.

As the 21st century continues, these differences in the work force will increase. Experts predict that the majority of new hospitality employees will be women, African Americans, Hispanic Americans, and immigrants. Many hospitality operations are also hiring older workers and people with disabilities.

Throughout their careers, hospitality employees will find that it is not enough simply to learn their jobs, they will also need to work well with co-workers, managers, and guests whose cultural backgrounds, behavior, and values may differ from the ones with which they are familiar.

Diversity

The terms multicultural and diversity are often used to describe today's work force. **Diversity** is the variety among people relative to age, race, gender, ethnicity, religion, physical ability, sexual orientation, marital status, work experience, income, thinking and learning styles, personality, personal appearance, job level, interests, education, etc., that forms the basis for bringing unique perspectives and creative contributions to the task at hand. In the hospitality industry, these unique perspectives and creative contributions help lead to success. Today's culturally diverse work force includes people who have been raised to view and react to the world around them in different ways.

Factors that produce the differences that make a lodging property's work force culturally diverse include:

Culture—Culture is a complex set of beliefs, customs, skills, habits, traditions, and knowledge shared by a group of people; a person's culture teaches him or her what is important and how to act in various situations.

Family—The family develops its own customs, rituals, beliefs, and values that direct its members' thoughts and actions.

Gender—Men and women have differences and different experiences based on gender and, in certain cultures, may be treated differently.

Age—People have different experiences based on what happens in the world and what happens to them as they age.

Race—People have different values, beliefs, characteristics, and experience based on their race. A race is a group of people with the same origins (such as the same ancestors, background, roots, or heritage).

Geographic area—People have differences based on where they are from and where they live.

Peers—Friends or co-workers often influence one's behavior.

Why Differences are Important

People learn about life and how to behave, eat, communicate, work, and have fun in many different ways. The language or languages they learn, the values they uphold, how they have fun, and how they view work may influence their behavior at work. For people from some cultures, for example, doing business with someone they don't know is unheard of, while such a practice is customary in the United States.

Behavior differs from one geographic region to another, from one culture to another, and from one family to another. For example, what is accepted as correct classroom or workplace behavior on the East Coast may be unacceptable on the West Coast; similarly, what is acceptable behavior on one side of town may be unacceptable on the other side of town.

Recognizing differences leads to understanding the reasons differences exist. Understanding the reasons for differences improves hospitality employees' ability to get along with a diverse staff.

Differences in the workplace are important and useful. They lead to new ideas and effective solutions to troublesome problems. If all hospitality employees were alike, their ideas would likely be similar; new ideas would not be introduced. And businesses need new ideas to succeed.

Diversity can increase productivity, and it can make work educational, interesting, and fun. For the hospitality industry in general, especially in the United States, differences and diversity among lodging staff can be a helpful business tool. When a guest from a certain country or culture visits a lodging property and sees a lodging employee who is like him or her, it makes them feel more comfortable and welcome. Furthermore, as it relates to languages, communication is infinitely more effective when a guest can speak to a lodging employee in his or her own language.

Getting Along in a Diverse Workplace

Uncomfortable situations can often occur when hospitality employees from different cultures work together. But these situations can be prevented if people have a better understanding of the cultural customs practiced by people with whom they work. As hospitality employees gain a better awareness and understanding of and respect for other employees' cultural traditions, their relationships with people from other cultures will likely improve.

Understanding factors that affect communication between people from different cultures is a good step in gaining an understanding of others. For instance, co-workers from different cultures may speak differently and have different ideas of appropriate on-the-job behavior. Some workers may have a casual conversational style; others may speak more formally. People from one culture might be taught to offer suggestions in a humble manner as a sign of respect, while people from another culture might interpret this humbleness as insecurity. Some workers may believe diligence and company loyalty are important values, while others value technical skills and moving up to higher-level jobs more.

The best way to work as part of a culturally diverse group is to admit that differences exist and then talk about them. If two co-workers have an approach or view that is different, they may try saying, 'With you being X and me being Y, we've had some different experiences. So, we are likely to do some things differently." Talking about differences and possible problems will help in managing them.

When working as part of a diverse lodging work force, it is common for one to believe his or her culture is "right" and all others are "wrong." To overcome this belief, hospitality employees should learn what people from other groups believe about their own group. For example, many Americans think they are part of the safest and cleanest culture in the world. But a large majority of automobiles made in the United States would not pass a safety inspection in Germany. And some cultures think Americans are unclean for placing the toilet and bathing facility in the same area.

A culture's rules and behaviors may seem odd, but they are usually based on historic or religious traditions. To succeed in a culturally diverse workplace, hospitality employees should learn as much as they can about the habits, actions, and reasons behind behaviors of other cultures. Learning about other cultures will help them begin to see the world through the eyes of others—and be more understanding, and professional, co-workers for their efforts. Another important consideration for hospitality employees is this: not only will they have co-workers who are different from one another; the guests whom they serve will also be different. Treating them with respect and consideration is a must.

Tips For Getting Along in a Diverse Workplace

Communication. Hospitality employees should:

- Make it easy for co-workers to admit that they do not understand something. For instance, say, "I know this is complicated; is there anything you're not sure about?"

- Try to match the speaking pace and timing of the people with whom they are communicating. If someone speaks slower, allow him or her to finish speaking before beginning to speak.

- Not read between the lines. The unwritten rules of other cultures may be very different. To assume that everyone has the same unspoken language may create an embarrassing situation.

- Look for clues that mean someone does not understand, such as a faraway look or a wrinkled forehead. If a listener nods and smiles often, this does not always mean he or she understands or agrees.

- Not talk louder to people who speak a different language. Yelling will not make English, Spanish, or any other language easier to understand. Speak slowly and use simple words.

- Not judge others based on their accent or speaking pattern. A co-worker is not slow because he or she speaks slowly and is not stuffy if he or she uses more formal words.

Working Together. Hospitality employees:

- Do not try to force others to work at their pace.

- Understand that there are many ways to approach a job and do it well.

- Take time to talk with others as part of getting ready to work. Show an interest in co-workers as people. Ask about their families or hobbies.

- Avoid topics such as politics or religion during casual conversations.

- Realize that some people are taught to separate work life from personal life, but that does not mean they do not care about others.

- Learn to be flexible and know that others may feel differently about space.

- Stay where they are when starting a conversation; let others move to where they feel comfortable.

- Learn the personal space and touching rules of co-workers. Until they understand these rules, they do not touch others; what one person from one culture thinks is simply a friendly

pat on the back may have a different meaning to others.

Putting Oneself in Another Person's Place

One technique that hospitality employees can use for getting along well with others and treating them with respect and consideration is putting themselves in another's place. They think about how they would feel if they were the other person. How would they want to be treated? What would make them feel comfortable? What would make them feel uncomfortable? With this technique as a basis, hospitality employees can use the following suggestions for dealing with differences based on gender, age, and disabilities.

Gender. Hospitality employees should:

- Avoid using "man" or "woman" and other gender-specific words when speaking. Substitute those words with appropriate—not clunky or outrageous—gender-neutral words. For example, use the term "bell services attendant" instead of "bellman" and "room attendant" instead of "maid."

- Offer to help if someone looks like they need assistance. Don't assume that people need or do not need help simply because of their gender.

Age. Hospitality employees:

- Do not refer to a person's age unless it is relevant For example, "the old man in room 317" should be "the guest in room 317."

- Do not assume that people have less ability or energy because of their age.

- Do not talk loudly to people just because of their age; they may have perfect hearing.

People with disabilities. Hospitality employees should:

- Never refer to someone by his or her disability; for instance, refer to the "switchboard operator," not the "blind switchboard operator."

- Ask first if someone looks like they need assistance, do not assume.

- Try to sit rather than stand when talking with people who use wheelchairs. Face them straight on so they don't strain their neck trying to look up.

- Speak slowly and clearly when talking with a person who has a hearing handicap. Always look the person in the eye and pause after each sentence.

- Invite people with disabilities to events even if they can't take part.

Diversity Awareness

So, what makes working as part of a diverse lodging work force different from working as part of any group, especially if all one must do is be polite and treat others with respect and consideration? The answer is *awareness*. It's important for hospitality employees to understand that if they think a co-worker who speaks their language is a better worker than someone who speaks another language, they are probably hurting their relationship with the co-worker who is different from them.

In addition to improving the way they treat others, it's equally important for hospitality employees to tell others when they are treated in a way they don't like. Sometimes people grow to accept names and behaviors they don't like and allow people to call them "girl," "kid," or unfavorable racial or other nicknames. If this happens, hospitality employees should speak up and tell others how they feel. They should try not to blame them or make them feel bad; but instead, tell them what they would prefer to be called.

Working as part of a diverse lodging work force gives everyone an opportunity to meet new people, learn about different groups, and look at life from a new angle. When hospitality employees realize that good co-workers may be of either gender or of any working age, or may have disabilities or be from any culture, they will begin to develop cooperative, productive, and professional working relationships.

Apply Your Learning 3.5

Please write all answers on a separate sheet of paper.

1. Why is it important to understand differences among people?

2. Define diversity.

3. How does diversity affect the workplace?

4. How should you treat all co-workers, guests, and others?

5. What is a good technique for learning how to treat others with respect and consideration?

6. What are two suggestions for dealing with differences based on gender?

7. What are three suggestions for dealing with differences based on disabilities?

8. What are three suggestions for dealing with differences based on culture?

Quick Hits

Chapter 3

SECTION 3.1—BUILDING A HOSPITALITY CAREER

- People choose careers in hospitality because of its varied career options and work, the opportunities to be creative, flexible hours, growth potential, and the perks.

- There are benefits to working for either a large chain or an independent operation, depending on what a person wants from his or her career.

- Independent restaurants offer great opportunities for people who want to be entrepreneurs while the chain restaurants offer a great deal of growth in a less risky environment.

- Club careers differ from other hospitality businesses because the guests are also the owners.

- The cruise industry offers careers both shore side and at sea.

- Each job you take is a stepping stone on a career path or career ladder.

- A résumé is an advertisement for yourself that helps to convince the person doing the hiring that they should interview you.

- An interview is an opportunity to sell yourself and sell the prospective employer on offering you a job.

SECTION 3.2—PRESENTING A PROFESSIONAL IMAGE

- Professionalism is the behavior or qualities that mark someone who is excellent in his or her field of work or who is an excellent hospitality employee.

- A professional image represents how other people perceive hospitality employees. Image is largely formed by appearance, personality, and posture.

- Good grooming, such as clean hair, hands, fingernails, and wardrobe is essential to the professional image.

- Personality refers to the way a person acts, looks, and thinks. Allowing one's pleasant personality to show through contributes to making a guest's stay memorable.

- Posture, such as standing upright and staying alert, is just as crucial to the professional image as grooming and personality.

SECTION 3.3—PROFESSIONALISM ON THE JOB

- Hospitality employers have certain expectations of their new employees. While most lodging properties have orientations to cover this information, new employees should still ask questions and watch carefully.

- Most lodging properties have professional standards of conduct that they expect employees to adhere to. In many cases, not adhering to these standards can lead to reprimands or dismissals.

- Getting along with the boss is important to job success. There are a number of different problems that hospitality employees can have with their supervisors. Likewise, there are just as many strategies for making these relationships better.

- Lodging employers have structured expectations related to work schedules, absences, dress regulations, and personal business, to name a few.

- Many properties offer such benefits as vacation time and sick pay to reward professional employees.

Section 3.4—Hospitality Teamwork

- To be successful, a lodging property needs each employee to work as part of a team so that everyone can do their jobs to the benefit of guests.

- Factors important in teamwork include a good attitude, cooperation, promptness, and loyalty.

- Formal work groups are necessary in the hospitality industry because of the large number of employees and services offered. Formal work groups include divisions such as food and beverage, and departments such as housekeeping.

- Informal work groups form because of similarities among co-workers. The informal groups are not inherently good or bad, but they do affect a hospitality operation.

Section 3.5—Differences and Diversity

- In the United States, the hospitality work force is made up of a wide variety of cultures, races, languages, and nationality.

- Hospitality work forces are culturally diverse. Diversity refers to the variety among people relative to age, race, gender, ethnicity, religion, sexual orientation, etc.

- Differences in the workplace are important because they lead to new ideas and effective solutions. They can increase productivity and make work educational, interesting, and fun.

- Getting along in a diverse workplace can be made easier by recognizing and being open about the differences. Being aware of our perceptions of these differences is also important. Putting oneself in another's place is one technique that can be very effective in getting along with others.

Safety and Security

Sections

Guests expect safety, security, and privacy when visiting a property. As a result, properties should provide reasonable security for guests, visitors, and employees. Making guests secure is part of providing excellent guest service.

Providing security in a lodging property means protecting people—guests, employees, visitors, and others who have a lawful reason to be at the property. It also means protecting items that belong to these people and to the property.

Lodging employees are a vital part of the property's security system. They watch who enters the property, look for unusual situations, and check locks and other security equipment to make sure they work properly.

They are also the property's security alarm. A dangerous situation can be prevented when they report what they see. They report burned-out light bulbs, broken windows and locks, people who seem suspicious or out-of-place, and other problems or possible problems.

Good security and safe working habits play a role in providing fairly priced rooms. In helping to reduce losses for the property through injury, theft, vandalism, or accidents, lodging employees help keep operating costs lower. These savings can be passed along to guests in the form of reasonable room rates.

4.1   Safety in the Workplace

AFTER SUCCESSFULLY COMPLETING THIS SECTION, YOU WILL BE ABLE TO:

◆ Describe safe methods for lifting, moving, and carrying items.

◆ Identify how OSHA regulations affect lodging properties.

◆ Explain how lodging employees protect themselves from bloodborne pathogens.

Safe Work Habits

Employees must be careful to lift, carry, and move items correctly so that they are not injured. When lifting items, they:

• Place their feet shoulder-width apart to maintain balance.

• Grasp the item with both hands.

• Bend their knees; don't bend at the waist.

• Keep their back straight.

• Use their leg muscles, keeping the item close to their body.

• Get help if an item is too heavy or is an awkward shape.

When moving or carrying items, they:

• Hold the item close to their body.

• Point their toes in the direction they are headed and turn their entire body in that direction.

• Step carefully.

• Watch where they are going.

OSHA Regulations

The **Occupational Safety and Health Administration** (OSHA) is a federal agency that helps keep employees safe by regulating sanitation, safety, and first aid in the workplace. OSHA regulations cover a variety of areas that concern lodging employees.

OSHA regulations deal with such areas as hallways, storerooms, and service areas. These regulations require that work areas be kept clean, neat, and sanitary. Regulations also require that hallways, passageways, and stairways have guard-rails and railings.

OSHA regulations require special signs for safety reasons. Three different types of signs are generally needed at a lodging property:

• **Danger signs** (red, black, and white)— used only in areas where there is an immediate hazard, such as where a caustic cleaning liquid has been spilled.

• **Caution signs** (yellow and black)—used to warn against a possible hazard, such as a wet floor.

- **Safety instruction signs** (green and white or black and white)—used to give general instructions, such as to tell employees not to eat in storage areas.

The OSHA **Hazard Communication Standard** requires all U.S. employers to tell their employees about hazardous materials that employees may be required to handle to do their jobs. The standard is commonly referred to as HazComm or OSHA's right-to-know legislation.

Material Safety Data Sheets (MSDSs) must be collected for each hazardous chemical used, and must be filed where employees may read them at any time. MSDSs are forms that list a product's hazardous components, health hazard data, and spill or leak procedures, as well as special precautions or protective gear required when using the product.

The MSDS form that OSHA developed has a section labeled "Health Hazard Data" that specifies first-aid procedures for accidents involving different chemicals. For instance, the form may say to flush a person's eyes with water for one to five minutes if a certain cleaner splashes into that person's eyes. These forms are useful for all accidents involving hazardous chemicals.

Lodging properties use a variety of chemicals that make HAZCOM compliance important. For example:

- Chlorine in pool areas

- Ammonia-based cleaners

- Chlorine-based cleaners

- Abrasives

- Acids, such as vinegar, which are used to clean glass and stainless steel

- Pesticides

- Disinfectants

Each chemical has an individual set of hazards to avoid.

Bloodborne Pathogens

Bloodborne pathogens are viruses, bacteria, and other microorganisms. These organisms are carried in a person's bloodstream and other body fluids and can cause the Hepatitis B Virus (HBV), the Human Immunodeficiency Virus (HIV), and other infections.

Lodging properties try to keep the workplace safe by having their employees take safety precautions. They give employees who must handle items that may contain bloodborne pathogens special training on safety policies, procedures, and equipment.

Lodging employees can protect themselves from bloodborne pathogens by:

- Covering cuts, scrapes, hangnails, rashes, and other open wounds with a bandage at all times while at work.

- Handling sharp objects (needles or other objects that can pierce the skin) carefully.

- Eating, drinking, smoking, handling contact lenses, and applying cosmetics and lip balms only in areas where bloodborne pathogens are not likely to be present.

- Washing your hands and skin immediately after contact with body fluids or objects that might be contaminated, and reporting the incident to security.

- Reporting any contaminated area to security or the manager on duty.

Equipment that can help protect employees from bloodborne pathogens includes masks and eye protection, aprons, pocket resuscitation masks, and gloves.

For gloves to provide enough protection, employees follow these procedures:

- Never reuse disposable latex or nylon gloves.

- Only reuse utility, vinyl, and leather gloves after they have been properly disinfected.

- Always examine gloves for tears, cracks, and holes before and after use. Do not use damaged gloves.

- Remove gloves properly and wash their hands.

Apply Your Learning 4.1

Please write all answers on a separate sheet of paper.

1. How can a lodging employee safely lift a heavy crate of linens?

2. What does OSHA stand for?

3. What type of sign is yellow and black?

4. What does MSDS stand for?

5. How can lodging employees protect themselves from bloodborne pathogens?

4.2 *Access and Key Control*

AFTER SUCCESSFULLY COMPLETING THIS SECTION, YOU WILL BE ABLE TO:

◆ Explain how a property maintains access control.

◆ Identify the types of keys a property uses.

◆ Describe how key control contributes to a property's security measures.

◆ List the important elements of guestroom security.

Access Control

Access control means watching the property's entrances, especially those that lead to guestrooms or guestroom areas. Access control helps protect the property, its guests, and employees.

Specially trained staff carry out most access control activities. But all hotel employees should be aware of possible access control problems.

Access control at a property may involve special equipment or **patrols** (regular checks of the building and grounds).

Access control equipment includes such things as:

• Hall mirrors

• Closed-circuit televisions

• Parking lot gates

• Exit doors and locks

• Fences

• Lighting

• Alarms

Access control equipment alone cannot stop security problems. It takes alert employees to respond to this equipment and report it if it is out of order.

Patrols are generally carried out by specially trained employees and can help prevent crime. Employees who conduct patrols could be members of the security staff, managers, or even the night auditor. All lodging employees should know who patrols your property and be able to tell the difference between that person and a possible intruder.

Security is a team effort. All lodging employees can contribute to this team effort when it comes to access control by:

• Being aware of the access control equipment the property uses and reporting it when it is out of order.

• Knowing who patrols the property.

• Knowing what doors in their areas should be kept locked at all times and reporting doors that they find unlocked.

• Knowing what areas are off-limits to employees.

- Allowing people into areas only if they have a right to be there.

Keys and Locks

Locks help ensure guest privacy, safety, and security. If the keys to these locks are not carefully watched and controlled, however, the security of the property and its guests could be at risk. Controlling the keys used at a property is an important way to prevent crime.

Different lodging properties use different types of keys and locks in guest areas:

- Card with magnetic strips and electronic locks

- Metal keys and mechanical locks

The vast majority of properties use cards and electronic locking systems.

Most properties also have several levels of **master keys** and submaster keys that are designed to open several different locks, and **emergency keys** that unlock all doors at a property, even deadbolts.

Who uses keys at a property?

- *Managers.* Typically, managers handle the keys to areas within their departments.

- *Employees.* Employees sometimes handle property keys. For example, room attendants may use master keys to unlock guestroom doors in their assigned work areas. And guest service representatives may give guestroom keys to registered guests and collect keys from guests when they check out.

- *Guests.* Guests have a room key that unlocks the door to their room. Sometimes the guestroom key also opens doors to the swimming pool, fitness center, elevators, or certain building entrances.

Key Control

Lodging properties have many procedures to help control key and lock use. These include:

- Giving room keys only to registered guests.

- Asking to see identification, such as a driver's license, before giving a registered guest a room key.

- Having a supervisor or manager go with a guest to his or her guestroom to get identification, if necessary.

- Putting notices in guestrooms or check-in folders that explain how to use room locks and remind guests to lock their doors and windows.

- Placing locked **key-return boxes** in the lobby and in the property's limousines or courtesy vans to remind guests to return room keys.

- Providing locked key boxes on room attendants' carts to store guestroom keys that have been left in guestrooms.

Lodging employees help control key use and keep the property safe by:

- Showing guests how to operate locks on their guestroom doors, windows, and connecting room doors.

- Never letting guests into a locked room. Send guests to the front desk if they need a room key.

- Returning any found keys to the proper department, the front desk, a supervisor, or a manager.

- Keeping any property keys attached to a belt, wrist band, or neck chain at all times during a shift.

- Signing keys in and out according to property procedures.

- Using keys only for their intended and approved purpose.

Guestroom Security

When you think of guestroom security, you probably think of locks and view ports on doors; window latches; or in-room safes. Guestroom security, however, covers much more.

It includes such things as:

- Good lighting in hallways

- Key control procedures

- Guestroom telephone

- Telling guests about security at the property

In simple terms, guestroom security includes all equipment and activities that keep guests and their belongings safe in the guestroom.

Most properties use special equipment in and out of guestrooms to keep them secure. This equipment includes many types of door and window locks and latches, view ports, house and guestroom telephones, alarms, hall lighting, **safe-deposit boxes**, and in-room safes.

Besides special equipment, properties have policies to keep guestrooms secure. These policies include such things as:

- Asking to see room keys before letting people into areas for guests' use only (for example, pools, playgrounds, spas).

- Giving room keys only to guests registered to a room.

- Not giving out guest or guestroom information to anyone.

Often, properties tell guests about the equipment and policies that help keep them safe. There are many ways properties can do this. They can:

- Give guests security reminders when they check in.

- Post security tips in guestrooms, on card key envelopes, on private television channels, in check-in folders, etc.

- Post emergency procedures on the back of guestroom doors.

- Answer guests' questions about the property's guestroom security.

- Require bell staff to explain in-room safety features when they escort guests to their room.

Finally, many properties assign patrols around corridors and stairways around guestroom areas.

Here are five things every lodging employee can do to help support guestroom security at their property:

1. Know what guestroom security equipment is used at the property and be able to tell guests how to use that equipment. They should also look for and immediately report any problems they find with guestroom security equipment.

2. Never unlock a door for someone who asks unless they are authorized to do so by their property's procedures.

3. Be thoroughly familiar with their property's guestroom security policies

and procedures. They follow these policies and procedures in a way that does not insult guests.

4. Report possible threats to guestroom security such as:

- Guns and weapons

- Bad smells such as smoke coming from guestrooms

- Pets that the property does not allow

- Unlocked guestroom doors or windows

- Dangerous electrical appliances in guestrooms

5. Tell guests how they can help keep themselves secure. Always be ready to:

- Tell guests not to leave valuables in their rooms or cars—unless they lock them in the trunk.

- Explain to guests where emergency information can be found in their rooms.

Once in a while, there will be guests who don't like to be away from home. These guests are sometimes nervous about staying in a strange place. Lodging employees take extra time to answer these guests' questions and concerns about security.

Apply Your Learning 4.2

Please write all answers on a separate sheet of paper.

1. What types of equipment do properties use to control access to its grounds?

2. What does a master key open?

3. What does an emergency key open?

4. What are two procedures that aid in key control?

5. What equipment can be used in a guestroom to keep the room more secure?

6. How can a lodging employee help support guestroom security?

4.3 Theft, Disturbances, and Suspicious People

AFTER SUCCESSFULLY COMPLETING THIS SECTION, YOU WILL BE ABLE TO:

◆ Identify ways that a property can prevent theft.

◆ Describe ways to deal with a disturbance.

◆ Explain how to respond to suspicious people.

Theft

It's a scary idea, but just about anyone at a property could be a thief. A thief could be:

• A guest who takes towels or bathrobes

• An employee who takes home anything from paper to food supplies

• A criminal hanging around the property looking for an opportunity to steal

Although most people are honest, some guests and employees do steal. Most properties deter guest theft in a number of ways. Three common ways are:

• Locking storage and supply rooms.

• Keeping track of the number of guestroom items such as towels. This helps properties track and sometimes get back stolen items.

• Bolting items such as pictures, television sets, and radios to guestroom floors, walls, and furniture.

The same methods listed above also help properties fight theft by employees. Additional methods are:

• Using a labeling system that helps separate employee belongings from those of the property.

• Conducting bag checks at employee entrances and exits.

• Enforcing a **package pass** policy that identifies employee belongings from those of the property.

• Installing devices that can tell who entered a particular room and when.

• Depending on honest employees to report dishonest ones.

Any theft costs the property money. But when guests' belongings are stolen, it could hurt the property's good name, too. And that could cost the property business.

All employees play a part in reducing theft of guests' belongings:

- Being alert to suspicious people, guest-room security, access control, and key and lock control

- Reminding guests not to leave valuables in their rooms or cars—unless they lock them in the trunk.

- Providing safe deposit boxes.

- Warning guests about high-crime areas around the property and the city.

Theft victims feel angry and frustrated. If the stolen item had special meaning to them, they feel even more upset. Lodging employees can help the theft victim and the property by responding sympathetically and calling a supervisor or manager right away so that the theft can be reported. They may also:

- Ask if the guest has other valuables that they can secure for him or her.

- Tell the guest what they will do according to their property's policies.

Never say things like:

- "If we had better locks at our hotel this wouldn't have happened."

- "This is the third theft reported this week; something's obviously wrong with our security system."

- "You had better let me lock up your valuables. Maybe there's a thief working at the hotel."

If reporters ask about a robbery, employees refer them to the manager.

Disturbances

A **disturbance** is anything that interrupts normal activities at the property or upsets the comfort of guests. When guests come to a property, they want a pleasant and safe visit. One example of a disturbance is when loud noises from the room next door keep guests awake. Another is when someone in the restaurant offends a guest by talking loudly and using vulgar language.

Procedures for dealing with disturbances are different from property to property. In some properties, employees are told to immediately telephone management or security when a disturbance happens. At other properties, employees deal with disturbances themselves.

Lodging employees should never put themselves in danger.

Disturbances happen in many different places and in many ways. Exhibit 1 gives three different situations and reviews actions that employees responsible for disturbances could take in each situation, but only if they feel safe doing so.

Suspicious People

A **suspicious person** is anyone—an employee, visitor, or guest—who gives you the feeling that something might be wrong. The way people look or the way they act may make you suspect them.

Properties may also have special equipment to help employees watch for suspicious people. Examples of special equipment include hall mirrors and **closed-circuit televisions**.

Special procedures and equipment may help, but it is up to each employee to look for anything that is not normal. They know better than anyone else what is normal in their work areas and what is not.

- Look lost, nervous, or out-of-place

- Hang around in one area

Exhibit 1
Handling Disturbances

Situation	If it is the property's policy, the employee might:
The employee is in the lobby when a disturbance happens.	1. Ask, "Can I help you?" 2. Ask the person causing the disturbance if he or she is a guest. 3. If so, ask to see the person's room key. 4. Explain the property's policy about the correct use of the property and grounds. 5. Be calm and polite, but firm. 6. If necessary, show the person off the property or call the correct staff person to do this. 7. Immediately report what happened to the supervisor or manager.
The employee is working alone when a guestroom disturbance is reported.	1. Ask, "Can I help you?" 2. Call the room where the disturbance is going on and ask to speak with the guest registered for that room. 3. Tell the guest that a complaint has been made, but do not say who made the complaint. 4. Tell the guest that further disturbances could result in his or her being asked to leave the property. 5. If more complaints are made about the room, tell the supervisor or manager or call the police, if this is the property's policy.

The employee is working with other employees when a guestroom disturbance is reported.	Go with another employee and check out the complaint, or call the police.
	• If checking out the complaint:
	  1. Knock on the door and state names and job titles. Do not enter the guestroom, even if the people inside open the door.
	  2. Do not make the situation worse by yelling or making threatening gestures; stay calm and reasonable.

(continued)

Exhibit 1
Handling Disturbances *(continued)*

Situation	If it is the property's policy, the employee might:

	3. Try to get the troublemakers to end the situation. Separate the people by asking the non-registered guests to leave.
	
	4. If the problem continues, leave the disturbance and tell the supervisor manager.
	
	• If police are called, write down as many details as possible about the situation:
	
	  1. The day and time the complaint came in
	  2. What happened
	  3. When and where it happened
	  4. Why it happened
	  5. Who was involved
	  6. What was done

A lodging property, although open to the public, is a private property. Lodging properties have three types of areas: public areas, guest areas, and employee areas. **Public areas** are places that are open to all people, such as hotel lobbies. **Guest areas** are places such as guestroom hallways where only guests, their visitors, and on-duty employees are allowed. **Employee areas** are those in which only employees on duty are allowed. Employees need to control the activity of people in all three areas of the property.

Suspicious people often act oddly. They may:

• Try to enter employee areas

• Go from room to room knocking on or trying to open doors

Many properties have special procedures to make it easier for employees to spot suspicious people. Some properties control entrances that are not in view of employees. Some properties require employees to wear uniforms or identification badges so they can be easily recognized.

It is almost impossible to know whether someone who seems a little odd is harmless or dangerous. If employees think someone is suspicious but are not sure, it is best they check things out. But they should never go up to someone who looks dangerous or makes them feel uncomfortable.

Several situations may come up where lodging employees have to deal with suspicious people. Here are some ways they can handle the situations:

- If the suspicious person is not an employee, they ask whether the person is a guest and ask to see his or her room key.

- If the person does not have a room key, they direct him or her to the front desk.

- If the person is not a guest, they ask politely what he or she is doing at the property. They avoid getting into an argument or long talk with the person.

- If the person should not be at the property, they show him or her off of the premises or call a supervisor or manager.

- If they find a co-worker in an off-limits area, they ask whether the person needs help. If he or she acts suspiciously, they report what they saw to a supervisor or manager.

Many properties ask employees to file—or help security staff write—a report about suspicious people according to the following guidelines:

- Complete the report (or give security staff information about it) as soon after the experience as possible.

- Tell what happened.

- Give the exact day and time of the incident.

- Identify the people involved.

- Tell where they saw the suspicious person and why the person seemed suspicious.

- Give only the facts; leave out their feelings and opinions.

- Re-read the report and make sure it tells what really happened.

- If they write the report themselves, they sign and date it, and give it to their manager.

Apply Your Learning 4.3

Please write all answers on a separate sheet of paper.

1. Who at the property could be a thief?

2. What is a package pass?

3. What is a disturbance?

4. Where can a disturbance take place?

5. Who is allowed in the guest areas of a property?

6. How should an employee respond to a suspicious person who is not an employee and does not have a room key?

4.4 Security Concerns

AFTER SUCCESSFULLY COMPLETING THIS SECTION, YOU WILL BE ABLE TO:

◆ Describe the procedures for handling lost and found items.

◆ Explain how the Americans with Disabilities Act affects security at a lodging property.

◆ Describe a lodging property's security department and the activities it performs.

◆ Identify the types of security documentation that lodging employees create.

◆ Explain how different types of special events affect the security of a lodging property.

Lost and Found

Most properties have policies and staff for handling misplaced items or items guests have left behind. Often, the housekeeping department handles lost and found items.

Guests appreciate it when lost items are returned to them. It shows the property is concerned about security and service.

State laws may require properties to follow certain procedures for storing, returning, and handling lost and found items. To make sure guests receive correct information, only the lost and found staff should talk about these items with guests.

If guests tell lodging employees that they have lost an item, employees direct them to the lost and found. If employees find an item, they take it to the lost and found area right away. If a guest gives an employee an item they have found, they:

• Thank the guest for giving them the item.

• Ask where and when the item was found.

• Write the guest's name down.

• Take the item to the lost and found area right away.

At many properties, lost and found items are tagged and put in a secure place. Some properties also have their employees record information about lost and found items in a **log book**.

Americans with Disabilities Act

The **Americans with Disabilities Act** (ADA) protects the rights of people with disabilities. A disability is a physical or mental impairment and may include:

• Physical handicap

• Vision impairment

• Hearing impairment

• Mental handicap

- AIDS and other illnesses, including cancer or leukemia

- Arthritis

In brief, ADA:

- Makes it illegal for employers to discriminate against hiring, promoting, or firing a qualified person with disabilities.

- Requires public businesses to make their workplaces more accessible to people with disabilities.

Lodging facilities must be accessible to people with various disabilities. Lodging properties often serve more people with disabilities than other public businesses. Lodging properties must provide convenient accommodations for their guests with disabilities. Convenient accommodations may mean:

- Ramps or elevators instead of stairs and escalators for people using wheelchairs

- Braille signs for the blind

- Automatic doors

- Drinking fountains and desks at appropriate levels for people using wheelchairs

- Text telephones and visual alarms for the hearing-impaired

Guests with disabilities provide special security challenges:

- Safety during emergencies

- Obstacles to the safety

- Communication

Have you ever tried to find your way around a place you've never been before? You probably had to ask for directions, and you might have taken a wrong turn or two before you got to where you wanted to be. How did you feel? Most people would feel a little nervous or anxious when dealing with a new environment and situation. Some people might even feel afraid.

Now imagine how you would feel if you were in a wheelchair, or if you couldn't see, or if you were unable to speak clearly. Your stress level would probably increase. In addition to facing the same challenges that you do, people with disabilities also face communication and mobility challenges.

Lodging employees can help make sure guests with disabilities stay safe during emergencies by doing the following:

- Making sure hallways and emergency exits are easily accessible, and not blocked.

- Explaining emergency procedures while escorting a guest with a disability to his or her room, and stating how far away emergency exits are.

- Making sure the front desk keeps track of the room numbers and types of disability of guests.

Security Department

You may have seen old movies that included a character called the house detective. The house detective was a tough-talking, one-man security force who wore a shoulder holster and slouchy hat, and chomped a cigar.

Lodging security has changed a lot since the days of the house detective. Today's lodging security officers are more likely to be female than they were 30 or 40 years ago. Today's officers are also expected to use advanced equipment such as closed-circuit television, computerized locks, and complex communication systems —inventions the house detective never dreamed of.

Lodging security officers may report directly to the general manager at the property, to the front office manager, or to the director of security, or even to a human resources manager, depending on the size of the property and how it is organized.

An in-house security department is only one way that a property may provide security. It may also contract security staff from the ranks of local off-duty police officers or from a local security company.

No matter who fulfills the security function at the property, the primary responsibility of a lodging security effort is to protect people and property by *preventing* crimes and accidents.

To prevent problems, most security officers are involved in the following six activities:

1. *Maintaining guestroom security.* Keeping guestrooms safe and secure includes:

   - Patrolling guest areas to spot suspicious people

   - Discouraging criminal activity by making sure hallway lighting is in working order

   - Making guests aware of and encouraging them to use security features in their rooms

2. *Controlling access to the property.* Security is responsible for making sure the building and grounds of the property are secure. This may involve such activities as:

   - Foot and vehicle patrols of areas around the property

   - Monitoring surveillance devices such as closed-circuit television cameras

   - Checking fences

   - Investigating suspicious people or situations reported by other employees

3. *Protecting assets.* **Assets** include items such as money, equipment, supplies, and the personal valuables of guests and employees. Protecting assets includes all the activities listed earlier for maintaining guestroom security and controlling access to the property. In addition, it involves things such as:

   - Lost and found procedures

   - Safe-deposit boxes and in-room safes

   - Credit and billing procedures

   - Inventory controls of food, alcoholic beverages, sheets and towels

4. *Handling emergencies.* Security provides guidance in handling emergencies such as heart attacks, injuries, fires, floods, and power failures. Security often develops emergency preparedness plans. In addition, many lodging properties encourage or even require officers to have first aid and CPR training.

5. *Investigating incidents.* If front desk employees notice a suspicious person, or room attendants discover an unconscious guest, or a guest discovers something is missing from his or her room, security staff are most likely to be called to investigate the situation and decide what action to take.

6. *Keeping security records.* Security must keep records of routine security activities as well as incident investigations. These records help the property identify ways to improve security and

provide essential information to local, state, and federal law enforcement agencies. These records are especially important in helping a property involved in a lawsuit.

Security Documentation

Because of the many legal risks in the lodging industry, security efforts must be well-documented to prevent and respond to lawsuits. This means taking notes and filling out daily logs, activity reports, and incident reports based on facts and observations rather than opinions or conclusions.

Taking notes for a job is similar to taking notes in class. Lodging employees need to pick out important pieces of information which may be hidden in a lot of other details. The information may be based on what someone tells them or on their personal observations.

For a lodging employee, taking notes means writing their observations about a situation immediately after they experience the incident. It also means writing down any actions they took to respond to the situation.

Lodging employees take notes in such situations as when they:

- Notice any unusual situations or suspicious individuals during a patrol.

- Investigate a crime.

- Respond to an emergency.

- Take action to prevent a fire or safety hazard.

- Communicate with a guest about a request, complaint, or security concern.

It probably sounds as though lodging employees could be constantly writing. Unless they know what kind of information is important, this could happen—and that would be a waste of time. Some incidents may require employees to take a lot of notes. For example, if someone tries to steal a car from the parking lot, they may need to remember information, such as a description of the criminal or the make, model, and color of the car. Other situations may not require extensive notes, such as when they spot a burned-out light in a hallway.

Notes can be used to help employees remember:

- Things that they need to do at specific times or places, such as locking pool area doors at 10 P.M.

- To recheck unusual details or hazards.

- Unusual or suspicious behavior, vehicles, or details that they spotted.

- Actions they took to respond to a situation.

- Descriptions of events.

- Observations made at incident or crime scenes.

- Facts that need to go on other forms.

Why are notes so important? Information employees pick up on the job may be needed to fill out activity reports and incident reports. Notes help employees keep track of details while they are still fresh in their minds. Memory can change details of events unintentionally. The more time that passes, the less likely it will be that employees can remember details accurately. Exhibit 1 contains tips for taking notes.

An **activity report** (sometimes called a daily log) gives detailed descriptions of what happened on a particular day and at a particular time during a shift. They are filled out at the end of a shift. Each activity report contains the employee's name, the exact time he or she started and ended a shift, and the badge number if appropriate.

Other information that may be included:

- Fire or safety hazards that were noticed and any actions taken to correct the hazard

- Emergencies

- Any suspicious, illegal or prohibited activities (including any by employees)

- Contact with law enforcement, fire, emergency, or medical personnel

- Accidents or injuries that were dealt with during the shift

- Any special guest or employee requests

Lodging employees may also have to fill out an **incident report** for any accidents, emergencies, or crimes that they handle during their shift. Incident reports are different from activity reports even though they contain some of the same information. An activity report covers all of an employee's activities for an entire work shift. An incident report focuses on one unusual event that happened during a shift and that directly affected security. Usually incident reports cover these events:

- Emergencies such as fires, weather or natural disasters, and medical emergencies

- Crimes reported on the property

- Conflicts between people, such as dealing with an intoxicated guest or a trespasser

- Civil unrest, strikes, or demonstrations

- Accidents

Special Events

The lodging industry is not just an endless stream of guests checking in and out. Most lodging properties also cater to a number of special events. Conventions, receptions, exhibits, and handling VIP guests are just a few of the special situations that employees may encounter at a property.

While it may be exciting to be involved behind the scenes of special events, there's a lot of work involved, especially from a security standpoint. Each event has its own set of security concerns.

Conventions

Conventions are part of the lifeblood of the lodging industry. They can bring a lot of people, publicity, and profit to the property. However, they can also bring a lot of security headaches to a property.

Preparation is the key to providing effective security during conventions. The more employees know about the convention group, the better they can predict problems that might develop during the event. For example:

- What kind of group is it? The type of group will affect the kind of security provided. A controversial group may encourage demonstrations or even terrorist threats.

- How many people are expected? The more people at the property, the greater the chance of problems developing.

- What types of events will be held during the convention?

- What are the demographics of the group? Ages? Occupations? There are different problems from a convention

Exhibit 1
Taking Notes

- Write your observations immediately, while they are still fresh in your mind.

- Write neatly and legibly. You don't want to have to figure out what you wrote later.

- Write in pen. If you make a mistake, cross out the mistake with one single line.

- Keep your observations professional. Never make slurs or write comments that you wouldn't want made public.

Provide details. Whenever you take notes, try to provide:

- The Five W's: who, what, where, when, and why

- Date, time and place of the occurrence and the time you arrived on the scene (if different)

- Detailed description of what happened

- Specific details about anyone who provides information, including the person's

    - Name

    - Address

    - Phone number

    - Title, department, and employee number if he or she is a property employee

    - Description of the person's role during the event, such as witness, victim, first on scene, etc., and his or her mood or emotional state (nervous, confused, alert, etc.)

- What happened or what was reported to you

- What actions you took

- Names of any official personnel (fire, police, ambulance) that you had contact with (if appropriate)

- What time you notified police, fire, ambulance, etc. and what time they arrived

- Unusual details or circumstances

- Sketch or diagram of the scene

- If and when your notes were transferred to another report

- Any language barriers that might affect your information

of student leaders than from a group of retired plumbers.

- Will alcohol be served or available to convention attendees?

- How will guests who are not part of the convention group affect the event? How will they be affected?

Alcohol can often be a problem during conventions. Some convention attendees look at the event as a vacation. Drinking often gets out of hand. Noise can also be a problem. Conventions can get boisterous and this can inconvenience other guests.

With so many people and the type of event, chances are increased for crime and accidents. Lodging employees must make every effort to limit access to the property to only those with legitimate reasons to be there.

Parties, receptions, and other special events

Lodging properties are often used to host parties, receptions, and other special events. Events such as these bring a lot of money and people to the property. They also bring security concerns. For example:

- Guests at a wedding reception may be dressed in their finest clothes and jewelry, and they might bring expensive presents for the bride and groom. It's part of a lodging property's job to make sure that no one steals the gifts or tries to rob the guests.

- A dinner to raise money for a local charity is being held at a property. Tickets are available at the door and large donations are expected. Thieves may try to steal the profits if property employees are not alert.

In most cases, the actions taken to provide security for parties, receptions, and other special events are the same as those taken for conventions. The biggest difference is that conventions usually last for a few days where special events usually go on for only one night.

VIPs

A VIP can be a rock star, a politician, a convention planner, a company executive, a famous author, an athlete, or a controversial religious figure. It may be someone whose face and name you recognize immediately or someone you may never have heard of before.

Information about VIPs staying at a property is confidential. Employees shouldn't tell relatives, friends, or employees not directly involved with the VIP's stay as it can create additional security problems, such as crowds of people, media coverage, or threats against the VIP.

Employees who are assigned to handle VIP guests investigate them just as they would conventions, especially if the guests are controversial. They might call the property where the VIP last stayed and ask about security problems that occurred or preventive measures they took.

Lodging employees also try to keep the commotion to a minimum as there are other guests at the property whose needs cannot be ignored.

Apply Your Learning 4.4

Please write all answers on a separate sheet of paper.

1. What should an employee do if a guest gives them a found item?
2. Who is covered under the ADA?
3. What sort of accommodations can be made for guests with disabilities?
4. What activities does a lodging security department perform?
5. When should a lodging security employee take notes?
6. What is recorded in an activity report?
7. What is recorded in an incident report?
8. What is often a security problem during conventions?
9. How can employees check out VIPs?

4.5 Handling Emergencies

AFTER SUCCESSFULLY COMPLETING THIS SECTION, YOU WILL BE ABLE TO:

♦ Identify topics on which lodging employees need training for handling emergencies.

♦ Demonstrate techniques for handling fires.

♦ Describe procedures for handling power failures.

♦ Handle elevator malfunctions.

♦ Explain how lodging employees respond to weather emergencies.

♦ Name actions employees may perform during a medical emergency.

♦ Explain what to do if an employee or guest dies.

♦ Describe how to respond to civil unrest.

♦ Identify ways to respond if weapons are found at the property.

An emergency is an urgent situation that requires immediate action. It can be stressful for anyone involved.

How do lodging employees prepare for a situation that they can't predict? It takes training, equipment, and regularly scheduled activities. This means learning how to handle given situations and how to use necessary equipment. It also means practicing emergency procedures on a regular basis.

Emergency Preparation Training

The most common basic emergency procedures that lodging employees are expected to know are:

• Evacuation techniques

• First aid

• Basic firefighting techniques (on a small scale)

• Power failure response techniques

• Crowd control

• Emergency equipment use

Many properties provide training on basic emergency procedures. In some cases, employees may have to get training before they are allowed to start work. At other properties, they may get their training on the job in the first few days or week.

Employees are also trained to use emergency equipment, such as:

• Fire extinguishers and hoses

• Manual elevator controls

• Emergency generators

• First-aid kits

- Oxygen in tanks

- Gas and electric shut-off valves

Each property has different characteristics—such as the size or number of employees—that affect how an emergency is handled. Because no two properties are exactly alike, each property's emergency procedures will be different. For example, procedures for responding to a tornado warning at a high-rise property will be different than procedures used by a one-story property.

Training may not come directly from a lodging property. For example, the fire department may provide training on how to use fire extinguishers, fire hoses, or other fire safety techniques. Local health organizations usually provide first–aid training, especially for serious procedures such as **CPR** or **mouth-to-mouth resuscitation**. Vendors of equipment or supplies may provide training on how to use their products.

Some organizations that may provide emergency preparation training are:

- Local branch of the American Red Cross

- Hospitals

- Police departments

- Fire departments

- Emergency medical teams

- Local health departments

- Community colleges

- Equipment or supply vendors

Emergency Drills

Because emergencies don't usually happen often at a property, there is no way to fully prepare for them. That's why properties conduct emergency drills. By simulating emergencies, everyone at the property can become familiar with the procedures for handling various situations. The more familiar employees are with procedures, the more prepared they will be to handle a real emergency. A prepared property is a safer property.

Some drills include:

- Fire drills

- Evacuation drills

- Medical emergency response drills

- Power failure drills

- Weather emergency and natural disaster drills

Usually emergency drills will be run by the manager-on-duty, the general manager, a supervisor, or the chief engineer or head of maintenance. Most properties conduct emergency drills every three to six months. Drills for weather emergencies may be held at the start of every weather season.

Fires

Fire alarms and power failures are the most common emergencies experienced in the lodging industry.

Lodging properties are encouraged to have written emergency plans which outline what needs to be done to protect people and property in a specific emergency. These plans can help each employee know exactly what he or she is expected to do in an emergency.

When you know in advance how to respond to a fire emergency or power failure, you not only make better decisions, but you can save time making the decisions. And when you save time, you have a better opportunity to manage the situation effectively. You can also increase guest satisfaction when you show guests that the property is prepared to handle these emergencies.

If a fire does break out at a property, every second counts. Fires can double in size every 60 seconds. Even a small fire can quickly rage out of control unless immediate action is taken.

Fire alarms may be triggered automatically by heat or smoke detectors, or manually.

Although some fire alarms turn out to be false alarms, lodging employees respond to every alarm as if it's the real thing. Every alarm should be treated as valid until a manager or emergency personnel confirm that it's a false alarm.

Initial actions should depend on the answers to these questions:

- Where is the fire?

- Are people in immediate danger?

- How big is the fire?

- Has the fire department been called?

If people are in immediate danger, lodging employees evacuate them at once if possible. If the fire does not pose an immediate threat to lives, they notify the fire department first. If possible, they notify the fire department and guests at the same time. Lodging employees usually notify the fire department in one of three ways:

- Trigger a pull station fire alarm.

- Radio or call the front desk or PBX operator and have someone call the fire department.

- Call the fire department themselves.

After lodging employees evacuate the area, they can try to keep the fire from spreading, but only if it's safe to do so. Their safety is as important as that of the people around them, so they are discouraged from trying to be a hero if it puts them at risk.

Lodging employees must use common sense when deciding whether it's safe to try to put out a fire. They consider the equipment they have on hand, how quickly the fire is growing, and the possibility of something in the area exploding. They attempt to put out only small, contained fires, and then only if they feel comfortable doing so. They make sure they have a safe escape route to use if they can't put out the fire. They also always make sure the fire department has been called before trying to put out a fire.

If it's not safe to put out the fire, there are still some things lodging employees can do as they leave the area to prevent the fire from spreading:

- Close windows, doors, and fire doors behind them.

- Remove **combustible** materials, such as gasoline or oily rags, from the area, but only if they have time.

- Shut off fans, air conditioners, or air circulators.

- If possible, shut off fuel to gas-powered equipment.

- If they think the fire is electrical, shut off electric current to the area.

If they do decide it's safe to try extinguishing the fire, they use the right equipment. Different types of fire extinguishers will put out different fires.

Fires are classified by the type of fuel that is burning, and fire extinguishers correspond to these classifications. For example, a wood fire can be put out with water. However, spraying water on a grease fire will only cause the grease (and the fire) to spread.

Lodging properties need to be concerned mainly with Class A, B, and C fires. Today many lodging properties use fire extinguishers that have been developed to put out fires in either Class A, B, or C. These extinguishers are clearly marked with the symbols "A-B-C" and can be used to put out all fires except those fueled by combustible elements.

When lodging employees find themselves in a fire area, they can protect themselves by:

- Making sure they always have an escape route and trying not to get cut off from an exit.

- Staying low in smoky conditions. Smoke rises and the air will be clearer close to the floor.

- If they get cut off, going into a guestroom and closing the door. They can seal around the door and vent openings with damp towels. They can try the phone to let someone know they are cut off. They can also fill the bathtub and sink with water to dampen towels and to keep the room door wet.

When firefighters arrive, lodging employees can help them as much as possible.

- Have master keys and a list of guests with disabilities available.

- Direct them to the fire.

- Answer any questions that they might have.

- Alert them to any potential dangers, such as hazardous materials, that might affect how they fight the fire.

- Follow their directions and obey their commands immediately—they are the experts in these situations and should have total command.

- Be prepared to leave the property if firefighters instruct them to do so.

Power Failures

Power failures are often triggered by some other emergency, such as severe weather, vandalism, or acts of terrorism. During a power failure, lodging employees have three major responsibilities:

1. Protect the safety of people at the property

2. Minimize vandalism

3. Secure money and valuable assets

The first priority is always the safety of the people at the property—including employees. Each property has a predesignated emergency command center (usually the front desk). Lodging employees should head to this command center. If they notice anyone trying to get around in the dark, they can help them get back to the main areas of the property, such as the lobby or evacuation areas.

If the problem is only in one area of the property, maintenance can try to fix it. Then other employees can concentrate on protecting the people around them.

- Post employees with flashlights at all ramps, escalators, and especially at stairways. The property may have battery-powered lamps that can be used as well.

- Notify guests about the problem. The front desk or PBX operator may do this by telephone or public address system, but if the systems are out, someone may be asked to go to guestrooms to give personal notice.

- Ask guests to remain in their rooms unless it is absolutely necessary that they leave. The more guests roaming around in the dark, the greater the chance that someone will get hurt. However, some situations, such as a fire, might justify the added risks of guests evacuating the guestroom areas.

- Some properties may advise guests to call the front desk for an escort if they need to leave their rooms.

- Be calm when speaking with guests. Reassure them that the situation is being taken care of and remind them of the danger of tripping or falling in the dark. The employees' attitudes will help keep them calm.

- Don't spend a lot of time talking to any one guest. There will probably be a lot of ground to cover and employees can't afford to waste time. Give guests only the information they need to know.

- Remind guests about the potential fire hazards of using matches, lighters, or candles for light. Tell guests to open drapes for external lighting during daylight.

Vandalism can be a big problem during power failures. The confusion in an emergency plus the poor lighting provide an excellent environment for wrongdoers, so employees need to maintain a visible presence on the property.

A power failure provides a perfect opportunity for criminals to try stealing property assets. Some employees will be asked to secure property valuables such as cash or important records.

Elevator Malfunctions

Elevator malfunctions can be caused by power failures, mechanical problems, or equipment failures. When an elevator isn't working correctly, it causes inconvenience and creates potential safety and security problems for a property.

If an elevator malfunctions, lodging employees try to find out what floors the car is trapped between. Then they try to communicate with anyone trapped inside.

- If the elevator's phone or intercom doesn't work, they call up the elevator shaft from below without entering the elevator shaft. Sound rises and will make it easier for passengers to hear.

- Reassure them of their safety. It can be frightening to be stuck in a small, enclosed space for even a short time.

- Ask them what happened when the elevator stopped. Try to find out anything that could help maintenance or the elevator company identify how to fix the elevator, such as sounds, strange vibrations or motions, or whether the emergency switch was accidentally activated.

- Tell the passengers what is being done and ask them to remain calm. Don't try to get them out of the elevator. Leave evacuation for the elevator company or the fire department.

Lodging employees then stay in communication with the passengers. Someone calls the maintenance department and gives them details about the problem so they can determine how to fix it. If the problem will take some time to fix, an employee updates the people trapped about any progress or lack of progress. If they are not kept posted, they may feel abandoned and start to panic.

Lodging properties must then keep people from using the elevator until it has been checked out and repaired. If possible, they lock the elevator with a key and place "Out of Service" signs near elevator doors until the elevator is fixed.

Weather Emergencies and Natural Disasters

Hurricanes. Floods. Tornados. Blizzards. Earthquakes. Ice and rain storms. All properties eventually experience some kind of weather emergency or natural disaster. Its location determines the type of weather it is most likely to experience. For example, hurricanes usually affect coastal areas, earthquakes happen more frequently on the West Coast, while tornados usually occur inland. The chances of a property in Kansas experiencing a hurricane are pretty slim. However, it has been known to snow in Florida, so you never know when or where a weather emergency may arise.

Properties may not get much advance notice of a potential weather emergency. Some weather situations such as hurricanes and floods usually take time to develop to danger stages, but others such as tornados develop quickly. No matter what type of weather emergency a property might experience, the key to handling it is planning.

- Know where emergency supplies are kept and when to get them out.

- Secure money, important papers, and other valuables in weather-tight areas.

- Prepare all hazardous materials. Be prepared to shut off gas if necessary.

- Carry out responsibilities using a property's emergency plan. This may include evacuating people.

- Make sure everyone has taken shelter in designated safe locations, if appropriate.

- Remain at assigned posts, as long as it's safe, until ordered to seek shelter, or until relieved.

- Keep people in shelters until the danger has passed.

Medical Emergencies

When confronted with medical emergencies, lodging employees need to make decisions quickly. In many cases, lives are at stake.

The first minutes in any emergency are critical. Lodging employees must quickly evaluate the situation by finding out what the problem is and trying to identify all important symptoms. Are the victims injured? Are they sick? They then send for emergency medical help immediately. This may mean contacting the front desk, security office, or the PBX operator to call emergency medical numbers, or it may mean any employee on the scene making the call themselves.

Sometimes lodging employees will need to provide first aid immediately. If the situation is life-threatening, they start first aid procedures at once if they have proper training, but have another employee or a bystander call for help as soon as possible.

They try to help the injured as much as possible without further endangering their condition. This means:

- Talk to them. Tell them that medical help has been called.

- Render whatever first aid possible.

- Keep them calm.

- Make them as comfortable as possible.

- Keep the victims still. Don't try to move them unless it's dangerous to stay in that area.

- Ask them if they have a relative or friend that should be called.

- Keep bystanders away from the scene. The victims need some breathing room and probably won't want people staring and hovering over them.

- While your primary concern is for the well-being of the injured, you also need to protect the property from liability in these situations. What you say or do at the scene can reinforce a case against the property. So follow these tips:

  - Don't apologize to the injured for the accident. An apology can look like an admission of guilt.

  - Don't take responsibility for the accident. For example, if an employee says something such as, "Mrs. Jackson, I've told them to fix that broken railing on the stairs," the victim could use the comment against the property in a lawsuit.

  - Don't discuss the property's insurance or reimbursement for medical expenses. A victim might consider this an agreement and the property might be obligated to pay.

  - Discuss the cause of the accident only with people who need to know. Don't talk to bystanders or employees unless they are involved.

Medical emergencies may require first aid. Under OSHA, properties are required to have someone trained in first aid at the property at all times, unless medical services are easily accessible on or near the property.

Some common first aid procedures that lodging employees can learn to help them in life-threatening situations are:

- The **Heimlich maneuver**—used when someone is choking

- Mouth-to-mouth resuscitation—used to restore breathing when the victim is not choking

- **Cardiopulmonary resuscitation** (CPR) —used to restore breathing and heartbeat

Handling the Death of a Guest

It's uncommon for guests to die at a property, but if they do, it can be very difficult to handle. Usually deaths at lodging properties happen with little or no warning, so there's no way to fully prepare.

Each property has its own procedures for handling a guest's death. Here are some tips that apply to most cases:

- Immediately alert property management and police.

- Notify emergency medical help and call the local law enforcement. A supervisor or PBX operator may make the calls.

- Find out if the guest is really dead. Check for a pulse or heartbeat, or breathing. Any death is unfortunate, but it is even more tragic if the death could have been prevented. A person who is "almost dead" may still be able to survive if medical help is brought in quickly.

- Try to disturb the scene as little as possible. Touch only what is necessary and leave everything exactly as found. Local police will try to determine a cause of death and details about how the guest died from clues in the room. These clues can easily be destroyed.

- Secure the area until police arrive. Only allow authorized people in the room until police arrive. Usually guests die in their own room. If this is the case, the room is double-locked so no one can get in without authorization. If a guest dies in a public area, the property attempts to lock the area if possible. If not, they block off the area so no one can disturb the scene.

Handling an Employee Death

Freak accidents, crime, and unknown health problems can cause an employee's death. Most techniques used to handle a guest's death are used when an employee dies at the property. Someone needs to notify management and the police, call emergency medical help, and secure the area.

Some additional problems might develop when responding to an employee death. When the property seals off the area in which the death occurred, it might affect guest service. For example, if a kitchen steward dies in the kitchen, sealing off the area will probably hinder meal preparation for room service and restaurant guests.

Employees who are distressed over a co-worker's death may not be capable of using equipment or performing their job responsibilities safely.

Terrorism and Bomb Threats

The lodging industry has an increased chance of being threatened by civil unrest and terrorism than at any time before. Arson, bombings, hostage-taking, and riots have become more common. Unfortunately, there are few ways to prevent these situations—all a property can do is be prepared and act to prevent injuries and damages.

Terrorism has grown as a concern since September 11, 2001. Lodging properties have begun taking new precautions to help prevent terrorist acts at their properties. Some of these actions include:

- Watching unattended baggage.

- Increasing security training.

- Locking all entry doors except lobby entrances.

- Do not allow any non-guest or non-hotel vehicles to park near the premises.

- Suspending valet parking during code-red or code-orange alerts.

- Hiring extra security officers.

Probably the most common type of threat experienced in the lodging industry is a bomb threat. Lodging properties are attractive targets for bomb threats because:

- The public nature of the lodging industry provides easy access for bombers.

- There is a potential for huge losses in life and property.

- The potential for publicity is great.

The majority of bomb threats are hoaxes. It's easy for pranksters to call up a business and claim to have placed a bomb. The number of bombs found is small compared to the number of threats received. Despite this, every threat must be taken seriously. No property wants to take the chance that the threat is a prank. It could be endangering lives if it does.

Most bomb threats are received by phone. Often the threats are called into the security office or a PBX operator.

Riots or Civil Unrest

Although riots and other types of civil unrest are not as common in the United States as they are in other countries, they do sometimes happen. Political situations, court rulings, and even a controversial VIP can quickly turn a quiet protest or peaceful street into a riot. For example, an angry crowd of students protesting against a religious dignitary speaking at a property might quickly turn violent when the dignitary disagrees with their opinions.

Properties that could be most vulnerable to civil unrest or riots are:

- In large cities, downtown, or urban areas

- Near low-income housing

- Near federal buildings or embassies

- Under foreign ownership

- Doing a large banqueting business

- Union properties or where union meetings are held

When a property is the target of such a threat, employees follow these general rules:

- Try to get as much information as possible. The more information available, the easier it will be to decide on a course of action.

- Notify the proper authorities. Start with a supervisor or the manager on duty. Then follow instructions for notifying other authorities such as local police, fire department, or FBI.

- Follow the instructions of the security supervisor or the manager-on-duty.

- Stay calm.

- Don't take any unnecessary risks.

- If a riot does start at or near the property, the employees' main concern is to follow police orders. Police will be involved and know more about handling any riot scene, so follow their directions. Usually those directions will involve keeping rioters out of the property buildings.

To protect the property:

- Secure all entrances except the main entrance to the lobby. Everyone, including employees, should use this door to enter and leave the building. Monitor this entrance to make sure rioters don't enter the building.

- Secure ground level windows and vulnerable windows or entrances on other floors. For example, windows near overhanging tree limbs might allow rioters to enter the property. Windows are often broken by objects rioters throw.

- Lock up alcoholic beverages and any valuables, such as cash or important papers.

- Patrol guest floors. Your presence on guest floors reassures guests and allows employees to prevent them from further inciting the crowd.

- Check fire equipment.

Demonstrations

Demonstrations may occur when people want to protest against something or someone at the property. For example, animal rights activists may protest against a convention of medical scientists who use animals for experimentation. Strikes, on the other hand, happen when an employee contract is unresolved and bargaining breaks down. Either situation is an unusual security challenge for the property.

Both strikes and demonstrations can be highly emotional. People protest because of what they feel is right. The property becomes the symbol of the opposing side, whether because of its employment practices or because it shelters a controversial figure or group. Any situation where people have conflicting beliefs has the potential to explode into violence.

Keep in mind that people who protest are not criminals, and the property cannot keep them from protesting. Strikes and demonstrations are protected by law, and the property could be sued for interfering with First Amendment or labor law rights. However, the property does have the right to keep protestors from coming onto the property.

Communication is a key to preventing peaceful demonstrations from becoming ugly riots. A property needs to make sure the crowd knows the limits that it will enforce and that appropriate people are kept informed of developments. But it can't be too heavy-handed or it will generate hostility among the protestors.

Demonstrators may ask to use the rest rooms or telephones, or to be allowed to get something to eat from a property restaurant. The reason they give may be legitimate, but it could also be a cover for some other action. They may try to cause damage to property assets or to confront or assault a person against whom they are protesting. If they get onto the property they become an even bigger security risk. For example, an angry striker may try to damage valuable machinery in order to force the property management to agree to the union's demands. Property staff should try to keep protestors off the grounds. If any protestor tries to trespass, they can notify the police to enforce trespassing laws.

Weapons at a Property

Guns and knives are sometimes found at lodging properties. Some properties ask guests carrying weapons to secure them in a safe deposit box at the front desk. Other properties have policies that employees will not be allowed to service guestrooms while a weapon is in the room.

Usually employees are directed to call security when they see a weapon on the property. State and federal laws about carrying weapons, especially guns, vary widely. These laws also can change frequently.

Apply Your Learning 4.5

Please write all answers on a separate sheet of paper.

1. What type of basic emergency procedures should lodging employees know?
2. What are some types of emergency equipment that lodging employees might use?
3. What type of emergency drills might a property conduct?
4. What are some ways that lodging employees notify the fire department of a fire?
5. What are the three major responsibilities of lodging employees during a power failure?
6. From where should employees try to communicate with guests stuck in an elevator if the phone or intercom doesn't work? Why?
7. When should a lodging employee start first aid on an injured guest?
8. When is mouth-to-mouth resuscitation used on a guest?
9. What are some actions properties are taking to reduce the opportunity for terrorist acts?
10. What is a key to preventing peaceful demonstrations from becoming riots?

Quick Hits

Chapter 4

SECTION 4.1—SAFETY IN THE WORKPLACE

- Lodging employees must be careful to lift, carry, and move items correctly so that they are not injured.

- The Occupational Safety and Health Administration helps keep employees safe by regulating sanitation, safety, and first aid in the workplace.

- Lodging properties use three different types of signs for safety reasons: danger signs, caution signs, and safety instruction signs.

- Lodging employees must take safety precautions when handling items that may contain bloodborne pathogens.

SECTION 4.2—ACCESS AND KEY CONTROL

- Access control means watching or controlling the property's entrances, especially those that lead to guestrooms or guestroom areas.

- Keys and locks help ensure guest privacy, safety, and security. Most properties have several levels of keys, including master keys, submaster keys, and emergency keys.

- Key control ensures that only those people who need keys have them.

- Guestroom security includes lighting, key control, telephones, information, and special equipment.

SECTION 4.3—THEFT, DISTURBANCES, AND SUSPICIOUS PEOPLE

- Properties deter guest theft by locking rooms, keeping good inventories, and bolting permanent items down.

- Properties also try to limit the opportunities for employees to steal.

- A disturbance is anything that interrupts normal activities at the property or upsets the comfort of guests.

- A property is divided into public areas, guest areas, and employee areas. Employees need to be alert to who is in each area and who is allowed to be there.

- Lodging employees need to watch for suspicious people and respond safely to them.

SECTION 4.4—SECURITY CONCERNS

- All employees need to know how to handle lost and found items.

- The Americans with Disabilities Act protects the rights of people with disabilities. Properties need to provide reasonable accommodations and be able to help people with disabilities during emergencies.

- A lodging security department may hire its own staff or contract with others. They perform six basic activities: maintain guestroom security, control access to the property, protect assets, handle emergencies, investigate incidents, and keep security records.

- Security efforts must be well-documented to prevent and respond to lawsuits. Documentation can include note-taking, daily logs, activity reports, and incident reports.

- Special events create specific security concerns for lodging properties. These special events might include conventions, parties, receptions, and VIP guests.

Section 4.5—Handling Emergencies

- All employees need to know basic emergency procedures for such things as evacuations, first aid, basic firefighting, power failure response techniques, crowd control, and emergency equipment use.

- Some common emergency drills include fire drills, evacuation drills, medical emergency response drills, power failure drills, and weather emergency and natural disaster drills.

- Fire alarms and power failures are the most common emergencies experienced in the lodging industry. Employees should respond quickly and safely.

- Power failures are often triggered by some other emergency. Lodging employees have three major responsibilities: protect people at the property, minimize vandalism, and secure money and valuable assets.

- If an elevator malfunctions, lodging employees should try to find out where the car is and communicate with anyone trapped inside.

- Lodging properties have to be prepared for weather emergencies and natural disasters since they may get very little warning.

- During a medical emergency, the response of employees could save a life. Common first-aid procedures include the Heimlich maneuver, mouth-to-mouth resuscitation, and cardiopulmonary resuscitation.

- When someone dies at the property, the police and management must be called immediately and the area secured.

- Properties are taking extra measures to reduce the chance of terrorist acts and respond to civil unrest.

- Demonstrations can be managed by communicating high and controlling access to the property.

- Employees are usually asked to call security when they see a weapon on the property.

Unit 2

Rooms Division

Rooms Division

Sections

In most hotels, the rooms division is the major division and the primary reason the property exists. Most of any hotel's square footage is devoted to guestrooms and areas that support the operation of those rooms.

Guestroom rentals are the single largest source of revenue for all hotels except casino hotels. Rooms occupy the most space, produce the most revenue, and generate the most profit.

No matter what the size or category of hotel, rooms divisions are organized and function in a similar manner. Large hotels have more departments and people within the division, but they still perform the same basic tasks.

In a small hotel, the general manager or owner directly oversees the rooms division. In a mid-size to large hotel (300 rooms or more) there is likely to be a rooms manager or an executive assistant manager in charge of rooms.

5.1 Getting to Know the Rooms Division

AFTER SUCCESSFULLY COMPLETING THIS SECTION, YOU WILL BE ABLE TO:

♦ List departments commonly found in a rooms division.

♦ Describe the function of the front office.

♦ Explain the purpose of the reservations department.

♦ Identify how technology has affected the communications department.

♦ Identify the most common positions within the uniformed service department and what they do.

♦ Explain the role of housekeeping in a lodging property.

A hotel's **rooms division** is often considered the heart and soul of a lodging property. It is the rooms division that sells the room to the guests, checks them in, cares for the room, and provides them with services throughout their stay. In most lodging properties, the rooms division generates more revenue than all other divisions combined.

Departments in the rooms division include:

- Front office
- Reservations
- Communications
- Uniformed service
- Housekeeping

Exhibit 1 shows a sample organization chart for the rooms division of a large hotel.

The Front Office

The **front office** is the most visible department in the hotel. Front office employees have more contact with guests than most other employees. The focal point of the front office is the front desk—a spot that is usually in a noticeable place in the hotel's lobby.

Guests come to the front desk to:

- Register
- Receive room assignments
- Ask about available services, facilities, and the community
- Check out

The front desk often acts as the command center for fielding guest requests and complaints. It may also be a base of operations during an emergency.

Exhibit 1
Organization Chart: Rooms Division of a Large Hotel

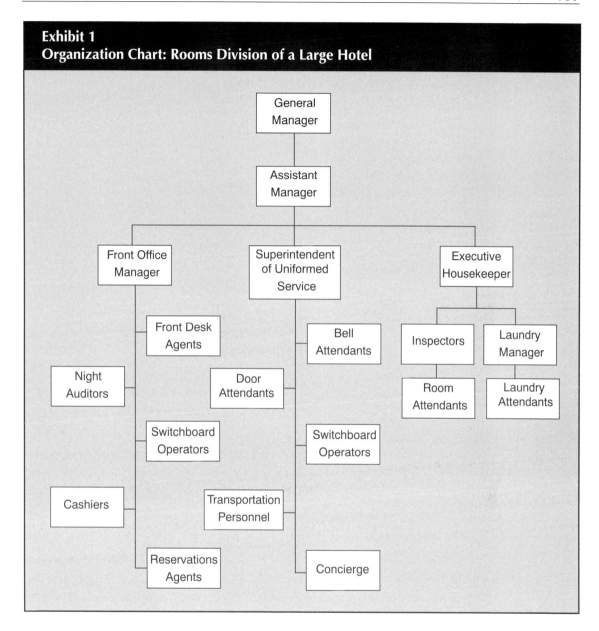

The functions of the front office are to:

- Sell guestrooms, register guests, and assign guestrooms

- Process future room reservations, when there is no reservation department or when the reservation department is closed

- Coordinate guest services

- Provide information about the hotel, the surrounding community, and any attractions or events of interest to guests

- Maintain accurate room status information

- Maintain guest accounts and monitor credit limits

- Produce guest account statements and complete proper financial settlement

Reservations

More than half of all lodging property guests make reservations. Reservations are made through:

- Toll-free telephone numbers

- Direct telephone lines

- Hotel sales representatives

- Travel agencies

- Property-to-property networks

- Postal delivery

- Telex and fax

- E-mail

- Internet

- Other communications services

Each lodging property has its own way of taking and tracking reservations. The reservations department receives and processes requests for future overnight accommodations.

Communications

The **telephone switchboard area** or department maintains a complex communications network. The telephone department may also be referred to as a private branch exchange or PBX.

Recent technology has made the PBX operator job easier and lightened the workload. Technology has made it possible for guests to handle room-to-room calls and most outgoing calls. Guest voice mail reduces the amount of messages PBX operators have to take. Call accounting systems can place direct-dialed calls over the least costly route available and automatically price calls. Technology can also be used to automatically place wake-up calls to guestrooms at preprogrammed times.

Uniformed Service

Employees who work in the **uniformed service** department of a hotel provide the most personalized guest service.

The most common positions within the uniformed service department are:

- Bell attendants: Persons who provide baggage service between the lobby area and the guestroom.

- Door attendants: Persons who provide curb-side baggage service and traffic control at the hotel entrance.

- Valet parking attendants: Persons who provide parking service for guests' automobiles.

- Transportation personnel: Persons who provide transportation services for guests.

- Concierges: Persons who assist guests by making restaurant reservations, arranging for transportation, and getting tickets for theater, sporting, or other special events and so on.

While these jobs may not seem complicated, they are critical to the smooth operation of a hotel. They are often the ones who make a lasting impression on guests. They are also the ones who can anticipate guest needs and communicate effectively with guests about the hotel's services.

Housekeeping

Housekeeping is often considered the most important support department for the front office. It is usually part of the rooms division, though at some hotels it may be its own independent hotel division.

Communication between the front office and housekeeping contributes to guest satisfaction while helping the front office monitor guestroom status. Housekeeping employees inspect rooms before they are available for sale, clean occupied and vacated rooms, and communicate the status of guestrooms to the front office.

The housekeeping department often employs the largest staff in the rooms division. Normally, an executive housekeeper is in charge aided by an assistant housekeeper. The department also includes inspectors, guestroom attendants, public space cleaners, and laundry personnel.

Frequently, guestroom attendants are assigned to specific sections of the hotel. If the hotel has its own laundry, housekeeping department staff may be responsible for cleaning and pressing the property's linens, towels, uniforms, and guest clothing.

Apply Your Learning 5.1

Please write all answers on a separate sheet of paper.

1. What departments can be found in the rooms division?

2. Why do guests come to the front desk?

3. How are lodging property reservations made?

4. Has technology given PBX operators more work or less?

5. What hotel employees are considered part of the uniformed service department?

6. What is often considered the most important support department for the rooms division?

5.2 The Guest Cycle

AFTER SUCESSFULLY COMPLETING THIS SECTION, YOU WILL BE ABLE TO:

♦ Identify the stages of the guest cycle.

♦ Describe what takes place in the pre-arrival stage.

♦ Explain the role employees play during the arrival stage.

♦ Identify how employees meet guest needs during the occupancy stage.

♦ Explain the departure stage process.

Lodging properties have traditionally divided the flow of business into a four-stage **guest cycle.** The four stages of the guest cycle are:

• Pre-arrival

• Arrival

• Occupancy

• Departure

Guests need to have good experiences in all four of the stages so that their expectations are exceeded and they leave wanting to come back.

Pre-Arrival

During the pre-arrival stage, the guest chooses which hotel to stay in and makes the initial contact. In this stage, the most crucial employees are the reservationists and PBX operators.

Reservationists must be sales-oriented and present a positive, strong image of the lodging property. The attitude, efficiency, and knowledge of the front office staff may influence a caller's decision to stay at a particular property.

It is also important that reservationists establish realistic expectations for the guest. If they over-sell the hotel or offer more than can be accommodated, they are setting up the guest for disappointment and dissatisfaction.

Arrival

The arrival stage of the guest cycle begins when the guest first sees the hotel's sign and parking lot. It includes registration and rooming functions. Employees who can make the arrival stage an excellent one for guests include valets, bell attendants, front desk representatives, and public space cleaners.

The guest should be greeted in a friendly and efficient manner. Each employee who sees an arriving guest can help make that guest feel welcome.

After the valet attendant takes the guest's car and the bell attendant opens the door with a warm greeting, the guest walks through the sparkling clean lobby to register at the front desk. The front desk representative checks on the guest's reservation status and creates a **registration record**. The registration record usually contains:

- Guest name and billing information
- Intended method of payment
- Planned length of stay
- Any special needs or preferred room location
- Guest telephone numbers
- Guest signature

The front desk representative then assigns a room type and a room rate (unless the room was already reserved and assigned a rate). Once a method of payment and the guest's departure date is established, the front desk representative alerts a bell attendant to show the guest his or her room and help with luggage.

Occupancy

When the guest arrives at the guestroom, the occupancy stage of the guest cycle begins. During the occupancy stage, guestroom attendants, laundry attendants, concierges, food and beverage employees, and retail cashiers all have ample opportunity to help the property shine. The front desk also continues to play a crucial role during the occupancy stage as it coordinates guest services and responds to requests and complaints in a timely and accurate way.

At this stage, the main objective of lodging property employees is to exceed guest expectations to encourage repeat visits. The front office must communicate clearly and constructively with all other hotel departments and the guest. The hotel has to be aware of a guest complaint in order to resolve it.

Departure

The departure stage begins even before the guest leaves the guestroom. It begins when an express check-out form is delivered and the guest begins packing to go.

At check-out, the guest vacates the room, receives an accurate statement of the settled account, returns the room keys, and leaves the hotel. After check-out, the front office updates the room's availability status and notifies the housekeeping department.

During check-out, the front office employees can find out whether the guest was satisfied with the stay and encourage the guest to return. Sometimes, a property will create a **guest history file** from expired registration records. This information can help the hotel anticipate and serve the needs of returning guests and help them develop marketing strategies.

Also during check-out, the guest will settle his or her account using the method established at check-in.

Apply Your Learning 5.2

For each of the following tasks, write whether they take place in the pre-arrival, arrival, occupancy, or departure stage. Please write all answers on a separate sheet of paper.

1. Create a guest history file.

2. Respond to guest requests.

3. Create a registration record.

4. Establish realistic expectations for a guest.

5.3 Knowledge for All Front Office Employees

AFTER SUCCESSFULLY COMPLETING THIS SECTION, YOU WILL BE ABLE TO:

♦ Describe courteous telephone behavior.

♦ Explain how front office employees help keep a property and its guests secure.

♦ Describe basic guestroom types.

♦ Identify the types of policies a property might have.

♦ Identify important information to know about the community.

♦ Explain how to give directions.

♦ Describe what front office employees need to know about property transportation.

♦ Describe courteous elevator behavior.

Telephone Courtesy

Front office employees try to make every caller feel important by being friendly, polite, and professional on the phone.

The following techniques help them leave a good impression with each caller. Front office staff:

• Smile when they talk. A smile helps them sound more relaxed and pleasant.

• Speak clearly into the receiver. They avoid slang, technical terms, or hospitality words that callers may not understand.

• Use proper grammar and diction. They avoid "yep," "uh-huh," and "OK." Instead, they use "yes," "certainly," or "absolutely."

• Answer the phone within three rings. A phone that rings more than three times gives a caller the impression that the property doesn't want to take the call.

• Always tell the caller their name, the property's name, and their department. Each property may have a specific way for employees to answer the phone.

• Give the caller a friendly greeting, such as "Good morning" or "Good evening," and ask how they can help him or her.

• Give the caller their complete attention. They pretend the guest is standing right in front of them.

• Talk only to the person on the phone, not to anyone around them.

- If the call is for a manager, they ask the caller if they may put him or her on hold. Then they get the manager immediately, or take a message if necessary.

- If the caller is looking for a guest, they ask a co-worker to help them locate the guest. If they can't find the guest within one or two minutes, they take a message.

- If a work-related call is for an employee, they ask the caller if they may put him or her on hold and then get the employee.

To take a message, they write down the caller's name, the time and date of the call, the message and their name as the message-taker in case there are any questions. Most of the time, callers will leave voice mail messages.

Sometimes, to take care of a request, front desk employees have to put callers on hold. Providing good guest service means they always ask callers first. If a caller gives them permission, they take care of the request quickly and then thank the caller for waiting when they return.

Each phone call is ended with a sincere "Thank you for calling." They offer to be of assistance in the future, and let the caller hang up first.

Security

The front office staff is a key part of a property's security system. They can watch who comes in and out of the property and can look for unusual situations.

Guests count on:

- *Reservationists* to tell them about property safety features.

- *Bell attendants* to secure luggage, show guests how to use security devices in their rooms, practice good key control, and keep their room numbers and other personal information private.

- *Front desk employees* to practice good key control and keep their room numbers private.

- *PBX operators* to guard their room numbers from callers and oversee emergency efforts.

- *Concierges* to help them meet special security needs.

Front desk employees are also the property's security alarm. They can prevent dangerous situations by reporting what they see: such as burned-out light bulbs, broken windows and locks, people who seem suspicious or out-of-place, and other problems or possible problems.

Guestroom Types

Front office employees help guests have a pleasant stay by helping them pick the best guestroom for their needs. How do they suggest a perfect room? They start by learning the types of rooms their property has and where they are located.

Some common room types include:

Accessible: A room designed for guests with disabilities. It may have a larger bathroom than bathrooms in standard rooms and a shower with bars and a removable shower head. The bar in the closet is usually lower than in standard rooms, as is the door view port. There is also typically a flashing light that can act as an alarm and doorbell.

Adjacent: Rooms next to each other with no connecting door, or rooms across the hall from each other.

Adjoining/Connecting: Rooms next to each other, connected by a door.

Balcony: A room with a glass door behind the curtains, opening to a balcony.

Business Class: A room for business travelers that may include amenities such as a computer modem, immediate priority fax service, and a daily newspaper.

Double: A room with two double beds.

King: A room with one king-size bed.

Suite: A sitting area connected to one or more bedrooms. When booking suites, front office employees note the number of bedrooms needed.

Smoking/Nonsmoking: Guestrooms designated for guests who smoke and for guests who do not smoke.

Property Policies

Every lodging property has certain rules that help maintain order. Front office employees have a special need to be familiar with those rules—they are the ones who will have to respond to guest questions about or problems with the policies.

Typically, a property might have policies about:

- Where buses park
- Fire code restrictions on where rollaway beds can be placed in guestrooms
- Maximum number of guests allowed to stay in a room
- Valet and self-parking charges

- Charges for cribs, rollaway beds, and other loaner items
- Policy regarding pets
- Check-cashing policy
- Guests who have confirmation letters at check-in, but no reservation
- Guests who don't have a credit card or driver's license to check in with
- Guests with nonguaranteed reservations who arrive after the cut-off time

Community

Guests expect front office employees to know about their community and all it has to offer. Whenever possible, employees want their guests to use the property's services. However, sometimes guests will want to leave the property. Front office employees can help meet guest needs by being prepared with suggestions about the area.

Front office employees can be prepared with information about:

- Area restaurants
- Night clubs
- Comedy clubs
- Movie theaters
- Theaters, symphonies, etc.
- Special events
- Other area attractions

Some areas of the community may not be very safe for guests to travel in. Front office employees are asked to suggest only those restaurants, entertainment sites, and other attractions that are in safe areas. If guests ask about places in unsafe areas, employees explain the potential danger and suggest an alternative spot. But they strive to be tactful, giving only the facts, and not trying to frighten guests.

Giving Directions

Most guests will be from out of town—and probably won't know the property's area very well or at all. Front office employees can remove some of the hassle from their trips by helping guests get to the property. Guests who arrive without getting lost are usually in much better moods than guests who can't find their way.

Here are some tips for giving directions:

- Keep directions as simple as you can. It's better to explain a longer way if the directions are easier to follow.

- Only give directions that take guests through safe areas.

- Talk slowly enough for the guests to write down what you're saying.

- Spell street names and mention other landmarks.

- Use "left" and "right" instead of "north," "south," "east," or "west."

- Ask guests if they understood you and if they'd like to repeat the directions back to you, just to be sure.

- If guests want directions from the property to local attractions, draw or use a map if possible. Maps are usually available at the front desk or from the concierge.

- Never point when giving directions.

It is especially important that front office employees can give directions from all major highways and from public transportation terminals.

Transportation

Whether the property drives guests to the airport, or an airline sends a van, front office employees learn airport transportation schedules. They have copies of the schedules and price rates in their work area. Those employees who are able to memorize the property's schedules are able to provide quicker quality guest service.

Guests need accurate information about the arrival and departure times of courtesy vans. If guests miss a ride—or the ride is later than they expected—they could miss a flight. The property wants guests to be satisfied with every stage of their visit—from making reservations to riding the van back to the airport.

Elevator Courtesy

Riding an elevator can often be socially uncomfortable. Guests may not be sure who should get off first, whether to make conversation, or who should push the buttons. Front office employees can help guests be more comfortable by being confident and knowing what to do. Riding the elevator with guests gives them a chance to provide superior service.

Lodging property employees are always the last one on the elevator and the last one off. This lets them hold the door open for all the guests each way. If they see guests approaching the elevator—even if they are moving slowly—they hold the elevator for them.

They then make small talk and eye contact on the elevator. Not only will it get rid of the uncomfortable silence, but they have a chance to sell the services of the property. Their friendliness makes good impressions on guests.

Apply Your Learning 5.3

Please write all answers on a separate sheet of paper.

1. How quickly should front office employees answer a phone?

2. How can bell attendants contribute to property security?

3. What is an adjacent guestroom?

4. When giving directions, should front office employees say "Go north" or "Turn right"?

5. Why should a lodging employee be the last one on an elevator and the last one off?

5.4 Knowledge for All Housekeeping Employees

AFTER SUCCESSFULLY COMPLETING THIS SECTION, YOU WILL BE ABLE TO:

♦ Explain how housekeeping employees can work as a team with other departments.

♦ Describe how housekeeping employees handle housekeeping keys and key cards.

♦ Explain how to properly handle cleaning chemicals.

♦ Identify how to respond to special cleaning needs.

♦ Explain how housekeeping manages inventories.

The housekeeping department is the key department in keeping the property pristine. It makes sure that the guest is comfortable by providing clean sheets, neat rooms, shining bathrooms, and fluffy towels. It puts the shine on the entire property from ceiling to floor.

Within the housekeeping department, there are many employees. The front-line employees include:

• Guestroom attendant

• Public space cleaner

• Laundry worker

Working closely with the housekeeping department employees are maintenance workers. This section will explore some of the essential information that all housekeeping employees need to know.

Housekeeping Teamwork

Housekeeping employees must be excellent team players as so many people throughout the hotel rely on them in order to do their jobs. Some of the ways that housekeeping helps other departments includes:

• Telling front office employees whether any of their cleaning will affect guests' movement through the property.

• Telling engineering employees about needed repairs and filling out a maintenance request form, if necessary.

• Helping banquet setup employees clean banquet areas and filling linen orders quickly.

• Learning the location and hours of operation of restaurants, lounges, health clubs, and other areas at the property so they can help guests enjoy everything the property has to offer.

Security

Housekeeping employees also have a key role to play in the property's security.

Guests count on housekeeping employees to keep room keys secure, to watch for suspicious people, and to keep their belongings safe.

The property depends on housekeeping employees to prevent the theft of linens, supplies, and other items. They are able to immediately report missing items to their supervisor or a security employee.

Housekeeping Keys

Housekeeping keys and key cards are the first line of defense against theft, guest harm, and room damage. It's very important that they stay in the hands of those who need them.

Housekeeping keys provide entry to guestrooms, storage closets, offices, and back-of-the-house areas. When housekeeping employees pick up their keys, they sign a register before a witness. This protects them from false charges.

Housekeeping employees follow some basic guidelines to help keep the property safe and secure for guests, fellow employees, and themselves:

- Always turn in their housekeeping key whenever they leave the property

- If anyone—even a supervisor—asks to borrow their key, they send him or her to the front desk or to the executive housekeeper. They don't loan their key to *anyone*.

- Keep their key on a belt around their waist or arm at all times. They don't leave it on a cart or caddy.

- If they lose a key, they report it immediately to the executive housekeeper.

- Lock boxes on room attendant carts are for keys they find in vacant guestrooms or in doors. If a cart does not have a lock box, they keep the keys in a secure area until they can return them to the front desk.

Housekeeping employees are careful to never open a guestroom for a guest. Instead, they explain to guests how they can get a spare key. This helps protect both the guest and the guest's belongings.

If a guest enters a room where guestroom attendants are working, attendants politely ask to see a room key. If the key is for the room that they are in, they let the guest in and offer to return later. If the guest cannot produce a key, they send him or her to the front desk, then report to security. If the room is registered to the guest, the front desk will be able to help him or her and still provide security.

Cleaning Supplies

Cleaning chemicals can be dangerous if they are not handled properly.

There are many ways housekeeping employees can protect themselves while working:

- Wear gloves and safety goggles when using cleaning chemicals.

- Never mix two chemicals together.

- Clearly mark all spray bottles with proper labels.

- Do not change spray heads.

- If they need to dilute a chemical, they do it in the storage room or in the housekeeping department, not in public areas or guestrooms.

Some of the most common chemicals that a housekeeping department uses are:

- *All-purpose cleaner* is used in the guestroom, in public areas, and to clean equipment.

- *Glass cleaner* is used to remove spots from chrome and to clean windows. It is not recommended for mirrors, since it streaks easily. Mirrors are cleaned best with just water.

- *Furniture polish* is used only on wood — and only in small amounts.

- *Bleach* helps remove stains, kills bacteria, and whitens fabrics. It can cause strong chemical reactions and can damage fabrics if it is not carefully controlled.

Special Cleaning Requirements

There are some extra jobs that housekeeping employees simply don't have time to do during a routine shift. These special cleaning jobs might include wiping down a dryer or removing a stain from a lobby wall.

Because housekeeping employees see a lot of the property, they'll often know better than anyone else what needs to be cleaned. The property relies on them to inform their supervisor about special cleaning needs. Some tasks will require immediate attention, and others can be put on a schedule to do later.

Housekeeping employees report such things as:

- Stains or dirt on carpets

- Pets or signs of pets

- Cigarette burns

- Air conditioner stains

- Vomit or other problems related to a sick guest

- Wet, stained, or damaged mattresses, furniture, or walls

- Missing furniture

- Broken lint screens

- Leaking valves on washing machines

- Low water levels in washing machines

Housekeeping Inventories

Typically, housekeeping departments take inventories monthly for guest supplies, and every three months for linens, towels, bath mats, and washcloths. When all department members work as a team, the inventory job is done well and quickly.

A pre-printed inventory form will list items that housekeeping employees need to count and where they are kept.

The cleaning supplies in the following areas may be counted during monthly inventory:

- Main back-up storage areas

- Housekeeping department's working storerooms

- Floor housekeeping closets

- Room attendants' carts and caddies

- Public area carts and caddies

- Laundry room

Housekeeping employees accurately count the supplies and linens in their areas. Sometimes they are also asked to count items in other areas too.

When directed by their supervisor, they check linens, towels, bath mats, and washcloths in the areas listed above and in these areas:

- Main linen room
- Laundry storage shelves
- Laundry room, linen bins, and chutes
- Mending area

They help make their job easier by sorting linens on shelves before counting, because each size is recorded separately.

New linens, towels, bath mats, and washcloths take a long time to arrive—especially if they have the property's logo. Keeping an accurate inventory lets the property know when to reorder. Lodging properties often try to keep enough of these items around to have one set in storage, one in the wash, one in housekeeping closets and carts, and one in use in the guestroom. If a property provides turn-down service, it should also keep a set of washcloths, towels, and bath mats on hand for this service. This system helps the linens, towels, washcloths, and bath mats last longer.

Apply Your Learning 5.4

Please write all answers on a separate sheet of paper.

1. What can housekeeping employees do for banquet setup employees?
2. What is the first line of defense against theft, guest harm, and room damage?
3. Where is all-purpose cleaner used?
4. What should a public space cleaner do if he or she sees an air conditioner stain?
5. Where are cleaning supplies counted during monthly inventory?

5.5 Concierge and Retail Cashier

AFTER SUCCESSFULLY COMPLETING THIS SECTION, YOU WILL BE ABLE TO:

♦ Describe the position of concierge.

♦ List the tasks a concierge might perform.

♦ Explain how ethics affect the job of a concierge.

♦ List the tasks a retail cashier is responsible for.

♦ Describe how retail operations are different in a lodging property than in a department store or mall.

Concierge Overview

The concierge is the key to hospitality at a lodging property. He or she brings luxury and personal attentiveness to each guest's stay.

The concierge was originally the castle doorkeeper. He made sure that everyone was locked in at night. Later, traveling royalty sent their concierge ahead of them to make food and lodging arrangements.

As luxury hotels developed in Europe, the concierge played an important role. In Europe today, concierges must go through years of apprenticeship. It wasn't until the mid-1970s that concierges began to play an important role in U.S. lodging properties.

The job of concierge is almost impossible to define—it includes providing whatever the guest needs or wants, if possible. They have the most extensive knowledge of the lodging property and the community. Guests, especially VIP guests and guests on a concierge-level floor, will expect concierges to have all the answers to their questions on the tips of their tongues. Whenever guests have an unusual request, they will be confident in the concierge's ability to meet it.

What makes a good concierge?

• Enthusiasm

• Organization

• Efficiency

• Sense of humor

• Sensitivity

• Stamina

• Discretion

• Warm and friendly personality

A Day as a Concierge

One of the joys of the concierge's job is that every day will be different. They never know what surprises may greet them as they work to make every guest experience a perfect one.

But that doesn't mean the days aren't without routine tasks. There are some things that must be done every day depending upon the shift.

A typical day for a concierge starts early in the morning. They begin by checking their mailbox. In their mailbox, they may find:

- An arrivals list

- A special requests list

- A concierge-level guest list

After reviewing their mail, they may need to set up a buffet breakfast in the concierge-level lounge. While the guests are eating, they usually have time to perform several tasks, such as:

- Running updates of the above lists.

- Preparing the daily count form for the kitchen staff. This must be done as early as possible so the kitchen staff can plan for the evening hors d'oeuvres and the next day's breakfast.

- Preparing welcome notes or cards to guests on the arrivals list. These should be in the guests' rooms by early afternoon, or as soon as possible. They check that the rooms are ready for arrival when they place the cards in the rooms.

After the breakfast buffet is over and the concierges have cleaned the breakfast area, they begin duty at the concierge desk. A property may have a concierge on duty in the lobby or other area from mid-morning to late afternoon every day. At the desk, the concierge helps guests as needed.

After duty at the concierge desk, they may be asked to set up a cocktail reception. If so, they will be the hosts until late evening.

In addition to this schedule, they must find time to visit restaurants, stores, and other local businesses; to host lunches for area business leaders; and to develop a network that includes anyone who might someday help your guests.

Exhibit 1 is a list of tasks that concierges are expected to be able to do.

Concierge Ethics

Concierge duties can sometimes put employees in tricky situations. They will develop close relationships with guests. They'll handle all sorts of requests, credit card numbers, meeting schedules, and other personal information.

To provide guests with the best service a lodging property has to offer, concierges will often be told much about guests' personal and business affairs. Guests will count on concierges to keep all information confidential. Concierges don't ever gossip about guests' business or use anything they know about guests in any way except to help them. They are discreet about what guests do while at their property.

Some guests expect concierges to be able to do *anything* for them. A good concierge, though, will do only those things that are legal and kind. They are careful to avoid ethical traps, such as:

- Supplying information about escort services

- Helping a guest pull off a practical joke

- Placing bets through a bookie

- Discriminating against guests based on gender, age, race, religion, or disability

Exhibit 1
Task List—Concierge

1. Use the Front Desk Computer System

2. Use the Printers

3. Use the Facsimile Machine

4. Use the Photocopy Machine

5. Use the Concierge Logbook

6. Use the Guest History System

7. Inventory and Requisition Supplies

8. Maintain and Use Equipment in the Concierge-Level Kitchen

9. Prepare Coffee

10. Provide Complimentary Concierge-Level Breakfast

11. Pick Up, Use, and Turn In Your Cash Bank

12. Post Guest Charges and Payments

13. Order VIP Amenities

14. Prepare and Place Welcome Notes in Guestrooms

15. Make Courtesy Calls to Guests

16. Maintain the Guest Information Directory

17. Learn About Local Restaurants

18. Respond to Guest Inquiries or Requests

19. Prepare Maps and Provide Directions

20. Prepare and Send Thank-You Notes

21. Help Guests With Future Reservations

22. Help Guests Make Airline or Railway Reservations

23. Rent Cars for Guests

24. Arrange Limousine Service for Guests

25. Arrange Taxi Service for Guests

26. Help Guests Arrange Business Services

27. Arrange Tours for Guests

28. Use Pagers and the Public Address System

29. Provide Complimentary Cocktail Service

30. Prepare Alcoholic Beverages

31. Respond to Dissatisfied Guests

32. Respond to Situations Requiring First Aid

33. Respond to Emergency Alarms Service

- Asking for special gifts or considerations from establishments that they recommend

- Going out to dinner or for drinks with guests

Retail Cashier Overview

Most lodging properties operate merchandise outlets such as gift shops and newsstands for the convenience of guests. A retail cashier is the employee who staffs a hotel's retail outlet, maintains inventory, and accepts payment for merchandise. In addition, a retail cashier must be knowledgeable about the property and the surrounding area. They represent their property to every guest who enters their location. Retail cashiers are challenged to give efficient, courteous service to every guest, every day.

Retail cashiers are responsible for:

- Assisting guests as they make purchase selections

- Ringing transactions using a variety of payment methods

- Stocking and maintaining displays

- Protecting cash and merchandise from theft and loss

- Answering guest questions and providing information to guests

Exhibit 2 lists the tasks that retail cashiers are called upon to perform.

Retail Operations in a Lodging Environment

Working in a retail store within a lodging property is quite different from working in a department store or mall location. These differences often can affect guest strategies, sales techniques, stocking frequency, and operational processes.

Vacationing guests are usually in a peaceful frame of mind and like to take a relaxed approach to shopping. With time to spare, these guests may demand more attention from store attendants and may want more detailed information about products. These guests may return to the store more than once during their stay and may expect to be recognized.

Other guests, such as business guests, may be in a more urgent frame of mind and may demand more immediate service. These guests may also become annoyed if certain items, such as daily newspapers, are not available. Many business guests will stay at the property for only one night.

Depending upon the amenities and services offered by the hotel, the store can expect to see either more leisure guests or more business guests. For example, a hotel with large amounts of meeting space, a business office, and several nice restaurants will attract large numbers of business guests. On the other hand, a beachside hotel with several swimming pools, a playground, and a food court will attract large numbers of vacationing families.

Items sold within stores will often reflect the needs and desires of the property's guests. These items can vary widely and include everything from toiletries, snacks, and office supplies to golf clubs, swimming accessories, and luggage. Depending upon the hotel's primary market segment (business or leisure), certain items may have to be replenished frequently. In a family-oriented hotel, the store may have to stock juices, sunscreen, or diapers on a daily basis. In a business-oriented hotel, the store may need to stock more office supplies and business gift items.

Exhibit 2
Task List—Retail Cashier

1. Prepare the Store for Opening	12. Process Travelers Checks
2. Prepare the Register and Cashier System	13. Process Gift Certificates
	14. Process Other Forms of Payment
3. Stock and Maintain Displays	15. Handle Returns and Exchanges
4. Greet and Assist Guests	16. Respond to Dissatisfied Guests
5. Use Effective Sales Techniques	17. Assist Guests by Telephone
6. Ring Transactions	18. Prepare Guest Purchases for Shipment
7. Process Cash Payments	
8. Process Credit Card Payments	19. Prevent Unnecessary Losses
9. Process Debit Card Payments	20. Close Down the Cash Register
10. Post Charges to House Accounts	21. Prepare to Close the Store
11. Process Personal Check Payments	22. Respond to Emergency Alarms

Retail operations within lodging properties are generally small, with as few as two to three employees running the location. In such small operations, a retail cashier may be alone most of the day with little or no supervision. Often the store manager will have other supervisory responsibilities on the property and may not always be available on short notice. For this reason, retail cashiers need to be independent and take on additional responsibilities such as:

• Interacting with vendors and shipping personnel.

• Resolving all or most guest complaints without the need for management involvement.

• Performing opening and closing procedures faithfully and accurately without exception.

• Devoting full attention to guests.

• Exhibiting the highest level of honesty and integrity regarding care of merchandise, cash handling, and loss prevention.

Apply Your Learning 5.5

Please write all answers on a separate sheet of paper.

1. What was the original, historical role of a concierge?

2. What might a concierge find in his or her mailbox in the morning?

3. What should a concierge do with guest information?

4. List at least two tasks that a retail cashier performs.

5. What sort of approach do vacationing guests take to shopping in a retail outlet?

Quick Hits

SECTION 5.1—GETTING TO KNOW THE ROOMS DIVISION

- Departments in the rooms division include front office, reservations, communications, uniformed service, and housekeeping.

- Guests use the front office to register, receive room assignments, ask questions, and check out.

- Reservations are made in many different ways and are processed by the reservations department.

- Technology has made the job of PBX operators much easier.

- Uniformed service includes bell attendants, door attendants, valet parking attendants, transportation personnel, and concierges.

- Housekeeping is an important support department and must have active communication with the front desk.

SECTION 5.2—THE GUEST CYCLE

- The four stages of the guest cycle are pre-arrival, arrival, occupancy, and departure.

- During the pre-arrival stage, the guest makes a reservation and learns about the property.

- The arrival stage begins when the guest first sees the property and lasts until he or she arrives at the guestroom.

- The occupancy stage is when lodging property employees have opportunity to help the property shine.

- The departure stage involves check-out and settlement.

SECTION 5.3—KNOWLEDGE FOR ALL FRONT OFFICE EMPLOYEES

- Front office employees must always be friendly, polite, and professional on the phone.

- Front office employees play many different roles in keeping the property secure and guests safe.

- There are many different types of guestrooms. Front office employees need to know what their property has and where each type is located.

- Property rules help the property run in an orderly fashion.

- Guests expect front office employees to be able to tell them about the surrounding community.

- Guests will often ask for directions from front office employees.

- Front office employees should be able to provide accurate information about airport transportation schedules.

- Front desk employees can make a good impression by showing courtesy on the elevator.

SECTION 5.4—KNOWLEDGE FOR ALL HOUSEKEEPING EMPLOYEES

- The housekeeping department helps keep the property in pristine condition and work with other departments to exceed guest expectations.

- Housekeeping employees help keep guestrooms secure. One way they do this is by protecting the housekeeping keys and key cards.

- Proper precaution is needed whenever chemicals are handled.

- Housekeeping employees need to report anything they see that falls outside of their routine duties.

- Housekeeping employees are often asked to help take inventory of cleaning supplies and linen.

SECTION 5.5—CONCIERGE AND RETAIL CASHIER

- A concierge provides whatever the guest needs or wants, if possible.

- Every day is different for a concierge, though some routine tasks include setting up buffets, checking and reviewing mail, writing welcome notes, preparing daily count forms, running updates on lists, serving at the concierge desk, and hosting receptions.

- Concierges must protect guest information and always act in a highly ethical manner.

- Retail cashiers work in a hotel's retail outlet, maintain inventory, and accept payment for merchandise.

- Retail stores in a lodging property differ from those in malls and department stores because of the types of guests and the items sold in a store. Retail operations are generally small and cashiers frequently work unsupervised.

Front Desk Representative

Sections

The most visible part of the front office is the front desk. The front desk can be a counter or, in some luxury hotels, an actual desk where a guest can sit down and register. Traditionally, the front desk was placed so that the person behind it had a view of both the front door and the elevator. This was so front desk representatives could discourage unwelcome individuals from entering and keep non-paying guests from departing. Because of modern credit and security procedures, such front desk placement is no longer necessary.

The duties of front desk representatives include:

- Greeting guests
- Registering guests
- Establishing a method of payment for the guestroom
- Assigning guestrooms
- Assigning guestroom keys
- Providing guests with information
- Calling a bell attendant to assist guests with their luggage

In small and mid-sized hotels, the front desk representative is also the cashier. These duties are usually separated in large hotels, though employees are often cross-trained to handle both jobs. Cashiers post charges to guest accounts.

6.1 Getting to Know the Front Desk Representative

AFTER SUCCESSFULLY COMPLETING THIS SECTION, YOU WILL BE ABLE TO:

♦ Describe how front desk representatives interact with other departments.

♦ Explain what a hotel target market is.

♦ Identify the types of equipment a front desk representative uses.

What is a Front Desk Representative?

Front desk representatives perform a vital service to everyone who stays at a lodging property. To many guests, the front desk representatives are the first contact with the property. They represent the lodging property to everyone who checks in, checks out, signs out safe-deposit boxes, and uses the front desk's other services.

The work of the front desk representative can make a difference in what type of stay the guest experiences. They have the chance to delight guests. Front desk representatives realize that guests are not an interruption of their work, *guests are the reason for their work*. Front desk representatives are challenged to give efficient, courteous service to every guest, every day.

Typically, someone works at the front desk 24 hours a day. Shifts are usually from 7 A.M. to 3 P.M., 3 P.M. to 11 P.M. and 11 P.M. to 7 A.M. The 7-to-3 shift takes care of most guest check-outs. The 3-to-11 shift takes care of most guest check-ins. The third shift does a little of everything, from handling late check-ins and early check-outs to running reports and express departures.

Exhibit 1 lists all the tasks that most front desk representatives may perform at one time or another.

Working as a Team

One secret of a property's success is that everyone works as a team to give guests great guest service. The front desk representative is part of a service delivery system. They must give guests and co-workers great service for the system to work.

Front desk representatives provide excellent teamwork by:

• Giving positive feedback to the reservations department when reservations information is detailed.

• Introducing guests to bell attendants. Returning bell equipment to the proper place after using it.

• Telling engineering staff members about needed repairs, and filling out a maintenance request form if needed.

Exhibit 1
Task List—Front Desk Representative

1. Use the Front Desk Computer System

2. Use the Front Desk Printers

3. Use the Front Desk Telephone System

4. Use the Facsimile Machine

5. Use the Photocopy Machine

6. Organize the Front Desk and Prepare for Check-Ins

7. Use the Front Office Logbook

8. Prepare and Use an Arrivals List

9. Block and Unblock Rooms

10. Set Up Preregistrations

11. Begin Guest Check-In

12. Establish the Payment Method During Check-In

13. Secure Authorization for Credit Cards

14. Issue and Control Guestroom Keys

15. Finish Guest Check-In

16. Use Effective Sales Techniques

17. Preregister and Check In Group Arrivals

18. Show Rooms to Potential Guests

19. Use a Waiting List When Rooms Are Not Ready for Check-In

20. Relocate Guests in Sold-Out Situations

21. Process Room Changes

22. Process Safe-Deposit-Box Transactions for Guests

23. Prepare a Cash-Only Report for Outlets

24. Run and Follow Up on Credit Check Reports

25. Process Guest Mail, Packages, Telegrams, and Faxes

26. Prepare Maps and Provide Directions

27. Help Guests With Special Requests

28. Respond to Questions About Services and Events

29. Handle Guest Service Problems

30. Cash Checks for Guests

31. Pick Up, Use, and Turn In Your Cash Bank

32. Post Guest Charges and Payments

33. Follow Guest Privacy and Security Measures

34. Operate the Pay Movie System

35. Process Guaranteed No-Shows

36. Update Room Status

37. Process Guest Check-Outs at the Desk

(continued)

Exhibit 1
Task List—Front Desk Representative *(continued)*

38. Adjust Disputed Guest Charges

39. Transfer Allowable Guest Charges

40. Process Automatic Check-Outs

41. Handle Late Guest Check-Outs

42. Process Late Charges

43. Keep the Front Desk Clean and Orderly

44. Update the Function Reader Board

45. Reconcile Room Status With the P.M. Housekeeping Report

46. Prepare a Current Status Report

47. Perform Bucket or Tub Checks

48. Perform a Night Audit

49. Inventory and Requisition Front Desk Supplies

50. Complete and Turn In the Shift Checklist

51. Use Pagers, Two-Way Radios, and Public Address Systems

52. Respond to Situations Requiring First Aid

53. Respond to Emergency Alarms

- Helping the concierge by responding to special requests. Updating the concierge with information about guest services.

- Learning the hours of operation and the location of restaurants, lounges, health clubs, and other areas at a property so they can help guests enjoy everything the property has to offer.

- Correctly transferring to the sales department inquiries about booking function rooms.

Target Markets

Two of the biggest questions facing lodging properties are "Who stays at our property?" and "Who else can we attract?" These questions determine a property's **target market**. Most lodging properties try to attract many types of people. For instance, a property may try to bring in business travelers, local business people who host conventions and meetings, families with young children, and newlyweds, among others. Any of these groups could be one of a lodging property's target markets.

Guestroom Equipment and Amenities

Every property has a different range of conveniences to offer guests. However, if the front desk representative doesn't tell guests about those conveniences, they may never find out about them. The more front desk representatives knows about the guestroom's special equipment and amenities, the more pleasant they can help make the guest's stay.

Some of the equipment that front desk representatives should understand how to use includes:

- Radios

- Free television channels

- Pay movie channels

- High-speed or wireless Internet service

- Heating, ventilation, and air conditioning system

- In-room mini-bars

- In-room hot tubs

- In-room safes

Point-of-Sale Equipment

A **point-of-sale** (**POS**) system is made up of a number of POS units, usually found in the lodging property's restaurants, gift shops, room service stations, and front desk area. Point-of-sale units are like cash registers. They add up guest charges and print a bill.

A property may use a manual, electronic, or computerized point-of-sale system. Most use a computerized system that prints the guest folio after all charges have been entered. The POS units at the front desk may be linked to the POS units in the food and beverage outlets. If so, when charges are entered on the food and beverage point-of-sale units, they will automatically be added to guest folios.

Properties program the keys on point-of-sale units according to standard room charges. This makes the job easier, because front desk representatives don't have to enter room rates.

The Front Desk Computer System

The **front desk computer system** is a tool to help employees serve guests better. Often, the front desk computer will be linked to point-of-sale equipment, the telephone system, and the in-room movie system. Each front desk representative is assigned an access code or given a card to swipe. The code or ID card allows the system to track and identify who performs each task.

When using the computer system to check-in a guest, a front desk representative will look at and talk with the guest as much as possible. Part of good service is making eye contact with guests as often as possible.

All front office computer systems do not operate identically. However, most systems include functions allowing for guest check-ins, check-outs, point-of-sale, adjusted charges, reservations, room assignment, and many other functions. Many of these functions are either automated and therefore performed automatically, or are performed by the computer upon data entry by the front desk representative. Information or data related to guests' stay will be updated to their electronic folio and will be printed out and presented to guests upon check-out.

As a component of the front desk computer system, many properties are now using rooms management software programs. The programs maintain current information on room rates, assist in room assignment, help coordinate guest services, or provide front desk staff with a summary of each room's status. Some room management systems even include maintenance and special request dispatch capabilities as well as a reservation function.

Front desk computer systems that combine these different systems are often referred to as a **property management system,** or a **PMS**.

Front Desk Printers

Front desk printers are part of the computerized equipment that front desk representatives use. They are easy to learn—the computer does most of the work. The computer's software tells the printers what to do. Front desk representatives just need to make sure that each printer is on and has paper.

Many front desk areas use two printers: one to print guest folios and another to print other items. Front desk representatives may have to routinely replace ink cartridges when they are empty or when toner is low. Most printers have an indicator light or a "toner low" message on the display when the ink cartridge needs replacement.

Apply Your Learning 6.1

Please write all answers on a separate sheet of paper.

1. What are the three most typical shifts for front desk representatives?

2. How can learning about a property make an employee a better teammate and co-worker?

3. List two possible target markets for a lodging property.

4. List equipment that might be found in a guestroom.

5. What does POS stand for?

6.2 Guestroom Terms and Rates

AFTER SUCCESSFULLY COMPLETING THIS SECTION, YOU WILL BE ABLE TO:

♦ Identify the primary guestroom reservation types.

♦ List the various terms for describing guestroom inventory, rates, and status.

Types of Reservations

Not all reservations are created equal. Different types of reservations mean different things for the property and the guest. All reservations can be confirmed, which means that the property agrees to hold the reservation for the guest. A property will assign a confirmation number to a guest to assure the guest that a reservation record exists. Two major types of guestroom reservations are guaranteed reservations and non-guaranteed reservations.

Guaranteed Reservations

When a guest makes a guaranteed reservation, the property agrees to hold a room on the guest's arrival date until check-out time the following day or until another time specified by the property's managers. The guest, in turn, agrees to pay for the room even if he or she never arrives, unless he or she cancels by a time specified by the property's managers.

Non-Guaranteed Reservations

When a guest makes a non-guaranteed reservation, the property agrees to hold a room until a cancellation hour (usually 6 P.M.) on the scheduled arrival date. After the cancellation hour, the room becomes available for sale to other guests. Some properties do not accept non-guaranteed reservations for dates on which the property has a high number of guaranteed reservations.

Reserving Function Rooms

In addition to guestrooms, groups may wish to reserve function rooms at a property. Function rooms are rooms where banquets, meetings, and receptions are held. Each function room may vary in size, style, and the number of people it will hold. Certain rooms may be used only for certain types of functions. A property's sales or convention staff can best reserve function rooms for guests.

Room Inventory and Status Terms

To communicate, people have to speak the same language. To communicate well with co-workers, front desk representatives have to know some "lodging language." Part of this language includes room status terms. These describe the current condition of a guestroom. Room inventory and occupancy are important concepts for all

Guests can use a variety of payment methods to guarantee a room:

Prepayment	Before his or her arrival date, the guest mails or brings in payment, plus tax, for all of the nights that he or she plans to stay.
Advance deposit	Before his or her arrival date, the guest mails or brings in payment, plus tax, for the first night's stay.
Credit/Debit cards	The guest gives the property his or her credit or debit card number. If the guest fails to arrive on the expected date and does not properly cancel the reservation, the guest is known as a "guaranteed no-show." The property can charge a guaranteed no-show the fee for one night's stay plus tax to the guest's credit or debit card account.
Travel agent account	A travel agent agrees to pay for a guest's room and tax if the guest does not show up or correctly cancel his or her reservation.
Corporate account	A company signs a contract with the property to pay for its employee no-shows.

front desk representatives. The first step in keeping room inventory and occupancy information organized is knowing the terms involved.

Below are some, but not all, of the terms that may be used at a property to describe the current inventory or status of a guestroom:

Arrival date	The actual date a guest will be checking into the lodging property.
Availability	A condition that describes the number of rooms available for sale on a particular day.
Block	A specific number of rooms set aside for members of a group planning to stay at the lodging property. These groups may include tour groups, conventions, or other functions. Also, front desk representatives may need to set aside special types of rooms, such as nonsmoking or accessible rooms. When rooms are set aside they are blocked, and no one else can reserve or check into them.
Cancellation	A reservation voided (canceled) at the guest's request.
Check-out	The procedures involved in the departure of a guest from the lodging property. The check-out time is usually noon.
Check-in	The procedures involved in the arrival and registration of a guest at the lodging property. Guests may not be able to check in until after the established check-out time if the property is full. Guests are required to fill out registration cards during check-in.

Departure date	The planned date a guest will be checking out of the lodging property.
Early make-up requests	Some guests ask to check in early. To help meet their needs, housekeeping cleans those rooms earlier than the normal time.
Late check-out rooms	This term lets housekeeping know that guests want to stay in their rooms past the standard check-out time.
Minimum stay	An inventory control that allows guests to make reservations only for a minimum number of days.
Same day	Guests who arrive at the lodging property on the same day they make their reservation.
Stayover	Guests who are not checking out that day.
VIP rooms	Very important guests receive special attention. Their reservation records need to be marked so the housekeeping department can provide extra touches.
Vacant and dirty rooms	This refers to rooms, which guests have checked out of, but which housekeeping has not yet cleaned. Front desk representatives won't be able to check anyone into these rooms until they are cleaned.
Walk-in	Guests who arrive at the lodging property without a reservation.

Room Rate Terms

Front desk representatives talk a lot about guestrooms. Sometimes guests can become confused by the many terms used to describe the different types of guestrooms, room rates, and reservations. A good way to avoid problems is to make every effort to understand what a guest needs, and to carefully explain special terms.

Special terms that relate to guestrooms and rates at a property may include but are not limited to the following:

Accessible rooms	Rooms with special features designed to meet the needs of people with disabilities.
Advance deposit	A type of guaranteed reservation in which the lodging property has received cash payment in advance for at least one night's lodging. This guest should be preregistered.
Children's or Family plan rate	A room rate whereby children age 18 and younger stay free if they share a room with an adult and do not require extra beds.

Corporate rate	A special room rate available by request to any person on company business.
Flat rate	A specific group rate agreed upon in advance by the lodging property and the group. The rate does not change based upon the number of guests staying in the room.
Government rate	A special room rate for government employees, including postal workers, who are traveling and can show official identification during check-in.
Late arrival	A guest with a reservation who tells the lodging property that he or she expects to arrive after the cut-off hour (usually 6 P.M.).
Preferred or Commercial rate	The room rate agreed upon by a company and the lodging property for all individual room reservations made by company employees or others on company business.
Preregistration	A procedure by which a front desk representative completes some or all of the registration process before the guest with that reservation arrives. This may or may not include pre-keying the room.
Rack Rate	The standard (non-discount) rate set by management for a specific type of room.

Frequent Flyer Programs

Many lodging properties have a frequent flyer program. This program makes sure that guests who travel a lot will return to the property again and again.

Lodging properties with frequent flyer programs typically offer frequent flyer guests bonus mileage points with the purchase of a guestroom at certain rates. Many airlines require flight within 24 hours before or after the guest's stay. The purpose of the program is to reward frequent flyers with free rooms, air travel, car rental, and other privileges. Guests enroll in airline frequent flyer programs directly through each airline.

Front desk representatives give each frequent flyer guest a warm welcome, and collect all the information needed to make the guest's check-in smooth.

Apply Your Learning 6.2

Please write all answers on a separate sheet of paper.

1. What are the primary types of guestroom reservations?

2. What does the room occupancy term "block" refer to?

3. List and define four of the common room rate terms.

4. List and define three of the room status terms.

5. How does a frequent flyer program reward guests?

6.3 Pre-Arrival and Arrival

AFTER SUCCESSFULLY COMPLETING THIS SECTION, YOU WILL BE ABLE TO:

♦ List the front office organizational tools and explain how they are used.

♦ Explain the procedures for checking in a guest.

♦ Describe how to establish payment methods.

Organize the Front Desk and Prepare for Check-Ins

Good organization at the front desk is important. If the front desk looks sloppy or unorganized, the guest will see the front desk representative—and the property—as unorganized. Front desk representatives keep their workstation and the entire front desk tidy. They also begin their shift by making sure they have enough cash for their duties and checking the day's room counts.

Use the Front Office Logbook

Most properties keep a **front office logbook** so that employees are aware of important events and decisions that happened during previous shifts. Logbooks are also legal documents that are used in investigations.

Most properties have a computerized logbook to record and communicate events.

Front desk representatives will need to review the logbook and make new entries as needed.

Arrivals Lists

An arrivals list typically includes:

• Arriving guests' names

• Type of room each guest requested

• Number of guests per room

• Special requests

Checking the arrivals list helps front desk representatives plan the day's activities. They will want to make sure it is free of errors, especially duplicates or misspelled names and VIPs who aren't identified. The arrivals list helps front desk representatives block rooms with special requests and inform housekeeping and the bell staff when they must help prepare for guests.

Block and Unblock Rooms

Rooms are typically blocked only on the days the guests plan to arrive. Front desk representatives never guarantee a specific room or give out a room number ahead of time. This allows the property maximum flexibility in issuing rooms to arriving guests and allowing for the accommodation of unexpected arrivals, stayovers, cancellations, or no-shows.

Front desk representatives block rooms by setting aside requested rooms for guests. This is most often done for rooms that are handicap accessible.

Set Up Preregistrations

Preregistration speeds up the registration process by limiting the time a guest must spend at the front desk. Guests like this service, and it should be used as often as possible. Front desk representatives determine who needs to be preregistered and create registration cards for these people.

Preregistration typically involves rate assignment, creating a guest folio, and printing a guest registration card. Preregistration lends itself to creative registration options. Guests being picked up from the airport might be able to sign the card in the van and immediately go to their room upon arrival.

Some hotels have centralized guest history systems that capture guest preferences. These preferences—such as a desire for extra pillows or a desire to have bottled water in the guestroom, are noted during the preregistration period. Front desk representatives can then notify housekeeping or room service about the requests.

Begin Guest Check-In

One of the most important tasks front desk representatives perform is to check in guests.

Exhibit 1 provides a step-by-step breakdown of how to begin checking in the guest.

Establish Guest Payment Method at Check-in

After check-in has begun, front desk representatives establish how the guest plans to pay for his or her visit.

Exhibit 2 provides a step-by-step breakdown of how to establish guest payment methods.

Authorize Credit Cards

A task front desk representatives perform often is getting approval for a credit card. The front desk accepts credit cards to set up guest credit at check-in and to settle guest accounts at check-out.

Some cards can be used only by the person named on the card. For these cards, the name of the employer is unacceptable.

Front desk representatives must ensure that a credit card is valid by examining it to make sure it is current, unaltered, and signed on the back. A property could lose large sums of money if a front desk representative accepts invalid credit cards.

Front desk representatives then must make sure that the estimated charges or the amount of a purchase is approved by using a magnetic strip reader. If the card is accepted, the front desk representative will receive an authorization number.

Credit cards are run through a magnetic-strip-reader machine. The machine reads information from the magnetic tape strip on the back of the credit card and sends the information to a verification service. The service will either approve or disapprove the credit card. If the machine doesn't respond to the card, the strip on the card may have been damaged. In that case, the front desk representative will need to type the credit

Exhibit 1
Begin Guest Check-In

Materials needed: Current status report, reservation records, registration cards, preregistration envelopes, the frequent flyer log, a computer, guestroom keys, and a pen.

STEPS:	HOW-TO'S:
1. **Greet guests.**	❏ Smile warmly and welcome guests. Say something such as: "Welcome to the property. How may I help you?"
	❏ Move toward guests and look them in the eye as you speak.
	❏ Call guests by name and welcome them back if you recognize them.
	❏ Be friendly, pleasant, and sincere about how happy you are that the guests have chosen your lodging property.
	❏ Make friendly conversation, but don't be chatty. Guests may be in a hurry to get to their rooms.
	❏ Once you've learned a guest's last name, use it with a courtesy title in your conversation: "Is this your first visit to Ohio, Ms. Tinker?"
	❏ Do not say the guest's name too loudly. You would be compromising a guest's security by speaking a name too loudly.
	❏ When there is a line at the front desk, try to make eye contact with each guest who joins the line. Welcome guests with a nod or a smile. Try to say "I'll be right with you."
2. **Ask guests if the property is holding reservations for them.**	
3. **If guests do not have reservations, check the house occupancy.**	❏ Be positive when arranging rooms for walk-in guests. Walk-in guests are an excellent chance to increase occupancy and income.

(continued)

Exhibit 1
Begin Guest Check-In *(continued)*

STEPS:	HOW-TO'S:
	❏ However, if walk-in guests look suspicious, excuse yourself and notify the security department and the Manager on Duty.
	❏ Check to see if the property has rooms available.
	❏ Ask guests how long they plan to stay and what type of room they prefer.
	❏ Do not sell reserved rooms to walk-in guests.
	❏ Quote available rates and point out the benefits of each room type according to your property's rate-quoting policy.
	❏ Do not quote discount rates too quickly because this can hurt your published rate structure. Make sure guests qualify for any discount rates they ask for.
4. **If guests have reservations, confirm information on the registration cards.**	❏ Get guests' preregistration envelopes from the file.
	❏ Verify guests' first and last names.
	❏ If you cannot find a guest's preregistration envelope:
	• Make sure you are spelling the guest's name correctly
	• Look for misfiled envelopes
	• Think of other ways the name may have been spelled, and look for the envelope under that spelling
	• Ask your supervisor for help
	❏ When you find the preregistration envelope, confirm the number of guests and the departure date.
	❏ Tell the guest the type of room you have reserved.
	❏ Suggest a room with more features.

(continued)

Exhibit 1
Begin Guest Check-In *(continued)*

STEPS:	HOW-TO'S:
5. **If guests are not preregistered, create registration cards.**	❏ If using a manual system, ask guests to fill out registration cards. ❏ If using a computer, ask guests questions so you can complete the registration screen.
6. **Handle guests with special room requests or needs.**	❏ Anticipate guests' needs. For example, if guests are walking slowly or need help, don't put them at the far end of a hall. And put families near recreational facilities. ❏ Follow these steps to handle requests for special rooms: • If guests have disabilities, ask them what room type would best suit them, and assign it if available. Typically, when guests with disabilities make reservations, special rooms are blocked (set aside) for them. • If guests request non-smoking rooms, assign them if available. • If guests request day-rental rooms, tell them the time period covered by the rate. If your property doesn't rent rooms by the day, explain that you'll need to charge the full rate. • If guests request special room numbers or locations, assign them when available. Tell guests if you must assign higher-priced rooms to meet requests. • If guests ask to share a room, put all names into the computer or on a registration card. If only one guest is checking in now, fill out a registration card and refile it so you can check in the other guests later.

(continued)

Exhibit 1
Begin Guest Check-In *(continued)*

STEPS:	HOW-TO'S:
7. **Handle guests with special room rates.**	❑ Follow these steps to handle guests with special room rates: • If guests belong to a group that gets discount rates, check their identification to make sure they qualify. • If guests request frequent flyer points, check their airline ticket, boarding pass, or membership card, if necessary. • Record on the property's frequent flyer log the frequent flyer number, name, airline, originating airport code, destination airport code, flight number, and dates of stay. • If guests have free rooms, enter the room rate as "COMP" on the registration record.
8. **Assign rooms and complete registration cards.**	❑ Based upon the guest's preferences, determined in steps 3, 4, 6 and 7, select a room that is vacant and clean for the guest. ❑ Enter the room number and room rate onto the registration card. ❑ If you are using a computer, print the registration card. ❑ If necessary, change the room's status to occupied. ❑ Do not say the room rate out loud, as it may be different from the rate of the next person in line. Instead, circle the rate in view of the guest. ❑ Ask the guest to sign his or her initials next to the room rate. ❑ Ask the guest to sign the registration card.

(continued)

Exhibit 1	
Begin Guest Check-In *(continued)*	
STEPS:	**HOW-TO'S:**
9. **Issue room keys.**	❑ If the room key is not in a preregistration envelope, get the key for each assigned room. ❑ Give guests the number of keys they request.
10. **Handle VIP guests.**	❑ As soon as you identify VIP guests, excuse yourself, if possible, and step to a phone away from the desk. However, do not leave the front desk unattended. ❑ Call a manager or sales person and have him or her come to the front desk to greet VIP guests and escort them to their guestrooms after check-in.
11. **Handle minors.**	❑ You may need to check in minors differently than other arriving guests. State laws may affect the property's policies about renting guestrooms to minors. Be informed so that you do not violate a policy or state law.

Exhibit 2
Establish the Payment Method During Check-In

Materials needed: Reservation records, registration cards, credit card vouchers, a pen, a credit card imprinter, a cash bank, and a group resume.

STEPS:	HOW-TO'S:
1. **Handle cash or personal check payments.**	❑ Collect the entire stay's room charges and tax in advance. Guests who plan to pay for their room by cash or check must pay during check-in or use a credit card to establish credit. Guests who pay cash and who do not establish credit are called "cash-only" guests.
	❑ Assure guests that they will be reimbursed if they check out earlier than expected.
	❑ If guests plan to pay by check, ask to see a driver's license, and note the license number and state on the check.
	❑ Recommend that guests leave a credit card imprint at the desk so they'll be able to charge items in the property's outlets and get keys to guestroom honor bars. Tell guests that they can always pay charges with cash during check-out.
	❑ Guests may also wish to leave cash or a personal check to establish credit. If guests *do* leave a credit card imprint, personal check, or cash, they are no longer treated as cash-only guests.
	❑ Collect parking fees in advance for the number of night guests are staying. Otherwise guests may leave without paying fees.
	❑ Give change and receipts to guests, and post payments to their accounts.
	❑ As you give change to guests, count it back to them.
2. **Handle credit card payments.**	❑ Verify signatures on the registration card and credit card to be sure they match. Most credit cards are non-transferable.

(continued)

Exhibit 2
Establish the Payment Method During Check-In (continued)

STEPS:	HOW-TO'S:
	❑ Verify the credit card for the estimated charges.
	❑ If a card is approved, imprint it on the back of the registration card and on a credit card voucher.
	❑ Write the estimated charge amount and the approval code on the registration card and on the credit card voucher.
	❑ Always hand the credit card back to the guest. Do not place it on the front desk.
3. Handle direct-bill payments.	❑ If direct-billing information is not marked, check to see whether guests are on their companies' direct-billing lists. The reservation record should note whether guests have direct-billing approval.
	❑ If a guest is not on the list, ask for another payment method. Advise the guest to contact the company to have his or her name added to the list.
	❑ If guests may only direct-bill room charges and tax, ask if they would like to leave a credit card imprint to establish credit for other charges. If so, see Step 2. If not, treat them as cash-only guests (see Step 1).
4. Handle scrip, coupon, voucher, or gift certificate payments.	❑ Treat these documents the same as cash. The property may purchase advertising and pay for it with room certificates or "scrip."
	❑ Read documents carefully to see what charges are covered.
	❑ Make sure the documents have not expired and that they are signed by the user, if necessary.
	❑ When you collect each document, mark it as void.
	❑ Collect cash or set up credit for items not covered by the document.

(continued)

Exhibit 2
Establish the Payment Method During Check-In *(continued)*

STEPS:	HOW-TO'S:
5. **Handle master account payments.**	❏ Check to see who the authorized signers are on the master account. Make sure the guest is authorized to make billing charges. A master account is set up by an organization for its members. The organization pays for part or all of guests' bills.
	❏ Refer to the group resume to see what charges will be paid by the master account. A group resume is prepared by the sales department when an organization sets up a master account.
	❏ Inform guests which charges are covered.
	❏ Establish credit for guests so they can charge items not covered by the master account.

card number into the machine. If the card is approved, he or she will receive an authorization number.

If a credit card is not approved, front desk representatives tactfully help the guest find another method of payment. If a guest's credit card is invalid, they politely and quietly inform the guest that the property cannot accept it.

Accept Checks As Payment

If a lodging property accepts checks to pay for rooms or other services, front desk representatives carefully follow the approval process to protect the property's money and answer any guest questions.

It is illegal to ask for a guest's credit card number to use as identification for check writing.

Issue and Control Keys

As part of check-in, front desk representatives give guests their keys. Guests may request more than one key for each adult in the guestroom.

Some properties have safe-deposit boxes and some have in-room safes. Metal keys, key cards or electronic touch-pad systems may be used to open and lock in-room safes. Front desk representatives may also give keys to guestroom honor bars if the guests have authorized credit.

Sometimes guests will need replacement keys. Front desk representatives politely ask to see the guests' picture identification and ensure that the guests are registered to the rooms. Keys are given *only* to registered guests—not to a guest's spouse, child, friend, boss, or anyone else.

Use Effective Sales Techniques During Check-In

During the check-in process, there are a number of ways in which front desk representatives can offer additional services or amenities to guests, which will make their stay more enjoyable and also bring in additional revenue for a property. At some properties, **upselling** can earn front desk representatives additional pay in the form of commission for a successful sale.

Upselling is a way of selling a more expensive guestroom than the one the guest originally requested. It never hurts to offer a guest a better room. Front desk representatives are showing guests that they want them to have a pleasant stay. They start by suggesting the better room when the guest checks in. They then describe the features and benefits. Depending on the guest, they can make suggestions regarding certain favorable aspects of the higher rated room. For instance, guests with children may prefer the extra space in a larger room; business travelers may prefer a larger room with a kitchen for holding meetings or entertaining clients; and vacationing couples may have a more memorable stay because of additional amenities. Anticipating what a guest wants is a large part of upselling.

In addition to upselling, they inform guests of the additional services, promotions, or restaurants that are available to them.

Relocate Guests

There may be times when front desk representatives are unable to accommodate a guest who has a reservation at a property. Current guests sometimes extend their taken more reservations that there are rooms available for arriving guests. In these situations, a property's policy may be to relocate guests to a similar property.

Most properties will keep a list of local lodging properties that are similar and routinely call them on sold-out days to determine if there is availability.

Guests who must be relocated for a night should be encouraged to return to the property for the following night or for the remainder of their stay. Front desk representatives will offer to arrange transportation for guests back to the property the following day. Often, these guests will receive a room upgrade upon their return, as well as a note of apology.

Finish Guest Check-in

Finally, front desk representatives give guests any waiting messages, mail, packages, telegrams, or faxes. Any property-specific policies, such as parking policies, will need to be explained.

In full-service properties, the front desk representative will then offer bell attendant assistance. In any property, they note special needs of guests with disabilities, file registration paperwork, and follow through on guest requests.

Apply Your Learning 6.3

Please write all answers on a separate sheet of paper.

1. List the items typically included in an arrivals list.

2. What is the first step in performing a guest check-in?

3. What are the two primary methods for securing credit card authorization?

4. Who is authorized to receive a key to a guestroom? Who is not authorized?

5. What is a common cause of having to relocate a guest with a reservation?

6.4 Occupancy

AFTER SUCCESSFULLY COMPLETING THIS SECTION, YOU WILL BE ABLE TO:

◆ Explain the procedures for providing services to property guests during occupancy.

◆ Describe how to handle any guest problems or emergencies.

◆ List the daily duties performed by front desk representatives.

Check In Group Arrivals

Front desk representatives prepare for the arrival of large groups so that there is less confusion and fewer long lines in the lobby when group members arrive. In some properties, the sales department helps the front desk prepare by providing a group résumé which explains how each group prefers to be checked in and out.

Preregistering groups may also include preparing registration packets that are given to group members when they arrive. By using the **arrivals list**, front desk representatives can create an individual packet for each group member. The packets would include a registration card that each guest would fill out and return.

It is helpful to block rooms for groups so that group members can be on the same floor or in the same area of the property.

Process Room Changes

Not every guest will be satisfied with his or her room accommodations. There may be times when guests request that they be changed to a different room.

Exhibit 1 provides a step-by-step breakdown of how to process a guestroom change.

Run Credit Check Reports

Front desk representatives can help a lodging property reduce losses by performing routine **credit check** reports on guests. While most guests are honest, some might run up a large bill and leave without paying. Because of those few, front desk representatives will need to run a credit check to make sure everyone's charges are within his or her credit limit.

A credit check will indicate whether:

• Cash-only guests have used the phone, watched pay movies, or charged items in any of the outlets

• Credit card guests have gone over their credit limits

• Credit card guests have gone over the property's floor limits

In situations where a cash-only guest's account needs to be reconciled to a zero balance, front desk representatives will need to contact the guest and politely request that he or she come down to the front desk to pay for the charged item.

Exhibit 1
Process Guestroom Changes

Materials needed: Guestroom keys, a room status report, and registration cards.

STEPS:	HOW-TO'S:
1. **Move unsatisfied guests to acceptable rooms.**	❑ If there's a problem with a guest's room, move the guest to a same-rate room.
	❑ If none are available, move the guest to a higher-rate room for no additional charge.
	❑ If there's a problem with the type of room, offer to move the guest to a room that will better meet the guest's needs.
	❑ If the new room has a higher rate, explain the extra charge to the guest and get his or her agreement to pay before moving him or her.
	❑ Enter the room change information into the computer or other front office rooming system before making the change of rooms.
	❑ If there are no other rooms available at the property, tell your supervisor about the problem right away.
2. **Provide bell attendant assistance for room changes.**	❑ Send a bell attendant to help guests change rooms.
	❑ Give the bell attendant the new guestroom key and have him or her bring back the first guestroom key.
	❑ Return the original guestroom key to its correct location.
	❑ About 10 minutes after a move is done, call the guest to make sure the new room meets his or her expectations.
3. **Change the room number on the registration card.**	
4. **Inform the housekeeping department of the change.**	

There may also be situations where a guest paying by credit card makes charges to the account that exceed the credit limit available on the card. Front desk representatives contact the guest to request an additional credit card to cover the difference. The guest may also choose to pay for the difference with cash.

Process Safe-Deposit Box Transactions for Guests

Many lodging properties provide free use of a **safe-deposit box** for their guests. These boxes can be used to store guests' valuables during their stay. Typically, properties set a maximum dollar amount for which they are liable for if something should happen to the valuables placed in the box. This amount is usually shown on the safe-deposit box card.

Front desk representatives assign a safe-deposit box to guests upon request. They ask for the guest's room number and then present the safe-deposit box card to the guest. The guest must fill out this card with his or her information and then sign the card. Front desk representatives must inform guests of the maximum dollar liability amount.

Once the box has been assigned and the key has been presented to the guest, the box is then removed from the vault and presented to the guest. Most properties will have a private location where guests can place their valuables into the box. Front desk representatives never handle these valuables themselves; only guests should place their valuables in the box.

Once a guest has finished placing items in their boxes, the front desk representative places the box back in the vault and presents the key to the guest, informing the guest

that he or she has the only key. By having only one key to the box, the guest knows that only he or she can access it. The front desk representative informs the guest that he or she will be held responsible if the key is lost and a new key hole must be drilled. Finally, the front desk representative must record on the card the date and time the items were placed in the box, along with his or her name or initials, and file the card in the proper location. This should be done every time the guest accesses the box.

Guests should be provided access to their boxes whenever they wish. Each occurrence should be recorded on the card. The contents of the box should never be discussed; someone may overhear and this might place the guest or the guest's property in danger. Only the guest who filled out and signed the card should be given access to the box. A key may be stolen or lost, meaning the person seeking access may not be the guest.

Before gaining access to the box, the guest must sign the card. If the signature doesn't match the one given when the box was issued, management or security must be notified immediately.

Each time a guest accesses the box, the front desk representative inquires whether the guest is closing the box out. If so, this should be recorded on the card, along with the date, time, and initials or name of the front desk representative. The guest will sign the card, indicating that he or she is removing valuables and closing the box out.

Respond to Questions About Facilities and Events

Some guests may ask for suggestions on where to go or what to do in the local area. Front desk representatives are often viewed as the face of the property and may have to field questions about events on property.

Guests may request help in choosing restaurants, attractions, and entertainment sites. Front desk representatives listen closely to what the guest wants and ask questions to clarify if they are not sure. If a guest asks about something that should be handled by another department, front desk representatives tell the guest that they will call someone from that department for the guest. They do not tell the guest to call the department.

Everyone is trained to respond immediately to guest needs within their area of responsibility. If possible, front desk representatives check back with the guest to make sure everything was handled correctly.

When possible, front desk representatives recommend the restaurants, lounges, services, and other facilities within the property first. They refer to the guest information directory if guests ask for help selecting local restaurants, attractions, or entertainment sites. They know whom in the community to call for more information, and contact them if necessary. To help guests make decisions, they show them any brochures, menus, or other promotional materials available. They write down the names, addresses, and phone numbers of all places guests are interested in.

Guests may also ask questions about function times and locations of meetings or events occurring on property. Many properties have daily and weekly function sheets that state what groups are meeting at the property and when. If guests ask for information that is not on one of the sheets, front desk representatives ask them to please wait a moment while they find the answer. They then call the department (catering, sales, convention services, etc.) responsible for organizing the function to find the information needed and present it to the guest, along with any directions necessary.

Currency Exchange

The lodging property welcomes guests from all over the world. The guests front desk representatives greet may be from halfway around the world or a few streets from the property. The money that guests bring with them is not always in the country's currency.

If a property exchanges foreign currency, front desk representatives will want to keep up with the exchange rates and what the property charges.

If a property doesn't exchange currency, front desk representatives should find out who does. They can provide quality service when they tell guests where they can exchange currency and where they can find the current exchange rates.

Use the Cash Bank

Front desk representatives have a **cash bank** at their station. It contains the smallest amount of cash that will allow them to do business throughout their shift. Only one person ever uses each bank and the front desk representative may be assigned a safe-deposit box for storage of the cash bank between shifts.

Exhibit 2 provides step-by-step guidance for picking up, using, and turning in the cash drawer.

Exhibit 2
Pick Up, Use, and Turn in Your Cash Bank

Materials needed: Cash bank, cash bank contract, cash drawer key, safe-deposit box, petty cash vouchers, a pen, receipts, paid-out vouchers, due-back vouchers, cash-deposit envelopes, and a drop safe logbook.

STEPS:	HOW-TO'S:
1. **Maintain security over your cash bank at all times.**	❏ Count the money you receive from a manager as your cash bank at least twice before starting your shift.
	❏ Sign a cash bank contract to assume responsibility for the cash in your bank the first time you receive a bank.
	❏ Count any money you give to or receive from guests and employees. Never give someone money without counting in front of him or her.
	❏ Lock your cash drawer when you leave the area. Keep the key with you and never leave it in the lock.
2. **Make approved petty cash disbursements.**	❏ Pay out petty cash from your bank: • When a guest has lost money in a vending machine • When accounting is closed and a cash purchase is required
3. **Document petty cash disbursements.**	❏ Prepare a petty cash voucher, date it, and initial it. Get a manager's approval before giving cash to a guest or employee.
	❏ Ask the person receiving the cash to sign the petty cash voucher.
	❏ Attach receipts for purchases reimbursed through petty cash.
4. **Process paid-outs.**	❏ When a guest asks you to pay for something for him or her (such as a flower delivery), pay for it with money from your cash bank. Cash given out by the property on behalf of a guest and charged to the guest's account as a cash advance is typically called a paid-out.

(continued)

Exhibit 2
Pick Up, Use, and Turn in Your Cash Bank *(continued)*

STEPS:	HOW-TO'S:
	❑ Fill out a paid-out voucher and attach a receipt from the guest's purchase.
	❑ Charge the money to the guest's account with the property.
	❑ If a guest charges a room service purchase to his or her account and includes the room service attendant's tip in that charge, pay the attendant the amount of the tip from your cash bank.
	❑ Fill out a paid-out voucher. The guest will pay back the money when he or she settles his or her account during check-out.
	❑ Do the following for all paid-out vouchers: • Fill in all of the information requested on the form. • Attach all back-up documents, such as receipts. • Stamp the voucher as "posted" after you post the charge to the correct account. • Sign it and get a manager's signature as approval.
	❑ Never "borrow" cash from your bank or "loan" cash to another employee. An "I.O.U." slip in your bank violates approved procedures.
5. **Prepare due-back vouchers.**	❑ Prepare a due-back voucher for the total amount of money you paid out of your cash bank. This includes petty cash and paid-outs. "Due back" is a situation that occurs when a front desk employee pays out more than he or she receives. The difference is due back to the front desk employee's cash bank.
	❑ Attach petty cash vouchers and paid-out vouchers to the due-back voucher.
	❑ If possible, take your due-back voucher to the general cashier to be reimbursed. Return this money to your cash bank.

(continued)

Exhibit 2
Pick Up, Use, and Turn in Your Cash Bank *(continued)*

STEPS:	HOW-TO'S:
6. **Prepare your shift deposit.**	❑ Separate out the amount of the initial cash bank.
	❑ Place the remaining cash, checks, and other negotiable items in a cash-deposit envelope.
	❑ Write down what's in the envelope on the outside of the envelope.
	❑ Seal the envelope and sign your name across the seal. Deposit the envelope in the drop safe. Another employee should witness your deposit.
	❑ Sign the drop safe logbook, and have the witness sign it also.
7. **Return your cash bank at the end of your shift, and ask your manager to count the cash.**	

Post Guest Charges and Payments

Many properties allow guests to charge expenses related to other property services or outlets to their room account. When these charges are incurred, it is the front desk representative's responsibility to make sure that they are recorded.

Exhibit 3 provides step-by-step guidance for how to post guest charges and payments.

Process Guaranteed No-Shows

Most lodging properties charge the guest with a guaranteed reservation for the guestroom even if the guest does not actually show. Because the property is telling the guest that the room will remain empty until they arrive, it only makes sense that the property should not lose out on revenue that could have been made by selling the room to another guest.

Exhibit 4 provides step-by-step guidance for how to process the payment of these guaranteed no-shows.

Keep the Front Desk Orderly

Keeping the front desk area clean and orderly is professional and helps front desk representatives do their jobs more effectively. There are several ways that front desk representatives can easily and efficiently keep their area clean:

- File paperwork as it is completed. Doing this right away will helps to avoid mixing up papers for different accounts. Front desk representatives finish filing before beginning another task. However, they don't make guests wait while they file.

- Arrange the work area so that everything is in a set place and can be accessed easily. Front desk representatives make sure the desk is constantly stocked with the necessary supplies.

- Clean while working. Front desk representatives throw out useless papers, dust the equipment and desktop frequently, and pick up any trash in the work area. If trash cans fill up, they empty them. If the desk is unusually messy, with a lot of trash or special cleaning needs, they contact the housekeeping department and ask that a public space cleaner be sent.

VIPs

VIPs (**V**ery **I**mportant **P**ersons) are guests who receive extra-special treatment. This special attention usually includes a daily morning newspaper, nightly turndown service, on-call transportation by the property's limousine or van, special amenities, and more. VIPs are offered the very finest services and accommodations a property has to offer.

Follow these procedures when checking in VIPs:

- Coordinate the VIPs arrival time with housekeeping.

- Preregister the VIP, and print his or her name and room number on a preregistration envelope.

- Pre-key the guestroom and test the key.

- Require only that the VIP *sign* the registration card, not completely fill it out.

- Notify the appropriate departments and co-workers, including concierge, room

Exhibit 3
Post Guest Charges and Payments

Materials needed: Point-of-sale equipment, guest folios, charge and payment voucher, and registration cards.

STEPS:	HOW-TO'S:
1. **Access the point-of-sale equipment.**	❏ Type in your access code or password. ❏ Make sure no one can see the keys you press.
2. **Set up a guest account.**	❏ Type in the guest's: • Last name • First name • Middle initial • Room number
3. **Access a guest's account by typing in the guest's room number or the first few letters of the guest's last name.**	
4. **Post guest charges or payments using a manual or electronic system.**	❏ Room and tax charges are automatically posted each night for occupied rooms.
5. **File back-up documents with the registration card or guest folio.**	❏ Back up all postings with a voucher or other document. ❏ Double-check your work to be sure the amounts are the same as those on the back-up paperwork.

Exhibit 4
Process Guaranteed No-Shows

Materials needed: Credit card validation machinr, credit card vouchers, a no-show report, canceled reservation documentation, and a travel agent no-show/cancellation form.

STEPS:	HOW-TO'S:
1. Research each guaranteed no-show to be sure that the reservation was not canceled, entered wrong, or a duplicate.	

2. Fill out credit card vouchers for no-show guests who used their credit cards to guarantee reservations, unless the property uses online verification.	❑ Imprint a credit card voucher.
	❑ Get an approval code using one of the following methods:
	  • Call a credit card authorization center and supply the card number, the amount of the charge, and the property's merchant number.
	  OR
	  • Enter the card number into a credit card validation machine.
	❑ Complete the voucher using the credit card information the guest supplied to guarantee the reservation.
	❑ Fill in the credit card number, expiration date, and guest's name.
	❑ Fill in the total amount for room and tax for one night.
	❑ In the signature blank, print "signature on file."
	❑ On the voucher, write "guaranteed no-show charge."
	❑ Process the vouchers with your shift deposit.

3. Complete the paperwork for no-show guests who used direct billing to guarantee their reservation.	❑ Note on the reservation whether it is a no-show from a sold-out or a projected sold-out night. This will be useful information if the charge is disputed.

(continued)

Exhibit 4
Process Guaranteed No-Shows *(continued)*

STEPS:	HOW-TO'S:
4. **Track no-show revenue.**	❑ Guaranteed no-show revenues should be shown as "no-show revenues" on the daily report the day the money is collected. No-shows can be a large income source if billed on a timely basis and properly tracked.
	❑ Maintain a no-show report to track the collection of all no-show billings.
	❑ Guaranteed no-shows should not be shown as occupied rooms on the housekeeping or room revenue report.
5. **Check your files to find out which no-show guests were booked by a travel agent.**	
6. **Fill out a travel agent no-show/cancellation form.**	❑ On the form, fill in the following:
	• Guest name
	• Original arrival date
	• Departure date
	• Confirmation number
	• Name of your property
	• Property's telephone number
	• Your name
	❑ Check the box on the form marked "Your client was a no-show."
7. **Mail one form to the travel agent and keep one for your records.**	

service, and the resident or general manager.

- Remember, when checking in VIPs and other guests, be courteous and professional, and provide quality service.

Key Control

Front desk representatives contribute to the property's key control policies. They issue keys only to registered guests and secure any guestroom keys that are not currently in use.

The front desk is often the area where master keys are stored. Because a master key can open all guestrooms, there are special procedures for getting master keys. Most properties use a logbook to record when master keys are checked out, who checked them out, why they were checked out, and any other details.

Apply Your Learning 6.4

Please write all answers on a separate sheet of paper.

1. List the three primary things that a credit check report can tell you.

2. What is the main purpose of a current status report?

3. How does the front desk contribute to the property's key control?

6.5 Check Out

AFTER SUCCESSFULLY COMPLETING THIS SECTION, YOU WILL BE ABLE TO:

◆ Describe the procedures for checking out a guest.

◆ Explain the processes for automatic checkouts such as express or video check outs.

◆ Describe how to process late check outs and their related charges.

◆ Explain how to adjust disputed guest charges.

When front desk representatives perform a check-out, one of their goals is to make that guest want to return. Therefore, they put as much guest service into a check-out as they would any other guest contact situation. This includes thanking the guest for staying at the property, inviting him or her to return, and encouraging the guest to fill out a comment card so the property can address any concerns or note any compliments.

When guests check out, front desk representatives collect their room keys and return them to the key rack. If a property has an electronic door system that creates new room keys for each guest, they simply throw the keys away. Front desk representatives also retrieve keys for in-room safes.

Process Guest Check-Outs

Most guests will take advantage of automatic check-out procedures. However, some check out in person because they have questions or are disputing a charge on the express check-out folio. They may also be settling the account with cash, check, or a credit card other than the one that was imprinted at check-in.

Exhibit 1 provides step-by-step guidance for how this service is provided.

Process Automatic Check-Outs

Many properties offer express check-out to the following guests:

• Credit card guests with approved credit authorization

• Approved direct-bill customers

• Paid-in-advance customers with a zero balance

To receive this service, guests may need to sign only the registration card at check-in, establish their signature on file, and allow their credit card to be imprinted on a voucher on their registration card.

Check-outs are usually accomplished with an in-room computer terminal, telephone or television screen to access and display folio data.

Exhibit 2 provides step-by-step guidance for how this service is provided.

Exhibit 1
Process Guestroom Check-Outs at the Desk

Materials needed: Computer, printer, pen, registration cards, credit card vouchers, paid-out vouchers, a group resume, guest folios, and a stapler.

STEPS:	HOW-TO'S:
1. Greet guests immediately as they approach the front desk, and ask how you can help.	
2. Use the guest's name throughout the check-out process.	❑ Ask for the guest's room number so you can bring up the account information on the computer or find it in the file. • Check that the total due is correct. • Ask if there were any charges made recently. If so, call the outlet for the amount and post the charges. • Read and reset the phone meter, and post charges in manual systems. • Print and present the folio to the guest for review of the charges.
3. Review accounts with guests.	
4. Locate the guest's registration card. Write the date, time, and your initials.	
5. Check for remaining mail or messages.	
6. Close out the guest's safe-deposit box, if appropriate.	
7. Collect room keys.	

(continued)

Exhibit 1
Process Guest Check-Outs at the Desk *(continued)*

STEPS:	HOW-TO'S:
8. **Settle the payment of the account balance.**	❏ Ask how the guest plans to settle the account: • *Cash payment:* Collect the correct amount of cash. Mark the folio as paid. Destroy any credit card vouchers imprinted at check-in. • *Personal check:* Collect the check and make sure it's correctly filled in. Ask for a driver's license. Write the state and license number on the folio. Compare the signature on the check with the signature on the license. Mark the folio as paid. Destroy any credit card vouchers imprinted at check-in. • *Credit card:* Fill in the total guest charges on the voucher. Ask the guest to sign the credit card voucher and the guest folio. • *Direct billing:* The guest's direct-billing status should have been approved during check-in. Ask the guest to sign the folio to verify and accept the charges. • *Gift certificate, scrip, coupon, or voucher:* Attach the document to a copy of the guest folio and file it with the day's work. Treat the canceled form as cash and include it with the shift deposit. • *Combined settlement methods:* Accurately record the combined methods on the folio. Attach all necessary items (checks, credit card vouchers, etc.) to the folio.
9. **Process group check-outs.**	❏ Refer to the group resume to find the preferred check-out method for the group and which charges are to be covered by the group.

(continued)

Exhibit 1
Process Guest Check-Outs at the Desk *(continued)*

STEPS:	HOW-TO'S:
	❏ Use express check-out with guests who established credit during check-in.
	❏ Ask guests who are sharing the cost of a room or paying with cash, personal checks, traveler's checks, gift certificates, scrip, coupons, or a voucher to check out at the front desk.
10. Post payments and provide receipts.	❏ Print a new folio for the guest to have as a receipt.
	❏ Ask the guest if he or she would like the credit card voucher copy stapled to the folio. If so, staple it. If not, give it to the guest separately.
	❏ Present the receipt to the guest and thank him or her for staying at the property.
11. Post payments and provide receipts.	❏ Offer bell service to guests.
	❏ If the guests accept, call "Service, please," or the appropriate phrase used at your property, and introduce guests to the bell attendant.
	❏ If guests decline bell service, be prepared to offer help with a taxi, courtesy transportation, limousine service, or luggage storage.
	❏ If your property has valet parking, offer to have the car pulled up.
	❏ Ask guests if you can make reservations for their next stay.
12. Thank guests again for visiting, and invite them back.	
13. File the check-out paperwork.	❏ File the remaining folio copies in the current day's check-out folios according to the method of payment.
	❏ File registration cards in the designated files.
	❏ Complete each check-out before beginning the next. Do not mix up your paperwork.
	❏ Don't make guests wait while you file.

Handle Late Guest Check-Outs

Late check-outs are a convenience to guests and are allowed whenever possible Typically the fee for a late check-out before 6 P.M. is 50 percent of the daily room rate, plus tax. The late fee for a check-out after 6 P.M. is usually the price of a full day's rental, plus tax.

Exhibit 3 provides step-by-step guidance for how this service is provided.

Process Late Charges

A late charge is a transaction that does not reach the front desk until after the guest has checked out. Unsettled guest accounts become the responsibility of accounting.

Exhibit 4 provides step-by-step guidance for how to process late charges.

Adjust Disputed Guest Charges

Sometimes guests dispute a specific charge on their bills. Front desk representatives apologize to a guest in this situation, regardless of who committed the error. They then determine whether the charge is worth challenging. For instance, if a guest is disputing a small amount, such as the charge for a pay movie, it is best to adjust the bill without question.

In situations where the charge should be challenged, front desk representatives research the charge, looking for documentation, such as signed chargers, to provide more information. Disputed charges usually are due to errors in posting or are, in fact, valid charges that the guest has forgotten. If documentation can be found showing the charge is legitimate, it should be shown to the guest.

In situations where the charge is an error, front desk representatives apologize for the mistake and make the correction to the bill on an adjustment voucher. Finally, the front desk representative attaches the documentation to the voucher, stamp the voucher as posted, and post a credit for the disputed amount to the guest's bill.

If the guest and the property cannot work out the dispute, the guest will likely call the credit card company. The credit card company typically sends an inquiry to the property. If the property doesn't produce back-up documents to support the charge, the company will not charge the guest or pay the property.

Apply Your Learning 6.5

Please write all answers on a separate sheet of paper.

1. In addition to room keys, what are some other types of keys front desk representatives should retrieve from guests?

2. What are the three types of guests that are eligible for express check out?

4. What is the typical fee for a late check-out before 6 P.M.?

5. Define a "late charge."

Exhibit 2
Process Automatic Check-Outs

Materials needed: Express check-out carriers, guest folios, guest comment cards, credit card vouchers, and property promotional materials.

STEPS:	HOW-TO'S:

1. **Handle express check-outs.**	❏ Print guest folios and place them in express check-out carriers along with a guest comment card and other promotional materials.
	
	❏ Ask bell attendants to put the carriers under the guestroom doors before 6 A.M. on the scheduled day of departure.
	
	❏ Change the status of the room to a check-out when:
	
	   • Guests call to say they are leaving the room
	
	   • The housekeeping department reports the room status as vacant-clean

2. **Process video check-outs.**	❏ Give the guest a printed folio copy if he or she stops at the front desk on the way out. ❏ If a guest does not stop, mail a copy of the folio to him or her.

Exhibit 3
Handle Late Guest Check-Outs

Materials needed: Occupancy report, an arrivals list, and a late check-out list.

STEPS:	HOW-TO'S:
1. **Determine whether a late check-out can be granted.**	❑ Look at the property's occupancy report and arrivals list to find out if a late check-out will prevent the property from having rooms available for arriving guests. ❑ If you cannot allow a late check-out, suggest other alternatives. For example, offer free luggage storage if the guest is attending a meeting that will run to the end of the day. ❑ If you are not sure whether you can allow a late check-out, check with a supervisor or manager.
2. **Inform guests of the late check-out policy.**	❑ Tell the guest the time by which he or she must check out to avoid a late fee. ❑ Tell the guest the amount of late fees. ❑ Most front desk computers require you to post by hand late check-out charges that are less than a full day's room charge and tax.
3. **Inform late check-out guests of additional late fees.**	❑ If the guest has not checked out in time to avoid a late fee, call the guest to see if he or she needs to stay longer. ❑ If so, tell the guest what the fees will be.
4. **Maintain a list of late check-outs and keep housekeeping informed of them.**	

Exhibit 4
Process Late Charges

Materials needed: Credit card vouchers, guest ledgers, and the city ledger.

STEPS:	HOW-TO'S:
1. **Find out if the guest settled the account with a credit**	❑ If the guest paid with a credit card, you may be able to complete a credit card voucher for the late charge and write "signature on file" on the signature line.
	❑ Mail a copy of the bill with any late charges to the guest. This will help the guest reconcile his or her accounts.
2. **If the guest settled the account with another payment method, transfer the account from the guest ledger to the city (non-guest) ledger.**	❑ Tell the guest the time by which he or she must check out to avoid a late fee.
	❑ Tell the guest the amount of late fees.
	❑ Most front desk computers require you to post by hand late check-out charges that are less than a full day's room charge and tax.
3. **Handle disputed charges.**	

Quick Hits

SECTION 6.1—GETTING TO KNOW THE FRONT DESK REPRESENTATIVE

- Front desk representatives are the first contact many guests have at a property.

- Front desk representatives are challenged to give efficient, courteous service to every guest, every day.

- A property's target market represents the type and location of guests that typically stay at the property.

- Front desk representatives should be familiar with the various guestroom equipment and amenities available to guests.

- Lodging properties possess unique POS and front desk systems that are designed and intended to make the front desk representative's job easier, as well as to provide excellent service to guests.

SECTION 6.2—GUESTROOM TERMS AND RATES

- Major types of guestroom reservations include guaranteed reservations and non-guaranteed reservations.

- Front desk representatives use room inventory and status terms to describe the current condition of a guestroom when communicating with each other or other departments on property.

- Many properties offer "frequent flyer" programs as an incentive to guests who travel a lot to stay at their property.

SECTION 6.3—PRE-ARRIVAL AND ARRIVAL

- Many lodging properties use a front office logbook to record important events or decisions that happened during a shift.

- Front desk representatives have a number of tasks that they perform to prepare for the day's check-ins, these include: checking the arrivals list, blocking or unblocking rooms, and setting up pre-registrations.

- Tasks performed by front desk representatives during a typical guest check-in include: establishing the method of payment, securing credit card or check approval, assigning a room, and issuing keys.

- "Upselling" refers to the concept of offering additional services or amenities to guests to make their stay more enjoyable and also to bring additional revenue for the property.

- In situations where a guest with a reservation cannot be accommodated for the night at a property, the property will relocate the guest to a similar lodging property and pay for his or her first night's stay.

SECTION 6.4—OCCUPANCY

- Preregistering large groups can prevent confusion and long lines in the lobby. Front desk representatives block rooms for these guests so that they can be on the same floor or in the same area of the property.

- Front desk representatives on occasion must accommodate guests not satisfied with their rooms by giving them a guestroom more to their liking.

- Front desk representatives perform routine credit check reports on guests to determine whether the guest's charges are within his or her credit limit. This can help the property reduce losses.

- Many lodging properties offer free use of safe-deposit boxes so guests can store valuables during their stay.

- Tasks typically performed by front desk representatives during the occupancy periods of a guest's stay include: currency exchange, posting charges and payments, and processing guaranteed no-shows.

- VIPs (Very Important Persons) are guests who receive extra-special treatment and are offered the very finest services and accommodations a property has to offer.

SECTION 6.5—CHECK-OUT

- Front desk representatives put as much guest service into a check-out as they would any other guest contact situation.

- Types of check-outs include: check-outs at the front desk, automatic check-outs, and late check-outs.

- Guests may dispute certain charges on their bill. The front desk representative must determine whether the charge is worth challenging. Regardless of who is at fault, the front desk representative always apologizes to the guest for the confusion.

Reservationist

Sections

The reservations department is staffed by skilled telemarketing personnel who are able to accept reservations over the phone, answer questions about the hotel and its facilities, and quote guestroom rates and available dates. Since some callers are shopping around, reservationists should be trained to sell the property as well as simply accept reservations.

Reservationists process reservations that arrive through a central computer reservation system (CRS) or through third parties such as travel agents and hotel representatives, who typically contact hotels by telephone or use the Internet. Many hotels have their own Web sites where guests can make reservations directly.

The largest percentage of advance reservations comes into hotels through direct inquiry, either by telephone or the hotel brand Web site. The remainder are received through the following sources:

- The Internet (e.g., Expedia, Orbitz, Travelocity)
- Travel agents
- Hotel representatives
- Tour operators
- Independent reservation systems
- Airlines, cruise lines, and other transportation companies

7.1   Getting to Know the Reservationist

AFTER SUCCESSFULLY COMPLETING THIS SECTION, YOU WILL BE ABLE TO:

♦ Explain the important role that reservationists play at a lodging property.

♦ Identify ways in which reservationists can be excellent team players.

♦ Describe the purpose and benefits of using a script.

♦ Explain the importance of group and travel agent reservation bookings.

♦ List the most common tasks that reservationists perform.

What Is a Reservationist?

Reservationists are a lodging property's goodwill ambassadors. They often provide the guest's first contact with the property. What reservationists say and do are critical to the guest's decision whether to stay at a property.

Every night that a room goes unsold, the opportunity to make money from that room on that night is gone. Reservationists have the unique ability to help a property fill every room every night. These skills can make a difference for the property.

How much of a difference can a reservationist make? By turning just one more call a day into a sale, a reservationist can help a property make a lot more money.

For example, if each day a property sells one more room at a rate of $100 per night, in one five-day work week the property will bring in an extra $500 ($100 × 5 days = $500).

And in one year, that property will bring in an extra $26,000 ($500 × 52 weeks = $26,000).

Reservationists can make a difference!

Working as a Team

One secret of the lodging property's success is that everyone works together—as a team—to give guests great service. Reservationists are part of a service delivery system. If they do their jobs well, co-workers can do their jobs well and can focus on giving guests the best possible service.

To be excellent team players, reservationists can:

• Explain reservation terms (such as adjoining vs. connecting rooms) to callers so that front desk employees won't have to deal with angry guests during check-in.

• Tell engineering staff members about needed repairs, and initiate a maintenance request, if necessary.

• Update the concierge with information about guest requests and VIP arrivals.

- Learn the hours of operation and the location of restaurants, lounges, health clubs, and other areas at the property so they can help guests enjoy everything the property has to offer.

Scripts

Many lodging properties provide **scripts** for reservationists. Scripts are powerful tools to help reservationists "ask for the sale." Scripts walk reservationists through a sale, providing suggested phrases to use when taking reservations. Scripts help reservationists ask for information in the order that is most efficient for them and the caller.

Scripts also help reservationists guide the caller through the conversation and keep control of the call. They are in charge of guiding callers to process their needs in a quick, professional manner, without seeming rushed or rude, and without overlooking any important information. This is no small task, but the scripts will help.

Reservationists remember that what the caller has to say is important, and don't interrupt. They practice good listening skills, giving callers time to respond to questions, and providing additional information.

Reservationists handle calls well because they practice the scripts before taking calls. The more familiar they are with the scripts, the more natural they sound. They don't just read the script to the caller. That would sound stiff and unfriendly. Instead, reservationists use the script as a guide. They try to picture each caller. This helps them remember that they are talking to a person, not just a voice.

Reservationists are like good actors who use a script to learn lines well, and then deliver those lines naturally after much practice.

Guest Credit Policies

Guests depend on reservationists to explain a lodging property's guest credit policies. They can keep guests satisfied by making sure they understand these policies.

If a guest makes a guaranteed reservation, reservationists explain the penalties for not showing up, and explain any cancellation policies. They make certain that the guest understands the importance of calling the property to cancel a guaranteed reservation if he or she is not going to make it.

Groups

Groups help keep occupancy levels high, and they bring in a lot of revenue. Because lodging properties want groups to return, they must give group members excellent service and as much attention as possible.

The sales department books groups and sets room rates. If someone calls the reservationist and asks to reserve more than 10 rooms for one night or five rooms for two nights, the reservationist will usually transfer the caller to the sales department.

Group rates vary depending on the number of rooms blocked, the type of group, how long group members plan to stay, and occupancy levels.

Reservationists have access to the information needed to take group member reservations. This information typically includes a list of all groups, rates, dates, Source of Business (SOB) codes, and reservation methods.

Travel Agents

Travel agents are important customers. They bring steady business and help fill the property. They often book high rates.

This improves the property's income and increases the travel agents' commissions.

Travel agents will usually introduce themselves when calling to make reservations for clients. To make their jobs easier, reservationists build good relations with travel agents. Some ways to do this include:

- Making sure they get the travel agent's IATA (International Air Transport Association) number and entering it into the Travel Agent area on their computer

- Asking for the travel agency's complete address

- Double-checking what the commission is

- Determining an agent's commission for booking groups

By setting up reservations correctly, reservationists allow travel agents to get their commissions quickly, making it more likely that the travel agents will continue to send business to the property.

Global Distribution Systems

Global distribution systems (GDS) have grown in popularity. Most airlines are connected to one of four GDSs: SABRE, Galileo International, Amadeus, or WorldSpan. GDSs provide worldwide distribution of hotel reservation information and allow selling of hotel reservations around the world. They link the reservation systems of hotels, airlines, car rental agencies, and travel agency companies on a world-wide basis through the Internet or a private network.

Hotels will often link their central reservations systems to the GDS which allows travel agents to book reservations directly into the hotel system while verifying room availability and rates. This is called seamless integration or seamless connectivity.

Internet Distribution Systems

Many airlines, hotels, and car rental firms offer online reservation services through an Internet distribution system (IDS). These include Expedia, Hotwire, Priceline, and Travelocity. This allows individual travelers to use their computers to book flights, reserve hotel rooms, and select rental cars. In short, to use the Web to do all the things they used to have to call a travel agent for.

Most hotels also make it possible for guests to reserve a room directly from their company's Web site.

Reservationist Duties

The primary job of a reservationist is to make arrangements for guests to stay at the lodging property at a future date. However, there are a number of other tasks, duties, and responsibilities that reservationists have to help make the property a success.

Some lodging properties require that reservationists use a daily checklist with specific times to perform each task listed. In some cases, there may also be a separate weekly checklist.

In general, reservationists are responsible for:

- Taking reservations by telephone, printed form, Internet, etc.

- Blocking rooms and arranging forecast reports

- Documenting and filing various reservation records

- Processing payment or cancellation of reservations

Exhibit 1 lists the most common tasks that reservationists are expected to be able to perform and perform well.

Exhibit 1
Task List—Reservationist

1. Use the Reservations Computer System
2. Use the Reservations Department and 800-Number Printers
3. Use the Facsimile Machine
4. Use the Photocopy Machine
5. Follow Yield Management Procedures
6. Greet Callers and Direct Calls
7. Take Reservations by Telephone
8. Take Reservations by Internet or E-mail
9. Take Reservations for Guests in Group Blocks
10. Use the Guest History System
11. Use Effective Telephone Sales Techniques
12. Promote Special Marketing Programs
13. Block Rooms for Guests With Special Requests
14. Process Reservation Records
15. Process Reservation Confirmations
16. Set Up and Monitor Group Reservation Masters
17. File Reservation Records
18. Document Reservation Calls
19. Give Directions
20. Mail Information to Potential Guests When Requested
21. Process Prepayments and Advance Deposits for Reservations
22. Process Reservation Changes and Cancellations
23. Process Travel Agent No-Show and Cancellation Forms
24. Complete and Run All Required Reports
25. Help Prepare Room Availability Forecasts
26. Prepare and Turn In the Reservations Department Checklist
27. Review the Arrivals List for Errors
28. Call Competitor Properties to Monitor Business
29. Keep the Reservations Area Organized and Clean
30. Respond to Emergency Alarms

Apply Your Learning 7.1

Please write all answers on a separate sheet of paper.

1. What is the primary responsibility of the reservationist?

2. How much extra money per year can a reservationist make for a property by selling one extra $200 room a night during the 5-day work week?

3. List four ways that reservationists can be excellent team players.

4. Why is it important for a reservationist to be familiar with a script before taking reservation calls?

5. List four items of information that reservationists should get from travel agents.

7.2 Getting to Know the Reservations Process

AFTER SUCCESSFULLY COMPLETING THIS SECTION, YOU WILL BE ABLE TO:

♦ Describe the use of the reservations computer system.

♦ List the forms typically printed out on the reservation and 800-number printers.

♦ Summarize the purpose and process of yield management.

♦ Describe the purpose of room forecasting.

♦ Explain the benefits of using the guest history system.

Reservations Computer System

The reservations computer system is a tool enabling reservationists to serve guests better. It is usually linked to the property management system.

Each lodging property's reservation computer system may be different. Reservationists receive training on their property's system. The reservations computer systems enable reservationists to do their jobs quickly and efficiently.

Revenue Management

Revenue management (also known as yield management) is the process of figuring out how to balance occupancy and prices to maximize room revenue—or get as much money from guestroom sales as possible. It increases revenue by:

• Managing the number of rooms filled

• Managing the number of discounts offered

• Booking guests who plan to stay longer than others

Reservationists are an important part of a lodging property's yield management strategy. It is their job to make sure that yield management tools such as rate controls and stay controls are used correctly. At most properties, the property management system will streamline yield management rates and availability.

Rate controls help the property to get the highest average rate. To bring in the most room revenue, hotel managers often charge a premium for better rooms. Hotels may offer deluxe rooms at standard rates to attract guests during times of low demand. As demand improves, the remaining deluxe rooms are then sold at or near full rack rate. Discounting may reduce the amount of business lost because of rate resistance and allows the hotel to sell rooms that might otherwise remain empty.

When discounting a deluxe room to a standard rate, the reservationist should tell the guest that he or she is being upgraded. This will add perceived value to the guest's stay. It also reduces guest confusion the next time he or she comes to the hotel and is quoted a higher rate.

One common rate control is called a **hurdle rate**. With this strategy, rack rates are always left open no matter what the demand is. The front office manager then sets the lowest rate for a given date based upon anticipated demand. Rates below this rate, called the hurdle rate, are not offered. Often the property management system won't even show the rates below the hurdle rate so that they can't be offered by reservationists. These rates can change from day to day.

Stay controls are used during periods of forecasted excess demand for rooms. The controls help determine which guests will bring in the most money for the property based on how long they plan to stay. These controls do not create business; they filter through excess business to find the ones that will pay the most for the available rooms.

Common stay control tactics are:

1. Minimum length of stay. **A minimum length of stay** tactic requires that a guest must stay for a specific number of nights in order to make the reservation. Resorts commonly use this tactic.

2. Close to arrival. A close-to-arrival tactic allows reservations to be taken for a certain date as long as the guest arrives before that date. For example, if a front office is expecting a 300-room check-in on a given date, the front office manager may decide that more than 300 rooms

checking in may be too much of a strain on the front desk and its related departments. Therefore, guests arriving before that date and staying through the date will be accepted; however, additional arrivals on the peak arrival date will not be accepted.

3. Sell-through. The **sell-through** strategy works like a minimum length requirement except that the required stay can begin before the date the strategy is applied. For example, if a three-night sell-through is applied on Wednesday, the sell-through applies to arrivals on Monday, Tuesday, and Wednesday. Arrivals on each of those days must stay for three nights in order to be acceptable.

Revenue management strategies or tactics are used to help sell the most rooms at the best possible rates. The ultimate goal is to meet guest needs, so revenue management tactics should not be overdone.

Room Forecasting

A room forecast is a prediction or estimate of how many rooms will be available for sale on a given day. When **room forecasting** is done well, everyone's job goes more smoothly and guests are better served. When room forecasting is done poorly, hotel employees have to deal with angry guests who are turned away from promised rooms; the lodging property loses money; and guests get a bad taste of the property.

Room forecasting helps reservationists:

- Sell rooms until the property is 100 percent full

- Sell the highest rates the occupancy levels will allow

Reservationists typically use the following forecast reports:

- **Ten-Day Forecast**—A report that uses the number of arrivals, walk-ins, stay-overs, no-shows, understays, check-outs, and overstays to help determine how many guests are expected at the property in the next 10 days. It is used to prepare weekly employee staff schedules for all departments, and to help figure out ordering needs.

- **Four-Day Forecast**—This report is an updated version of the 10-day forecast, reflecting a more current estimate of room availability. It is used by the front desk for managing arrivals, departures, walk-ins, and same-day reservations. They also use it to plan for alternate rooms in oversold situations. The food and beverage department uses the form for buying perishables, and housekeeping uses it to set up amenities, plan VIP arrivals, and adjust room attendant schedules.

These forecast reports list information about:

- Today's arrivals, today's stayovers, and tomorrow's arrivals

- The number of arrivals, departures, and occupied rooms; the percentage of occupied rooms; and the guest count every day for the next four days

- Confirmed reservations for the 10 days covered by the forecast

- Projected rates based on these reservations

- VIP arrivals for the next 10 days

- Number of complimentary rooms for the next 10 days

- Any other information requested

Forecasts consider the following information:

- Historical information (what happened on the same day of the month last year)

- Market conditions (new properties, properties closing, remodeling, etc.)

- Special promotions planned

- New market groups (new businesses, new sports facilities, etc.)

- Rate strategies

- Special events such as concerts, festivals, sporting events, and conventions

Forecasting the number of rooms for sale is the most important short-term planning task performed by the front office.

The Guest History System

Most lodging properties make use of a **guest history system** to track when and how often guests stay at their properties. Depending on the capabilities of the system, reservationists can access their caller's preferences for room type, location, rate, and any special requests. When used with the reservations system, a guest history system can help reservationists give a personal touch for repeat guests.

Reservationists start out by asking the caller if he or she has stayed at the property before. If so, the caller's name should appear in the guest history system. To verify accuracy, reservationists confirm the callers' address and compare it to the record. From this point, reservationists can personalize the reservation by describing the room the caller reserved for a previous stay and asking if he or she would care for a similar room or perhaps an upgrade.

Apply Your Learning 7.2

Please write all answers on a separate sheet of paper.

1. What must each reservationist have in order to use the reservations computer system?

2. What are the four common revenue management techniques?

3. What is the purpose of room forecasting?

4. What function of the reservations system allows reservationists to provide a more "personal touch?"

7.3 Taking Reservations

AFTER SUCCESSFULLY COMPLETING THIS SECTION, YOU WILL BE ABLE TO:

♦ Describe the various methods of taking guestroom reservations.

♦ Identify the procedures for documenting reservation calls.

♦ Identify effective telephone sales techniques.

♦ Describe how to handle guests' special room requests.

♦ Summarize the steps for mailing information to potential guests.

Taking Reservations

Reservationists make reservation arrangements for guests. Typically, they book reservations using the telephone. However, there are other methods. Reservation requests may arrive in the following forms:

• Reservation cards

• Letters

• Memos

• Faxes

• Telegrams or telexes

• Central reservations office printouts

• Group rooming lists

For group bookings, a **group reservation master**—usually part of the reservation computer system—is used.

Many reservations are booked using a lodging property's Website. Most lodging companies offer online reservation services. This enables travelers from many different market segments to use their personal computers to reserve hotel rooms.

The variety of potential guests accessing Internet sites to place reservations has prompted travel and hospitality companies to develop simple, user-friendly reservation procedures. Large and small hotels alike have a presence on the Internet. Chains often have a Web site focusing first on the brand and its features, then on the individual properties. Most chain Internet sites allow visitors to book reservations. Independent hotels have Web sites that may not be as sophisticated as chain sites, usually due to the cost of operating such sites, but they normally provide similar information and allow visitors to make reservations.

Exhibit 1 provides a step-by-step breakdown for taking reservations using the above methods.

Documenting Reservation Calls

Throughout each day's shift, reservationists document all the phone calls they have received on a **reservation call conversion form** or in a file on the property management system. This form usually has a space to document converted calls and a space for non-converted calls. **Conversion** refers to turning a reservation into a booked room.

For converted calls, reservationists enter the number of room nights converted and the rate at which they were booked. For non-converted calls, reservationists enter one of the following:

- Number of room nights canceled
- Number of room nights denied due to stay controls
- Number of room nights adjusted (date of arrival, number of rooms, etc.)
- Number of room nights not converted for other reasons

Many properties also use a room nights denied report to record all reservations that were denied. Reservationists include the date of the night denied and the reason it was denied. Reasons may include close outs, stay controls, and rate controls. Unless the property knows why business is being turned away, it cannot effectively manage rates and arrival patterns.

Using Effective Sales Techniques

Reservationists employ effective telephone sales techniques to help their properties succeed. This involves listening well, knowing all guestroom features and rates, and matching them to a caller's needs. Successful reservationists know that they don't sell rooms or services—they sell the benefits that guests receive when they choose a certain type of room. In other words, when reservationists hear what callers want, they describe a room's features and tell the callers how they would benefit from these features.

Reservationists never dwell on drawbacks that the property may have. If callers bring up negatives about the property, reservationists counter with at least two benefits.

Reservationists are expected to help promote any ongoing marketing programs. Many lodging properties develop marketing promotions to attract guests from competitors. The success of these promotions depends on the ability of reservationists to accurately explain the features and benefits and to help callers book programs that will best meet their needs.

One of the most important components of effective telephone sales techniques is the practice of upselling. **Upselling** is a way of selling a more expensive guestroom than the one the guest originally requested. When using upselling techniques, reservationists take into account the needs of the caller, the available room types, and rates.

Three upselling techniques are:

- *Top-Down*—The reservationist recommends the room with the highest rate that fits the caller's needs. If the caller does not take the room, the reservationist then describes the room with the next highest rate, and so on until the caller chooses a room. When occupancy is low, it is common for supervisors to tell reservationists to freely negotiate downward to capture as much business as possible.

- *Bottom-Up*—Upon request by the caller, the reservationist describes the lowest priced room, then suggests extra amenities and benefits that the caller could enjoy in a more expensive room.

For example, a reservationist might say, "For only $10 more, you could have a king-sized bed for a better night's rest." This sales technique may upsell callers to a middle rate when they might otherwise choose a lower rate.

- *Choice-of-Alternatives*—The reservationist gives the caller a choice of two or three rooms—two high-priced and one mid-priced. The reservationist describes the benefits of each room, states the differences in each rate, and then asks the caller which room he or she prefers.

In situations where the property is full, reservationists can still sell by offering guests an alternative date or placing callers on a waiting list.

Reservationists can sell many other property facilities, features, services, and events to callers. This includes selling callers on the property's restaurants as well as entertainment and recreation options. Other property features may include:

- Coffee shops, room service, and snack bars

- Lounges or entertainment venues

- Gift shops, barbershops, and beauty shops

- Health clubs, golf courses, and swimming pools

- Laundry and valet services

- Banquet facilities, meeting rooms, and catering services

Reservationists always think about the needs of callers, and do their part to arrange for a pleasant stay with great food and fun.

Handling Special Room Requests

It is common for callers to request a special arrangement or room feature when they make a reservation. Reservationists tell these callers that they will do their best, but that they can't guarantee a specific room. Instead, reservationists tell these callers that what they *can* guarantee is a certain *type* of room, and that if the room is not available on the day of their arrival, a front desk employee will try to put him or her in the same type of room on a different floor, a similar room on the same floor, or an upgraded room.

Once these requests are taken, reservationists note the specific request on the reservation record, block the room, and in the case of requests for accessible rooms, pre-assign the room to the caller to ensure that one will be available.

Special requests may include any of the following:

- Accessible room (equipped for guests with disabilities)

- Room by the pool

- Specific view (mountain, ocean, skyline, etc.)

- Specific bed type, such as a king, queen, double, etc.

- Specific amenities, such as a kitchenette, wet bar, microwave oven, etc.

- Smoking or nonsmoking room

- Specific floor, such as the lowest or highest floor

- Specific room for sentimental reasons ("We spent our honeymoon in that room.").

- Room away from the elevator

- Room with good lighting or desk space, room for a crib, etc.

Mailing Information

When guests are deciding at which lodging property to stay or spend their vacation, they may request information such as brochures or rate sheets be sent to them via regular or electronic mail. When guests make these requests, reservationists gather this information and send it to the guest's address on the same day.

This information may include:

- General brochures about the property

- Brochures about property promotions

- Brochures about property facilities and rooms for guests with disabilities

- Copies of the restaurant menus

- Rate information

- Brochures of local attractions

- Maps with directions to the property

Reservationists can also provide guests with the phone numbers of local area attractions. The phone number of the local tourism association may also be beneficial to guests.

Apply Your Learning 7.3

Please write all answers on a separate sheet of paper.

1. What method for taking reservations has become more common in recent years?

2. What term is used to describe a phone call that was turned into a reservation?

3. List three upselling techniques used by reservationists.

4. List five special room requests that callers may make.

5. When guests request information about the property, when is it be mailed to them?

Exhibit 1
Take Reservations

Materials needed: The reservations computer system, a telephone, a reservation record, and the availability calendar.

STEPS:	HOW-TO'S:
1. Greet callers.	
2. Use effective telephone sales techniques.	
3. Bring up the reservations screen on your computer.	
4. If you're not working on a computer, ask your supervisor or trainer what supplies you need to take reservations.	
5. Check room availability.	❏ Ask callers when they plan to arrive and leave.
	❏ Ask callers if they are part of a group.
	❏ Input the caller's arrival and departure dates into the computer. It will tell you if rooms are available.
	❏ If you must check room availability without using a computer, ask your supervisor or trainer how to do so. Non-automated properties may use a reservations wall chart or control book to track room availability.
6. Ask the caller about his or her guestroom needs.	❏ Find out if the caller has previously stayed at the property.
	❏ Ask what type of room the caller wants.

(continued)

Exhibit 1
Take Reservations *(continued)*

STEPS:	HOW-TO'S:
	❑ Ask if the caller has any special requests.
	❑ Ask if the caller is traveling for business or pleasure.
	❑ Ask how many adults and how many children will stay in the room.
7. Quote room rates.	❑ Use the information on your availability calendar to quote room rates and upsell.
	❑ Be positive about your property.
	❑ Know the rooms and their furnishings. Sell the benefits of each feature your property offers. Create a positive image of the caller enjoying these features. For instance, callers like to know that the room has a desk, a remote control TV, in-room movies, a mini-bar, free coffee service, etc.
	❑ If a caller is not rate-sensitive, book the best room at the highest available rate.
	❑ Follow your property's yield management strategies in quoting rates.
	❑ In high-demand situations, be courteous but firm in stating that you have no rooms available at lower rates, unless:
	• The caller is requesting multiple rooms or multiple nights (generally three or more rooms or nights)
	• The reservation is for a regular guest and you may lose this relationship by being inflexible
	• You have reason to believe that the current forecast will not hold (such as the slow pickup of a group coming in that week or the potential for a weather-related delay that could result in no-shows)

(continued)

Exhibit 1
Take Reservations *(continued)*

STEPS:	HOW-TO'S:
8. Each time you describe a room and quote a rate, ask if the caller would like to reserve that room. This is called "asking for the sale."	
9. Process the reservation record when the caller decides to reserve a room.	
10. Process a printed reservation record for each guest who is part of a group.	
11. For individual guests, check room availability.	❑ Input the guest's arrival and departure dates into the computer. It will tell you if rooms are available.
	❑ If rooms are available, process a reservation record for the guest.
	❑ If the property is full on the requested date, call the guest and try to adjust the arrival date to match available dates. If no phone number is provided, send a written note to tell the person that rooms are not available on the date requested. If the central reservations office booked the reservation, the reservation must be honored.
12. Send printed reservation confirmation forms to guests.	❑ Process reservation confirmation forms for guests who request them. Mail confirmation forms to U.S. addresses if the guests will not arrive within five to seven days. Mail forms to non-U.S. addresses if the guests will not arrive within two weeks.

(continued)

Exhibit 1
Take Reservations *(continued)*

STEPS:	HOW-TO'S:
13. **Bring up a group reservation master on your computer screen.**	❑ If you cannot find a group reservation master for the name the caller gives you, don't turn the caller away. ❑ Get the caller's name, number, group name, dates of stay, and rate quoted. Tell the caller that someone from the property will call back soon. ❑ Call your sales department and explain the situation. ❑ Ask a salesperson to call the guest back.
14. **Confirm the prenegotiated group rate to the caller.**	❑ Read the information on the screen to find the room rate and any special instructions for making reservations. Group rates vary depending on the number of rooms blocked and how many nights the group will be at the property. ❑ If callers question the rate, write down their names, phone numbers, and the rate they think is correct. ❑ Tell the caller you'll look into the situation and that someone from the property will call back soon. ❑ Call the sales department and find out the correct rate. ❑ Ask a salesperson to call the guest back.

7.4 Processing Reservation Information and Reports

AFTER SUCCESSFULLY COMPLETING THIS SECTION, YOU WILL BE ABLE TO:

◆ Describe the procedures for processing reservation records and confirmations.

◆ Explain how to set up group reservation masters.

◆ Summarize the steps for processing prepayments and advance deposits.

◆ Identify the steps for making changes to or canceling reservations.

◆ Explain the importance of processing travel agent no-show and cancellation forms.

◆ List the reports that reservationists are typically required to complete.

Processing Reservation Records and Confirmations

Lodging properties try to keep accurate records of their reservation histories. These histories are kept in **reservation records,** usually on the property management system. The reservation record is where reservationists input reservation information. Reservationists ask guests to repeat themselves or to spell words or names as necessary. Confirming any and all reservation information prevents potential problems.

Reservationists ask for the following information from guests:

• Guest's last name, first name, and middle initial

• Guest's title (if applicable)

• Guest's complete mailing address

• Guest's e-mail address

• Travel agent's IATA number, address, and phone number (if reservation is booked by travel agency)

• Telephone number of person to be contacted about the reservation

• Arrival and departure dates

• Number of people sharing the room (and, if necessary, their names)

• Room type, rate, and any special requests (nonsmoking room, king-sized bed, etc.)

• Rate code

Once reservationists have recorded all the necessary guest information in the reservation record, they inform guests that they can guarantee their reservations by using a credit or debit card. Guaranteed reservations reduce no-shows and guarantee the money if the room is canceled. Reservationists usually try to secure a guarantee. They explain to guests that a guaranteed reservation is also to their benefit. It guarantees that the lodging property will hold the room until checkout time on the day after the arrival date. Conversely, a non-guaranteed reservation will hold the room only until the property's cancellation hour (usually 6 P.M.).

Besides using a credit or debit card, guests can also guarantee a reservation by using an approved direct-billing account that is set up with the lodging property's accounting department before the guest arrives. Also, a guest can mail in an advance deposit of the charges for at least one night's room and tax.

Lastly, reservationists inform guests of the property's check-in and check-out times, repeat the details of the reservation, note the payment method, provide the guest with a confirmation number, enter the date and their initials, and thank the guest for calling and encourage him or her to call again.

Some guests may request an electronic or hard copy confirmation be sent to them. This confirmation confirms the important points of agreement: dates, rates, number of guests, etc. This is documented on a **reservation confirmation form** that can be printed from the reservation computer system and mailed or faxed to the guest. Some confirmation forms are printed ready-to-mail, while others may require envelopes.

Guests who book a reservation on a lodging property's Internet site or who provide an email address may receive an email confirmation. At some properties, these email confirmations are sent automatically and do not have to be requested by the guest.

Group Reservation Masters

Lodging properties that get heavy group business may make use of a **group reservations master.** This group reservation master is a part of the reservation computer system and provides one folio for the entire group. Group reservation masters are set up with the following information:

- Group name and address
- Name and number of group contact
- Market segment code
- Single, double, and suite rates
- Extra person charge
- Cut-off date for when the rooms will no longer be available
- Names of guests who will receive free rooms
- Designated VIPs in the group
- Master billing instructions
- Number of rooms of each type required for each night of the booking

If enough rooms are available, reservationists will then block the agreed-upon number of rooms, one room for each of the group's individual guests. The computer will treat the blocked rooms as out of inventory unless the block is canceled. Once each individual group guest reserves a blocked room, the room becomes booked.

Prepayments and Advance Deposits

When guests make reservations, they may provide an advance deposit or a repayment. The accounting department informs the reservations department of these postings. Reservationists then update the reservation records of these guests who prepay or who send advance deposits to guarantee their reservations.

After the record has been updated, reservationists write the guest's name, deposit date, and reservation confirmation number on an advance deposit list. They then sign and date the list and give the list to the accounting department. This lets the accounting department know that the reservation records have been updated.

In situations where a guest did not send or provide an advance deposit in the allotted time to guarantee a reservation, reservationists change the guaranteed reservation to a non-guaranteed reservation.

Reservation Changes

Guests with reservations may need to make changes or adjustments. At times, they may even have to cancel their reservation entirely. Guests do a property a service when they call in advance to cancel. This allows the reservationist to free up a previously reserved room and make it available for sale to another guest. If handled well, a guest who cancels will probably call the property again when he or she needs a room.

Today's reservation systems make it very easy for reservationists to make these changes to the reservation record.

Exhibit 1 shows the step-by-step procedures for processing reservation changes and cancellations.

Travel Agent No-Show and Cancellation Forms

When reservations are booked through a travel agency, any cancellations must be processed differently than cancellations from other sources. Reservationists check the canceled reservation file and determine which cancelled reservations were booked through a travel agency. Travel agents are not credited for cancellations or no-shows. Therefore, reservationists promptly notify travel agents of cancellations and no-shows to prevent complaints.

Reservationists fill out a **travel agent no-show/cancellation form**, which includes:

- Guest name

- Original arrival date

- Departure date

- Confirmation number

- Name of property

- Property's telephone number

- Name of reservationist

No-show forms are also used if the rate or number of nights differs from the original reservation. If the guest was a no-show, reservationists check the box on the form marked "Your client was a no-show." If the guest canceled the reservation, they check the box on the form marked "Your client canceled the reservation."

Once the form is completed, it is mailed to the travel agent. Reservationists keep a copy of the form for the property's records.

Completing and Running All Required Reports

At some lodging properties, the reservations department may prepare reports for use by the front office, housekeeping, and other departments. These reports include:

- Expected arrivals lists

- Expected departures lists

- Reservation confirmation forms

- Group rooming lists

- VIP reports

- Special requests reports

- Room availability reports

These reports are usually printed out at the end of each day. However, these reports may be requested or may need to be printed at any time of the day.

When printing out the **expected arrivals list**, reservationists carefully check it for errors. An error in the arrivals list can result in losing the sale of one or more rooms. Errors that are checked for include:

- Duplicate or multiple reservations for one person under the same or similarly spelled names

- Misspellings (keying errors)

- Strange reservations (names or details that look like the reservation might be fake)

- Inadequate guarantee information

The arrivals list for the next day is also compared with the list for the current day to check for:

- Duplicate reservations for the same person with different dates of arrival.

- Guest on today's list that also appears on tomorrow's list. If the guest isn't registered, it may indicate that the arrival date is an error.

Apply Your Learning 7.4

Please write all answers on a separate sheet of paper.

1. List five items of information that must be included on each guest's reservation record.

2. In what manner are group reservation record files typically arranged?

3. Why is it important to handle a cancellation with the same degree of guest service as a reservation?

4. Why is it important for reservationists to promptly notify travel agents of cancellations or no-shows?

5. List five reports that reservationists are typically required to prepare or complete.

Exhibit 1
Process Reservation Changes and Cancellations

Materials needed: The reservations computer system, a pen, reservation records, reservation files, and the cancellation number log.

STEPS:	HOW-TO'S:
1. Find out the name of the person the reservation is for, the original arrival date, and the original departure date or confirmation number.	
2. Bring up the reservation record on your computer or get the record from the file.	
3. Ask for and record the name of the caller, if the caller is not the guest.	❑ When reservations are guaranteed by a corporation or travel agency, the caller is probably not the guest, but an employee of the corporation or agency.
4. Ask what the caller would like to change.	❑ If a caller changes the arrival or departure date to a date that is sold out, save as much of the reservation as possible. You may need to reserve a room at another lodging property for the nights you can't accommodate the guest.
5. Make the change.	
6. Read the changes back to the caller to make sure everything is correct.	
7. Give the caller a new confirmation number based on the changed reservation, if necessary.	❑ At some lodging properties, the confirmation number stays the same.

(continued)

Exhibit 1
Process Reservation Changes and Cancellations *(continued)*

STEPS:	HOW-TO'S:
8. **Update the reservation record.**	❑ Enter or write the date you made the change and the new confirmation number, if there is one. The reservations computer may perform this step automatically.
	❑ Write or type your initials next to the change.
	❑ Return the reservation record to the file if necessary, and file it alphabetically by arrival date.
9. **Cancel reservations.**	❑ Assign a cancellation number to the reservation and tell the caller the number.
	❑ If the reservation was guaranteed, encourage the caller to keep the cancellation number as proof of cancellation. Most credit card companies will only pay no-show billings if the property issues cancellation numbers for reservations that are canceled correctly. This means that credit card companies aren't likely to incorrectly bill people who cancel their reservations.
	❑ Ask if the caller would like to make a reservation for another date.
	❑ Mark the reservation record as canceled. Initial and date it. Add the cancellation number to the reservation record.
	❑ Write or type the cancellation number on the cancellation number log.
10. **Thank the person for calling and invite him or her to call your property again.**	

(continued)

Exhibit 1
Process Reservation Changes and Cancellations *(continued)*

STEPS:	HOW-TO'S:
11. **File the reservation record.**	❑ File the canceled reservation record by the arrival date given when the person made the reservation.
	❑ Put the record at the back of the file.
12. **Send printed reservation confirmation forms to guests.**	❑ Process reservation confirmation forms for guests who request them. Mail confirmation forms to U.S. addresses if the guests will not arrive within five to seven days. Mail forms to non-U.S. addresses if the guests will not arrive within two weeks.

Quick Hits

Chapter 7

SECTION 7.1—GETTING TO KNOW THE RESERVATIONIST

- Reservationists are a lodging property's goodwill ambassadors. They often provide the guest's first contact with the property.

- Scripts are powerful tools that help reservationists ask for the sale.

- Lodging properties have policies about how guests reserve and pay for rooms. Reservationists are responsible for explaining these policies.

- Groups are very important to lodging properties. Because of the revenue that groups bring in, they are provided a high level of service and attention.

- Travel agents provide steady business to lodging properties, usually at high rates. Reservationists help travel agents get their commissions quickly, increasing the likelihood of future business.

- Reservationists' duties include taking reservations, blocking rooms, preparing or completing reports, documenting reservation records, and processing payments, changes to, or cancellations of reservations.

SECTION 7.2—GETTING TO KNOW THE RESERVATION PROCESS

- The reservations computer system is a powerful tool enabling reservationists to perform their duties quickly and efficiently. It is often linked to the front desk computer system.

- Revenue management is the process of balancing occupancy and prices to maximize room revenue—or get as much from guestroom sales as possible.

- Room forecasting involves predicting or estimating how many rooms will be available for sale on a given day.

- The guest history system is a component of the reservation system that allows reservationists to provide repeat guests with a more personal touch.

SECTION 7.3—TAKING RESERVATIONS

- Rerservationists can book reservations for guests through any of the following methods: telephone, printed forms, or a group reservation master. In addition, many lodging properties now offer their guests the option of booking a reservation through the Internet.

- Reservationists document all calls they receive each day on a reservation call conversion form.

- Reservationists can provide guests with a better stay and the property with additional revenue by using upselling techniques when booking reservations.

- Reservationists may be asked to make special room arrangements for guests or to mail information about the property.

SECTION 7.4—PROCESSING RESERVATION INFORMATION AND REPORTS

- Reservationists keep accurate records of the property's reservation history.

- Reservationists use group reservation masters to properly document and file group reservation information.

- Reservationists are responsible for processing data for the advance deposits and prepayments guests place when guaranteeing a room.

- When changes or cancellations are made to a guest's reservation, reservationists promptly make these changes so that rooms become available to sell to other guests.

- When reservations made through a travel agent are cancelled, reservationists promptly inform the travel agents and fill out a travel agent no-show/cancellation form.

- Reservationists prepare and complete a number of forms throughout their shifts, including expected arrivals lists, group rooming lists, and room availability reports.

PBX Operator

Sections

The telecommunications switchboard area or department maintains a complex communications network similar to that of any large company. The telecommunications department may also be called a private branch exchange or PBX. Hotel switchboard or PBX operators may have responsibilities that extend beyond answering and distributing calls to the appropriate extension.

PBX operators may also place wake-up calls, answer questions about the hotel, monitor automated systems (such as door alarms and fire alarms), and coordinate emergency communications. Operators also protect guests' privacy, thereby contributing to the hotel's security program by not divulging guestroom numbers.

Some hotels now instruct guests to call the hotel operator or a special guest service department for all service requests, including housekeeping, room service, and even bell service. Another trend involving guest safety with telephone systems is to have all house phones (telephones in public areas of the hotel used for calling within the hotel) ring the operator for call processing. This reduces the risk of unwanted or mistaken guestroom telephone calls. Many hotels also provide guest paging services over a public address system.

Recent technology has considerably decreased the responsibilities and workloads of PBX operators. Hotels have installed technology that allows guests to place their own room-to-room or outgoing phone calls. Most guestroom phones offer touchtone convenience and may feature call waiting or caller ID. Also available is guest voice mail, reducing the reliance on hotel operators to record messages for guests and turn on message waiting lights in guestrooms.

8.1 Getting to Know the PBX Operator

AFTER SUCCESSFULLY COMPLETING THIS SECTION, YOU WILL BE ABLE TO:

◆ Explain the role the PBX operator plays in the lodging operation.

◆ Identify the qualities that make up an excellent PBX operator.

The primary job of a PBX operator is operating the property's telephone switchboard. In this capacity, the PBX operator is the primary source of information for property guests and employees.

Exhibit 1 lists the most common tasks that the PBX operator is expected to be able to perform and perform well.

There are several characteristics common to successful PBX operators:

Friendliness. When talking on the telephone, the PBX operator relates information to the caller and attitude. A cheerful voice will make all callers feel welcome.

Confidence. A PBX operator is familiar with the property and ready to answer any questions about its services and amenities. This enables operators to speak with confidence.

Thoughtfulness. Operators must remember that they may be talking with people of different backgrounds and education levels. They speak with callers on their level and are always polite, never talking down to anyone.

Clarity. It is embarrassing if a listener must ask for a statement to be repeated. A PBX operator pronounces words carefully, and speaka at a normal rate — not too fast and not too slow.

Creativity. PBX operators creatively solve problems whenever possible by using their skills and knowledge to offer ideas others may not have thought of.

Enthusiasm. PBX operators should be sold on the property. If not, how can a guest be sold on it? They must project the positive things about a property.

Integrity. PBX operators are honest if they do not know the answer to a caller's question. They admit it, and offer to find the answer. They don't mislead callers.

Tact. It is better to say nothing than to say something that's inappropriate.

Pride. PBX operators take pride in the property and in their work. This pride is reflected in their voice. This pride instills interest and confidence in the caller.

Working as a Team

PBX operators can be excellent team players by:

Exhibit 1
Task List—PBX Operator

1. Use the Front Office Computer System

2. Use the Front Office Printers

3. Use the Switchboard

4. Use the Facsimile Machine

5. Use the Photocopy Machine

6. Restrict Guest Telephones

7. Maintain and Use the Guest Information Directory

8. Respond to Questions About Services and Events

9. Give Directions

10. Help Guests Make International Telephone Calls

11. Process Guest Telephone Charges

12. Process Wake-Up Calls

13. Follow Guest Privacy and Security Measures

14. Use Pagers, Two-Way Radios, and Public Address Systems

15. Issue and Control Property Master Keys

16. Process Guest Mail, Packages, Telegrams, Faxes, and Messages

17. Read and Make Entries in the Front Office Logbook

18. Complete the PBX Shift Checklist

19. Complete or Run All Required Reports and Forms

20. Keep the PBX Area Organized and Clean

21. Respond to Fire Alarms or Smoke Alarms

22. Respond to Non-Fire Emergencies

23. Respond to Bomb Threats

24. Respond to Weather Emergencies

25. Help Evacuate the Property

26. Respond to Threatening, Obscene, or Prank Telephone Calls

27. Respond to Dissatisfied Guests

• Helping front desk employees make wake-up calls.

• Telling engineers about needed repairs.

• Learning the location and hours of operation of restaurants, lounges, health clubs, and other areas of the property to help guests enjoy everything available.

• Processing all business calls in an efficient, courteous manner.

Apply Your Learning 8.1

Please write all answers on a separate sheet of paper.

1. What is the primary job of the PBX operator?

2. List the nine qualities that make up an excellent PBX operator.

3. Why is it important for pride to be reflected in the PBX operators' voices?

8.2 Performing PBX Operator Functions

AFTER SUCCESSFULLY COMPLETING THIS SECTION, YOU WILL BE ABLE TO:

♦ Explain how to use the front office computer and switchboard system.

♦ Describe the information available in the PBX information directory.

♦ Explain how to restrict guest phones and process wake-up calls.

♦ Identify guest privacy and security measures.

♦ Describe the use of pagers, two-way radios, and public address systems.

♦ Define ways to keep the PBX area organized and clean.

Use The Front Office Computer System

The front office computer system is a tool to help PBX operators serve guests better. Even if someone has never worked with a computer, with a little training they can become skilled at using it.

Often, the front office computer will be linked to the telephone system and the in-room movie system.

The PBX operator often has a list of abbreviations and code words the computer uses. This acts as a cheat sheet during training until it is memorized. Memorizing the list will increase speed, skill, and confidence. The PBX operator has a personal access code for using the PBX and computer system.

Use the Switchboard

Different lodging properties use different telephone systems. Some may have only one incoming line or several. It may be capable of only basic functions, or be as complex as an advanced switchboard.

In general, the front office telephone system consists of the main switchboard and the multi-line telephones at the front desk, in reservations, at the bell stand, and throughout the front office area.

Exhibit 1 shows a step-by-step breakdown for using the telephone switchboard.

Use the PBX Information Directory

It would be nearly impossible to memorize all of the telephone numbers and information a

PBX operator is asked about every day. That's why an information directory is kept in many PBX workstations to provide the following information:

- Emergency phone numbers

- Fire, bomb-threat, and weather-emergency procedures

- Power failure and switch failure procedures

- Medical emergency procedures

- Paging system number assignments and paging instructions

- Directions to the property from major airports and highways

- Department manager home phone numbers

- Facility hours

- Three listings of department phone extensions: (1) in order of number, (2) in alphabetical order by department, and (3) in alphabetical order by employee name

- Telephone problem and procedures manual

- Daily and weekly schedule of all property functions

- Airport transportation schedules

- Daily VIP list

Very often the information directory will be on the computer with a back-up copy on paper at the PBX station.

Restrict Guest Telephones

At times it may be necessary to restrict the telephone service of cash-only guests, minors, or high school or college groups. In these cases, the front desk usually provides a list of restricted guests. By checking the list of restricted guests, the PBX operator can then restrict those guests' phones via the switchboard or computer, depending on the phone system in place. It may be necessary to politely inform these guests that to place their call they will need to use a public pay phone, a calling card, or a credit card.

Typically, phone restrictions include the following:

- Area code—callers can be barred from making calls in a specific area code

- Fully restricted—the phone can make only internal calls

- Hotline to console—phones will immediately connect to the switchboard when the handset is picked up

- Six-digit toll restrictions—this allows calls only to specific exchanges within an area code

Process Wake-Up Calls

Wake-up calls are an extremely important guest service. If a guest does not receive a wake-up call and oversleeps, a formal complaint is sure to follow. Many guests will call PBX operators from their room to request a wake-up call for the following morning. When receiving these calls, they record the following information:

- The day and date the call will be made

- The guest's name and room number

- The exact time of the wake-up call

This information is usually recorded on a **guest call sheet.** PBX operators repeat the information to the guest to check for accuracy.

Most properties now have automated wake-up call systems as a component of the front desk telephone system and switchboard. At these properties, the information for a guest's wake-up call is put into the system. The system makes all the wake-up calls to the guests' rooms, except in VIP situations a personal call is still made.

At properties without an automated system, the PBX operator makes the wake-up calls manually. They dial the guestroom and allow the phone to ring several times—some guests are deep sleepers and may need time to wake up and answer the phone. Once the guest answers, PBX operators say something such as, "Good morning, Mr. Smith, it's 7:30. Enjoy your day," or "Good morning, Mrs. Carlos, this is your 7:30 wake-up call." The guest always hangs up first. If a guest requests a second call later in the day, PBX operators record the time of the new call and make the call again later.

Manual wake-up calls are tracked as they are made. This is done by highlighting or drawing a line through the guest's name and room number on the guest call sheet. The PBX operator signs his or her initials next to each guest's name after the guest has been called.

If a manual wake-up call is made but not answered by the guest, PBX operators typically wait 10 minutes and try the guest's room again. The guest may have already awakened on his or her own and may be in the shower or otherwise getting ready. If a second call still produces no answer, they send an appropriate employee to the guest's room to check the status of the guest.

It is a good idea to keep track of guests' responses to their wake-up calls. This can be recorded on the guest call sheet. By keeping accurate records, the PBX operator can properly respond to any potential problems or complaints.

Follow Guest Privacy and Security Measures

When a guest stays at a lodging property, they are paying for a warm bed, a comfortable room, and a measure of security and privacy. A PBX operator has a responsibility for helping ensure that property guests enjoy this privacy and security.

There are several ways that PBX operators help protect the guest. They include:

- *Protecting room numbers.* Guest's room numbers are given only to registered guests or other staff members. PBX operators should not give out room numbers even to spouses or business associates unless the guest has given permission. Instead, they should connect callers or visitors to the guest's room.

- *Protecting guest information.* Some of the information that PBX operators keep confidential include how many people are registered to a room, whether a guest was registered during specific dates, guests' home address, and guests' telephone numbers or other personal information.

- *Reporting suspicious people.* A suspicious person is anyone—an employee, visitor, or guest—who makes a guest or employee feel something might be wrong. PBX operators report when they see suspicious people and respond to guest reports.

Use Pagers, Two-Way Radios, and Public Address Systems

PBX operators have a number of communication devices at their disposal. These devices allow PBX operators to act as the hub of communication and information for the entire property. These devices include:

- *Pagers or beepers*—Small electronic devices that are assigned a telephone number and beep or buzz when they are called. Some pagers are exclusively for receiving phone numbers, while others can receive voice messages.

- *Two-way radios*—Sometimes called walkie-talkies, these radios must be kept in good condition because they are often needed in emergency situations. They are called two-way because the open channel can receive and send messages; however, the transmit button must be released in order to hear the other party's response. It is important to always be professional when communicating with these devices. You never know who may hear a transmission when talking on a portable unit or the base station.

- *Public address system*—The PA system is usually used only in the case of an emergency, such as an evacuation. However, some properties may use them for locating guests or making general announcements.

Exhibit 2 shows a step-by-step breakdown for using these devices to communicate and send information throughout the property.

Keep the PBX Area Organized and Clean

Keeping the PBX station clean and orderly is not only professional, it also enables PBX operators to more effectively do their jobs and provide service to guests. There are several ways that PBX operators can easily and efficiently keep the area clean:

- File paperwork from a completed activity before beginning a new one. This will help prevent confusion from mixed-up papers. Knowing where to file copies of posting slips, telephone vouchers, occupancy reports, guest mail or messages, and registration cards is a necessity.

- Maintain a stock of necessary supplies, arranged neatly. Usually, backup supplies are maintained on a par stock basis. Daily supplies should be drawn from these par stocks. Arrange the contents of the work area so that everything has a place and can be located and accessed quickly and easily. Have a set place at the desk for everything needed to perform the job.

- Keep the PBX station clean and orderly by cleaning while working. Throw out or recycle useless papers, dust the equipment and desktop frequently, and pick up any trash in the work area. If trash cans fill up, empty them. If the desk is unusually messy, with a lot of trash or special cleaning needs, contact the housekeeping department and ask that a public space cleaner be sent to clean the area.

Apply Your Learning 8.2

Please write all answers on a separate sheet of paper.

1. Where can the PBX operator find the code words that the front office computer system uses?

2. List four items of information usually found in the PBX information directory.

3. When placing wake-up calls, why is it important to allow multiple rings?

4. List two uses of a property's public address system.

5. When is the best time to clean the PBX station?

Exhibit 1
Use the Switchboard

Materials needed: Telephone console (switchboard), telephones, operating manuals, a message pad, a pen, and rack slips.

STEPS:	HOW-TO'S:
1. **Answer calls from outside the property.**	❑ Answer calls within three rings.
	❑ Greet the caller with your property's standard greeting.
2. **Answer in-house lines.**	
3. **Place the caller on hold only when necesssary.**	❑ Ask for the caller's permission to place them on hold.
	❑ Do not place callers on hold before listening to their requests. It is faster to listen to requests and process them than to ask callers to hold and return to the line later.
	❑ Return to callers as soon as possible and apologize for the delay.
4. **Route calls to guestrooms.**	❑ If you are using a manual system, search the alphabetical rack slips for the guest's name to find the room number.
	❑ If you are using an automated system, type in the first few letters of the guest's last name. A caller might misspell a name. If you only type in the first few letters of a name, it will save you time and repeated efforts.
	❑ Do not give out guestroom numbers to callers under any circumstances.
	❑ Always acknowledge a request before transferring, saying, "Certainly. One moment please."
	❑ Enter the room number, and press the correct button to connect.

(continued)

Exhibit 1	
Use the Switchboard *(continued)*	
STEPS:	**HOW-TO'S:**
	❑ If the guestroom line is busy, say, "I'm sorry, but that line is busy. Would you like to leave your name and number so that I may ask (name of guest) to return your call? Or would you like to hold?"
	❑ If the caller decides to hold, return to the caller every 30 to 40 seconds and make sure he or she wishes to continue holding.
5. **Route calls to in-house extensions.**	❑ Never ask for the caller's name before saying whether the person requested is available.
	❑ Explain to the caller that you will transfer his or her call, and then do so.
	❑ Pick a route if your switchboard is automated. Try to learn the extensions for all the departments in the property. It will help you provide efficient, faster service.
	❑ If your system has a **Call Accounting System (CAS)**, it will automatically pick the **Least Cost Route** (LCR).
6. **Take messages.**	❑ All messages are confidential, and you should never discuss them with co-workers or anyone else. Write the following information on a message pad:
	• Name of the person who will receive the message
	• Date and time of the call
	• Name of the caller
	• Name of the caller's business or organization
	• Caller's telephone number
	• The message the caller wants to leave

(continued)

Exhibit 1
Use the Switchboard *(continued)*

STEPS:	HOW-TO'S:
	❑ Repeat the message to make sure you have the correct information—especially the correct name and phone number.
7. **Alert guests to messages.**	
8. **Make outgoing calls.**	
9. **Perform special telephone functions. These may include:**	
• **Changing voice-mail-recorded messages.**	
• **Responding to call waiting.**	
• **Breaking on calls.**	
• **Using call-back queuing.**	
• **Using call forwarding.**	
• **Setting up code numbers for speed calling.**	
• **Placing guestroom phones and meeting room phones out of service and into service.**	
• **Placing DND on guest phones. DND stands for "Do Not Disturb."**	

Exhibit 2
Use Pagers, Two-Way Radios, and Public Address Systems

Materials needed: A pen, pagers, two-way radios, and the public address system.

STEPS:	HOW-TO'S:
1. **Use pagers to contact guests and employees.**	❏ Call the pager number and follow the instructions you receive when you reach the pager. ❏ If the pager doesn't give you instructions, you probably need to dial a phone number where you can be reached. Enter the number followed by the # sign.
2. **Communicate using the base station or portable unit of a two-way radio.**	❏ If you are responsible for maintaining the radios, make sure the rechargeable batteries are kept fully charged. ❏ Hold down the "transmit/send" button when speaking. Release the button when receiving a response. ❏ For the best reception, adjust the "squelch" button until it squeals, and then reduce it just enough to stop the squealing. ❏ Turn the "volume" switch to the desired level. ❏ Speak clearly. Do not yell into your radio. Adjust it for clear reception, or instruct the other party to move into an open area.
3. **Send emergency information by two-way radio.**	❏ Know the emergency codes for radio transmissions. ❏ Use these codes to communicate emergency information by radio. ❏ Do not use a walkie talkie during a bomb threat —it could cause the bomb to go off.

(continued)

Exhibit 2
Use Pagers, Two-Way Radios, and Public Address Systems *(continued)*

STEPS:	HOW-TO'S:
4. **Communicate using a public address system.**	❑ Find out if announcements can be made in selected areas of the property or if the system covers all public spaces at once.
	❑ If possible, avoid interrupting guests by limiting the areas reached by the announcement.
	❑ Organize your announcements before making them.
	❑ Ask your supervisor to show you how to work the public address system.
	❑ Speak clearly using good grammar and diction. Pronounce names correctly. If you are unsure of any pronunciations, ask someone for the correct pronunciations.
	❑ Give each announcement once. Wait three to five minutes and repeat the announcement, if necessary.
	❑ If you are asked to page an individual and there is no response, inform the person who made the request.

8.3 Providing Guest Service as a PBX Operator

AFTER SUCCESSFULLY COMPLETING THIS SECTION, YOU WILL BE ABLE TO:

◆ Explain how to use the guest information directory.

◆ Describe how to process guest mail, packages, telegrams, faxes, and messages.

◆ Explain how to answer guests' questions about the property, services, and events.

◆ Identify the procedures for giving good directions.

◆ Describe the procedures for placing international calls for guests.

◆ Summarize the procedures for responding to dissatisfied guests.

Using Guestroom Equipment and Amenities

PBX operators can help guests learn to use the equipment in their rooms. They should be familiar with each type of guestroom and its special equipment and amenities.

Some of the guestroom equipment PBX operators should be familiar with includes:

• Wireless Internet service, radio, free television channels, and pay movie channels

• Heating, ventilation, and air conditioning system

• In-room mini-bars

• In-room hot tubs

• In-room safes

Maintain and Use the Guest Information Directory

As an additional service to guests, many properties provide a directory, usually located at the front desk, which details many of the local restaurants, attractions, and recreation options. To give guests excellent service, PBX operators must be very familiar with the directory and study it until they can quickly find all the information it provides.

The **guest information directory** is usually a set of file folders or a three-ring binder with tabs. Part of the information may be stored on a computer. PBX operators know how the information is organized so that they can use it to turn quickly to needed information.

The directory should include information about:

- Special events
- Art and cultural attractions
- Theaters and cinemas
- Night clubs and entertainment
- Shopping centers
- Restaurants
- Lounges and taverns
- Recreation and hobby activities (bowling centers, gyms, etc.)
- Transportation
- Medical services
- Personal services (babysitters, hair salons, etc.)
- Business services (typists, equipment rental firms, etc.)
- Churches, synagogues, and mosques
- Maps of the area

When collecting brochures, maps, and other information about local events, services, and attractions, PBX operators try to make sure that the following information is included for each establishment:

- Name and location
- Directions from the property
- Telephone number
- Hours of operation
- Type of establishment
- Whether reservations are needed
- Whether there is a dress code
- Name of owner and/or manager

- Approximate cost of taxi fare to reach the site
- Entry fee or cost of the attraction
- Public transportation available to the site

Process Guest Mail, Packages, Telegrams, Faxes, and Messages

While staying at a lodging property, some guests receive correspondence in a number of forms such as mail, packages, faxes, telegrams, or other messages. It is important that guests receive this correspondence quickly and accurately. For packages, many properties will use a date and time stamp to answer questions about how promptly these items are delivered.

Certain packages or messages may be of an urgent nature and may be marked to indicate this. All packages marked as "priority" or sent overnight delivery or by priority mail should be treated as urgent. If an overnight delivery is delayed, it could cost the property a repeat guest.

Exhibit 1 shows a step-by-step breakdown for processing guest mail, packages, telegrams, faxes, and other messages.

Respond to Questions

Imagine that you've been invited to the White House to see the president. You call ahead and ask what door you should use to enter the building and where you should wait to be greeted. The operator pauses and says, "I don't know. Let me check."

You'd be surprised if someone working at the White House didn't know where guests should enter the building. Likewise, guests at your property expect PBX operators to be able to tell them where they need to go.

PBX operators are a guide to guests visiting the property for the first time. They tell guests where to find exercise rooms, meeting rooms, pools, ice machines, banquet rooms, and property restaurants.

Along with providing information about the property and places in the local area, some guests may request suggestions for where to go or what to do. PBX operators first listen carefully to guests to find out what they want to know. They ask questions to clarify, if necessary, and always give help with a clear and helpful tone of voice. When possible, they suggest the property's restaurants, lounges, services, and other facilities first. It may be necessary for PBX operators to get help from a co-worker if they are unable to make a suggestion. However, they do not leave the guests waiting for long. If it is necessary to call the guest back with the information, they do so quickly.

Guests may also ask for information about function times and locations of meetings or events both on and off property. Many properties provide daily and weekly function sheets that list groups that are meeting on property, as well as their meeting times and locations. This function sheet should always have the most current information. If the information requested by the guest is not on the function sheet, PBX operators call the department in charge of the function and find out the information.

In situations where a guest requests a service that another department provides, the PBX operator should coordinate with that department to make sure the guest's need is met. A guest should not have to call the department themselves.

Give Directions

It is almost a guarantee that at least once a day, a guest will call the PBX operator and request driving directions to a location in the area. It is therefore important that PBX operators not only be familiar with how to get around the local area, but also be skilled at providing good directions. When guests need more thorough directions or need a map for where they are going, the PBX operator can coordinate with the front desk to have a map drawn for the guest.

Exhibit 2 provides a step-by-step breakdown of how to provide directions.

Help Guests Make International Telephone Calls

International guests often need some assistance in placing a telephone call back home. PBX operators can help these guests by placing the call for them. The guests may provide the operator the country code or phone number, but most local telephone directories include country and city codes of major cities in the customer information section. Some properties also have charts at the workstations listing all the international codes. If all else fails, the local operator can be called for this information as well as for instructions for placing the call.

PBX operators need the following information:

- **International access code** (usually 011)
- **Country code** (such as 33 for France)
- City code (such as 1 for Paris)
- Local number

PBX operators are very careful when dialing the numbers. There is often a slow response time, in some countries as long as 45 seconds. If the guest should reach the wrong number or be disconnected, they call the local operator to request credit for the call.

Respond to Dissatisfied Guests

Because of the frequency with which PBX operators speak with guests, the operator is more likely to interact with a dissatisfied guest than other positions on the property. When responding to a dissatisfied guest, PBX operators listen intently to the details of the complaint. They allow the guest time to explain how he or she feels and what he or she wants. While listening, PBX operators stay calm and do not react angrily or argue with the guest.

Once the guest finishes, PBX operators apologize to the guest and acknowledge the guest's feelings, regardless of who's at fault. PBX operators never argue, criticize, ignore, or challenge a guest's complaint. They make sure that they properly understand the guest's complaint. The guest does the property a favor by complaining—it allows the property the chance to fix the problem. A guest with a problem who doesn't complain to a property employee is probably complaining to other potential guests!

PBX operators take appropriate action by thanking the guest for bringing the problem to their attention and informing the guest that the problem will be resolved immediately. They then either take care of the problem themselves or coordinate with the appropriate department or manager to handle the problem.

Finally, PBX operators follow up with the guest to determine that the matter was resolved to the guest's satisfaction.

Apply Your Learning 8.3

Please write all answers on a separate sheet of paper.

1. List four guestroom items that a PBX operator should be able to show a guest how to use.

2. Where should a PBX operator look for information about a group meeting happening on property?

3. List the four items of information a PBX operator should have when placing an international call.

4. What is the first thing a PBX operator should do when receiving a call from a dissatisfied guest? What is the second thing?

Exhibit 1
Process Guest Mail, Packages, Telegrams, Faxes, and Messages

Materials needed: A pen, a date/time stamp, envelopes, reservation records, registration cards, the incoming mail logbook, a scale, receipts, a miscellaneous charge voucher, and the switchboard.

STEPS:	HOW-TO'S:
1. **Log in all guest mail, packages, telegrams, faxes and messages when they arrive.**	❑ Open the incoming mail logbook to the correct date. ❑ Write down what arrived (mail, telegram, package, fax, or message) and the name of the guest it arrived for. ❑ Stamp the item with the date and time of arrival. ❑ Place faxes, telegrams, and messages in an envelope for privacy. ❑ If the delivery is a Western Union telegram, write the Western Union telephone number on the envelope.
2. **Determine if a guest has checked in.**	❑ Write the guest's arrival date on the outside of each delivery. ❑ Store the delivery in a secure place.
3. **Process deliveries for arriving guests.**	❑ Write down in the incoming mail logbook the guest's arrival date and where the delivery is stored. ❑ Make a note about the delivery on the guest's reservation record or on the registration card in the preregistration envelope.
4. **Process deliveries for registered guests.**	❑ Write the guest's room number on the outside of each delivery. ❑ If your property uses voice mail, turn on the guest's message light and enter a voice-mail message. ❑ Keep the delivery in a secure place until the guest picks it up.

(continued)

Exhibit 1
Process Guest Mail, Packages, Telegrams, Faxes, and Messages *(continued)*

STEPS:	HOW-TO'S:
5. Route calls to in-house extensions.	
6. Deliver urgent mail, packages, telegrams, faxes, and messages.	❏ Ask a bell attendant or another appropriate employee to deliver the item to the guest right away.
	❏ If the guest cannot be reached in the guestroom, check whether he or she is part of a function (meeting, reception, etc.). If so, have the item delivered to the correct function room right away.
	❏ If the guest cannot be found, store the urgent delivery in a secure place. Turn on the guest's message light and leave a voice-mail message, if possible.
7. Help guests mail items.	❏ Make sure guests have proper postage on their mail and packages. If necessary, tell guests where they can buy stamps.
	❏ If your property mails items for guests, deliver mail and packages to the mailbox as soon as possible.
	❏ If your property does not mail items for guests, direct guests to a nearby mailbox.
8. Help guests use other delivery services.	❏ Know which package services pick up at the property.
	❏ Know the pickup deadline for guaranteed overnight delivery.
	❏ Handle packages with extreme care. Process them for pickup as quickly as possible.
	❏ Weigh packages and write the required information in the correct logbook.

(continued)

Exhibit 1
Process Guest Mail, Packages, Telegrams, Faxes, and Messages *(continued)*

STEPS:	HOW-TO'S:
	❑ Post the correct charges to the guest account.
	❑ Give guests receipts for each package. Receipts should include a trace number in case the package is lost.
	❑ Prepare a miscellaneous charge voucher as a backup document when charges are passed along to guests. Each package service has a special logbook.
	❑ When a delivery service arrives, check the logbook to see which packages should be sent. When guests use their own account number for the carrier charges, the property may charge only for arranging pickup. A package may have been dropped off before you began your shift. Make sure all packages are turned over to the driver.
	❑ The driver will note in the logbook which packages were picked up, making it easy to figure out which packages are still at the property.
9. **Help guests send telegrams.**	❑ Give the guest the telephone number for the Western Union office in your area.
	❑ If a guest needs more help, call Western Union for the guest.
10. **Help guests send faxes.**	

Exhibit 2
Give Directions

Materials needed: A local map, a highlighter pen, a pen, paper, and a photocopy machine.

STEPS:	HOW-TO'S:
1. **Get a clear local map.**	❑ Ask your supervisor if the property has a local map that shows side streets. ❑ If not, ask if you may call your local chamber of commerce, visitor's bureau, or a taxi company and have one sent to the property.
2. **Mark with a highlighter pen the best routes to the property from the airport, train station, and major highways into the city.**	
3. **Use the map to give clear directions to the property.**	❑ Ask for the caller's exact location or where the caller will be arriving from. ❑ Find the caller's location on your city map. ❑ Ask if the caller has a pen and paper for writing the directions. If not, allow time for the caller to get a pen and paper. ❑ Use "right," "left," and "straight," instead of "north, "south," "east," and "west" to direct guests. ❑ Give street names, but also include landmarks such as important buildings and physical features. ❑ Explain the simplest route—not necessarily the shortest one. ❑ Estimate how long it will take for the caller to arrive.

(continued)

Exhibit 2
Give Directions *(continued)*

STEPS:	HOW-TO'S:
4. **Explain how to enter the front drive of the property if it is not obvious.**	❑ If a building near your property is more noticable than the property, use the building as a reference point.
	❑ Tell the caller where to park to unload and check in, and where to park for longer periods of time.
5. **Be patient and ask the caller to repeat your directions.**	
6. **Give directions from the property to other places.**	❑ Know where on your map to find major attractions.
	❑ Write directions down, or photocopy a section of the city map and mark the best route with a highlighter pen.
	❑ Leave the directions at the front desk for the guest to pick up.

8.4 Responding to Emergencies and Alarms

AFTER SUCCESSFULLY COMPLETING THIS SECTION, YOU WILL BE ABLE TO:

♦ Describe how to respond to alarms, emergencies, and threats.

♦ Explain the procedures for alerting the property to weather emergencies.

♦ Summarize the procedures for evacuating the properly safely and effectively.

♦ Describe how to respond to threatening, obscene, or prank phone calls.

The PBX station is the property's command center during all emergency situations. The more PBX operators know about emergency procedures, the more prepared they will be when emergencies happen. When an emergency occurs, someone at the property will notify the PBX operator. The operator will then play a key role in keeping the property safe and the guests calm. Everyone will depend on him or her to stay calm and in control, and to contact help.

Emergency phone numbers and emergency codes are kept visible at all times. **Emergency codes** are numbers that identify the type of emergency the property is facing. These codes, which typically begin with "10," are transmitted to police, firefighters, and other officials by means of two-way radios. Whenever PBX operators communicate using two-way radios, their conversation can be picked up by anyone who is tuned to that channel. Codes are used so that private citizens, who may have overheard the transmission on their cellular telephones, televisions, and other electrical communication equipment, won't panic.

At the start of their shift, PBX operators check the schedules and duties of the Manager on Duty (MOD) and the security staff. For instance, if they know that at 11 P.M. the security staff checks the pool area, they would be able to more quickly locate security in an emergency. A list of all of the pager numbers of the MOD and security employees on duty is kept handy.

Some properties may have a manager on duty (or emergency procedures) manual that lists information about handling emergencies. The following pages cover a few of the basics.

Respond to Fire Alarms or Smoke Alarms

When a fire or smoke alarm goes off, it is important for PBX operators to remain calm. Most properties have occupancy reports that must be immediately printed so that management will investigate the alarm to find out the nature of the emergency. If it is a false alarm, the PBX station is notified immediately so they can relay this information to other areas of the property.

Guests that call regarding the alarms are reassured that the situation is under control and investigation. The calls are kept short so that the phone lines remain open.

When the fire captain arrives, he or she should be handed a copy of the occupancy report as well as a set of master keys. The fire captain must sign out the master keys.

Respond to Non-Fire Emergencies

Many properties have an **emergency hotline** available for guests to use in need. This line should be answered quickly and with full attention. Typically, operators answer it by saying, "Emergency hotline. Where are you calling from?" Until this emergency has been addressed, they do not answer other lines.

PBX operators try to calm the guest as much as possible so that he or she can give a specific description of the emergency. The caller's name, location, and any other pertinent details should be written down.

If the emergency is life threatening, PBX operators instruct the caller on how to evacuate the area—if necessary—and immediately call 911 or the local emergency number.

If the emergency involves someone other than the caller who is injured or ill, the operator requests that the caller remain with the person until help arrives. If possible for the caller to do so, the operator will ask the caller to remain both on the phone and near the injured or ill person.

If the situation is not life threatening, the operator places the caller on hold and calls 911 or the local emergency number.

Once the proper emergency number has been called and help is on the way, the PBX operator notifies management and/or security and alerts them to the situation. Finally, the PBX operator records an accurate record of the emergency and its subsequent response in the front office logbook. An accurate record will help protect the property in case it is sued. It will also help the property improve its response process for the next emergency.

Respond to Bomb Threats

If a situation arises in which a PBX operator receives a bomb threat call, he or she should attempt to communicate the situation to another PBX operator while remaining on the line. If possible, he or she should write a note asking the other operator to call 911 or the local emergency number, as well as the property's security and engineering departments. The caller should be kept on the phone as long as possible. The operator should remain calm and courteous, and should not interrupt the caller nor be the first to hang up. The caller should be informed that the property is occupied and that the bomb could cause injury or death.

It is imperative to gain as much information from the caller as possible. If the switchboard displays the caller's telephone number, it should be written down. The operator should try to ask questions to find out where the bomb is, the time of its detonation, the caller's location, and how the caller knows about the bomb. The operator listens for any background noises that might provide clues to the caller's location. He or she notes whether the caller is male or female, adult or child. He or she notes the caller's accent, how fast he or she speaks, and his or her manner and voice characteristics. Once the caller hangs up, the operator immediately calls 911 or the local emergency number if this has not already been done. Also, he or she notifies property security and management. Walkie-talkies are avoided as they could set off a bomb.

Most properties have information sheets for recording details of events such as bomb threats. These are filled out soon after the event so that no details are forgotten.

Respond to Weather Emergencies

PBX operators often have access to weather updates via radio, television, or the Internet. These updates are monitored routinely whenever there is a possible weather emergency in the area, such as tornadoes, thunderstorms, hurricanes, floods, and snowstorms. It is the responsibility of PBX operators to alert the other property departments—security, engineering, and management—if a weather emergency looms. Guests should also be notified of the weather emergency. Most properties have specific procedures for alerting guests to weather emergencies.

Help Evacuate the Property

Many emergencies, whether they are fire, weather, or terrorism related, require the property to be evacuated. PBX operators must remain calm at all times. They print the occupancy report and notify guests that they must evacuate the property.

Evacuations begin on the floor on which the emergency is happening. It continues with guests on all the floors above that floor, then all the guests on the floors below the emergency.

When alerting guests, PBX operators give the following or similar message:

> *"This is (their name), the switchboard operator. We are evacuating the lodging property. Stay calm and please use the stairs. Leave personal belongings in your room. Take your room key and close the door as you leave. Come to the lobby (or other designated location). You must act quickly. Do you understand?"*

In addition, make sure of the following:

- Ask for cooperation, and confirm that the guests will do as asked.

- Avoid any discussions. If guests ask for details, simply say that other guests must be called and there is no time to talk. Time is very important once the evacuation has been ordered.

- If a guest sounds panicky, acts belligerent, or states that he or she will not leave the building, note this so that a firefighter, police officer, or security officer can follow up. If a guest doesn't answer his or her phone, note it on the occupancy report.

- If a guestroom line is busy, interrupt the guest's call to inform him or her of the emergency and request the evacuation.

- Note on the occupancy report each guest that answers the call and says that he or she will leave the building.

- Highlight on the occupancy report the names called.

- Do not put calls from outside the property through to guestrooms if the building is being evacuated. Keep the telephone lines open for emergency help.

In some cases or at some properties, it may also be necessary to use the public address system to inform guests and employees of the evacuation. PBX operators work at sounding calm and saying only what is required so that guests do not panic.

PBX operators remain at the PBX station until told to evacuate or when they see immediate danger such as a fire. When told to evacuate, they proceed to the designated area so they can be counted.

Respond to Threatening, Obscene, or Prank Telephone Calls

Unfortunately, there are times when PBX operators must deal with callers who make threatening, obscene, or prank telephone calls. In the case of threatening calls, PBX operators take these seriously. They keep the caller on the line and try to determine his or her identify and location. They record any information about the threat or the person making the threat such as the number of where the person is calling from, the time of the call, the name of the caller, and what the specific threat is.

These calls are reported to management and security immediately along with as many facts about the call as possible. In some cases, it may be necessary to call the police as well.

When PBX operators are directly threatened, they should have security escort them to their car at the end of their shift.

Obscene or prank callers that are nonthreatening should be hung up on immediately. PBX operators should still record the details of the call in the front office logbook and report the matter to management. The matter should then be forgotten unless the same caller calls back. In this case, the PBX operator should inform management so that they can handle the situation.

Apply Your Learning 8.4

For each of the following statements, write "true" if the statement is correct or "false" if the statement is wrong. Please write all answers on a separate sheet of paper.

1. When a fire alarm sounds, a PBX operator should immediately leave the building.

2. The fire captain does not need to sign out the master keys.

3. When a guest calls with an emergency, he or she should be kept on the line as long as possible.

4. If there is a bomb threat, managers should be informed via walkie-talkies.

5. Weather emergencies can include hurricanes and tornadoes.

6. When evacuating the property, the PBX operator should still put outside calls through to guestrooms.

7. When an obscene caller calls, the PBX operator should try to keep him or her on the line as long as possible.

Quick Hits

SECTION 8.1—GETTING TO KNOW THE PBX OPERATOR

- The PBX operator, while operating the property's switchboard, acts as the voice of the lodging property.

- The following nine qualities make up an excellent PBX operator: friendliness, confidence, thoughtfulness, clarity, creativity, enthusiasm, integrity, and tact.

SECTION 8.2—PERFORMING PBX OPERATOR FUNCTIONS

- The PBX operator uses the front office computer system and switchboard to process information via telephone throughout the lodging property.

- The PBX information directory contains important information such as emergency phone numbers, directions, and daily or weekly schedules.

- PBX operators use the switchboard to restrict phone access to cash-only guests.

- PBX operators process wake-up calls to guests by either programming an automated system or by manually placing the wake-up calls.

- PBX operators, like the rest of a lodging property staff, have a responsibility to help ensure the security and privacy of guests.

- Pagers, two-way radios, and public address systems are three additional devices that PBX operators use to communicate information across the lodging property.

- PBX operators maintain a clean and organized workstation by filing paperwork regularly, cleaning while they work, and maintaining a stock of necessary supplies.

SECTION 8.3—PROVIDING GUEST SERVICE AS A PBX OPERATOR

- PBX operators assist guests by showing them how to use guestroom equipment and amenities such as televisions and in-room safes.

- The guest information directory provides guests with a wide range of information about the local area.

- Guest mail, packages, and messages is processed and delivered to guests as soon as possible.

- PBX operators need to be very familiar with the property, events, services, as well as the local area, so they can provide great guest service and proper directions.

- PBX operators place international phone calls for guests.

- PBX operators respond to calls from dissatisfied guests by listening, apologizing, and informing the guests that the problem will be resolved to their satisfaction.

SECTION 8.4—RESPONDING TO EMERGENCIES AND ALARMS

- The PBX station becomes the command center during emergency situations. The PBX operator is responsible for keeping calm and relaying information across the property.

- PBX operators should be very familiar with the property's emergency and evacuation procedures.

- During a fire alarm, the PBX operator is responsible for notifying emergency personnel.

- When guests needing help contact the PBX operator, the operator assesses the situation, gets as much information as possible, maintains phone contact with guests, and contacts the appropriate emergency personnel.

- PBX operators respond to bomb threats by keeping the person making the threat on the line as long as possible. Meanwhile, they gather as much information about the caller and the threat as possible.

- PBX operators receive regular weather updates so that they can alert the property if there is a weather emergency.

- During an evacuation, the PBX operator remains at his or her station so that he or she can continue to coordinate the evacuation and communicate with guests, property employees, and emergency personnel.

- PBX operators respond to threatening calls by gathering as much information as possible about the caller and the threat and communicating this to management. Prank or obscene callers are hung up on, noted, and then forgotten.

Bell Attendant

Sections

Bell attendants work in the uniformed service department, sometimes called the guest service department. Employees in this department include bell attendants (so called because they were originally summoned by a bell), a concierge, and transportation or valet-parking employees. Some large hotels have door attendants who move luggage from cars or taxicabs into the hotel.

Bell attendants move guest luggage to and from guestrooms. They also escort guests to their rooms, inspect guestrooms while rooming the guest, and explain the features of the room and the hotel to guests. Bell attendants should possess a detailed knowledge of the hotel, including the hours of operation of the hotel's restaurants, lounges, and other facilities. They should also know the local community.

Transportation services include valet parking, either in the hotel's own garage or a nearby facility. If other transportation services are provided, such as airport shuttle service, these are normally handled by the same department. In most large hotels, garages and limousines are handled by outside contractors.

9.1 Getting to Know the Bell Attendant

AFTER SUCCESSFULLY COMPLETING THIS SECTION, YOU WILL BE ABLE TO:

◆ Explain the important role bell attendants play in the hospitality industry.

◆ Describe the purpose of a posting system.

◆ Summarize the use of the bell stand logbook and front sheets.

◆ Explain the procedures involved when a guest's luggage is lost.

◆ Describe how to respect guest property.

◆ List the special rules involved in key control.

◆ Summarize tip accepting and reporting procedures.

What Is a Bell Attendant?

A bell attendant provides luggage service to and from the lobby and guestroom, and valet parking service. Because of the level of contact bell attendants have with guests, bell attendants must be knowledgeable of all areas of the property and its services. This way, they can answer any and all questions that guests may have and also perform a wide range of services.

Think about this: Would you rather come home to an empty house with no one to greet you, or a comfortable house filled with friends who welcome you warmly and help you find what you need?

Bell attendants make guests feel welcome. Successful bell attendants are:

• Friendly and cheerful

• Sensitive to the needs and feelings of others

• Able to interact well with strangers

• Tactful and considerate

• Reliable and trustworthy

• Good communicators

• Excellent team players

• Organized

• Ready to react quickly

• Able to handle change well

• Able to handle tasks carefully and correctly

• Able to calmly deal with frustrating situations

• Even-tempered, even in difficult situations

Bell attendants are often the first hotel employee that a guest sees upon arrival and the last they see upon departure. Therefore, bell attendants must provide guests with a positive first impression and a positive last impression. How the guest perceives the bell attendants can determine how much the guest enjoys his or her visit. It all starts with a smile. By being friendly, courteous, helpful, and sensitive to the guests' needs, bell attendants make a guest's stay more pleasurable every time.

Working as a Team

Bell attendants are part of a service delivery system. They must give guests *and* co-workers great service for the system to work.

To be excellent team players, the bell services department can:

- Respond quickly when guests need valet or luggage service.

- Deliver emergency messages to guests when the PBX operator gives these messages to a bell attendant, and help locate guests in the lobby when they receive telephone calls.

- Tell engineering and housekeeping about needed repairs or cleaning problems, and fill out a maintenance request form, if necessary.

- Learn the location and hours of operation of restaurants, lounges, health clubs, and other areas at the property to help guests enjoy everything the property has to offer.

- Take guest laundry and dry cleaning to housekeeping in a timely fashion, and help housekeeping employees deliver irons, ironing boards, and other items to guestrooms.

- Help deliver materials to function rooms for the banquet department.

- Help the banquet staff move tables and chairs when setting up for or breaking down a function.

Bell Services Posting System

Most lodging properties have a **posting system** which allows the bell attendants to stage themselves so they can quickly help guests. This enables bell attendants to observe guest or vehicle traffic and respond immediately to guests who need help. It also allows all bell attendants a fair chance to earn tips.

The system uses these five terms:

"Service, Please!"—A phrase called out by a front desk employee when a bell attendant is needed to perform a task that will likely earn a tip.

"Courtesy, Please!"—A phrase called out by a front desk employee when a bell attendant is needed to perform a task that will *not* likely earn a tip.

Post Position—Where bell attendants will stand while not helping guests or co-workers. By standing at this assigned spot, they will be available whenever someone needs help.

Front—The post position from which bell attendants are called to perform service tasks for guests. When in the front position, a bell attendant will be the first attendant called to help a guest with a task that will likely earn a tip.

Last—The post position from which bell attendants are called to perform courtesy tasks for guests. When in the last position, a bell attendant will be the first attendant called to help a guest with a task that is not likely to earn a tip.

Some lodging properties may have several other post positions.

When the bell attendants in the front position goes to help a guest, all other bell attendants rotate to the next posting position, leaving the last position open. When the bell attendant returns from an assignment, he or she takes the last position on the posting system.

Bell attendants stay alert while at the bell stand. They stand erect; they never slouch at their posts or lean against anything. They greet guests who pass by and invite them to enjoy their day.

Logbook and Front Sheets

Most properties have a logbook and **front sheets** located at the bell stand for recording the duties and services that were performed during a shift. In addition, any important item of information will be recorded. Often it is in a file on the property management system.

Bell attendants check the logbook at the beginning of their shifts and pay close attention to entries about current activities, situations that require follow-up, and guest complaints. The bell stand logbook should be treated and used with great care; during investigations, it can be used as a legal document.

Information recorded in the logbook may include incidents involving lost luggage, intoxicated guests, or accidents in front of the property. The information should include:

- The date of the incident
- The time of the incident

- Details of the incident
- The action taken
- Name or initials

Bell attendants use the front sheets to record any guest services performed. Information recorded includes the time, room number of the guest, guest name, the service, and the name of the bell attendant who performed the service.

Noting the guest's name is a good way to track whether bell attendants are given the guest's name when called for service.

Information That Guests Want to Know

All guests are special and they all have their own special needs and desires. Bell attendants must be able to respond to each guest individually. How? By learning to **read** guests. Bell attendants find out why guests are at the property and what kind of things they're looking for.

While assisting guests, bell attendants can chat with them and ask questions such as "Where did you fly in from?" "What areas of town will you be visiting while you're here?" and "Have you been to the city before?"

While not everyone belonging to a category wants the same thing, listed below are certain types of guests, and the features they generally are interested in.

Bell attendants also get the chance to introduce many guests to their rooms. Bell attendants answer questions about the radio, free television channels, and pay movie channels; heating, ventilation, and air conditioning system; in-room mini-bars, in-room hot tubs, in-room safes, and Internet or e-mail access.

Business people	Health clubs, restaurants, dry cleaning and laundry services, newspapers, CNN and ESPN availability, express breakfasts, shoe shines, quick haircuts, gift shops, airport transportation, faxing, making copies, mail, messages, and jogging trails.
Senior citizens	A coffee shop, fire exits, door locks, a pharmacy, a gift shop, shopping, and bus tours.
Younger people	Health clubs, night clubs with dancing, lakes, outdoor recreation, bike rentals, restaurants, tennis courts, golf courses, jogging trails, movie theaters, comedy clubs, and entertainment.
Couples	Restaurants, plays, events, shows, shopping, piano bars, entertainment, and dancing.
Single travelers	Safety features, bus tours, health clubs, shopping, and room service.
Sports teams	Restaurants, restaurants, restaurants! If the team doesn't have a scheduled pre-game meal at the property, the players will probably ask for restaurant recommendations.
Musical groups	All-night cafes, privacy features, and restaurants.

Lost Luggage

It is unfortunate, but once in a while, a guest's luggage gets lost. The guests rely on the bell attendants to help find it.

The following are some steps bell attendants take for finding luggage that is lost at the property. Bell attendants:

- Get a complete description of the bag: the type, size, color, markings, luggage tag, etc.

- Look in the luggage storage area.

- Allow the guest to look for the bag in the luggage storage area, if the bell attendants can't find it. Searching for the bag will help the guest feel better than just standing around waiting.

- Check overflow areas for the bag. Find out whether a large group checked out today, and whether their bags were stored somewhere other than the primary luggage storage area.

- Call the airport shuttle company or cab companies that the property uses. The dispatcher may be able to find whether the luggage was accidentally sent with the cab or shuttle. Check with other bell attendants and the concierge to see if anyone remembers loading that bag into another car.

- If the wrong guest has the bag, work with a front desk employee to call that guest.

Once the bell attendant is sure the luggage is lost, and none of the above methods has found it, he or she follows these steps:

- Contact the bell captain for help.

- Notify security and the manager on duty so that they can get information from the guest about what the luggage looks like, its contents, its value, etc. This is very important for insurance purposes.

- Get the phone number and address of the guest. If the guest is traveling, find out where else he or she will be staying so the luggage can be sent there once it is found.

Respecting Guests' Property

At properties that provide valet parking, bell attendants will park and have access to many guests' vehicles and their personal property. Giving respect to guests and their property is a necessity for a successful bell operation.

Bell attendants use the following guidelines to show respect to guest vehicles and property:

- Operate guest vehicles in a safe, steady manner. Never accelerate or brake quickly while driving a guest vehicle.

- Leave all guest possessions in the vehicle as they were. Do not alter settings on the various vehicle controls or disturb any other item in the vehicle. Never remove anything from a guest vehicle without permission from the guest or management.

- Protect the security of the guest's vehicle and its contents by securing the vehicle once it is parked. This includes closing all windows, removing keys, and locking doors.

- Carefully open vehicle doors so as not to chip paint on the car while exiting or entering a vehicle.

- Do not search through or remove items from guest luggage. This is a severe invasion of the guest's privacy.

- Secure guest vehicle keys in the valet key cabinet. Do not keep keys in pockets or loose on the bell stand. If the keys should be lost or stolen, the security of the guest's vehicle is compromised.

Key Control

Bell attendants can help maintain key control by asking guests they are assisting whether they have turned in their room keys at check-out. If they've forgotten, bell attendants offer to return the keys for them. They turn room keys in to a front desk employee right away.

Some properties have in-room safes for storing guest valuables. Metal keys, key cards, or electronic touch-pad systems may be used to open and lock the safes. At properties that use metal keys or key cards for in-room safes, bell attendants help control these in the same way they help control room keys, by asking guests at check-out whether they've turned in their in-room safe keys. If they haven't, they offer to return the keys for them.

Bell attendants may occasionally need a master key. With a master key, bell attendants can deliver luggage or other items to guestrooms and help guests if their keys do not work. Because a master key can open all guestrooms, there are special rules to protect bell attendants and guests:

- Never leave a master key in a door's lock, and never set it down; bell attendants keep their master keys with them at all times.

- If anyone—even a supervisor—asks to borrow the key, bell attendants send that person to the front desk—they *don't* loan anyone their key.

- Always turn in the key before leaving the property for any reason.

- Report any lost keys immediately to the front desk.

With valet parking, key control takes on an added dimension. Guest vehicle keys are kept secure in the valet key cabinet. Valet key cabinets are usually stored in an area where only property employees have access. Many also can be locked. Some properties may designate a specific person to store and retrieve keys from the cabinet.

Cash Payment, Tips, and Tip Reporting Procedures

Tips are a guest's way of thanking a bell attendant for a job well done. Some guests may give a large tip upon arrival to ensure great service throughout the visit. Bell attendants may get tips for escorting guests to their guestrooms, carrying luggage, parking and retrieving guest vehicles, providing courtesy transportation, delivering newspapers, calling a taxi, or any number of other services.

Unlike the wages bell attendants get from the lodging property, no taxes are withheld from tips. However, the federal government still considers tips as income and taxes them. The federal tax law requires that workers report any tips that add up to $20 a month or more.

When accepting a tip from a guest, bell attendants always look at the guest, not at the tip. They thank the guest but never comment on the amount of a tip, small or large. Bell attendants never wait for a tip

if the guest forgets and they do not show dissatisfaction toward a guest who does not tip them. They also never let this affect the level of service they provide.

Lodging properties may have differing policies related to tips. Some properties require their bell attendants to share or pool tips with each other. These **tip pooling** policies allow all bell attendants to split the shift's tips evenly. Other properties do not have a policy—all bell attendants keep the tips given to them by guests. Some properties may have a policy on sharing tips between two bell attendants who have helped the same guest.

Lodging properties that offer valet parking may have an additional charge for this service. For guests staying at the hotel, this may be charged to their room account. For guests visiting the hotel for dinner or other entertainment venues, cash may be required. In most situations, the property will have an employee whose duty is to accept guests' payment for valet and give back change as needed. However, guests may have cash ready to pay for the charge as they are exiting their vehicles. They may offer this cash to the bell attendant who assists them. Bell attendants should not assume that the guest is handing them a tip. If guests offer cash upon getting out of their vehicle, bell attendants ask the guest if the cash is for the valet charge.

Bell Attendant Duties

Below are just a few of the tasks or services that a bell attendant may perform for guests:

- Assisting guests with luggage, including luggage storage and retrieval

- Parking and retrieving guest vehicles

- Delivering luggage and other items to guestrooms

- Transporting luggage and/or guests in a courtesy vehicle

- Providing guests with directions and other useful information

- Performing many other miscellaneous tasks including performing errands, arranging for guest reservations, or escorting guests around the property, to name just a few

And, of course, all employees are responsible for performing other reasonable duties as requested by a supervisor or manager.

Exhibit 1 lists the most common tasks that bell attendants are expected to be able to perform and perform well.

Apply Your Learning 9.1

Please write all answers on a separate sheet of paper.

1. What are the primary responsibilities of a bell attendant?

2. List three ways that bell attendants can be excellent team players.

3. What is the post position?

4. What are the bell stand logbook and front sheets used for?

5. What features of the local area are couples usually interested in?

6. What is the first thing a bell attendant should do when dealing with a lost luggage item?

7. List two ways in which bell attendants show respect for guest property.

8. List two of the special key control rules that bell attendants obey.

9. Describe the differences between tip pooling and no sharing.

Exhibit 1
Task List—Bell Attendant

1. Use the Bell Stand Telephone System
2. Follow the Property's Posting Positions
3. Maintain the Bell Stand Logbook and Front Sheets
4. Handle Cash Payment and Tips
5. Welcome Guests and Offer Assistance
6. Load and Transport Luggage
7. Valet Park Guest Vehicles
8. Provide Storage For Guest Luggage
9. Assist in Rooming Guests
10. Assist With Luggage for Group Arrivals and Departures
11. Assist Guests at Check-out
12. Retrieve Vehicles That Have Been Valet Parked
13. Assist Guests During Room Changes
14. Use the Guest Information Directory
15. Prepare Maps and Provide Directions
16. Arrange for or Hail Taxis for Guests
17. Arrange Limousine Service
18. Provide Courtesy Transportation
19. Arrange for Services Requested by Guests
20. Handle Guest Service Problems
21. Show Rooms to Potential Guests and Check Rooms for Occupancy
22. Process and Deliver Mail, Messages, Facsimiles, or Packages
23. Deliver Express Check-Out Packets to Guests
24. Process Guest Laundry
25. Deliver Guest Service Equipment and Supplies to Guestrooms
26. Maintain Clear Drive-Up/ Drop-Off Area
27. Perform Errands
28. Process Lost and Found Items
29. Clean the Drive-up, Entrance, Lobby, Bell Services Stand, and Luggage Carts
30. Report Vehicle Accidents

9.2 Assisting Guests During Check-In and Check-Out

AFTER SUCCESSFULLY COMPLETING THIS SECTION, YOU WILL BE ABLE TO:

♦ Describe how to welcome guests and assist them.

♦ Summarize the procedures for loading, transporting, and storing guest luggage.

♦ Explain how to park and retrieve guest vehicles.

♦ Describe the procedures for assisting guests to and from their rooms.

♦ Summarize ways to handle group luggage.

Welcome Guests

As guests enter the property, be it through the lobby or the drive-up area, bell attendants make eye contact with the guests, greet them, and make them feel welcome.

Bell attendants open the lobby doors for guests and greet them or offer assistance. When a vehicle arrives at the drive-up area, bell attendants step up to the vehicle, open the door, and welcome the guest. They use a friendly greeting such as "Good afternoon! Welcome to _____ Resort. My name is John. How may I be of assistance to you?"

They then inquire whether the guests are checking in and assist anyone who needs help getting out of the vehicle.

Guests may have many questions. They expect the bell attendants to know all the answers. Therefore, bell attendants are well informed about all aspects of the property's hours, services, and amenities. If they are unable to answer a guest's question, they are at least able to point them toward someone who can.

Bell attendants assist guests with their luggage and inform guests who have arrived before the check-in time that they will store their luggage while they are checking in and that their luggage will be brought to their room once it is ready. Bell attendants suggest things the guests can do on property while they are waiting for their room to be available. If guests have arrived after the check-in time, it may not be necessary to take the guests' luggage to the storage area.

When storing luggage for guests, bell attendants tear a two-part **luggage claim ticket** into its two parts and give guests one part of the claim ticket. Bell attendants also use baggage tags which help them quickly locate luggage when guests are ready to go to their room or to leave.

If guests prefer to carry their own luggage, bell attendants politely direct them to the front desk, offer future aid, and wish them a good stay.

At properties offering valet parking, bell attendants ask the guests whether they would like to have their vehicle parked. If yes, bell attendants provide the guest with a valet parking ticket and inform guests of any parking charges.

If the guest prefers to park his or her own vehicle, bell attendants politely ask them to park their vehicle in the guest parking area before checking in. They also provide the guest with clear directions to the guest parking areas. Asking guests to park before check in helps keep the property's drive-through/drop off area from getting congested.

When guests have no further questions, bell attendants direct them to the front desk and then immediately store the guests' luggage in a secure area. If the guests have requested valet parking, bell attendants store their luggage before parking their vehicle.

Load and Transport Luggage

Bell attendants always handle luggage and other articles safely and with care. These following steps are followed when loading a courtesy van, car trunk, or **luggage cart**:

- Put heavier or larger items on the bottom. When using a luggage cart, place the heaviest items over the rear stationary wheels. This will provide more stability for the cart, making it easier to steer.

- When lifting items, bend at the knees. In addition, bell attendants never assume a luggage item is as light as it looks.

- Keep their back straight and use legs to lift.

- Set the item down carefully.

- Hang soft garment bags from luggage cart bars or place them on top of other

luggage to help protect them from wrinkles and damage.

- Secure fragile items between other bags, and do not put other items on top of fragile items.

- Check that all luggage is secure on the cart before moving it.

- Push heavy luggage carts instead of pulling them.

- Move slowly, especially around corners, so items don't shift and fall off the cart.

- Never allow guests to use luggage carts by themselves. If guests hurt themselves while using the luggage cart, the property is liable.

Children's items such as toys, games, and dolls may be loose. Successful bell attendants keep a supply of plastic bags handy to store items. The bag can then be hung from the luggage cart bars.

If guests ask to use a cart, bell attendants ask the guests to let them help. They explain to the guests that assistance with luggage is one of the services that the property provides.

Valet Park Guest Vehicles

Valet attendants—who are part of the bell staff—are responsible for parking guest vehicles.

Exhibit 1 provides a step-by-step breakdown of the steps for valet parking guest vehicles.

Store Guest Luggage

The luggage storage area usually contains numbered closets or bins in which luggage items are placed. A checklist listing the bin numbers records the guest's name and in which bin their luggage is stored.

Bell attendants provide guests with one portion of a two-part claim check or baggage tag. This tag is numbered on both portions. One portion is placed on the luggage, making it easier to locate luggage quickly when guests are ready to leave.

Exhibit 2 provides a step-by-step breakdown of the steps involved in providing storage for guest luggage.

Assist in Rooming Guests

Rooming guests refers to the entire procedure of guest check-in and taking guests and their luggage to the guestroom. When guests check in, their first concern is usually to get to their room as soon as possible. Bell attendants are quick, informative, and friendly.

Exhibit 3 provides a step-by-step breakdown of the steps for assisting in rooming guests.

Assist with Luggage for Group Arrivals and Departures

When a large group is checking in to a lodging property, the front desk usually provides the bell staff with a rooming list for the group with each guest's name and assigned room number. Bell attendants make sure to:

- Have enough luggage claim checks or tickets when unloading the motorcoach, bus, or van.

- Tag all luggage with the guests' names before guests go to the front desk for check-in.

- Arrange luggage onto luggage carts by room numbers.

- Assist guests who return to the entrance and insist on handling their luggage. Help them find their bags.

- Match names on claim checks with the rooming list and deliver luggage by floors to save time.

When these guests are departing, bell attendants will:

- Take a luggage cart and go to each guestroom on the rooming list to pick up the luggage.

- Introduce themselves when guests open the door and enter the guestroom when invited in.

- Quickly check each guestroom for personal articles that might have been forgotten.

- Take the luggage to where it will be easy to load the tour bus or van.

Large groups are often be on a tight schedule and are in a hurry. Bell attendants work quickly when handling group luggage. Because of their busy schedules, it is very common for group guests to be out of their rooms during luggage delivery. Therefore, bell attendants may have to use a master key from the front desk. However, they always knock first to ensure the room is empty. Bell attendants never touch guests' personal property in their guestrooms.

For most large groups, a tip is included in the package price. In these cases, bell attendants do not expect an additional cash tip when they provide bell services. The group tip will be passed out later among the bell staff who helped the group or may be distributed on the next paycheck.

Exhibit 1
Valet Park Guest Vehicles

Materials needed: Valet parking tickets, a pen, guest vehicle keys, and a luggage cart.

STEPS:	HOW-TO'S:
1. Offer valet parking service to the guest.	❑ A valet must park and retrieve all guest vehicles. Guests should not be permitted to either park or retrieve their own vehicles from valet parking areas. If a guest is injured while driving in the valet parking lot, the property could be liable.
2. Separate the guest portion of the valet parking ticket and give it to the guest.	❑ Instruct the guest to retain this portion of the ticket and present it when he or she is ready to pick up the vehicle.
	❑ Most valet parking tickets have two portions: one that is presented to the guest, and one that is retained with the vehicle keys. A number on the guest portion corresponds with a number on the key portion so that the two can be matched when the guest requests the vehicle. In addition, the guest portion will include a telephone number to call to pick up the vehicle. At some properties, valet parking tickets may contain multiple portions or copies for placing in the vehicle or for filing purposes.
3. Fill out the remaining portion of the valet parking ticket.	❑ Write the number of the parking space on the portion of the valet ticket retained with the keys. It will be easier to quickly find a vehicle in the parking lot with all ticket portions filled out correctly.
	❑ Leave one portion of the ticket face up on the dashboard of the parked vehicle, if applicable.
	❑ Turn in the appropriate portion of the ticket to the front desk, if applicable. The front desk will use the tickets to charge the guest for valet parking, if applicable.

(continued)

Exhibit 1
Valet Park Guest Vehicles *(continued)*

STEPS:	HOW-TO'S:
4. **Operate guests' vehicles.**	❑ Look at the car before driving. Make a note of any body damage and report it. The property may be liable for any damage you cause to a guest's vehicle. ❑ Be extremely careful and respectful when driving guests' vehicles. Do not adjust radio dials or seats. ❑ Do not touch or remove anything from the guest's vehicle. ❑ Do not speed when driving guests' vehicles. ❑ Do not accelerate or brake quickly. ❑ Report all accidents immediately.
5. **Park guests' vehicles.**	❑ Park all vehicles in the valet parking area. Some properties may have an overflow parking lot to accommodate peak business hours. ❑ Back vehicles into parking spots when time permits. Backing vehicles into parking spaces will save time when you are retrieving the vehicle. It also reduces the likelihood of accidents caused by poor visibility when backing out of a parking space. ❑ Park vehicles with manual transmissions in neutral and vehicles with automatic transmissions in park. ❑ Park with the front wheels straight, unless parking on a hill. If parking on a hill, turn the steering wheel so the front wheels are slanted. ❑ Set the parking brake firmly on all vehicles. ❑ Be sure the lights are turned off, unless the vehicle has an automatic turn-off device. ❑ Remove keys. ❑ Be careful when opening vehicle doors to avoid hitting another vehicle, a concrete post, or anything else.

(continued)

Exhibit 1
Valet Park Guest Vehicles *(continued)*

STEPS:	HOW-TO'S:
	❑ Lock all vehicle doors.
	❑ Close vehicle doors securely and double-check to see that they are locked. Make sure all windows are rolled up.
6. **Store guests' car keys in the valet key cabinet.**	❑ Check that the guest's car keys are labeled with the appropriate identification, including the guest's name, description of the vehicle, and parking space number.
	❑ File or hang the guest's keys in the space for the letter of the guest's last name. If you should notice keys stored in the wrong letter location, place them in the proper one.
7. **Inform guests of any mechanical problems you notice with their vehicle.**	❑ If a guest asks for an auto repair shop, recommend the nearest dealer or a garage approved by the property.
8. **Escort guests to their vehicle if they want to retrieve items.**	
9. **Accept tips.**	❑ Look at the guest, not at the tip.
	❑ Say "Thank you very much," but never comment on the amount of a tip, small or large.
	❑ Do not look at or count the tip in view of the guest.
	❑ Never wait for a tip if the guest forgets.

Assist Guests at Check-Out

Guests should be given the same level of service when they check-out that they receive when they check-in. It is just as important to leave a guest with a positive *last* impression as it is to make a good first impression. This will go a long way in determining whether the guest makes a return visit.

If guests are departing immediately upon checking out, a bell attendant will escort them from the room with their luggage. However, some guests may check out of their room but not leave the property right away. These guests may ask to have their bags stored in the luggage storage area. They will then ask a bell attendant to retrieve their bags once they are ready to leave.

Exhibit 4 provides the step-by-step procedures for assisting guests at check-out.

Retrieve Vehicles

At check-out, guests who have had their vehicle valet parked will ask a bell attendant to retrieve their vehicle.

Exhibit 5 provides the step-by-step procedures for retrieving vehicles that have been valet parked.

Apply Your Learning 9.2

Please write all answers on a separate sheet of paper.

1. What do bell attendants do first when a vehicle arrives at the property?

2. What is done with each of the two parts of a luggage claim ticket?

3. Where should heavier items be placed on a luggage cart?

4. List three things that bell attendants should tell guests while escorting them to their guestroom.

5. What is a typical tipping policy for large groups?

Exhibit 2
Provide Storage for Guest Luggage

Materials needed: Luggage claim checks, a pen, damp cloths, a broom, a vacuum cleaner, and a mop.

STEPS:	HOW-TO'S:
1. **Check in luggage.**	❑ Attach a luggage claim check to each piece of luggage. At large properties, the shelves in the luggage area may be coded to match the numbering system on the claim checks.
	❑ Tear off luggage claim check stubs and present them to guests. Explain to guests how to pick up checked luggage.
	❑ If valuable items are being checked, note where you stored them on your part of the claim check stub. Some properties may have a special area for storing items that require additional security.
	❑ Store the luggage and note the number or location of the luggage bin.
	❑ Use care and caution when storing guest luggage.
	❑ When storing luggage in an overflow area, mark it on the claim check stub.
2. **Return checked luggage to guests.**	❑ Ask guests for their luggage claim check stubs.
	❑ Find the bags and turn them over to guests or help guests move them, if necessary.
	❑ If guests have lost their claim checks, escort them to the luggage area to identify bags.
	❑ Politely ask to see identification such as a driver's license to compare with the name and address on the bags. Many bags look alike, and guests will appreciate your attention to security.
3. **Maintain the luggage area.**	❑ Straighten all items.
	❑ Make sure items belonging to the same guest are grouped together.

(continued)

Exhibit 2
Provide Storage for Guest Luggage *(continued)*

STEPS:	HOW-TO'S:
	❑ Arrange luggage according to claim checks or according to the guests' last names.
	❑ When possible, store luggage off the floor to make cleaning easier.
	❑ Dust shelves or bins with a damp cloth and pick up all trash and debris.
	❑ Sweep, vacuum, or mop floors as appropriate or move luggage so that the floors can be cleaned by custodial or housekeeping personnel.
	❑ Replace luggage in an orderly arrangement.
4. **Transfer abandoned luggage to the lost and found department.**	❑ If you suspect that luggage has been left behind, check with a front desk employee and find out when the guest checked out.
	❑ Take luggage that has been left behind to the lost and found department.

Exhibit 3
Assist In Rooming Guests

Materials needed: Luggage cart, the front sheet, the bell services logbook, pen, and guestroom key.

STEPS:	HOW-TO'S:
1. Step to the front desk from the "front" post position when "Service, please" is called.	
2. Greet guests when the front desk employee introduces you and gives you a guestroom key.	❑ Use a greeting that is comfortable to you, such as: "Good morning, Mr. and Mrs. McCann. My name is Rudy" or "Hello, I'm Claire." Be sure guests know your name. They can then contact you for service.
	❑ Use guests' last names with a courtesy title. Courtesy titles include Miss, Ms., Mrs., and Mr.
	❑ Ask how to pronounce names you're unsure of. If guests' names are difficult, guests will be used to repeating them.
	❑ To protect guest security, do not say the guestroom number aloud.
3. Assist with guests' luggage.	❑ Load luggage onto a luggage cart.
	❑ If guests ask to borrow your cart to move their own luggage, ask them to let you help.
	❑ Be careful not to run into furniture, walls, or guests while using the luggage cart.
4. Direct guests to the elevator.	❑ Walk with guests as much as possible. Try not to walk in front of them. The first few minutes you are with the guest are important to "reading" that person.
	❑ While still in the lobby, ask guests if this is their first stay at the property. If you find out why the guest is staying at the property, you can better direct your conversation on the way to the room.

(continued)

Exhibit 3
Assist In Rooming Guests *(continued)*

STEPS:	HOW-TO'S:
	❏ If so, point out restaurants, lounges, and gift shops. Explain the hours of operation and the food and services provided.
5. **Start the elevator.**	❏ If your property has concierge-level floors, explain to guests the limited access to their floor. Show them how to reach their floor.
	❏ If there is not room for you, the luggage cart, and the guests in the elevator, give the key to the guests and send them ahead.
	❏ Take the next elevator to the guestroom floor.
6. **Escort guests from the elevator to the guestroom.**	❏ Point out emergency exits and ice and vending machine areas.
	❏ Allow guests time to consider how they will exit in an emergency.
7. **Enter the guestroom.**	❏ Show guests how to use the guestroom key and locks.
	❏ The key may not have the room number on it. If not, point out that this is for security reasons and that the guest will need to remember the room number.
	❏ Enter the guestroom ahead of guests, when possible.
	❏ Turn on the light and make sure the room is ready and not occupied by someone else.
	❏ Hold the door open so guests can enter.
8. **Make sure guests are satisfied with the room.**	❏ If guests do not like the room, call the front desk and tactfully explain the situation.

(continued)

Exhibit 3
Assist In Rooming Guests *(continued)*

STEPS:	HOW-TO'S:
	❑ Do not promise the guests anything until you have contacted the front desk.
	❑ If the front desk assigns a new room, allow guests to wait in the first guestroom while you get a key for the new guestroom.
9. **Put away the guests' luggage.**	❑ Ask guests whether they would like their garment bags hung. If not, place them where the guests indicate. Some guests will want to unpack right away and would prefer that you place the garment bag on the bed.
	❑ Place the largest suitcase on the luggage rack. Place smaller bags in the closet or beside the luggage rack.
10. **Check lighting and equipment.**	❑ Turn on all lamps to make sure they work.
	❑ Turn on the television with the volume low.
	❑ Review the in-room movie system.
	❑ Ask guests if they want the television left on.
	❑ Check the thermostat setting. Ask guests if they would like you to adjust the temperature.
	❑ Explain specialized equipment such as a whirlpool tub, in-room safes, wireless internet connections, a mini-bar, etc.
	❑ If major items, such as the television, heat, or air conditioning do not work, call the front desk to arrange for a new room.
	❑ Point out literature in the room, such as a room service menu, guest directory, and television listings. Be careful not to be too chatty. The guest may be in a hurry or may be a frequent guest.
	❑ Notify the appropriate department if you notice missing amenities or anything that is not working properly.

(continued)

Exhibit 3
Assist In Rooming Guests *(continued)*

STEPS:	HOW-TO'S:
11. Offer to get ice for guests.	❑ If guests would like ice, take the ice bucket and clean liner to the nearest ice machine. Line the bucket and fill it with ice. ❑ Put the lid on the bucket and return to the room. Place the bucket on the tray. ❑ If guests don't want you to get ice for them, explain where ice and vending machines are.
12. Check the number of glasses in the room.	❑ Make sure there are enough glasses for all guests. ❑ Call the appropriate department if extra glasses are needed, or get more glasses from a housekeeping closet.
13. Present the room key to the guest.	
14. Thank guests politely for all tips.	❑ Look at the guest, not at the tip. ❑ Say "Thank you very much," but never comment on the amount of a tip, small or large. ❑ Do not look at or count the tip in view of the guest. ❑ Never wait for a tip if the guest forgets. ❑ If a guest tips you in the middle of your room orientation, it usually means that the guest is ready for you to leave.
15. Wish guests a pleasant stay and tell them how they can reach you.	❑ Let guests know that you can be reached at the valet stand: "I'm Troy, and if there's anything else you need, you can reach me at extension ____. Enjoy your stay."
16. Record the assignment on the front sheet or in the bell stand logbook as appropriate.	❑ Return to the bellstand. On the front sheet, fill in the information about rooming the guest. ❑ Record any unusual incidents in the logbook and discuss such matters with your supervisor as appropriate.

Exhibit 4
Assist Guests at Check-Out

Materials needed: Luggage cart, luggage claim receipts, valet claim receipt, map, and guest vehicle

STEPS:	HOW-TO'S:
1. **Retrieve luggage for guests who are checking out.**	❑ Take luggage claim receipts from the guest.
	❑ Ask the guest how they will be leaving the property. Guests may be leaving in their own vehicle or may need you to hail a taxi for them. Some properties may also provide a shuttle service to the airport.
	❑ If the guest has a vehicle in the valet lot, ask for their valet receipt if it has not already been offered.
	❑ Inform the guest that you will be right back with their luggage and then you will retrieve their vehicle. Always retrieve guests' luggage before their vehicle. This will keep the drive-up from congesting unnecessarily and will also give the guests time to sort their luggage or put away items.
	❑ Bring the luggage out to the guest on a luggage cart.
2. **Retrieve the guest's vehicle.**	
3. **Load the guest's luggage into the vehicle.**	❑ Ask the guest if there are any specific items they wish placed in the trunk or in the cabin of the vehicle.
	❑ Place heavy items on the bottom and lighter, more fragile items in the trunk.
4. **Ask the guest if they need directions.**	
5. **Thank guests for staying at the property and invite them to return.**	

Exhibit 5
Retrieve Vehicles That Have Been Valet Parked *(continued)*

Materials needed: guest portion of a valet parking ticket, guest vehicle keys.

STEPS:	HOW-TO'S:
1. **Obtain the guest's claim ticket.**	❏ Do not release a vehicle without a claim ticket. If a guest does not have a claim ticket, contact a supervisor. The guest's portion of the valet parking ticket may also be called a "claim ticket."
	❏ If a guest calls to request that his or her car be retrieved, ask for the valet parking ticket number, guests' names, and the make of the vehicle. Collecting information about the vehicle provides security in case the guest has lost the valet parking ticket and someone is trying to steal the vehicle.
2. **Retrieve guests' car keys from the valet key cabinet.**	❏ Match the guest's number on the guest portion of the valet parking ticket with the portion retained with the guest vehicle keys. Several of your guests may have the same or similar names or vehicles. Always double check that you have retrieved the right keys for the right guest.
3. **Retrieve guests' vehicles.**	❏ Take the keys to the parking lot.
	❏ Inspect the vehicle's exterior for damage that may have occurred since it was parked. Report any problems to your supervisor right away.
	❏ Unlock all doors.
	❏ Start the vehicle and warm it up slowly. Do not race the engine.
	❏ Release the parking brake and carefully drive the vehicle to the guest pickup area.
	❏ Set the parking brake when you park.
	❏ Turn off the ignition. If the guest has luggage, open the trunk. If the key is needed to open the trunk, make sure to return it to the ignition.

(continued)

Exhibit 5
Retrieve Vehicles That Have Been Valet Parked *(continued)*

STEPS:	HOW-TO'S:
	❏ Open vehicle doors, depending on the number of guests using the vehicle. When presenting a vehicle to a guest, always leave the guest with a good lasting impression. You never know when it will be the guest's final departure.
4. **Load luggage for departing guests.**	❏ Ask guests whether they have all their luggage. ❏ Ask guests whether they need directions.
5. **Smile, thank guests, and invite them back.**	
6. **Accept tips.**	❏ Look at the guest, not at the tip. ❏ Say "Thank you very much," but never comment on the amount of a tip, small or large. ❏ Do not look at or count the tip in view of the guest. ❏ Never wait for a tip if the guest forgets.

9.3 Assisting Guests During Their Stay

AFTER SUCCESSFULLY COMPLETING THIS SECTION, YOU WILL BE ABLE TO:

♦ Describe the procedures for assisting guests during room changes.

♦ Explain how to arrange for taxi or limousine service for guests.

♦ Describe the process of providing courtesy transportation to guests.

♦ Explain the proper way to handle guest service problems.

Assist Guests During Room Changes

There may be times when bell attendants are asked to help move guests who are unsatisfied with their current room to a new, more acceptable room. Bell attendants are sensitive to the fact that these guests may feel that their stay has gone poorly so far. By providing quick and friendly service, bell attendants can improve the guest's mood and send them on their way to a pleasant stay.

Exhibit 1 provides the step-by-step procedures for assisting guests during a room change.

Arrange for or Hail Taxis

Some guests use taxis to get around. Bell services staff may arrange for or hail taxis for guests. Larger properties will often have a staging area—sometimes called a **taxi line**—where taxis can wait for a guest who needs a ride. This ability to provide prompt taxi service helps everyone involved. Bell attendants simply hail the taxi at the front of the taxi line outside the property.

If there is no taxi line at the property, bell attendants will call a taxi company's taxi dispatcher. Many properties have specific taxi companies they use, either by contract or by preference. However, bell attendants honor special guest requests and call the taxi company of the guest's choice, if necessary. Bell attendants give the taxi dispatcher the guest's name and destination so that the driver will pick up the right person when the taxi arrives.

Guests may request in advance for a taxi to pick them up at a specific time. These requests are often noted in the bell stand logbook. Bell attendants then can call the taxi dispatcher and make these arrangements. The entry in the logbook will serve as a record that the taxi was ordered.

When the taxi arrives, bell attendants open the right rear door for guests and help them board the taxi. They then load the

Exhibit 1
Assist Guests During Room Changes

Materials needed: Luggage cart, front sheet, pen, room key, bell services logbook.

STEPS:	HOW-TO'S:
1. **Respond quickly when you are asked to help a guest change rooms.**	❏ Ask for the guest's name, current room number, and new room number. ❏ Get a luggage cart. ❏ On the front sheet, write the current room number, that the request is a room change, and your initials. ❏ Pick up the key for the new room from a front desk employee.
2. **Go to the guestroom.**	❏ Knock on the guestroom door with your knuckles, not your key, and announce yourself. ❏ When the guest opens the door, introduce yourself and enter the room when invited in.
3. **Gather and load the luggage.**	
4. **Secure the guestroom.**	❏ Make sure windows and sliding doors are closed and locked. ❏ Adjust the thermostat according to property policy.
5. **Walk with the guest to the new guestroom.**	❏ Point out emergency exits and ice and vending machines.
6. **Enter the guestroom.**	❏ Enter the room ahead of the guest if possible so you can turn on the lights. ❏ Hold the door open so the guest can enter.

(continued)

Exhibit 1
Assist Guests During Room Changes *(continued)*

STEPS:	HOW-TO'S:
7. **Make sure the guest is satisfied with the room.**	❑ Ask the guest if he or she is satisfied with the room. ❑ If the guest does not like the room, call the front desk and tactfully explain the situation. ❑ Do not promise the guest anything until you have spoken with a front desk employee or front desk supervisor. ❑ Follow the front desk employee's instructions about how to handle any problems.
8. **Put away the guest's luggage.**	❑ Ask the guest if he or she would like the garment bags hung. If not, place them where the guest indicates. ❑ Place the largest suitcase on the luggage rack. ❑ Place smaller bags in the closet or beside the luggage rack.
9. **Check lighting and equipment.**	❑ Turn on all lamps to make sure they work. ❑ Check the thermostat setting. Ask the guest if he or she would like you to adjust the temperature. ❑ Ask the guest if he or she would like you to explain how to use any of the room's equipment or amenities. The guest may have already been told how to operate the equipment when he or she checked in to the original guestroom. ❑ Notify the appropriate department if something does not work properly or if amenities are missing.
10. **Offer to get ice for the guest.**	❑ If the guest would like ice, take the ice bucket and clean liner to the nearest ice machine. Line the bucket and fill it with ice.

(continued)

Exhibit 1
Assist Guests During Room Changes *(continued)*

STEPS:	HOW-TO'S:
	❏ Put the lid on the bucket and return to the room. Place the bucket on the tray.
	❏ If the guest doesn't want you to get ice, explain where ice and vending machines are located.
11. **Put away the guest's luggage.**	
12. **Thank the guest politely for all tips.**	❏ Look at the guest, not at the tip.
	❏ Say, "Thank you very much," but never comment on the amount of a tip, large or small.
	❏ Do not count the tip in view of the guest.
	❏ Never wait for a tip if the guest forgets.
13. **Wish the guest a pleasant stay and explain how you can be reached.**	❏ You might say, "Please enjoy the rest of your stay. If there's anything else you need, please call me at extension _____."
14. **Return the guest's original room key to a front desk employee right away.**	
15. **Record any unusual incidents in the bell stand logbook.**	

guest's luggage into the taxi's trunk. From a guest service standpoint, it is preferable for bell attendants to load the guest's luggage into the taxi trunk instead of the taxi driver.

Finally, bell attendants tell the driver the guest's destination and make sure the driver knows how to get there. Bell attendants always treat taxi drivers with respect, this way the drivers will be more likely to treat the guests with respect.

Arrange Limousine Service

There are three types of limousine services:

- Scheduled airport limousine service

- Unscheduled airport limousine service

- Unscheduled luxury limousine service

Airport limousines are often vans or buses. Guests using the limousine service to get to the airport will need to be told the airport limousine's scheduled pickup times. If the airport limousine company does not have a scheduled stop at a property, call the company to schedule a pickup for guests.

When the airport limousine arrives, bell attendants clearly announce in both the lobby and drive-up, drop-off areas:

> "The airport limousine is now boarding and will depart in _____ minutes."

Bell attendants then load the luggage for departing guests and wish them safe travel and invite them back.

At properties with concierges, they will likely help guests rent luxury limousines. However, bell attendants still must be familiar with the procedures. For unscheduled luxury limousine service,

bell attendants explain to guests that the guests will pay the limousine service directly unless they have arranged for it to be charged to their account. When the limousine arrives, bell attendants assist guests with departure.

Provide Courtesy Transportation

Many properties have a vehicle for courtesy guest transportation. This may be a shuttle for transporting guests to and from the airport at scheduled times, or it could be a van or car used for miscellaneous trips or other property business. Bell attendants are usually the employees who drive these vehicles and transport guests. Depending on the vehicle, a chauffeur's license may be required to operate it.

Before they leave the property in the courtesy vehicle, bell attendants enter the time of the trip, their name, the destination, and the number of passengers in the vehicle logbook. The vehicle logbook is a legal record of trips, how many passengers there were, and when events took place. Bell attendants also perform a radio check and establish radio contact with the PBX operator and/or bell stand. This radio contact is useful in case of emergencies.

When driving guests in the courtesy vehicle, bell attendants maintain a positive and friendly attitude the entire time they are with the guests. They talk to guests while traveling and offer to answer any questions. They point out places of interest in the area and inform guests about the property's services, facilities, and restaurants. If guests do not respond to conversation, then bell attendants do not disturb them. If guests are reading, they do not interrupt them unless it is essential.

While driving, bell attendants make sure to:

- Signal before pulling into traffic

- Use extra care in inclement weather

- Never exceed safe and legal speeds

- Obey all traffic signs, signals, and speed limits

- Watch for cars and people behind, in front of, and on both sides of the vehicle

- Stay alert and prepared for sudden stops or turns

- Make a complete stop at stop signs and red lights

- Set the emergency brake firmly before exiting the vehicle

At each stop, bell attendants get out of the vehicle, open the doors, and help guests with their luggage. They leave the engine running with the heater or air conditioner on. They smile, thank guests, and invite them back. They close and secure the rear and passenger doors, get back in the vehicle, release the emergency brake, signal, and merge safely into traffic.

When bringing guests to the property, bell attendants will help guests exit the vehicle, assist them with any luggage, and inform them of check-in procedures. Once they have finished assisting the guests and have parked and secured the vehicle, they remove the key, lock all doors, return the key to the designated location, and make an end-of-trip entry in the vehicle logbook.

Arrange for Guest Services

Because of the amount of contact that bell attendants have with guests, many guests will come to them with requests for services. In these situations, bell attendants listen carefully to determine exactly what the guest wants. It's very important for bell attendants to understand exactly what the guest expects before making a suggestion. If bell attendants cannot answer a guest's questions, satisfy a guest's request, or resolve a problem, they alert a supervisor.

When guests ask questions about restaurants, bell attendants recommend the property's restaurants first. Bell attendants may call a restaurant or other venue and make reservations or purchase tickets for guests. They then provide guests with good directions, as necessary.

For certain guest requests, bell attendants may need to coordinate with other departments. If a guest requests a service that involves another department, bell attendants call the appropriate employee and explain the situation. Bell attendants then work with the other department to meet the guest's needs.

Properties usually have specific procedures for performing errands off the property. If guests ask them to perform an errand that is illegal, immoral, or violates a property rule, bell attendants politely explain that they are not allowed to perform such a request. They then notify their supervisor.

Apply Your Learning 9.3

Please write all answers on a separate sheet of paper.

1. What is a "taxi line?"

2. What are the three types of limousine services?

3. List four things bell attendants make sure to do while driving a courtesy vehicle.

4. What do bell attendants do if asked to perform a service they are uncomfortable with?

9.4 Assisting the Front Desk

AFTER SUCCESSFULLY COMPLETING THIS SECTION, YOU WILL BE ABLE TO:

♦ Describe how to show rooms to potential guests.

♦ Explain how to process and deliver guest mail, messages, or packages.

♦ Summarize how to process and deliver such items as express check-out packets, guest laundry, and other guest equipment or supplies.

Show Rooms to Potential Guests and Check Rooms for Occupancy

Potential guests may visit a lodging property and request that they be shown a vacant room. Seeing a room is important to some guests when deciding on where to stay.

Most properties have their front desk or bell staff show appropriate rooms to these potential guests. Only vacant and clean rooms are shown. A front desk employee will use the room status report to determine which rooms are vacant and clean.

When showing rooms, bell attendants point out the positive features and benefits of the room. If a guest points out a negative feature, bell attendants draw attention to a positive feature, or show a room that does not have the feature the guest doesn't like.

Bell attendants describe the restaurants, pool, health club, or other property features while walking to and from the rooms.

Sometimes housekeeping and the front desk may not have the same status for a guestroom. The front desk may then ask a bell attendant to check a guestroom to see whether it is occupied. Bell attendants knock on the guestroom door and announce themselves. If a guest opens the door, they introduce themselves. If no one answers the door, they use the key to unlock and open the door. They then look around the room to determine whether it is occupied and then report their findings to the front desk.

Process and Deliver Mail

At some lodging properties, bell attendants, not front desk employees, process mail, packages, messages, and faxes. There is usually a logbook to record information about mail, packages, messages, etc. that arrive. Bell attendants will log in all guest mail, packages, messages, and facsimiles (faxes) as they arrive, including what arrived (mail, message, package, or fax) and the name of the guest it arrived for. They then find out whether the guest has checked in and arrange to deliver the item or message to the guest. If the guest hasn't arrived, the delivery is stored in a secure place.

Many properties use a time stamp on deliveries or on tags which are then placed on deliveries. This helps answer questions about how promptly items are delivered.

Urgent mail, messages, facsimiles, or packages are given top delivery priority. The content or delivery method usually determines the urgency of the mail, message, fax, or package. For instance, overnight deliveries are considered urgent. The guest may be waiting for the information. Emergency messages may concern life-threatening situations, such as messages regarding an illness or death.

Deliver Express Check-Out Packets to Guests

Most lodging properties now offer express check-out service to guests who have approved credit. Bell attendants deliver **express check-out packets** to guestrooms, usually early in the morning.

The front desk usually has the packets—which contain the guest's charge statement and a blank copy of a guest comment card—arranged by floor and room number so they can be delivered efficiently. Bell attendants slip an express check-out packet under each door, sliding it all the way under. They do not knock on guestroom doors and are careful to place the correct packet under each door.

Process Guest Laundry

At properties that offer laundry service to guests, the bell department coordinates it with the front desk and housekeeping staffs.

Guests will call to request laundry pickup. A bell attendant will then go and pick the laundry up from the guestroom. Bell attendants always take some extra laundry slips with them to guestrooms. A slip should be filled out for each bag of laundry. Some properties will place laundry bags and slips in each guestroom, so that guests can place laundry in the bags, fill out the slip, and have housekeeping pick it up during their daily service.

If guests bring laundry to the bell stand, bell attendants make sure a completed laundry slip is in each bag. The bags are then stored in a secure place until the laundry service picks it up.

Bell attendants sort any incoming clean laundry packages and check off each guest's name in the laundry logbook. The laundry service person takes the laundry invoice to the front desk so that front desk employees can post the charges to the guests' accounts.

When delivering guest laundry, bell attendants arrange laundry packages on a luggage cart by room number.

Deliver Guest Service Equipment and Supplies to Guestrooms

Items that bell attendants may deliver to guestrooms include pillows or other bed linens, towels, ashtrays, cribs, ironing boards, and rollaway beds.

When guests are not in the guestrooms, bell attendants will place the item in an appropriate spot. For instance, they will:

- Place pillows on a bed

- Place towels in the bathroom

- Place ashtrays on a table

If guests are in the guestroom, bell attendants hand items to guests or ask them where they should place items.

For certain items such as cribs, or rollaway beds, bell attendants may set them up. To do so, bell attendants place clean sheets and blankets on the crib mattress or rollaway mattress, and tuck in and straighten the corners of the sheet. Rollaway beds receive an extra pillow. Cribs do not receive pillows.

When delivering a crib or a rollaway bed, bell attendants supply extra towels and soap. When removing the crib or rollaway bed, bell attendants strip the linens and carry it to the housekeeping closet. If it is a folding crib, they fold it first.

Apply Your Learning 9.4

Please write all answers on a separate sheet of paper.

1. Why is it necessary for bell attendants to occasionally check a room to see if it is occupied?

2. How are urgent mail, messages, or packages different from others?

3. What is an express check-out package and what is its purpose?

4. List four guest service items that bell attendants may deliver to guestrooms.

9.5 Duties Performed When Not Assisting Guests

AFTER SUCCESSFULLY COMPLETING THIS SECTION, YOU WILL BE ABLE TO:

♦ Explain the importance of maintaining a clear drive-up/drop-off area.

♦ Describe the procedures for processing lost and found items.

♦ Summarize the procedures for performing general errands.

♦ Explain the importance of cleaning the entrance, lobby, and drive-up areas of the property.

♦ Describe the procedures for reporting vehicle accidents.

Maintain Clear Drive-Up/Drop-Off Area

At properties with valet service and large drive-up areas at the front entrance, bell attendants keep the lanes of drive-up traffic flowing. If the drive-up area gets congested with parked cars, other vehicles won't be able to get through. This could lead to long waits for guests.

Bell attendants can help prevent this in a number of ways.

1. Bell attendants always guide vehicles up to the end of the drive-up area and instruct guests, taxi drivers, and other drivers to pull as far forward as possible. This ensures that the highest number of vehicles possible can fit into the drive-up area.

2. Bell attendants maintain at least one open traffic lane at all times. Most properties providing valet parking have a drive-up area with at least three vehicle lanes. By keeping one lane open, departing vehicles can exit the drive-up area. Vehicles just passing through, bell attendants parking guest vehicles, and emergency vehicles will all make use of the open lane.

3. Bell attendants promptly park guest vehicles. If the guests have luggage to store, bell attendants will pull their vehicle forward before storing the luggage. During busy periods, bell attendants may be able to park a guest's vehicle on their way to retrieve another guest's vehicle.

4. Bell attendants pull up retrieved vehicles in a designated lane. Some properties

may have an outside lane exclusively for guest or vehicle drop-offs.

Process Lost and Found Items

At some lodging properties, bell attendants take care of the lost and found area. Many guests find it convenient to turn found items in to bell attendants.

Bell attendants tag found items and place it in the lost and found area. Many properties use numbered tags to identify items. They will then fill out the lost and found log with information about the found item. This usually includes the following information:

- Item's tag number

- Date and time the item was found

- Description of the item, including color, size, brand, etc.

- Location where item was found

- Who found the item

Lost and found items are always kept in a secure place for at least 90 days. Many states have laws that determine exactly how long found items must be kept. After the 90 days are up, some properties will donate unclaimed items to local charities.

When a guest reports a lost item in person, bell attendants ask the guest to fill out a loss report. If a guest calls on the telephone, bell attendants ask the guest the following questions and record the answers on the loss report:

- What is your name, address, city, state, and zip code?

- What did you lose?

- On what date did you lose the item?

- Where did you lose it?

- What is/was your date of departure?

- What is/was your room number?

- What does the item look like?

- What is your home telephone number?

When a guest claims an item from the lost and found area, bell attendants make sure to establish ownership of the item before returning it to the guest.

Perform Errands

Others at the property may occasionally request that bell attendants run errands for guests or for the lodging property. These services are recorded on the front sheet, including the time it was performed.

If bell attendants must leave the property while performing an errand, they usually inform their supervisor before doing so. When performing errands for the property's managers, bell attendants give the same level of service that they would give to guests. If the request appears to be of a strictly personal nature, such as picking up the manager's children from school in the courtesy van and taking them home, bell attendants check with their own supervisor first. However, it is appropriate for managers to send bell attendants on business-related errands.

Clean Bell Areas

When bell attendants are not assisting guests, they are always on the lookout for anything that could be thrown away or made tidy at the entrance, lobby, and drive-up areas of the property. It is a source of pride for all property employees to keep the property presentable to guests. And since the drive-up and entrance areas are the first part of the lodging property that most guests see, cleanliness and orderliness are critical.

When bell attendants are walking through the drive-up area, they look at it from a guest's perspective. They pick up trash, empty ashtrays, and clean up spills. If needed, they will clean the glass on entrance doors and plate glass windows and dust ledges, benches, and furnishings around the entrance.

At properties with an exterior bell stand, bell attendants keep it clean and orderly at all times. They remove all trash, and dust and polish the exterior surface to remove dirt and fingerprints. All papers are arranged and stored in drawers or on shelves.

Bell attendants clean luggage carts daily. The shelves, frame, and wheels of the luggage cart are cleaned by wiping with a damp cloth. Bell attendants vacuum carpeted carts or sweep them with a stiff broom as needed. Brass luggage carts are polished with an approved brass polish at least once each week. Finally, bell attendants lightly lubricate any squeaky wheels as needed.

Report Vehicle Accidents

Accidents involving bell attendants can happen. When they do, the safety of the bell attendant and any guests involved is of utmost importance.

Bell attendants stop for all accidents they are involved in; this is required by law. Someone at the property is notified immediately, either by radio, cell phone, or by another bell attendant. The property can then notify police and medical help as needed.

Most properties equip their courtesy vehicles with emergency road flares. Bell attendants should place these emergency flares around the accident. Bell attendants ask uninjured passengers to exit and move off the road if the vehicle cannot be moved out of the traffic lane. Until help arrives, bell attendants help injured people or direct traffic around the accident. They also write the names and phone numbers of witnesses, making sure to spell names correctly.

Bell attendants are careful regarding what they say about the accident. They do not sign anything, admit responsibility, or say anything that could put the property at risk. When the investigating police officer arrives, they provide the following information to the officer and other involved drivers:

- The name of the property
- Their complete name and home address
- Their driver's license number and state
- The vehicle registration number
- The registered owner of the vehicle if other than the property

They also collect the following information from the others involved in the accident:

- Driver's name
- Driver's home and business addresses and phone numbers
- Driver's license number and state
- Model and make of vehicle, license plate number, and state
- Vehicle registration number
- Name and address of registered owner if different from driver

- Insurance company and policy number

- Names of all passengers in each vehicle

If any driver refuses to provide information, bell attendants will ask the police officer for help.

Once they are back on property, bell attendants will complete an accident report. They will then meet with management and describe the accident, and draw a diagram of all vehicles and points of contact. The accident report is needed for insurance purposes.

Apply Your Learning 9.5

Please write all answers on a separate sheet of paper.

1. Describe one way that bell attendants can maintain a clear drive-up/drop-off area.

2. List the five items of information that bell attendants make sure to get for a lost item.

3. What should bell attendants do if a manager requests them to perform an errand that appears to be of a personal nature?

4. Why is it important for bell attendants to help maintain the clean appearance of the entrance and lobby areas?

5. What information should bell attendants provide when they have been involved in a vehicle accident?

Quick Hits

SECTION 9.1—GETTING TO KNOW THE BELL ATTENDANT

- Bell attendants are responsible for assisting guests with their luggage and vehicles, and for providing many other important guest services.

- Bell attendants make use of a posting system that provides maximum visibility and opportunity to help guests.

- Bell attendants make use of a logbook and front sheets to keep track of services they perform for guests.

- Successful bell attendants are knowledgeable of what guests want to know and what their interests may be.

- When guests lose their luggage, bell attendants help them find it.

- Bell attendants respect guest property and guest vehicles.

- Because of their access to guests' car keys and guestroom and master keys, bell attendants practice proper key control procedures at all times.

- Bell attendants often receive tips from guests because of the duties they perform. They understand the proper etiquette involved in accepting tips as well as their property's policies regarding sharing and reporting tips.

SECTION 9.2—ASSISTING GUESTS DURING CHECK-IN AND CHECK-OUT

- As guests enter a lodging property, bell attendants make eye contact, greet

them, and provide assistance such as luggage and valet parking service.

- When handling guest luggage, bell attendants practice proper safety procedures so that the guest luggage, and the bell attendant, is not harmed.

- Bell attendants store guest luggage in a secured area. The luggage is properly marked and logged so that the luggage can be retrieved quickly.

- Bell attendants park and retrieve guest vehicles with caution. They take the necessary key control steps so that the vehicle is safe at all times.

- When assisting guests to and from their guestrooms, bell attendants practice exceptional guest service skills; providing both information and service to their guests.

- Bell attendants practice the specific procedures involved with handling luggage service for large groups staying at a lodging property.

SECTION 9.3—ASSISTING GUESTS DURING THEIR STAY

- Occasionally, guests may request a different room other than the one they have received. Bell attendants typically escort these guests from their old room to their new one.

- Bell attendants are often responsible for hailing taxis for guests, or for arranging for taxi or limousine service.

- At some properties, bell attendants will provide courtesy transportation for guests, as needed.

Section 9.4—Assisting the Front Desk

- The front desk may request that bell attendants escort potential guests to a clean, empty room so that the guests can view a room before making reservations.

- At some lodging properties, bell attendants process and deliver guest mail, messages, and packages.

- Bell attendants often deliver express check-out packages, laundry, and guest service equipment and supplies to guestrooms.

Section 9.5—Duties Performed When Not Assisting Guests

- Bell attendants understand the importance of maintaining a clear drive-up and drop-off area so that they can provide luggage and valet assistance at the hotel entrance as efficiently as possible.

- At some lodging properties, bell attendants maintain the lost and found area.

- Bell attendants may perform a number of miscellaneous errands for other hotel employees or management staff. These errands may even take bell attendants off property.

- Bell attendants are constantly maintaining the appearance of the lobby, entrance, and drive-up areas of a property. By picking up trash, emptying ashtrays, and cleaning any spills, they help present a positive first impression of the property to guests.

- When bell attendants are involved in vehicle accidents, they practice proper safety and vehicle reporting procedures.

Guestroom Attendant

Sections

No other feature or service a property provides will impress the guest more than a spotlessly clean and comfortable guestroom. The condition of the guestroom conveys a critical message to guests. It shows the care that the property puts into creating a clean, safe, and pleasant environment for its guests.

This places a big responsibility on guestroom attendants. After all, the guestroom is the main product that a property sells. Housekeeping plays a greater role than any other department in ensuring that this product meets the standards that guests need and expect.

To maintain the standards that keep guests coming back, guestroom attendants must follow a series of detailed procedures for guestroom cleaning. A systematic approach can save time and energy—and reduce frustration. In this respect, room cleaning procedures not only ensure quality for the guest, but ensure efficiency and satisfaction for the employee performing the task.

Guestroom attendants should recognize the value and logic behind the organization of cleaning activities. Sticking to a careful routine can save time and ensure a professional job.

10.1 Getting to Know the Guestroom Attendant

AFTER SUCCESSFULLY COMPLETING THIS SECTION, YOU WILL BE ABLE TO:

♦ Describe the essential role guestroom attendants play in a lodging property.

♦ Provide superior performance standards that enhance the guest's overall experience.

♦ Identify tasks guestroom attendants typically perform at lodging properties.

What Is a Guestroom Attendant?

A guestroom attendant could be defined as a housekeeping department employee who cleans guestrooms. While this definition is technically correct, it doesn't begin to describe the effect guestroom attendants have on guests.

Many studies have shown that clean rooms and public areas are the most important factors in determining whether guests will return to a lodging property. By cleaning guestrooms, attendants make a difference in the success of their property and in the comfort of the guests.

Guestroom attendants have a job to be proud of—without them, the property would be empty. No one would check into a room that had dirty sheets, damp towels, or a bathroom floor with loose hair in the corners.

The guestroom attendant makes sure each guest has a room complete with all the comforts that amenities can offer, and all the warmth that a clean room can bring.

Superior Performance Standards

The condition of each guest's room should enhance the guest's overall experience. Making sure guestrooms are clean, neatly arranged, and inviting at all times is the ultimate goal of a guestroom attendant. Superior performance standards help them achieve that goal.

Guestroom attendants are hired for their ability to meet superior performance standards. What are some of these standards? Guestroom attendants must:

• Thoroughly clean mirrors, glass surfaces, windows (inside and out), ashtrays, walls, telephones, and wastebaskets.

• Thoroughly clean and dust baseboards, pictures, window sills, drapes, chairs (legs and rungs), dressers and drawers, desks and drawers, night stands, lamps, lamp shades, light bulbs, headboards, closet poles and hangers, closet shelves, and televisions.

- Neatly make beds, and make sure there are no stains, holes, or loose threads in bedding materials.

- Thoroughly vacuum guestroom carpeting, and make sure it doesn't have any stains or holes.

- Make sure each guestroom's electrical and mechanical functions are in proper working order.

- Thoroughly clean and sanitize the bathroom.

- Wash hands after taking a break.

- Change their apron after a break if they smoke while on break.

Tip Sharing

Tips are the guests' way of thanking guestroom attendants for a job well done. Guests may leave a tip for guestroom attendants when they check out of the property.

Properties have many different ways for their guestroom attendants to share tips. If tipping is not common at a property, it may be the policy for each guestroom attendant to keep their own tips. However, some properties require guestroom attendants to report all of their tips and share them with other guestroom attendants.

Think about this situation: A guest stays at a property for three nights. John cleans the guest's room after the first two nights and Mariana cleans the room on the last day. The guest leaves a tip before checking out and Mariana keeps it. How does this make John feel? Keeping the few extra dollars from a tip is not worth the bad feelings it could create among co-workers.

Unlike typical property wages, no taxes are withheld from tips. But the federal government still considers tips as income, and guestroom attendants are required to report any tips that add up to $20 or more a month.

Guestroom Attendant Duties

The primary job of a guestroom attendant is to clean the guestroom. This involves them performing many specific tasks in the guestroom and some outside the guestroom to support the cleaning of the room.

Exhibit 1 lists the most common tasks that guestroom attendants are expected to be able to perform and perform well.

Apply Your Learning 10.1

Please write all answers on a separate sheet of paper.

1. What is the guestroom attendant's primary job?

2. Why is the job of guestroom attendant so important to the hotel?

3. List some of the things guestroom attendants are responsible for cleaning.

Exhibit 1
Task List—Guestroom Attendant

1. Use Your Room Assignment Sheet
2. Get Guest Amenities for Assigned Rooms
3. Get Cleaning Supplies for Assigned Rooms
4. Keep Your Cart and Work Areas Organized
5. Enter the Guestroom
6. Prepare the Guestroom for Cleaning
7. Begin to Clean the Bathroom
8. Clean the Tub and Shower Area
9. Clean the Toilet
10. Clean the Sink and Vanity
11. Clean the Bathroom Floor
12. Finish Cleaning the Bathroom
13. Clean the Guestroom Closet
14. Make the Bed
15. Dust the Guestroom
16. Replenish Supplies and Amenities
17. Clean Windows, Tracks, and Sills
18. Put Finishing Touches on the Guestroom
19. Vacuum the Guestroom and Report Room Status
20. Exit the Guestroom
21. Correct Cleaning Problems Found During Inspection
22. Complete End-of-Shift Duties
23. Rotate and Flip Mattresses
24. Set Up or Remove Special Guest Service Equipment
25. Clean Multi-Room Guest Suites
26. Provide Evening Turn-Down Service

10.2 Preparing to Clean

AFTER SUCCESSFULLY COMPLETING THIS SECTION, YOU WILL BE ABLE TO:

♦ Explain how to use a room assignment sheet.

♦ Describe ways to stock a cart.

♦ Identify the correct method for entering a guestroom.

♦ Describe how to handle unusual guestroom situations.

Use Room Assignment Sheet

The **room assignment sheet** lists all the rooms that each guestroom attendant needs to clean during his or her shift. It typically includes room status codes and terms that can help a guestroom attendant decide which rooms to clean first.

Guestroom attendants' jobs go more quickly and easily when they use short codes for room status terms. Each property uses a different code for terms. See Exhibit 1 for room status explanations.

Guestroom attendants can keep track of their work on the room assignment sheet by writing the correct codes in the status column. They will mark whether a room is occupied or vacant when they clean it. This also helps the front desk update room statuses for arriving guests.

Exhibit 2 provides a step-by-step breakdown of how to use a room assignment sheet.

Get Guest Amenities for Assigned Rooms

The guestroom attendant is responsible for putting guest amenities into each room. **Guest amenities** are delivered to each guestroom on an amenity caddy on the cart. **Amenity caddies** are the containers that hold amenities and are usually stocked centrally in the housekeeping department.

An amenity caddy may contain:

- Breakfast menus
- Stationery folders
- Guest comment cards
- Arrival magazines
- Stationery paper
- Stationery envelopes
- Wastebasket liners
- Room service menus
- Pens
- Deodorant soap bars
- Hand soap bars
- Notepads
- Plastic cups or glassware lids

Exhibit 1
Room Status Explanations

Term	What It Means
Early make-up requests	Guestroom attendants can help make a guest's stay an excellent one. When a guest requests an early make-up, or puts the "make up room" sign on the doorknob, guestroom attendants have the opportunity to shine by cleaning this room first.
VIP rooms	Many properties have "very important persons" who receive extra attention. Guestroom attendants are a big part of making these guests feel at home.
Blocked rooms	These rooms have been set aside for guests with special requests—connecting rooms, nonsmoking rooms, etc. When guestroom attendants clean these rooms together, they are helping the front desk meet guests' special requests.
Vacant and dirty rooms	Cleaning vacant rooms before stayover rooms helps arriving guests get into their rooms more quickly. Guestroom attendants provide quality guest service by making rooms available as soon as possible. These rooms are also called check-out rooms.
Stayover rooms	These rooms can be done later in a shift, because the guest has already unpacked and probably isn't waiting for the guestroom attendant to clean.
Late check-out rooms	Guestroom attendants can save themselves time and energy by cleaning these rooms late in the shift. They should not need to be cleaned until the guest has left.
DND (Do not disturb)	The property always respects the guests' wishes in these rooms. If the sign is still up after checkout time in a room where the guest is due to check-out, guestroom attendants should inform their supervisor.
No-service room	If a guest requests that a room not be cleaned, the guestroom attendant should tell his or her supervisor and mark the sheet. The supervisor will find out whether there is another time to clean or if there are any special requests.

Exhibit 2
Use Your Room Assignment Sheet

Materials needed: A room assignment sheet and a pen.

STEPS:	HOW-TO'S:
1. Review your room assignment sheet before beginning to clean. At the beginning of your shift, you will receive a room assignment sheet that lists the rooms you need to clean. The sheet also has a place to indicate the condition of each room at the end of your shift.	
2. Set priorities for cleaning assigned rooms using the codes in the sheet's "A.M. Status" column.	
3. After you clean a room, note under "HSKP Status" whether the room is vacant clean or occupied clean.	
4. Write any housekeeping or maintenance needs beyond your routine duties.	
5. Handle rooms that display "Do Not Disturb" signs or have guests who refuse service.	❑ If you see a "Do Not Disturb" sign, check back later. ❑ Report to your supervisor rooms that: • Show a "Do Not Disturb" sign at the end of the shift • Have guests who tell you they don't want service • Are double-locked Your supervisor will verify that the guest requested no service; will schedule an alternate time for cleaning; and will tell you about any special guest requests.

- Shampoo bottles
- Hand lotions
- Shoe mitts
- Valet laundry bags
- Trash bags

Get Cleaning Supplies for Assigned Rooms

Cleaning supply caddies, like amenity caddies, are restocked in the housekeeping department. A fully stocked cleaning caddy may contain the following:

- Spray bottle of all-purpose cleaner
- Spray bottle of glass cleaner
- Furniture polish
- Other approved cleaning chemicals
- Scouring sponge
- Scrub brush
- Cleaning cloths
- Johnny mop (a Johnny mop is a special brush used for cleaning toilets. It can pump the water and swab the toilet)

Keep Carts and Work Areas Organized

Carts are typically stored in the linen room along with the housekeeping supplies. Most carts have three shelves—the lower two for linen and the top for supplies.

It is important to stock a cart correctly. Overstocking increases the risk that some items will be damaged, soiled, or stolen. An under stocked cart means that a guestroom attendant will have to return to the supply closet, increasing the time it takes to clean rooms.

Items typically found on a guestroom attendant's cart include:

- Clean sheets, pillowcases, and mattress pads
- Clean towels and washcloths
- Clean bath mats
- Toilet and facial tissue
- Fresh drinking glasses
- Soap bars
- Clean ashtrays and matches
- Hand caddy with cleaning supplies
- Amenity caddy with amenities

Each property will have a specific way that they stock their carts depending on the make and model of a cart. Some general guidelines for stocking a cart include:

- Use a checklist.
- Count the linens so that the number equals the number of rooms on the room assignment list plus a few extras in case of damaged or stained linen.
- Stack the linens so that the folds face outward. This will make it easier to remove them and easier to count them.
- Keep your cart clean by wiping it at the end of each shift.
- Keep glasses on a shelf at least six inches above cleaning supplies.

See Exhibit 3 for a step-by-step breakdown on keeping a cart and work areas organized.

**Exhibit 3
Keep Your Cart and Work Areas Organized**

Materials needed: A stocked housekeeping cart and supplies to restock your cart at the end of your shift.

STEPS:	HOW-TO'S:
1. **Check the supplies on your housekeeping cart.**	❑ Make sure you have a guest amenity caddy and a cleaning supply caddy.
	❑ Make sure you have enough linens, towels, and other supplies.
	❑ Stock items on your cart as your supervisor directs.
2. **Dump soiled linens often.**	❑ Dump linens often to reduce the weight of your cart and help the laundry department keep up with its work.
	❑ Dump soiled linens every two or three hours. A good guideline is to empty linens at 10 A.M., before your lunch break, at 2 P.M., and at the end of the workday.
3. **Restock your cart at the end of your shift.**	❑ Reorganize and clean your cart at the end of your shift. Your cart tells a lot about you. Keep it neat and well-maintained throughout the day. A clean, well-organized cart will help you work better and look neater to guests.
	❑ Load fresh linens
	❑ Empty trash and reline your garbage bag.
	❑ Keep chemicals at least four inches away from clean glassware.
4. **Keep the linen closet clean at all times.**	❑ Store personal items in your locker or other assigned areas. Do not store personal or flammable items in the linen closet.
	❑ Dust and sweep the linen closet when the housekeeping department schedules it.
5. **Keep work areas secure.**	

Cleaning Sequence

Guestroom attendants follow a system to produce spotlessly clean guestrooms every time. A plan saves time and prevents the guestroom attendant from overlooking a cleaning task—or even from cleaning an area twice.

To be most effective, guestroom cleaning should be logical and follow a flow from entering the guestroom to the final check and departure. Exhibit 4 shows a general sequence that some properties follow for guestroom cleaning tasks.

Enter a Guestroom

Guestroom cleaning begins the moment the guestroom attendant approaches the guestroom door. It is important to follow certain procedures when entering the guestroom that show respect for the guest's privacy.

Exhibit 5 shows a step-by-step breakdown for entering a guestroom.

For many years, the standard in the hospitality industry was for guestroom attendants to leave the door open with the cart in front of it while cleaning. This let the guest know that the room was being cleaned and gave the guestroom attendant easy access to the cart. However, concerns for security have started to change this standard. Now, many properties require that guestroom attendants lock themselves in guestrooms while they clean. This helps protect the guestroom attendant from harm and makes it more difficult for anyone to steal things from the room while the guestroom attendant is cleaning.

Unusual Guestroom Situations

Guestroom attendants often have bizarre stories to tell of what they've found in

Exhibit 4
Cleaning Sequence

Step 1: Enter the guestroom.

Step 2: Begin cleaning. Tidy and air out the room.

Step 3: Strip bed.

Step 4: Clean the bathroom.

Step 5: Make the bed.

Step 6: Dust the guestroom.

Step 7: Vacuum.

Step 8: Make the final check.

Step 9: Close the door and make sure it is locked.

Step 10: Note or report room status and proceed to the next room.

guestrooms. Guestroom attendants respond to a lot of different situations. While they can't predict everything, they can try to be as prepared as possible. That way, they are able to respond calmly and reduce their stress level.

Here are some suggestions for responding to unusual guestroom situations:

- *Sick guest.* Ask if the guest wants medical attention. If so, call the PBX operator and explain the situation to him or her right away. If there is vomit to clean up, wear gloves, goggles, and aprons, and follow the other bloodborne pathogen safety procedures.

- *Dead guest.* Leave the room right away. Don't touch anything in the guestroom.

Exhibit 5
Enter the Guestroom

Materials needed: A stocked housekeeping cart, a room assignment sheet, a pen, a doorstop, and your housekeeping key.

STEPS:	HOW-TO'S:
1. Find out if the guest is in the room.	❑ If a "Do Not Disturb" sign is on the doorknob, return later. A policy at many properties is to never knock on a door or call a room when a "Do Not Disturb" sign is displayed.
	❑ If the sign is still on the door when all your other rooms are done, ask your supervisor to find out if the room is occupied. The guest may have forgotten the sign.
	❑ If the lock system has a pin to show that the room is locked from the inside, return later.
2. Announce yourself before entering the room	❑ Knock on the door with your knuckles and say "Housekeeping." Don't use a housekeeping key or other metal object to knock on the door. These objects will damage the door's surface.
	❑ If no one answers, knock again and say "Housekeeping."
	❑ Use your housekeeping key to unlock the door.
	❑ As you open the door, loudly say "Housekeeping" and turn on the room's entrance light.
3. Find out when you can clean if the guest is in the	❑ Introduce yourself and politely ask when you may clean the room.
	❑ If the guest gives a later time, note that time on your room assignment sheet. Thank the guest, leave, and return at that time.
	❑ If a guest in a stayover room says you may clean now, do so.

(continued)

Exhibit 5
Enter the Guestroom *(continued)*

STEPS:	HOW-TO'S:
	❑ Sometimes a guest will be sleeping or in the bathroom. If so, leave quietly, close the door, and return later to clean the room.
4. **Prop the guestroom door open with a doorstop.**	❑ Never use a towel or your vacuum cleaner as a doorstop.
	❑ If you see a guestroom door propped open and there is no guest or employee in the room or in the immediate area, please close the door.
5. **Position your cart.**	❑ Place your cart in front of the open guestroom door. Positioning your cart properly is one of the best ways to prevent an intruder from entering a room. Also, it gives you easy access to your supplies.
	❑ Keep the open side of the cart toward the room.
	❑ Some properties require room attendants to place a "Maid on Duty" sign on the door and close the door when working in an occupied room. If so, put your cart in the guestroom.

Call security and the PBX operator. They will handle the situation.

- *Firearms, illegal substances, or large amounts of cash.* Guestroom attendants need to protect themselves by letting their supervisor know right away when they find these things.

- *Sleeping guest.* Some guests are sound sleepers and won't hear knocking. When this happens, provide quality service by quietly leaving the room and marking on the sheet the time you tried to clean the room and why you were unable to do so.

- *Guest who wants to stay while you clean.* Some properties allow guestroom attendants to clean a room while a guest is in it. To protect the guestroom attendant, some properties have a policy that two guestroom attendants will work together whenever a guest is in the room. However, you should do this only if you feel safe and should leave the room if you become uncomfortable.

- *Intoxicated guest.* Drunken guests represent a danger to guestroom attendants. Protect yourself by leaving the room immediately.

- *Abused guestroom.* Some guests will destroy a room just for fun. This is costly to the property, and it takes a lot longer to clean that room. Guestroom attendants inform their supervisor about the abused room so that someone else can clean some of their other scheduled rooms while they work on the damaged room. Also, the front desk may be able to charge the guests for the damage.

- *Partially dressed guest.* The guest may not have heard the knock or may have ignored it. Whatever the reason, apologize for the interruption and leave quickly. Never gamble with your safety.

- *Guest who suggests a sexual encounter.* Guestroom attendants must quickly and politely refuse the suggestion and leave immediately. Any such suggestion should be reported to a supervisor and possibly to security.

- *Flooded bathroom.* This may happen from a toilet overflow or leaky plumbing. Inform maintenance immediately. They will probably take the room out of service to fix it.

- *Unauthorized pet.* Report to your supervisor or the front desk any pets or signs of pets. You may be given specific policies about what to do, though you should never risk a bite or scratch while cleaning.

Apply Your Learning 10.2

Please write all answers on a separate sheet of paper. Put the rooms in the order that they should be cleaned according to their status.

1. Room 101 Stayover

2. Room 102 Blocked for incoming group manager

3. Room 103 Vacant and dirty

4. Room 104 Do not disturb

5. Room 105 Late check-out

6. Room 106 VIP room

7. Room 107 No service room

8. Room 108 Early makeup request

10.3 Cleaning the Guestroom

AFTER SUCCESSFULLY COMPLETING THIS SECTION, YOU WILL BE ABLE TO:

♦ Explain how to prepare a guestroom for cleaning.

♦ Describe the process for cleaning the guestroom closet.

♦ Explain how to make a bed.

♦ Describe the process for dusting a guestroom.

♦ Identify ways to replenish supplies and amenities.

♦ Explain how to clean windows, tracks, and sills.

♦ Identify ways to put finishing touches on a guestroom.

♦ Describe how to exit a guestroom.

Prepare the Guestroom for Cleaning

Once guestroom attendants enter the guestroom, they must work efficiently to clean. They begin by setting up supplies and equipment such as the vacuum cleaner and the cleaning supply caddy in the room where they will be most useful.

They then turn on lights and replace any burned-out or missing light bulbs. This is also the time when they check the television, remote control, and radio to make sure it works. However, after checking them, they always turn them off while cleaning. If a guest returns while guestroom attendants are cleaning and the television or radio is on, it will look like they are entertaining themselves rather than working efficiently.

Guestroom attendants also open the drapes and check the rods, cords, or wands. In full-service hotels, guestroom attendants may also need to gather room service equipment and move it to outside the guestroom door. They first check to make sure there are no guest items on it.

Stripping the bed right away—removing the bedspread, blanket, pillows, and sheets—allows it to air while the guestroom attendants clean the bathroom. Guestroom attendants wear heavy latex utility gloves during this step to protect them from exposure to any body fluids in bed linens. All linens are placed on a chair or table to protect them from being damaged and prevent the guestroom attendant from tripping over them.

All soiled linen from the bed and from the bathroom are then removed and placed in the linen bag on the cart. This is also a good time to remove used guest amenities and drinking glasses, collect trash, and empty ashtrays.

Clean the Guestroom Closet

Although guestroom attendants normally avoid moving any guest items, they do have to remove wet items that are hanging in the closet and hang them on the bathroom showerhead or shower curtain bar. Guests may hang wet bathing suits or other wet items in the closet. Dripping water from these items will damage the carpet.

If guest clothing is not on the luggage rack, the rack is wiped with a damp sponge or dusted with a dust cloth. The closet shelf and door are then wiped with a damp sponge. Any missing or rumpled laundry bags and slips are then replaced.

Every property has a standard number of hangers. The guestroom attendant counts the hangers and replaces any that are missing.

Make the Bed

Properties differ on whether the bed should be made immediately—so that any returning guest will see a freshly made bed, giving the room a neat appearance—or whether the bed should be made after the bathroom is cleaned so that it has time to air.

Many properties upgraded their beds and now require guestroom attendants to triple sheet the bed—add an extra sheet above the blanket that is folded over the edge. These properties often also add extra pillows, dust shams, and larger, down-filled comforters.

Exhibit 1 gives the step-by-step breakdown of how to make a bed.

Dust the Guestroom

A guestroom attendant begins dusting by spraying a clean cloth with a dusting solution. The most efficient way to dust is to follow a system of starting at one side of the room and working around in a circle from the top down.

Some of the things that guestroom attendants dust include:

- Doors
- Walls and ceiling moldings
- Mirrors
- Pictures
- Drapes
- Dressers
- Nightstands and beds
- Telephones
- Tables, chairs, and lamps
- Television and stand

The guestroom attendant will also set the air conditioner and heater controls to property standards in a check-out room. In an occupied room, the settings are left the way the guest had them.

Replenish Supplies and Amenities

The guestroom attendant will check and replace as needed the room supplies and amenities such as:

- Gideon Bible
- The Book of Mormon
- Writing supplies (envelopes, stationery, notepads, pens)
- Guest comment cards
- Glasses
- Travel magazines
- Room service menus

Clean Windows, Tracks, and Sills

Guestroom attendants are responsible for cleaning and polishing windows. This is usually done with either water or an approved glass cleaner and a clean cloth. A fresh cloth is then used to polish the windows once they are clean. If the outsides of windows need cleaning, it will be noted on the room assignment sheet.

Guestroom attendants also need to remove any built-up dirt from window tracks and sills with a small brush and then wipe it with a damp cloth.

Any possible safety or security problems with windows need to be reported to a supervisor right away while other maintenance needs are typically noted on the room assignment sheet.

Put Finishing Touches on the Guestroom

Additional cleaning tasks in a guestroom might include:

- Vacuuming or dusting upholstery

- Cleaning balconies and patios

- Checking all room clocks in check-out rooms to be sure they are set correctly

- Making a final check that all supplies and equipment are properly loaded back on the cart and that no cleaning supplies or trash is left behind in the guestroom

The guestroom attendant's last impression of the room will be the guest's first impression. Sometimes using a room inspection form can help an inexperienced guestroom attendant make sure that all of the details have been completed.

If the air smells odd, the guestroom attendant sprays air freshener.

The guestroom attendant also secures any guestroom keys that were left behind by putting them in a lock box or a secure place on the cart.

Vacuum the Guestroom and Report Room Status

Before vacuuming each day, the guestroom attendants check to make sure the vacuum cleaner bag is empty and replace or empty it if it is full. They also check it for safety, removing knots and tangles from cords and turning off any equipment that sparks, smokes, or flames.

A vacuum cleaner should not be used if the cord is damaged. The guestroom attendant could be injured or a short could start a fire.

Before vacuuming, guestroom attendants use a small, stiff broom to brush dirt away from room corners and carpet edges to a carpeted area that the vacuum can reach. The vacuum cleaner is then plugged into the outlet nearest the guestroom door.

Guestroom attendants begin vacuuming the room at the point farthest from the guestroom door. They then work back toward the guestroom door so that they can vacuum over their footsteps.

Chairs and tables are moved if necessary to vacuum underneath them. While vacuuming, the guestroom attendant typically checks under and behind the dressers, nightstands, and beds for trash and left-behind items. Any lamps or light switches that are on are turned off as the guestroom attendant vacuums past them.

Once guestroom attendants have completely vacuumed the guest room, they record the room status on their sheets or call in to the property management system to report the room is clean.

Exit the Guestroom

Finally, the guestroom attendant turns out the lights at the door, closes the guestroom door and makes sure it is locked. They then wipe any fingerprints or other marks from the guestroom door.

Apply Your Learning 10.3

Please write all answers on a separate sheet of paper.

1. What tasks should a guestroom attendant perform upon first entering a guestroom?

2. What is mitering?

3. What is the most efficient way to dust a guestroom?

4. What should a guestroom attendant do if the vacuum sparks or smokes?

Exhibit 1
Make the Bed

Materials needed: A mattress pad, clean linens, and a room assignment sheet.

STEPS:	HOW-TO'S:
1. **Check the mattress pad, mattress, and box springs.**	❑ Look at the mattress pad to see if it is stained, torn, or damaged. If it is not, straighten it and make sure the mattress and box spring are even. Adjust them if necessary. Whenever you adjust the mattress, lift with your legs, not your back, to avoid injuries.
	❑ If the mattress pad is stained, torn, or damaged, remove it.
	❑ Look at the mattress and box springs to see if they are also stained, torn, or damaged. Tell your supervisor about any problems right away.
	❑ If the mattress and box springs are not stained or damaged, make sure the mattress and box springs are even. Adjust the mattress as needed.
	❑ Get a clean mattress pad from the linen closet. Mattress pads are about the same size as the mattress. Different size pads are required for double and king-size beds. Be sure to get the correct size. Place it on the mattress:
	• Lay the fresh pad on the bed
	• Unfold the pad right-side up and spread it evenly over the center of the bed
	• Smooth out wrinkles
2. **Center the bottom sheet on the mattress so that an equal amount of sheet hangs over each side of the bed.**	
3. **Miter the bed corners.**	❑ Tuck the bottom sheet along one side of the bed except for the corners. Do not use a stained or torn sheet. Place it in your soiled linen bag.

(continued)

Exhibit 1
Make the Bed (continued)

STEPS:	HOW-TO'S:
	❑ Take the loose end of the sheet, about a foot from the corner at the head of the bed, and pull it straight out, forming a flap. Pull up the flap so it is flat.
	❑ Tuck in the free part at the corner.
	❑ Pull the flap out toward you and down over the side of the bed. Tuck the flap in.
	❑ Move to the corner at the foot of the bed on the same side of the bed, and repeat the procedure.
	❑ Move to the other side of the bed. Miter both corners.
4. **Put the top sheet on the bed.**	❑ Center the top sheet on the bed with the hem-side up.
	❑ Position the sheet so that the top edge is at the top of the mattress.
5. **Put the blanket on the bed.**	❑ Arrange the blanket so that its top edge is about one palm-length below the top of the sheet.
	❑ Fold the top edge of the sheet over the top edge of the blanket. Smooth the sheet and blanket. By folding the top sheet over the top edge of the blanket, guests may pull the blanket up around their neck without touching the blanket. This keeps the blanket cleaner and protects it from added wear.
	❑ Go to the foot of the bed. Tuck in the sheet and blanket smoothly.
	❑ Miter the corners of the blanket and sheet together at the foot of the bed. Do not tuck in the sides of the top sheet.

(continued)

Exhibit 1
Make the Bed *(continued)*

STEPS:	HOW-TO'S:
6. **Put pillowcases on the pillows.**	❑ Insert pillows into the pillowcases and tuck in the loose ends. Double beds often have two standard-size pillows. King-size beds have three standard-size pillows or two king-size pillows.
	❑ Place the pillows on the bed with the tucked edges, facing the center and the tucked flaps on the underside of the pillows. Use your hands, not your chin or teeth, to put pillows into pillowcases.
7. **Put the bedspread on the bed.**	❑ Position the bedspread on the bed with equal amounts hanging over both sides and the foot of the bed.
	❑ Smooth the bedspread over the pillows to the head of the bed. Notify your supervisor if there are stains on or tears in the bedspread.
	❑ Tuck the remainder of the bedspread under the front edge of the pillows.
	❑ Smooth the surface of the bed.
	❑ Check the bedspread for evenness on both sides and at the foot of the bed.
8. **Place menus or property materials on the bed. Sometimes important materials with information about fire exits or emergency procedures will be placed on pillows so that guests will be sure to see them.**	
9. **Make sofa beds.**	❑ Sheets and blankets, but not bedspreads, are used on sofa beds. Your room assignment sheet will tell you whether you are to set up a sofa bed.

(continued)

Exhibit 1
Make the Bed *(continued)*

STEPS:	HOW-TO'S:
	❑ Follow the same basic procedures for making a standard bed. Place the blanket, and tuck it and the top sheets tightly at the foot, and then on both sides of the bed. Sheets may be larger than the sofa bed mattress and may require special care when tucking on all sides to give a smooth appearance.
	❑ Place the pillows neatly on the bed and check the overall appearance of the bed.
	❑ Leave the completed bed open.
	❑ If a guest plans to use the room during the day, remove the pillows, make the bed, then fold it into a sofa. In this case, place the pillows on the closet shelf or in a bottom dresser drawer.
10. **Set up Murphey or Sico fold-up beds.**	❑ Be careful to avoid injury when opening Murphey or Sico fold-up beds. Make sure everything is out of the way before you lower the bed. Your room assignment sheet will tell you if you are to set up a Murphey or Sico bed.
	❑ Open Murphey or Sico beds completely and then make them up like a sofa bed. A Murphey or Sico bed folds up into the wall and looks like a bookshelf when it is put away
	❑ Fold up the bed.
	❑ Put clean pillowcases on the pillows and store them in the closet or in a bottom dresser drawer.

10.4 Cleaning the Bathroom

AFTER SUCCESSFULLY COMPLETING THIS SECTION, YOU WILL BE ABLE TO:

♦ Describe how to clean a tub and shower area.

♦ Explain how to clean the toilet.

♦ Explain how to clean the sink and vanity.

♦ Identify ways to clean the bathroom floor.

Cleaning the bathroom is an important part of the work of a guestroom attendant. It is also one where safe work practices are especially important. Guestroom attendants need to work carefully to avoid injuring themselves by falling, strains, or chemical misuse.

Begin to Clean the Bathroom

There are several special tasks that a guestroom attendant may need to do when cleaning a bathroom. These include soaking soiled ashtrays, cleaning vents, and cleaning the ceiling. These tasks are almost always done first so that the rest of the bathroom is not dirtied by these tasks.

Hair dryers can cause hair to blow against and cling to the ceiling—which means guestroom attendants will need to use a feather duster or dry cleaning cloth on a broom to remove hair, dust, lint, and

cobwebs from the ceiling. It is important that guestroom attendants stand on the floor to clean. They should not climb on the toilet or the edge of the bathtub nor should they use chairs from the guestroom for cleaning the bathroom ceiling. Detailed cleaning is important, but personal safety is more important. If needed, a public space cleaner can help a guestroom attendant by providing a ladder and holding it in place.

Clean the Tub and Shower Area

Guestroom attendants will typically place guest belongings left in the bathtub on the vanity with other toiletries while scrubbing the tile and bath area. If there is guest clothing left in the tub or shower area, it is often moved out of the way until guestroom attendants have finished cleaning.

Guestroom attendants begin by removing hair from the tub or shower with a tissue and using a soap and water solution to scrub the grout, soap dish, fixtures, faucets, showerhead, shower towel rack, and tub. Shower doors are wiped carefully with a cleaning solution and a sponge. They then clean the track with a brush and wipe all surfaces with a dry cloth.

The next task is to clean the shower curtain liner. This is done with a cleaning solution and sponge. If a shower curtain is stained or damaged, it will have to be replaced.

To scrub the tub and skid strips, guestroom attendants run about one inch of water into the tub. They then add cleaning solution and scrub the strips as necessary with a scrub brush or sponge. They spray the remainder of the tub with an all-purpose cleaner and wipe it with a cleaning cloth.

Fixtures are polished with a dry cloth. Abrasive cleaning compounds or vinegar and water solutions on chrome fixtures can damage them and must be avoided.

Clean the Toilet

Protective gloves and goggles are an essential part of toilet cleaning. Guestroom attendants must protect themselves from bloodborne pathogens and chemicals.

The cleaning begins by testing to make sure the toilet flushes and then spraying cleaning solution on the inside and outside of the toilet, the walls beside and behind the toilet, and under the vanity.

The most sanitary system for cleaning a toilet is to begin on the outside and work inward. Guestroom attendants wipe the outside of the toilet bowl and the walls around the toilet with a damp sponge that is used for cleaning only the toilet. They also wipe the pipes leading to the toilet and then rinse the sponge in the toilet.

A toilet bowl brush is used to scrub the inside of the toilet bowl and under the rim and seat. A dry cloth is then used to wipe the outside of the toilet and polish the walls and pipes. Most properties recommend leaving the cleaning solution in the toilet water until after all the other tasks in the bathroom are done. This gives the chemicals a chance to work on the toilet.

Clean the Sink and Vanity

In stayover rooms, guestroom attendants should handle the guest's toiletries as little as possible, though they may have to clear a spot on the vanity to wash it. If so, properties usually ask guestroom attendants to place a clean washcloth or hand towel on the vanity and move the guest's toiletries to the washcloth or towel.

A sponge is used to wipe the light fixture, towel racks, and other bathroom fixtures. If there are ashtrays in the room, they should be washed with a sponge, rinsed out in the sink and dried with a clean cloth. Wastebaskets should also be washed in the sink. Ashtrays should be placed in the wastebasket and set aside until the rest of the bathroom is cleaned. This saves guestroom attendants extra trips in and out of the bathroom.

The next step is to spray cleaning solution on the sink, stopper, overflow and main sink drains, fixtures, and vanity. Guestroom attendants use a stiff brush to clean overflow holes in the sink where dirt often collects. Then a sponge is used to wipe all surfaces. The final step is to polish the area with a dry cloth to prevent water spots.

Clean the Bathroom Floor

The steps to cleaning a bathroom floor are:

- Spray the bathroom floor and baseboards with an all-purpose cleaning solution

- Scrub away grime

- Dry the floor with a clean cloth

Many properties recommend that guestroom attendants kneel on a towel while washing the floor to protect their knees and keep them from slipping. Also, it is important to start with the farthest corner and work toward the door while scrubbing the floor with a sponge or cleaning cloth.

Baseboards can be wiped as the guestroom attendant moves backward.

Special attention must be paid to the areas around the toilet, behind the door, and in corners.

Finish Cleaning the Bathroom

Other tasks in the bathroom include:

- *Cleaning mirrors.* Mirrors are cleaned with a damp sponge and water only. Glass cleaner is not recommended for cleaning mirrors because it may leave streaks.

- *Cleaning the ice bucket and replacing water glasses.* Used glassware should be removed. Glasses and covers should never be wiped out and reused. Glassware must be washed and sanitized through a dishwasher to meet sanitation codes and ensure guest safety.

- *Picking up supplies and restocking fresh bath towels and washcloths.* To work efficiently, guestroom attendants want to make every trip in and out of the room count. Therefore, guestroom attendants will often pick up clean bed linens when they get the towels to save them a trip when they make the bed.

- *Restocking paper bath supplies.* Guestroom attendants must check the supply level of facial tissues and toilet paper. Tissues are folded into a VIP point as are toilet paper rolls. Attention to details, such as the supply of facial or toilet tissue, is very important.

- *Restocking guest bathroom amenities.* Guest bathroom amenities will always include a bar of soap. Other amenities vary by property.

- *Returning the clean bathroom wastebasket and ashtrays to their correct locations.*

Apply Your Learning 10.4

For each of the following statements, write "true" if the statement is correct or "false" if the statement is wrong. Please write all answers on a separate sheet of paper.

1. Room attendants should stand on the toilet when cleaning the ceiling.
2. Guest clothing left in the tub or shower area is usually moved out of the way until cleaning is complete.
3. Goggles are not necessary when cleaning a toilet, but rubber gloves are.
4. Light fixtures are cleaned with a sponge.
5. Bathroom floors are cleaned with water only and a damp cloth.
6. Glass cleaner is used to clean mirrors.
7. Room attendants often pick up clean bed linens when they get towels for the bathroom.
8. Every property has the same type of amenities for the bathroom.

10.5 Special Guestroom Attendant Duties

AFTER SUCCESSFULLY COMPLETING THIS SECTION, YOU WILL BE ABLE TO:

♦ Identify how to correct cleaning problems found during inspection.

♦ List end-of-shift duties.

♦ Explain how to set up or remove special guest service equipment.

♦ Describe how to clean multi-room guest suites.

♦ Explain how to provide evening turn-down service.

The primary task of a guestroom attendant is to clean the guestroom. However, there are several other tasks that guestroom attendants may be asked to do during their shift. These tasks include:

• Correcting problems found during inspection

• Performing end-of-shift duties

• Setting up or removing special guest service equipment used in guestrooms

• Cleaning multi-room guest suites

• Providing evening turn-down service

Correct Cleaning Problems Found During Inspection

When a guestroom attendant gets a less-than-perfect score on inspection, they end up doing extra work. Doing it right the first time makes guestroom attendants feel less tired at the end of a shift and makes the property more profitable.

When a supervisor or inspector finds a cleaning problem, the guestroom attendant needs to go back to the room and correct that problem. Once the problem is corrected, the guestroom attendant notes the correction on the room assignment sheet and moves on to the next room.

Complete End-of-Shift Duties

At the end of the shift, there are several tasks a guestroom attendant needs to do to finish up and prepare for the next day. These tasks include:

• Empty dirty linens and trash bags from the housekeeping cart

• Restock the housekeeping cart

• Clean the vacuum cleaner

• Clean and arrange the housekeeping closet as needed

- Take supplies and amenities back to the housekeeping department

- Find out if the supervisor has any other tasks to complete

- Sign in the housekeeping key with at least one witness present

- Return any guestroom keys collected while cleaning

- Get a package pass, if the property uses it, for anything that will be taken from the property

Set Up or Remove Special Guest Service Equipment

It is usually the housekeeping department that is responsible for placing such special guest service equipment as cribs, rollaway beds, bed boards, and irons and ironing boards (if not already kept in the room).

Cribs and crib linens will usually be stored in the housekeeping closets. Some guests may request cribs when they make reservations. If so, the room will be marked on the room assignment sheet. Cribs should be placed where they won't block the main walkway that leads to the guestroom door. Clean sheets and blankets are placed on the crib mattress. Pillows are not supplied with a crib.

Many properties direct guestroom attendants to place extra towels in the bathroom whenever a crib is delivered.

When a crib is being removed from a room, all linens should be stripped from it when the bed is stripped.

Bed boards are usually stored in housekeeping closets or a nearby storage closet. Bed boards are placed between the mattress and box springs on the side of the bed with the phone or television remote control.

Irons and ironing boards are usually stored in housekeeping closets, storage closets, or in the main housekeeping office. Ironing boards should be set up near a wall socket in a place where it does not block the main walkway. When removing an iron and ironing board, the guestroom attendant must empty the water from a steam iron before placing it on the cart or into storage.

Rollaway beds and linens are usually stored in the housekeeping closet. The process for setting up a rollaway bed will vary according to the model the hotel has purchased. Also, in some properties, it may be standard procedure to make the rollaway bed in the housekeeping closet before delivering it to the room. If not, it will need to be made up in the room.

Clean Multi-Room Guest Suites

VIP guests most frequently use multi-room suites, so guestroom attendants must pay close attention to details in these rooms. When guestroom attendants are assigned to clean multi-room suites, they will be assigned fewer rooms than usual.

For the most part, the same procedures used to clean a standard room will be used to clean a suite. If there are live plants, they will need to be carefully cleaned and watered without damaging the leaves or stems.

It may also be necessary to clean wet bars and kitchenettes. Clean cloths and cleaning solutions will be used to clean all surfaces in wet bar and kitchen areas. The cleaning supplies for the kitchenette areas must not be mixed with the bathroom supplies. Special sanitary cloths will be provided for polishing surfaces and fixtures. If there is an ice tray in the freezer, the guestroom attendant should fill it.

Provide Evening Turn-Down Service

Turn-down service is a special service provided to VIP guests. It is called such because the guestroom attendant turns down the bedspread and blankets on the bed. Turning down the bed involves:

- Folding back the top of the bedspread

- Pulling the top corner of the top sheets and blanket back to form a triangle

- Turning down both sides if two people are sharing a bed

- Fluffing the pillows so that they look fresh and firm

- Leaving a terry bathrobe neatly folded on the foot of the bed (not all properties do this)

Some properties provide turn-down amenities such as a flower, a piece of chocolate, or pieces of candy. Along with the amenity, the guestroom attendant may place a note or business card from the general manager or director of sales and marketing.

The guestroom attendant will also tidy the room while he or she is in the room turning down the bed. This involves:

- Replacing dirty ashtrays

- Replacing dirty glasses

- Collecting any foodservice trays

- Emptying the trash

- Vacuuming, if needed

- Removing used terry from the bathroom

- Straightening and wiping the vanity area

- Straightening and wiping down the tub area

- Refilling toilet tissue and facial tissue as necessary

- Closing the drapes

- Turning on the bedside lamp

- Turning on the radio to a recommended easy-listening FM station

Apply Your Learning 10.5

Please write all answers on a separate sheet of paper.

1. What is the most important task a guestroom attendant performs?

2. How do guestroom attendants benefit from having perfect scores on their inspections?

3. List three tasks that a guestroom attendant might do at the end of the day.

4. List some of the special equipment a guestroom attendant might place in a guestroom.

5. What are some of the special features that guestroom attendants might have to clean in a multi-room guest suite?

6. What does a guestroom attendant do when providing turn-down service?

Quick Hits

Section 10.1—Getting to Know the Guestroom Attendant

- Guestroom attendants clean guestrooms.

- The superior performance of guestroom attendants make a difference in the success of a property and the comfort of guests.

- Many properties require guestroom attendants to share tips with everyone who cleaned a room during a guest's stay.

Section 10.2—Preparing to Clean

- A room assignment sheet lists all the rooms that each guestroom attendant needs to clean during a shift. It includes room status codes to help a guestroom attendant decide which rooms to clean first.

- Guestroom attendants place guest amenities into each room. Amenities are usually stored on an amenity caddy.

- Cleaning supply caddies carry the cleaning supplies guestroom attendants need to clean rooms.

- Correctly stocking a cart helps a guestroom attendant perform more efficiently and safely.

- Cleaning systems help save time and prevent the guestroom attendant from overlooking a task or repeating a task.

- Procedures for entering a guestroom help protect the room attendant and show respect for guest privacy.

- Guestroom attendants must be especially careful and courteous when unusual guestroom situations arise.

Section 10.3—Cleaning the Guestroom

- A check of the room to make sure everything is in working order is one of the first steps in guestroom cleaning—followed by stripping the bed and removing all soiled linen.

- The guestroom closet should be wiped with a damp sponge or dust cloth.

- Beds should be made up with clean linen and mitered corners.

- The most efficient way to dust is to start at one side of the room and work around in a circle from the top down.

- All guestroom supplies must be checked and replaced as needed.

- Guestroom attendants are responsible for cleaning and polishing the inside of windows, tracks, and sills.

- Finishing touches on a guestroom include vacuuming or dusting upholstery, cleaning balconies or patios, checking clocks, and ensuring that all cleaning supplies and trash has been removed.

- Guestroom attendants begin vacuuming at the point farthest from the guestroom door and work their way out.

Section 10.4—Cleaning the Bathroom

- Guestroom attendants clean tubs by removing hair and applying a soap and water solution to the tub surfaces. The shower curtain, tub, and skid strips also must be washed.

- Toilets are sprayed with cleaning solutions and washed from the outside in.

- The sink and vanity is cleaned with a sponge and cleaning solution.

- Typically, room attendants kneel on a towel and wash a bathroom floor from the farthest corner back to the door.

- Other tasks include cleaning mirrors, cleaning the ice bucket, replacing water glasses, and replenishing towels and amenities.

Section 10.5—Special Guestroom Attendant Duties

- Guestroom attendants need to correct any mistakes that inspectors find in their rooms.

- End-of-shift duties include restocking the housekeeping cart, putting away supplies, and signing keys back in.

- Some of the guest service equipment that guestroom attendants may be asked to place include cribs, rollaway beds, bed boards, irons, and ironing boards.

- Multi-room guest suites typically have extra things that need cleaning such as bars or kitchenettes.

- Turndown service is a special service for certain guests. It prepares their room for their evening return.

Maintenance Worker

Sections

Taking care of the hotel's physical plant and controlling energy costs is the job of the engineering division. The physical upkeep of the building, furniture, fixtures, and equipment is important to:

- Slow a hotel's physical deterioration

- Preserve the original hotel image established by management

- Keep revenue-producing areas operational

- Keep the property comfortable for guests and employees

- Preserve the safety of the property for guests and employees

- Create savings by keeping repairs and equipment replacements to a minimum

The engineering division is also responsible for heating and air-conditioning systems and the systems that deliver electricity, steam, and water throughout the property.

In order to accomplish the many tasks of the engineering division, several types of technicians may be employed: electricians, plumbers, carpenters, painters, refrigeration and air-conditioning engineers, and others. In small hotels, one all-purpose engineer may perform all engineering functions or subcontract work as needed. In a large hotel, the chief engineer may be called a plant manager.

The maintenance and repair work performed by the engineering staff is one of two kinds: preventive or as needed. Preventive maintenance is a planned program of ongoing servicing of the building and equipment to maintain operations and prolong the life of the facility. Maintenance workers also perform routine repairs.

11.1   Getting to Know the Maintenance Worker

AFTER SUCESSFULLY COMPLETING THIS SECTION, YOU WILL BE ABLE TO:

♦ Explain the important role that maintenance workers play in a lodging operation.

♦ Describe how preventive maintenance can save a property time and money.

♦ Identify basic key control and security procedures.

♦ Identify general maintenance worker duties.

What Is a Maintenance Worker?

Having a comfortable guestroom in which the lights operate properly, the toilet flushes, the shower works, and door locks securely is very important to the guests of a lodging property.

A maintenance worker makes certain that each guest is able to experience a pleasant night's stay in a room that is free from any malfunctions or problems that can complicate the guest's visit.

A maintenance worker is also responsible for maintaining the function of all areas on the lodging property's premises. This may include the lobby, meeting spaces, laundry facilities, or guest recreation areas such as a pool or lounge.

Superior Performance Standards

The condition of the guestrooms and guest areas at a lodging property should enhance each guest's overall lodging experience. Keeping these areas properly maintained is a goal of the property as well as every maintenance worker. Adopting superior performance standards help maintenance workers achieve that goal.

What are some of these standards? Maintenance workers:

• Behave professionally within the property.

• Properly maintain, service, or repair the various areas, equipment, and machinery of the lodging property.

• Greet warmly any guests encountered on the property.

• Respond quickly to guests' maintenance requests.

• Practice appropriate safety procedures at all times.

A maintenance worker's alertness keeps the property in excellent condition. They see the facility up close every day. Guests will often come to them when they know of a maintenance problem.

Working as a Team

The property can succeed if everyone works together—as a team—to give guests great service.

To be excellent team players, maintenance workers and the maintenance department can:

- Inform front office employees whether any maintenance work will affect guests' movement through the property.

- Inform the front office and housekeeping when a room will be unavailable for sale or for cleaning.

- Inform the front office and housekeeping when a room is available for sale or for cleaning.

Preventive Maintenance

Preventive maintenance (PM) is the practice of inspecting, servicing, adjusting, or performing minor repairs to machinery, equipment, and areas of a lodging property before major damage or malfunction occurs. Preventive maintenance keeps the property and its equipment in top shape for a longer period of time. Ideally, all maintenance would be performed before any equipment failure or property damage occurs. A few of the benefits to a preventive maintenance program are:

- *Decreased maintenance costs.* Maintenance workers save the cost of having to repair the equipment or damage, or perhaps making costly replacements if damage is beyond repair.

- *Decreased downtime for maintenance workers.* By maintaining a PM schedule, they will always have duties to perform on property as opposed to waiting for the next maintenance request.

- *Decrease in maintenance requests.* Maintenance workers can reduce the future likelihood of having to make repairs. An additional side effect is that guests are able to have a positive stay in a room that is well maintained.

Preventive maintenance is scheduled for the areas of the property that are most crucial to guest satisfaction, safety and security, and to the performance of other departments' duties. Maintenance workers often find that some areas may require PM more frequently than others.

Maintenance workers often perform PM during time periods when day-to-day lodging operations and guests' comfort will be least disrupted. Preventive maintenance work should be scheduled around the daily performance of maintenance requests and emergency repairs.

Most properties conduct routine preventive maintenance of all guestrooms. Maintenance workers refer to a "guestroom preventive maintenance checklist" while they are performing the work. In addition, there is usually a **preventive maintenance log** to store the checklists and to also document when the preventive maintenance is scheduled and completed.

Exhibit 1 provides a step-by-step breakdown of preventive maintenance tasks in guestrooms.

Most properties also conduct routine preventive maintenance of the public areas. Maintenance workers refer to a "public areas preventive maintenance checklist" while they are performing the work.

Key Control

Because their maintenance duties take them to all areas of the property, including guestrooms, maintenance workers properly sign out the master key, according to the property's procedures.

Because a master key can open all guestrooms, there are special rules to protect maintenance workers and guests. Maintenance workers:

- Never leave a key in a door's lock, and never set it down; they keep their keys with them at all times.

- Do not allow anyone—even a supervisor—to borrow their keys. They send anyone who asks for keys to the front desk.

- Always turn their keys in before leaving the property for any reason.

- Report any lost keys immediately to the front desk.

Guests sometimes forget to turn in their room keys when checking out of the property. Maintenance workers can help by returning any room keys they find in vacant guestrooms or elsewhere on property to the front desk.

Security and Safety

Providing security means protecting people —guests, employees, visitors, and others who have a lawful reason to be at the property. It also means protecting items that belong to these people and to the property.

Maintenance workers are a key part of a lodging property's security system. For example, because they may be in many areas of the property while performing maintenance duties, maintenance workers can watch who comes in and out of the property, and can look for unusual situations or people who seem suspicious or out-of-place.

By regularly checking and testing the smoke alarms on property, maintenance workers ensure that a destructive, potentially fatal fire does not spread across the property. Likewise, maintenance workers routinely check the emergency strobe for damage or malfunction to ensure that their hearing-impaired guests will be alerted in the case of an emergency.

Maintenance Worker Duties

The primary job of a maintenance worker is to keep the lodging property in good repair. This involves them performing many specific tasks in all areas both inside and outside the property. In general, maintenance employees are responsible for:

- Performing preventive maintenance on guestrooms and public areas

- Handling maintenance requests from guests or co-workers

- Maintaining pars of all necessary maintenance supplies

- Repairing damage to the property

- Maintaining the physical structure of the property

Exhibit 2 lists the most common tasks that the maintenance worker is expected to be able to perform well.

Apply Your Learning 11.1

Please write all answers on a separate sheet of paper.

1. What is the primary responsibility of a maintenance worker?

2. List three benefits that can be derived from a good preventive maintenance plan.

3. What should a maintenance worker do if a supervisor has requested his or her master key?

4. List tasks that maintenance workers are responsible for.

Exhibit 1
Perform Preventive Maintenance on Guestrooms

Materials needed: A guestroom preventive maintenance checklist, a notepad and pen/pencil, and maintenance request forms   .

STEPS:	HOW-TO'S:
1. **Conduct routine annual and seasonal maintenance inspections of guestrooms.**	❑ Remove a guestroom preventive maintenance checklist from the preventive maintenance log. ❑ Use the checklist for the guestroom to be inspected. ❑ Mark items on the checklist that are satisfactory. ❑ Complete the entire checklist. ❑ Take a notepad and pen or pencil to write down any observed discrepancies.
2. **Fill out a maintenance form for every problem found.**	❑ Mark items on the checklist that require repair and schedule the repairs as soon as possible. ❑ Complete a maintenance request form for items requiring repair. ❑ Turn the form in to the appropriate person according to property policy.
3. **Inspect interior doors.**	❑ Check the overall condition of knobs, hinges, and door trim. ❑ Check the operation of locks, peepholes, doorstops, and door closure devices. ❑ Open and close the doors to make sure they don't squeak. ❑ Verify that the pile of the rug or tension on the door stopper does not prevent the door from latching properly. ❑ Verify that the doors are properly locked or secured after your inspection.

(continued)

Exhibit 1
Perform Preventive Maintenance on Guestrooms *(continued)*

STEPS:	HOW-TO'S:
4. Inspect lights.	❑ Turn lights on and off to make sure they work. ❑ Check the switch cover. Make sure it is on tightly. ❑ Check the light fixture and power strips.
5. Inspect the walls.	❑ Evaluate the overall condition of the walls. ❑ Check for holes in the walls. ❑ Determine the type of wall covering and its condition. ❑ Check wall-mounted equipment, pictures, baseboards, and receptacle covers. Make sure they are secured tightly and aren't scratched. ❑ Inspect the telephone cover and wire. Make sure the wire isn't loose. ❑ Inspect walls for water damage or any indication of leaks.
6. Inspect the closet.	❑ Check that the door glides operate properly and smoothly. ❑ Inspect the closet handles to determine that they are on tight. ❑ Check that hanger rods are secure. ❑ If an ironing board and iron are provided, check that they are safely stored and easily accessible.
7. Inspect the air conditioning units.	

(continued)

Exhibit 1
Perform Preventive Maintenance on Guestrooms *(continued)*

STEPS:	HOW-TO'S:
8. **Check the heating system.**	❏ Determine that the thermostat is working properly. Depending on need and condition of calibrated thermostat units on premises, have an outside contractor perform regular re-calibration service on all appropriate thermostat units.
9. **Inspect the windows and coverings.**	❏ Check the drapes, blinds, shades, and shutters. Look for tears or loose hinges. Make sure the mechanisms for opening and closing them work.
	❏ Open and close the windows to make sure they work.
	❏ Inspect the screens, window mechanisms, window locks, window hinges, and window closures for damage. Take note of rust stains, or signs of mold and mildew, so appropriate corrective action can be taken.
10. **Inspect the ceiling.**	❏ Check the overall condition of the ceiling.
	❏ Look for leaks.
	❏ Check for chipping paint.
	❏ Look for broken ceiling tiles.
	❏ Inspect the sprinkler system.
	❏ Test the smoke detector.
	❏ Check any ceiling-mounted light fixtures.
	❏ Check any ceiling-mounted HVAC items such as filters, grills, ducts, insulation, or hangers for dust or grease.
	❏ Inspect ceiling-mounted piping.

(continued)

Exhibit 1
Perform Preventive Maintenance on Guestrooms *(continued)*

STEPS:	HOW-TO'S:
11. Inspect the bathroom.	❑ Check the mirror for scratches or chips.
	❑ Inspect the showerhead. Make sure it is attached tightly.
	❑ Inspect the toilet. Flush it to make sure the water drains and doesn't keep running. The toilet bowl should clear with a single flush. Adjustment may be required so the high-pressure/low water flush will adequately clear the bowl while staying within the EPA's mandatory limit of 1.6 gallons of water used per flush. Toilets requiring multiple flushes to clear are counterproductive to water conservation efforts.
	❑ Inspect the towel bars. Make sure they are firmly attached to the wall
	❑ Where grab bars are installed, be sure they can withstand a 200-pound pull test.
	❑ Inspect the sinks. Look for chips or scratches in the basin. Make sure the faucets and stoppers work correctly.
	❑ Inspect the toilet paper dispenser.
	❑ Check the caulking. Make sure it is not peeling or missing. Check for mold or mildew.
	❑ Inspect the drains. Make sure all water drains quickly.
	❑ Check the shower curtain and rod. Make sure they are in good condition. Look for tears in the curtain or mold or mildew.
	❑ Inspect the shower doors. Make sure they slide and lock correctly. Shower doors should be made of shatterproof glass.
	❑ Check the soap dispenser. Make sure it is dispensing soap correctly and is not clogged.

(continued)

Exhibit 1
Perform Preventive Maintenance on Guestrooms *(continued)*

STEPS:	HOW-TO'S:
	❑ Inspect the soap and toothbrush holders. Make sure they are firmly attached to the wall.
	❑ Inspect the hair dryers. Make sure they are working, properly mounted, and that the cords are not frayed.
	❑ Inspect the cabinets. Look for scratches and make sure the hinges are tight.
	❑ Inspect the condition of the tub/shower stall.
	❑ Inspect the sink and tub stoppers.
	❑ Inspect the urinal. Make sure it is working correctly.
	❑ Inspect the water pressure to ensure that it meets property standards.
	❑ Inspect the ground fault circuit interrupter (GFCI)/ test receptacle.
	❑ Inspect the ventilation system and the heat lamp. Make sure they are working properly.
	❑ Inspect the exhaust system.
	❑ Check the medicine cabinet for wear.
12. **Inspect beds.**	❑ Make sure headboard is attached tightly to wall or bed frame.
	❑ Check bed for proper assembly.
	❑ Check for broken bed boards or mattress springs.
13. **Inspect common electrical wiring (all electrical repairs must be performed by a properly certified technician).**	❑ Check for receptacle discoloring.
	❑ Listen for lights humming.
	❑ Listen for any popping or crackling near electrical wires.

(continued)

Exhibit 1
Perform Preventive Maintenance on Guestrooms *(continued)*

STEPS:	HOW-TO'S:
	❑ Look for frayed cords.
	❑ Check the ground fault circuit interrupters (GFCI).
	❑ Check that there are no electrical cords placed under carpets or rugs where they may be stepped on or run over by wheeled equipment.
14. Inspect furniture.	❑ Make sure tables and chairs do not wobble.
	❑ Check seat cushions for broken or visible springs.
	❑ Check for loose rungs.
	❑ Check for missing/broken parts.
	❑ Check drawer handles and make sure they open/close properly.
	❑ Check wood for warping, slivers, and broken parts.
	❑ Check upholstered items for stains, rips, tears, frays, warping, sagging, or exposed springs or batting.
	❑ Check to make sure items are properly assembled.
15. Conduct any other necessary inspections.	

Exhibit 2
Task List—Maintenance Employee

1. Document Maintenance Requests
2. Prepare Tools for Maintenance Work
3. Perform Preventive Maintenance on Guestrooms
4. Perform Repairs to Guestroom Furniture
5. Inspect and Service Guestroom AC Unit
6. Perform Interior Installations
7. Replace Sink in Guestroom
8. Change Shower Head
9. Repair Wash Basin Drain
10. Repair Faucet Leaks and Drips
11. Service or Repair Toilet
12. Replace Mirror
13. Install Ceiling Fan
14. Replace Light Bulbs
15. Replace Out-of-Order TV Sets
16. Repair Door Hardware
17. Communicate Out-of-Order Room Status
18. Repair Damaged Carpet
19. Apply or Repair Wallpaper
20. Repair Drywall
21. Perform Preventive Maintenance of Public Areas
22. Maintain and Service Ice Machines
23. Clean Pool
24. Paint Walls and Other Surfaces
25. Clean and Paint Property Signs
26. Make a Surface Skid-Free
27. Perform Preventive Maintenance on Roofs
28. Replace Ceiling Tiles
29. Repair Ceramic Tile and Grout
30. Basic Carpentry Repairs
31. Perform Pressure Washing
32. Replace Corner Guide
33. Perform Visual Check of Air Compressor
34. Inspect Flood Pump
35. Service Sump Pump
36. Perform Water Valve Maintenance
37. Test Water Heater
38. Perform Lockout/Tagout Procedures During All Repairs
39. Inspect Power Supply After Power Failure
40. Perform Basic Generator Service
41. Troubleshoot Vacuum Cleaner
42. Maintain and Service Laundry Equipment
43. Inspect Laundry Carts
44. Keep Maintenance Shop Organized
45. Maintain Chemicals Properly

11.2 Preparing to Perform Maintenance Work

AFTER SUCCESSFULLY COMPLETING THIS SECTION, YOU WILL BE ABLE TO:

♦ Describe the OSHA regulations regarding safety in the workplace.

♦ List basic personal protective equipment.

♦ Explain the importance of lockout/tagout procedures.

♦ Describe how maintenance requests are documented.

♦ Identify basic procedures for preparing tools for maintenance work.

♦ Describe the basic guidelines for keeping the maintenance shop organized.

♦ Describe the procedures for maintaining chemicals properly.

♦ Explain how to communicate out-of-order room status.

When maintenance workers prepare to perform their maintenance duties each day, they take into consideration several factors such as tool preparation, supply or par levels, and most importantly, safety.

OSHA Regulations

The **Occupational Safety and Health Administration (OSHA)** is a federal agency that helps keep workers safe by regulating sanitation, safety, and first aid in the workplace.

Maintenance workers use the proper protective equipment when working with tools. Properties provide personal protective equipment whenever there is a "reasonable probability that the use of the equipment will prevent or reduce the severity of injuries or illnesses."

Personal protective equipment does not make the tool or piece of equipment less hazardous. Instead, it provides a last line of defense.

Some protective equipment maintenance workers may use includes:

• *Eye and face protection.* **Eye protection** should be worn at all times in designated eye-hazard areas. A maintenance worker's eyes or face could be injured by flying particles and chips, or by splashes from liquids such as acids, caustics, and solvents.

• *Respiratory protection.* Respiratory hazards occur through exposure to harmful dusts, fogs, fumes, mists, gases, smoke, sprays, and vapors. The best protection is local exhaust ventilation. When that is not practical or applicable, maintenance workers wear personal respiratory protection equipment.

- *Head protection.* Helmets and hats can protect maintenance workers from falling and flying objects and from limited electric shock and burn. They wear head protection at all times in designated head-hazard areas.

- *Foot protection.* Maintenance workers wear safety shoes or boots whenever they are exposed to foot and toe hazards. Types of foot protection might include:

  - Safety shoes with a built-in protective toe box for protection from heavy falling objects

  - Semi-conductive safety shoes used to dissipate static electricity

  - Electrical hazard safety shoes with a built-in protective toe box to guard against electrical shock hazards when performing electrical work on live circuits not exceeding 600 volts

- *Hand protection.* Maintenance workers wear hand protection whenever their hands are exposed to (or are likely to be exposed to) hazards such as harmful substances, severe cuts or lacerations, severe abrasion, punctures, chemical burns, thermal burns, harmful temperature extremes, and so on.

- *Electrical protective devices.* Maintenance workers wear and use appropriate rubber protective devices when working on energized or potentially energized electrical systems. These might include rubber insulating gloves, rubber matting for use around electrical apparatus, rubber insulating blankets, rubber insulating line hose, rubber insulating covers, and rubber insulating sleeves.

- *Hearing protection.* Some hearing protection devices include earplugs or safety headphones.

- *Back support braces/devices.* Maintenance workers wear these whenever they do heavy lifting.

Lockout/Tagout

When performing any type of electrical maintenance, safety comes first. This means following proper **lockout/tagout procedures.** The term lockout/tagout refers to the isolation of equipment during maintenance work. In other words, removing or blocking the source of energy being provided to the equipment. In addition, locks or tags are placed on equipment as a warning so there are no injuries due to accidental machine start-ups.

Machinery or equipment requiring lockout/tagout procedures that maintenance workers may encounter includes:

- High voltage power supplies

- Boilers

- Elevators

- Fan systems

Maintenance work that may require lockout/tagout includes installation or set-up of equipment and the inspection, maintenance, repair, and service of machines and equipment. Even though maintenance workers may not routinely perform this type of maintenance, they are still familiar with proper safety and lockout/tagout procedures.

Document Maintenance Requests

Maintenance workers usually find when their shift begins several maintenance requests wait for them. These requests may be regular requests for routine or non-urgent maintenance, or they could be requests for immediate maintenance assistance.

Most lodging properties make use of a **maintenance request log** to document calls or requests from guests requiring maintenance-related assistance.

Some properties also have a maintenance request or priority form, which is used when the request requires immediate action. These forms are usually marked or colored differently to designate the priority status of the request.

Exhibit 1 provides a step-by-step breakdown of how to document maintenance requests.

Prepare Tools

Tools, spare parts, and operating supplies are high-cost items. Proper care of these items protect property assets.

Maintenance workers check tools out each day. Additional controls for protecting tools include:

* Locking up carts and tools in a secure area

* Taking routine inventory of all tools

* Keeping all tools on the lodging premises

It is not uncommon for maintenance workers to supply some of their own tools.

Maintenance workers know what tools they have and what each tool is used for.

Maintenance workers always check with the operator's manual before using any tool or piece of equipment for the first time. Some tools and equipment require special safety precautions. When manuals aren't available for a tool or piece of equipment, maintenance workers check with the local safety office.

Exhibit 2 lists many of the tools maintenance workers use as well as a description of the tool and its use.

When maintenance workers prepare to leave the maintenance shop to perform a task, they collect the tools needed. They sign out the tools on the maintenance tool log and then place the tools on the maintenance cart. Some maintenance workers use a maintenance tool belt, a toolbox or tray, or bucket in place of a maintenance cart.

Once the maintenance task is completed, maintenance workers return all the tools to their proper place and then check the tools back in on the maintenance tool log.

Keep the Maintenance Shop Organized

Maintenance workers need a clean and organized work area to work efficiently. The maintenance shop is organized so that maintenance workers can quickly find the tools or supplies they need.

Some basic guidelines for organizing the maintenance shop include:

* Keep items stored on shelves straight.

* Do not store items on the floor.

* Do not store items on upper shelves within 18 inches of a fire sprinkler head.

* Open cases of supplies that have been received and shelve them in the correct locations.

Exhibit 1
Document Maintenance Requests

Materials needed: Maintenance request forms, a pen or pencil, and the maintenance request log.

STEPS:	HOW-TO'S:
1. Record maintenance requests in the maintenance request log.	❏ Document pertinent information about the request, such as the problem, room number, and time of call. ❏ Call the front desk to report a problem as an emergency if it involves safety or health.
2. Fill out a maintenance request form in response to a maintenance request.	❏ Ask for a maintenance request form from the front desk whenever a problem needs to be reported. ❏ Fill out as much information as possible on the form. ❏ File active maintenance request forms according to property procedures.
3. Track status of maintenance requests.	❏ Check the maintenance request log to determine daily outstanding requests. ❏ Keep logs updated by writing in any changes in status to maintenance requests. ❏ Keep guests informed of maintenance request status so they know that the problem is being taken care of. ❏ If a maintenance request is not complete within the appropriate time limit, tell the affected guest when the work is expected to be complete.
4. Follow up on completed maintenance requests.	❏ Check the maintenance request log for completed maintenance requests. ❏ Call the guest or staff member who turned in the request.

(continued)

Exhibit 1	
Document Maintenance Requests *(continued)*	
STEPS:	**HOW-TO'S:**
	❑ Ask if the work performed is satisfactory. If not, correct the problem as soon as possible.
	❑ If the work performed is satisfactory, follow property procedures to close out the maintenance request form.

- Store new items in the back to permit first-in, first-out rotation of supplies. **First-in, first-out (FIFO)** storage makes sure that older supplies are used before newer ones.

- Store heavier or larger items on the floor level or on lower level shelves.

Maintain Chemicals Properly

There are many chemicals that maintenance workers use. These properly labeled chemicals are stored in the maintenance shop. OSHA requires proper labeling of all chemicals, including labels that designate a particular chemical's potential hazards. Maintenance workers refer to the chemical's Material Safety Data Sheet when labeling it.

Chemicals are stored in a cool, dry area. Flammable and combustible liquids are stored in appropriate containers. Paints, cleaners, flammable liquids in aerosol cans, and other similar materials are kept in an approved explosion-proof cabinet or storeroom. Maintenance workers check that compressed gas cylinders are in safe condition.

Maintenance workers properly seal chemicals before and after use.

Communicate Out-of-Order Room Status

When maintenance workers receive a request to perform a maintenance task in a vacant guestroom, they communicate with the front desk and housekeeping departments to let them know that the room will not be available to be sold. Once they have completed the work in the guestroom, maintenance workers then inform the departments that the room can now be returned to inventory.

Many properties have automated their work order systems so that room status is communicated to all departments in real time.

Exhibit 3 provides a step-by-step breakdown of how to communicate out-of-order room status.

Exhibit 2
Commonly Used Tools

Tool	Description	Use
Cold chisel	Tempered forge steel in various lengths	Cutting bolts, rivets, nails, etc.
Woodworking chisel	Plastic handles with steel caps	General wood and structural repair and installation
Auger bit set	Set of 13 drills, ¼- to 1-inch, in 1/16-inch increments	Wood boring with brace
Brace, bit, and ratchet	10-inch sweep for tapered wood bits	Wood boring
Masonry drill	Set of drills 3/16- to ½ inch, by 1/16-inch increments	Drilling brick, marble, etc.
Claw hammer	Carpenter's 1-pound hammer with curved claw	Nailing and nail remover
Cross peen hammer	2-pound engineer's hammer	Metal work
Tack hammer	5-ounce hammer with magnetized head	Upholstery
Mallet	Hard rubber mallet, 2- by 4-inch head, 24 ounces	Adjusting and positioning structural elements or furniture parts with delicate surfaces
Straight-nose pliers	6-inch	General repairs
Combination pliers with cutter	8-inch	General repairs, electrical work
Angle-nose pliers	10-inch	General repairs
Lineman's pliers	6-inch wire skinner	Cutting wire
Needle-nose pliers	6½-inch straight round nose with cutter	Electrical repairs
Channel-lock pliers	10-inch	General repairs
Pipe and sewer auger or snake	½-inch by 50 feet, with bulbous type head	Opening clogged pipes
Rip saw	Quality saw, 26-inch blade	Cutting wood with the grain
Keyhole saw	Quality saw, 10-inch blade	Cutting wood from a drilled hole

Exhibit 2
Commonly Used Tools *(continued)*

Tool	Description	Use
Hacksaw	Adjustable 10- to 12-inch pistol grip hacksaw and blades	Cutting metal rods
Electrical saw	Circular 8-inch blade, 2 5/8-inch cut, capable of rip and cross cut with many speed control and safety features	Heavy-duty cutting
Mitre box and saw	Metal or wood mitre box with attached saw, capable of taking 4-inch wood	Making square or angled wood joinings
Soldering gun	Pistol-type soldering gun and solder	Light soldering of electrical connections
Crescent wrench	Open-end adjustable wrench set including at least: • ½ by 4 inches • 15/16 by 8 inches • 1 15/16 by 12 inches • 2 1/16 by 18 inches	Heavy-duty repair
Basin wrench	T-handle wrench with interchangeable jaws	Lavatory repair
Pipe wrench	Adjustable jaw wrenches: • ½ by 6 inches • 1 by 10 inches • 2 by 18 inches • 2 ½ by 24 inches	Plumbing repair
Allen wrench	Set	Tightening Allen bolts
Combination box and open end wrenches	Set of wrenches from 5/16 to 1 ¼ inches	General repairs
Socket wrench	Set with square drive, handles, extension, ratchet	General repairs

Exhibit 2
Commonly Used Tools *(continued)*

Tool	Description	Use
Caulking compound and gun	Caulking compound in gun cartridges, approximately 12 ounces	Filling cracks in wood, stone, or metal; sealing windows or doors
Grease gun	Lever-type hand grease gun	Lubricating equipment
Level	Side-reading 18-inch aluminum carpenter's level	Determining whether a surface is inclined
Roller	Assorted sizes, as appropriate	Applying paint, floor sealer
Screwdrivers	Set of flat-tip screwdrivers; set of rotating-tip, slot-gripping screwdrivers; set of Phillips screwdrivers; set of hexagonal wrench grip screwdrivers	Light and heavy tightening of screws and bolts with various heads
Carpenter's square	24- by 2-inch body, 16- by 1 ½ -inch tongue	Ruling wood
Steel tape	Spring-loaded ruler	Measuring
Vise	5-inch replaceable jaw, 4½ - inch jaw width, to accommodate pipe and tubing from ¼ to 3½ inches	Holding pipe and other materials
Wrecking bar	Offset pinch point, 30 inches long	Pulling nails, opening crates

Exhibit 3
Communicate Out-of-Order Room Status

STEPS:	HOW-TO'S:
1. **Determine out-of-order room status.**	❑ Designate a guestroom as "out of order"—so that the room is not sold to guests—if it contains damage or is in need of extensive or lengthy repair.
	❑ Inform the front office as soon as possible of the need to make the room unavailable.
	❑ Notify the housekeeping department about the change in the room's status.
	❑ Complete a maintenance request form detailing what needs to be done to the room and why it is "out of order."
2. **Perform work on out-of-order room.**	❑ During service, continue to communicate work progress and room status to both the front desk and housekeeping.
	❑ Inspect the room one final time to make sure that the work is complete and satisfactory.
3. **Notify housekeeping that the room is ready for cleaning.**	
4. **Notify front desk of the availability of the room.**	

Apply Your Learning 11.2

Please write all answers on a separate sheet of paper.

1. List four forms of personal protective equipment.

2. What should come first when performing any type of electrical maintenance?

3. What are the two basic types of maintenance requests?

4. List three controls for protecting a property's tools and equipment.

5. List five tools that may be found in most properties' maintenance shops.

6. List three basic guidelines for keeping a maintenance shop organized.

7. What should maintenance workers refer to when labeling a chemical?

8. What two departments should a maintenance worker communicate out-of-order room status to?

11.3 Performing Guestroom Maintenance Tasks

AFTER SUCCESSFULLY COMPLETING THIS SECTION, YOU WILL BE ABLE TO:

◆ Describe the procedures for performing interior installations.

◆ Explain the steps for replacing a mirror.

◆ Identify the steps for replacing light bulbs.

◆ Describe how to replace an out-of-order TV set.

◆ List procedures for performing guestroom door maintenance.

◆ Explain how to repair damaged carpet.

◆ Describe how to apply or repair wallpaper.

◆ Identify the steps for replacing corner guards.

◆ List the steps for troubleshooting a vacuum cleaner.

Perform Interior Installations

The following basic interior installation procedures are common to most, but not all, lodging properties:

- Installing a curtain rod
- Mounting Venetian blinds
- Mounting a window shade
- Hanging a picture

These are all tasks that are often done in teams. Maintenance workers begin by holding the item to be installed against the wall or window casing. They then mark with a pencil where the item sits—usually the corners of the item or where it touches the wall. Maintenance workers then carefully measure from the edges to the bracket that will hold the rod, blinds, shade, or picture in place.

For a curtain rod and Venetian blinds, maintenance workers drill holes into the casing or wall at the pencil outline. They then screw in the curtain rod or headbox brackets. If a curtain rod is more than 48 inches long, an intermediate rod support is mounted halfway between the two curtain rod brackets. Shade brackets are usually attached to the window casing or wall with a hammer and small nails. The curtain rod, blinds, and shades are then mounted onto the bracket holders.

Pictures are slightly more complicated to hang. One method for doing so follows these steps:

1. Write a small 1 in pencil on one of the side frames on the back of the picture, 1/3 of the way down from the top of

the frame. Regardless of picture size, it is advisable to have a partner for this task, as this will permit better alignment of the picture on the wall.

2. Write a small 3 in pencil on the other side of the frame on the back of the picture, 1/3 of the way down from the top of the frame.

3. Write a small 2 in pencil ¼-inch below the top of the picture frame, halfway between the two side frames.

4. Measure from point 1 to point 2, and from point 2 to point 3 with a tape measure or ruler. Add the two numbers together to determine the correct wire length for the picture. Determining the wire length in this manner ensures that the wire will have the proper slack.

5. Cut the wire to the correct length using heavy-duty scissors or wire cutters.

6. Attach the wire to the picture frame by screwing a small screw eye into the 1 on the back of the picture frame. A screw eye is a wood screw with a head in the form of a loop.

7. Screw a small screw eye into the 3 on the back of the picture frame.

8. Tie one end of the wire to one of the screw eyes, using two pairs of pliers to tighten the knot.

9. Tie the other end of the wire to the other screw eye, using two pairs of pliers to tighten the knot.

10. Mark the picture location on the wall by holding the picture against the wall in the location and use a pencil to outline the top edge of the picture.

11. Draw a small X ¼-inch below the midway point of the pencil mark. Make very light lines when marking on the wall in pencil.

12. Hold the picture hanger flush against the wall, with the hanger's lower hole placed over the X. A picture hanger is a small metal hook with two holes that attach to the wall. The picture hangs on the hanger.

13. Hammer a small nail through each of the hanger's holes, securing the hanger to the wall. If the picture is especially large, two hangers may be needed.

14. Place the center of the hanging wire on the picture hanger.

15. Adjust the sides of the picture so that it is level.

Replace Mirror

Mirrors are replaced because of discoloring, cracks, or other damage. It may be necessary for two maintenance workers to perform mirror replacement.

The basic procedures for replacing a mirror are as follows:

1. Remove the old mirror from the sink or vanity area using suction cups. Use extreme care.

2. Clean the mirror space of any dust or dirt.

3. Inspect the back of the old mirror for scratches or holes that might allow for a view of the bathroom from an area outside the bathroom, such as a corridor or crawl space. Report any holes or scratches to management.

4. Discard the old mirror in the property trash.

5. Inspect the back of the new mirror for any scratches or holes.

6. Measure the new mirror to make sure it will fit in the mirror space. Make sure that the new mirror is the correct size and shape.

7. Install the new mirror using mirror adhesive.

8. Check that the mirror hangs evenly.

9. Inspect the new mirror. Make sure the mirror is free of dirt, fingerprints, and smudges. Wipe the mirror if necessary.

Replace Light Bulbs

Before either removing or installing a new light bulb, maintenance workers make sure the switch is turned off and that the replacement bulb is of the correct wattage. Light bulbs are removed by turning them counter-clockwise and installed by turning them clockwise. Bulbs are always handled gently and never over-tightened.

Fluorescent tubes are replaced in a similar manner. They are turned until the pins slide out of the sockets on either side of the light fixture. They are handled carefully as they can explode if dropped or broken. The new tube is installed by carefully inserting the pins on either side of the tube into the vertical slots and then turning it clockwise until the pins sit horizontally.

To replace halogen light bulbs, maintenance workers disconnect the power supply to the lamp, making sure that the halogen lamp on/off switch is not defective and the proper power is being applied to the lamp. They then open the bulb cover of the lamp and remove it using a piece of plastic or paper foil. Halogen bulbs are not touched with bare hands or fingers. This damages the bulb. Maintenance workers use a meter to measure the resistance of the halogen bulb. If there is no resistance, they replace the bulb. They then brush the bulb connector pins on the lamp to make sure they are free from dust or dirt. After installing the new bulb, they put the bulb cover in place, restore power to the lamp, and switch the lamp on.

Replace Out-of-Order TV Sets

Televisions, like any other electrical appliance, sometimes need replacing. When lifting heavy, bulky objects like TV sets, maintenance workers use proper lifting techniques. When replacing out-of-order TV sets, maintenance workers unscrew the cable wire from the back of the set and loosen any screws or brackets holding the TV in place. The old TV set is removed on a dolly or luggage cart. They then clean away any dust or debris found in the TV set housing or shelf before placing a new TV set onto the shelf or installing it onto the wall. Maintenance workers check to make sure all screws are tightened and the set securely installed so that it doesn't crash or fall.

The maintenance worker then checks the set and makes sure that it works and there is clear reception on all channels. All information (including model type, TV number, room number, and replacement/installation dates) about both televisions is recorded in the maintenance log.

Repair Door Hardware

Guestroom doors have several components that often require maintenance.

Two of the most common maintenance tasks performed on doorways are servicing a sticking doorknob and replacing door thresholds.

To service a sticking doorknob, a maintenance worker would:

1. Remove the screws holding the doorknob in place. Using an offset screwdriver allows easier access to the screws.

2. Pull the two halves of the doorknob off of the door.

3. Remove the screws that hold the bolt in place and remove the bolt.

4. Place the doorknob parts on a paper towel and spray them thoroughly with penetrating oil.

5. Leave the doorknob parts to soak in the penetrating oil for several minutes.

6. Wipe the doorknob parts clean with a lint-free shop towel and a cotton swab.

7. Replace the doorknob back on the door by reversing the removal steps.

To replace a door threshold, a maintenance worker would:

1. Swing the door open as far as it will go.

2. Pry the door trim near the threshold loose, if necessary for removal of the threshold.

3. Remove the old threshold. For aluminum thresholds, a screwdriver may be needed to remove the screws holding the plating in place.

4. Clean out the threshold recess thoroughly, making sure to remove all dirt and debris from the area.

5. Apply a good coat of caulk to the bottom of the threshold. Caulk will help provide an airtight seal between the joint and the threshold.

6. Install the new threshold. If the new threshold came with screws, use the new screws. Make sure that the new threshold is the same size as the old threshold.

7. Replace the door trim, if it was removed.

8. Secure the threshold and make sure the door opens and closes without striking the threshold. Make sure that the threshold does not hinder passage of a wheelchair across it.

9. Clean the area.

Repair Damaged Carpet

No guest wants to walk into a guestroom and see holes, runs, or stains in the carpet. Damaged carpet not only looks bad, but it could cause injury if guests or guestroom attendants catch their feet on the damaged area. In general, repair should be attempted only on smaller sized rips and tears. Major carpet damage requires replacement of carpet for the entire room. Newer carpeting is available in carpet tiles. A bad spill or torn area can be quickly replaced by inserting the proper matching carpet tile.

Minor carpet burns are trimmed away with carpet scissors. Larger pieces of carpets are repaired with a carpet knife. Maintenance workers set up barriers to keep others from entering the repair area while they are working and then they cut out the damaged area. The replacement carpet piece is placed front to back with the damaged piece (making sure that the piles on both pieces face the same direction). They then cut the replacement piece to the right size, using the damaged piece as a pattern. The replacement piece is then placed where the damaged piece used to be and trimmed to the exact size.

Carpet seam tape is placed around the edge of the hole with half under the existing carpet and half exposed. The existing carpet and tape is glued together with a hot glue gun. Hot glue is then spread on the exposed tape. The replacement piece is glued into place and a tractor tool run across the seam to blend it. Maintenance workers often place a board over the replacement piece and stand on it for about 30 seconds so that the glue will bond.

Apply or Repair Wallpaper

As with damaged carpet, a guest does not want to see rips, tears, or stains on the guestroom wallpaper. In cases where guestrooms are being renovated, an entire wall or room will have new wallpaper applied to it.

Prepare the room

1. Move furniture to the center of the room. Cover the furniture with drop cloths, if necessary.

2. Place a cloth or old blanket on the floor to protect the carpet.

3. Remove any electrical outlet and light switch plates using a screwdriver.

Remove the existing wallpaper

1. If paper is already loose, begin to peel.

2. If the paper will not peel easily, use a wallpaper-perforating tool over the wallpaper to be removed. A wallpaper-perforating tool is a roller with small teeth that perforate the paper, allow-

ing for the use of adhesive-dissolving solvent.

3. Apply wallpaper-removing solvent over the old wallpaper using a paintbrush.

4. Allow the solvent to soak into the paper. Refer to the solvent label for the proper length of time.

5. Scrape at a seam or edge of the wallpaper with a putty knife or drywall knife and begin peeling the wallpaper. Apply additional solvent, as needed, until all of the wallpaper is peeled free.

Prepare the wall

1. Clean the surface of any adhesive, dirt, stains, dust, or wallpaper remnants. Make sure the wall is dry.

2. If there is not an existing coat of primer under the old wallpaper, prime the wall with an oil-based primer using a paintbrush, making sure to coat the wall evenly.

Apply the new wallpaper

1. Match the new wallpaper to the wallpaper in the rest of the room or other guestrooms. Most wallpaper is vinyl. Wallpaper can come pre-pasted with adhesive or paste-free. Pre-pasted wallpaper is easier to work with. Refer to the manufacturers instructions for hanging the wallpaper.

2. Measure a strip of wallpaper several inches longer than the wall to be covered.

3. Cut the paper with a utility knife or razor.

4. With a pencil, mark a spot a few inches out from the top of a corner of the wall.

5. Using a level, draw a plumb line from the mark down the length of the wall.

6. Roll the strip back up with the adhesive side out and soak it in a wallpaper tray filled with water for 15 seconds.

7. Remove the strip and roll it out pattern side down on the blanket.

8. Apply the wallpaper strip to the wall, leaving a few inches above and below the edges of the wall. Make sure to apply the paper flush with the plumb line.

9. Smooth out the wallpaper strip using a wallpaper brush so it is free of bubbles, rips, or tears. Start at the top of the strip and move downward. Use vertical strokes whenever possible. Horizontal strokes may stretch the wallpaper.

10. Use a straight edge to press the wallpaper tightly into the corners.

11. Use a razor to neatly cut away excess wallpaper at the top and bottom.

12. Apply subsequent strips flush with the first strip. Make sure to match the patterns at seams and corners.

Apply wallpaper around windows and doors

1. Press the wallpaper strip being applied around a window or door over the casing. The strip should overlap the casing.

2. Cut diagonal slits at the corners of the casings. Use a flat or broad knife to press or tap the wallpaper against the casing, then use the broad knife as a straightedge for creasing the edge of the wallpaper into the casing seam.

3. Using a straightedge and a utility knife, cut the wallpaper where the wallpaper meets the casing.

Apply wallpaper around corners

1. Measure the distance from the last strip of wallpaper to the next corner. Cut the next wallpaper strip an inch wider than the distance just measured. To ensure accuracy, it may be necessary to measure in several places.

2. Apply the strip into the corner carefully, pressing it cleanly into the corner. Use a straightedge to trim down the length of the wallpaper.

3. Measure a plumb line on the adjacent wall a distance of one inch shorter than the width of the wallpaper from the corner.

4. Hang the next wallpaper piece so that it overlaps the edge of the previous piece. Press or tap the paper in to make sure it fits snug in the corner. By overlapping the wallpaper, maintenance workers can compensate for areas where the wall isn't plumb. This method can be used when applying wallpaper to both inside and outside corners.

5. Using a utility knife, cut through both layers of wallpaper strips about a ¼ inch from the corner.

6. Peel away the outer piece of wallpaper. This extra piece is called the selvage.

7. Lift up the outer wallpaper strip just enough to allow access to the inside selvage. Remove the selvage and lay the outer piece of wallpaper back onto the wall.

8. Smooth the outer piece down with a seam roller.

Apply wallpaper around electrical outlets

1. Hang the strip of wallpaper that will cover a light switch or electrical outlet over the opening. Make sure that the electric current to the outlet is either locked or disconnected.

2. Using a utility knife, cut an "X" out of the wallpaper covering the opening. Peel back the edges and trim them to expose the opening.

3. Smooth the wallpaper strip over the wall, pressing firmly around the edges of the opening.

4. Reinstall the outlet or light switch cover using a screwdriver.

Apply finishing touches

1. After the wallpaper has set for 15 minutes, use a seam roller to press the seams between the strips together.

2. Wipe off any excess adhesive with a damp sponge or cloth.

3. Check that the wallpaper adheres securely to the wall.

4. Clean the area of adhesive drippings or splatters on the carpet or on the furniture.

Repair a damaged section of wallpaper

1. Find a remnant that matches the wallpaper or take a piece from an inconspicuous area.

2. Cut a square patch from the replacement wallpaper. Make sure the patch is larger than the damaged area.

3. Move the replacement piece over the damaged area until the pattern matches. Tape the replacement piece in place.

4. Cut through both the replacement piece and the damaged wallpaper.

5. Untape and remove the replacement piece. Pull off the damaged piece.

6. Apply wallpaper adhesive to the wall at the damaged spot.

7. Place the replacement piece over the adhesive and line up the seams.

8. Use a roller to smooth out the repair and blend the seams.

9. Let adhesive set for one minute. Then wipe off excess adhesive with a sponge before it dries.

Replace Corner Guard

Corner guards are very useful in preventing injury to guests or damage to wall corners. Corner guards are usually made of strips of plastic. They are mounted or installed along the length of a wall corner. Because they take the brunt of any impact a corner may take, they can be damaged and occasionally may need replacing.

Generally speaking, old corner guards are either unscrewed or pried away from the wall with a knife. The old caulk or adhesive is scraped away and a new corner guard is installed with silicon caulk. Masking tape can be used to keep the guard in place until the caulk has time to set.

Troubleshoot Vacuum Cleaners

Guestroom attendants and public space cleaners rely heavily on vacuum cleaners to make guestrooms and other public areas clean for guest use. Because of their heavy use, vacuum cleaners require routine maintenance and often need belts or other parts replaced. Maintenance workers must work swiftly to repair any problems to a vacuum cleaner so that it can be returned to action.

Exhibit 1 provides a step-by-step break-down of how to troubleshoot a vacuum cleaner.

Exhibit 1
Troubleshoot Vacuum Cleaner

Materials needed: Brush, belt, filter bags, and vacuum hose attachments.

STEPS:	HOW-TO'S:
1. **Clean the brush.**	❑ Turn the vacuum cleaner upside down and remove the plastic cover over the brush assembly. ❑ Lift the brush and remove the belt from the motor. The vacuum cleaner brush is sometimes referred to as the agitator. ❑ Remove any dust or particles.
2. **Inspect the bearings.**	❑ Inspect the bearings on the brush rollers. Both ends of the brush should turn freely. If they don't, the bearings may need replacing.
3. **Install new belt.**	❑ Install the new belt by connecting it to the motor and wrapping it around the brush. Insert the brush into the vacuum cleaner. Most vacuum cleaner assemblies provide a clear indication of where the new belt should be installed.
4. **Replace brush assembly cover.**	
5. **Replace filter bag.**	❑ Remove the filter bag from the vacuum canister or arm. Most upright vacuum cleaners have either a filter bag or canister stored in a plastic casing or a filter bag located inside a bag connected to the vacuum arm exterior. ❑ Clean away any dust or dirt left inside the canister or around the filter housing. ❑ Insert a new filter bag into the vacuum canister.

(continued)

Exhibit 1
Troubleshoot Vacuum Cleaners *(continued)*

STEPS:	HOW-TO'S:
6. Remove obstructions from vacuum brush or hose attachment. For vacuum cleaners with hose attachments, obstructions can be removed by sticking a broom handle through the straightened hose.	
7. Perform additional inspections.	❏ Inspect the electrical cord. Make sure it is not frayed and wires aren't exposed.
	❏ Check that the wheels turn easily and grip handles are not broken.

Apply Your Learning 11.3

Please write all answers on a separate sheet of paper.

1. What type of equipment do maintenance workers often have to install?
2. Why should the back of a mirror be inspected?
3. List two reasons why is it important to repair damaged carpet.
4. What is the benefit gained from overlapping one piece of wallpaper over the previous piece?
5. What is the purpose of a corner guard?
6. List two things that may require replacement on a vacuum cleaner.

11.4 Performing Bathroom Maintenance Tasks

AFTER SUCCESSFULLY COMPLETING THIS SECTION, YOU WILL BE ABLE TO:

♦ Explain the procedures for changing a showerhead.

♦ List the steps for repairing a wash basin drain.

♦ Explain the process of repairing faucet leaks and drips.

♦ Describe the procedures for servicing or repairing a toilet.

Because of the amount of water typically used in a guest bathroom, the majority of maintenance tasks performed in a bathroom involve water or water damage. Because excessive leaking or overflowing water can quickly damage a guestroom, guestroom attendants and maintenance workers must routinely check for leaks or damage to pipes, basins, and faucets.

Change Showerhead

If a guestroom is occupied 365 days a year and the shower is used every day, the showerhead may quickly need replacement due to wear or water damage. The basic procedures for replacing a showerhead are:

1. Turn off the water.

2. Remove the old showerhead. If the showerhead has been attached for a long time, there may be water deposit buildup, requiring extra force to remove. A pair of pliers may be necessary. If pliers are used, wrap a cloth around the showerhead stem to prevent potential damage.

3. Clean the showerhead stem of any corrosion or buildup.

4. Wrap Teflon tape around the showerhead stem threads. Wrap in a clockwise direction at least three times around the threads.

5. Once the tape has been wrapped around the threads once, begin to stretch the tape while wrapping.

6. Tighten the new showerhead onto the showerhead stem. When tightening with pliers, wrap a cloth around the showerhead neck to avoid scratching the surface.

7. Turn on the water and make sure the showerhead works properly, the mixer valve is working properly, and that water pressure is satisfactory.

Repair Wash Basin Drain

Because of the amount of water flowing through them, wash or sink basin drains are extremely susceptible to corrosion or other damage.

1. Turn the water supply to the wash basin off and inspect the wash basin drain for damaged or corroded piping.

2. Place a bucket and a towel under the wash basin drain to catch any excess water.

3. Loosen the wash basin drain trap.

4. Allow any water and dirt to drip into the bucket.

5. Loosen and remove all bad piping as well as the bad trap.

6. Determine that the remaining drain piping is clear from debris.

7. Wipe all piping clean with a towel.

8. Install the new drain trap and drain piping using the manufacturer's installation instructions. Make sure the replacement drain is the same quality, size and design as the previous one.

9. Turn the water supply to the wash basin back on and run the water to check the piping for leaks.

10. Clean up the work area, making sure no water or dirt is left under or around the drain.

Repair Faucets

Faucet leaks are very common. Most leaks are caused when the faucet handle repeatedly pushes the disc washer against a seat when the guest turns the handle. It is important to repair leaky faucets quickly. Tightening the fixtures is only a temporary solution and only prolongs the problem. In fact, it could cause additional damage.

Leaks and drips are usually repaired by replacing the entire assembly on cartridge-type faucets, greasing the seals before the new one is put in place. Cracked seats are replaced with a seat wrench.

Leaking stoppers are fixed by clearing away any blockage underneath it. If there is no blockage, the screw and strap assembly is adjusted.

Service or Repair Toilet

Damage from an overflowing or leaky toilet can be excessive and costly. Toilets have many different components that can be damaged or worn. Maintenance workers turn off the water supply before beginning work. The shut-off valve is usually on the bottom left-hand side of the toilet.

Maintenance workers typically perform the following tasks related to the toilet:

• Fix a running toilet. They first check to make sure the flush handle isn't stuck and loosen the nut on the back of the handle if it is. They then check the lift chain and either uncatch it, untwist it, or trim off excess chain to prevent tangling. If that doesn't work, they check the flapper for pitting and wear. The **flapper** is the rubber piece that opens and closes on the valve seat when the toilet is flushed. Also, if necessary, the washer at the top of the float ball assembly or the assembly itself is replaced.

• Unclog a toilet. The first line of defense is to plunge the toilet and then turn the water back on. If that doesn't work, they use a plumber's snake to loosen up whatever has clogged the toilet. If this doesn't work, they call a plumber.

- Replace a broken toilet handle. After removing the toilet tank cover, the chain is removed from the float ball. Maintenance workers then remove the nut on the back of the handle with channel lock pliers. The handle can then be removed and a new one put in place. The new nut is tightened back on before reconnecting the chain the replacing the tank cover.

- Fix loose toilet seats. The nuts on the toilet seat are removed with a wrench. Garden hose washers are then placed at the top and bottom of the seat bolts and the nuts are screwed back on tightly.

Apply Your Learning 11.4

Please write all answers on a separate sheet of paper.

1. What kind of tape is used when replacing a showerhead?

2. Why is a bucket needed when repairing a wash basin drain?

3. What is the main cause of guest bathroom faucet leaks?

4. List four common maintenance tasks performed on guestroom toilets.

5. What is a flapper?

11.5 Performing Exterior/ Outdoor Maintenance Tasks

AFTER SUCCESSFULLY COMPLETING THIS SECTION, YOU WILL BE ABLE TO:

♦ Describe the basic procedures for performing preventive maintenance of public areas.

♦ Explain the procedures for painting walls and other surfaces.

♦ Explain how to replace ceiling tiles.

♦ Identify the proper steps for performing pressure washing.

♦ Describe how to inspect a laundry cart.

Long before a guest has entered the guestroom, he or she has developed an impression of the lodging property based on the outside or exterior of the property.

Regardless of a lodging property's size, there will be a number of tasks that maintenance workers must perform to the exterior of the property.

Public Area Inspections

Maintenance workers typically use a preventive maintenance checklist and mark each item that is satisfactory. Any discrepancies are noted on the list as are items that require repairs. Maintenance workers fill out a maintenance request form for items requiring repair.

Inspect Building Exteriors

Maintenance workers typically inspect the following areas:

• Exterior building surface

• Window ledges, parapets, decorative surfaces, carvings, etc.

• Parking and exterior building area lighting

• Drainage system

• Support of outdoor stairwells, overhead walkways, balconies, and bridges

• Doors, locks, peepholes

• Walkways

• Mailboxes

• Parking lot painted lines, signs, and pavement

• Fences

• Exterior windows and coverings

• Alarm system

Inspect the Lobby and Vending Area

Maintenance workers inspect the lobby and vending area by:

1. Checking any artwork to make sure it is hung correctly, at the proper height, using the proper anchors.

2. Checking any plants for broken limbs and ensuring there are no leaves or petals on the floor.

3. Inspecting any seasonal decorations.

4. Checking the support of any chandeliers, spotlights, or any other overhanging fixture in the lobby area.

5. Checking the carpeting to make sure it is clean and in good repair.

6. Inspecting handicap-accessible items to ensure they are working properly.

7. Inspecting the vending machines, making sure everything over 700 pounds is bolted to the floor.

8. Inspecting the glass or mirrors on the machines for dirt or damage.

Paint

Generally, painting is not performed as frequently as other maintenance tasks. Lodging properties instead schedule specific times of the year to paint large sections of the property.

Common interior paints include: latex, rubber-based, oil-based, varnish, shellac, lacquer, enamel, epoxy, aluminum, and stains.

Maintenance workers follow safety practices when painting:

- Do not smoke or allow anyone to smoke in areas where paint is stored, prepared, or applied. This prevents sparks from igniting paint fumes.

- Open windows, doors, or vents, or run a fan.

- Wear an air-supply respirator if there is no ventilation.

- Wet down paint sweepings, cloths, and waste. Store them in a closed metal container until they are discarded. Paint sweepings are flammable and represent a potential fire hazard.

- Place a safety lockout tag on electrical switches until work is completed.

- Ensure that electrically powered equipment in a paint shop is properly grounded.

- Check that the lighting is explosion-proof.

- Keep fire extinguishers nearby. The fire extinguisher must be chemical or foam for "B" or "C" class fires. A water-based extinguisher will spread the fire and be ineffective.

When preparing to paint, maintenance workers cover all trim, light fixtures, electrical outlets, and doorknobs with masking or painters tape. They then cover furniture and carpeting with plastic, newspapers, or drop cloths. They also cover fire sprinkler heads with a bag to avoid getting paint on the sensors. Any objects on the wall are removed and "wet paint" signs are posted.

Walls are thoroughly cleaned before painting or paint removal takes place. Any nails are pulled out of the wall and spackle is applied to holes or cracks using a putty knife. Maintenance workers then apply a primer or sealer to any new wallboard surfaces.

There are many methods used for painting, including:

- Painting with a brush

- Painting with a roller

- Spray painting

If an entire room is being painted, the ceiling is painted first to keep the walls free of dripping. Any drips are wiped up before being painted over.

Painting with a brush is slower than rolling or spraying, but it is ideal for odd shapes and spot painting. Brushes are dipped one-third of the length of the bristles into the paint and then surplus paint scraped off. Typically, paint is then laid on with horizontal brush strokes and laid off with vertical strokes from top to bottom. Laying on and laying off makes the paint spread more evenly with the least amount of paint. Maintenance workers can minimize brush marks by using strokes directed toward the last area finished and gradually lifting the brush near the end of the stroke, while the brush is still in motion.

Rolling is faster than brushing but slower than spraying. It is most efficient on large, flat surfaces and requires the least amount of training. Rolling can leave a stippled—or spotted—effect. Brushes are first used to paint the corners and the trim around the mouldings. Then the roller is immersed in paint in a paint tray and moved back and forth along the ramp of the tray. It is then run across a newspaper to remove trapped air. When rolling paint on the wall, maintenance workers are careful to never roll too fast or completely in the same direction. Rolling too fast will cause the roller to spin at the end of a stroke, while rolling in the same direction will distribute paint unevenly. Paint is rolled from a dry area

into the just-painted area. The final stroke is rolled with minimal pressure, to pick up excess paint.

Spraying is the fastest and most efficient way of painting large flat surfaces. It is not recommended in areas where there are fire hazards or equipment that can't be covered. It requires the most training of all three painting methods.

The typical spray gun mixes air under pressure with paint or forces paint through a hole at high pressure. When using an airless-spray system, maintenance workers first strain the paint. They check the adjustments on the gun before starting to spray by testing the spray on a surface similar to what will be painted. They stand six to ten inches from the wall, hold the gun perpendicular to the surface and apply as little pressure as necessary. The paint stroke is started before squeezing the trigger. Maintenance workers squeeze the trigger and move in a straight line, staying the same distance away from the surface. At the end of the stroke, they release the trigger.

After painting, brushes, rollers, and spray heads are all thoroughly cleaned.

Replace Ceiling Tiles

Ceiling tiles may need to be replaced in many different areas of a lodging property: guestrooms, hallways, the lobby, meeting rooms, and back-of-house areas. The same procedures for replacing ceiling tiles should apply to all areas. Maintenance workers always practice safety precautions when ascending, standing on, and descending ladders.

1. Remove the damaged ceiling tile by lifting it up and then sliding it at an angle downwards and out of the ceiling frame.

2. Discard the damaged ceiling tile.

3. A ladder may be needed to replace ceiling tiles.

4. Inspect for water leaks if the damage to the tile was caused by water.

5. Find the source of the leak and repair it prior to inserting the new ceiling tiles.

6. Check the measurements of the new ceiling tile to make sure it matches the old tile. The new piece of ceiling tile should be cut to the same measurement as the one removed.

7. Use an undamaged piece of tile from the ceiling to measure the cut of the new tile.

8. Cut the new tile using a sharp utility knife (if the new tile requires cutting). Lay down a cloth or towel when cutting the ceiling tile to avoid getting the floor or carpet dirty.

9. Install the new tile by sliding it above the ceiling frame at an angle and then lowering it into the ceiling frame. New ceiling tile fits snugly into ceiling frame; no gaps.

10. Clean the area.

Perform Pressure Washing

Pressure washing is an extremely useful and efficient technique for cleaning exterior surfaces at a lodging property. Maintenance workers use pressure washers to clean sidewalks, walls, windows, and can even use them to quickly remove old paint from various surfaces.

Because of the nature of the work, pressure washing is usually performed when guest traffic is low. Maintenance workers wear protective eyewear and a raincoat while pressure washing to avoid injury from the spray.

Maintenance workers maintain a safe distance from the surface they are cleaning. Pressure washers can remove paint very easily if the stream of water is too close to the surface. Brick or cement walls and sidewalks can be damaged if the stream of water is too close to the surface.

Inspect Laundry Carts

Laundry attendants would not be able to properly perform their duties if they did not have laundry carts. Because of the heavy lifting that laundry carts do, they are susceptible to wear, tear, and damage. There are some basic steps maintenance workers take when inspecting laundry carts:

1. Test the wheels to make sure they are in good working condition.

2. Make sure that the wheels' **zerk fittings** are sufficiently lubricated. (Zerk fittings are where one can lubricate the bearing in the wheel or swivel section of the caster.) When lubricating the wheels, one or two shots of grease is sufficient.

3. Replace wheels if necessary.

4. Check that casters and hitches are in good condition.

5. Replace the casters and hitches if necessary.

6. Check that laundry cart wire frames are unbent and undamaged. Laundry carts with bent frames or wire should be replaced or taken out of service.

Apply Your Learning 11.5

For each of the following statements, write "true" if the statement is correct or "false" if the statement is wrong. Please write all answers on a separate sheet of paper.

1. Any vending machine over 300 pounds should be bolted to the floor.

2. Painting with a brush is slower than painting with a roller.

3. Rolling is the fastest and most efficient way to paint large flat surfaces.

4. Maintenance workers should stand close to a wall that they are pressure washing to keep control of the washer.

5. To be properly lubricated, a laundry cart wheel needs three or four shots of grease.

Quick Hits

SECTION 11.1—GETTING TO KNOW THE MAINTENANCE WORKER

- Maintenance workers are responsible for maintaining the function of all areas of a lodging property's premises.

- The superior performance of maintenance workers makes a difference in the success of a property and the comfort of guests.

- Maintenance workers save their properties time and money by performing routine preventive maintenance.

- Maintenance workers contribute to the security of the property and its guests by exercising key control procedures.

SECTION 11.2—PREPARING TO PERFORM MAINTENANCE WORK

- The isolation of electrical equipment—lockout/tagout—during maintenance procedures is essential.

- Lodging properties use maintenance request forms and a maintenance request log to document all maintenance requests.

- Proper care and preparation of help maintenance tools is vital to protecting property assess and ensuring guest satisfaction.

- An organized maintenance shop helps maintenance workers work more efficiently.

- Maintenance workers must communicate a guestroom's status to the front desk and housekeeping departments both before and after maintenance work.

SECTION 11.3—PERFORMING GUESTROOM MAINTENANCE TASKS

- Interior installations that can be performed in a guestroom include installing curtain rods, mounting blinds or shades, and hanging pictures.

- Guestroom maintenance duties include replacing light bulbs or television sets, repairing door hardware or damaged carpet, and applying wallpaper.

- Newer carpet now is available in tiles which more easily permit the repair of a damaged section of carpet.

- Corner guards take the brunt of any impact a corner takes and therefore can receive damage and need to be replaced.

- Vacuum cleaners receive heavy use and must be routinely repaired or maintained.

SECTION 11.4—PERFORMING BATHROOM MAINTENANCE TASKS

- Maintenance tasks performed in the guest bathroom usually involve water damage.

- Because of water deposit buildup, pliers may be required to remove an old showerhead.

- When repairing a wash basin drain, a bucket and towel are useful for catching drips and cleaning spills.

- When a faucet is leaking or dripping, it is important to repair or replace the damaged part. Tightening the fixtures is only a temporary solution and will prolong the problem.

- Maintenance tasks performed on a guestroom toilet may include: fixing a running toilet, unclogging a toilet, replacing a broken toilet handle, and fixing a loose toilet seat.

Section 11.5—Performing Exterior/ Outdoor Maintenance Tasks

- When painting, it is important to follow the specific safety procedures such as venting the area being painted and wetting down old paint chips.

- Painting can be performed using a brush, roller, or spray. Brushing is the slowest method; spraying is the fastest method.

- When replacing ceiling tiles, it is also important to check for water leaks or damage.

- Pressure washing is an extremely useful technique and can be used both to clean walls and other surfaces and also to prepare those surfaces for painting by removing old paint.

- Because of their value to laundry attendants, it is important to keep laundry carts well maintained.

Laundry Attendant

Sections

Doing the laundry at home or at the Laundromat may not be your favorite chore, but it is not a difficult one. Once or twice a week, you sort a basket of wash, select a detergent and the proper washer setting, and then dry and fold the items.

But imagine doing laundry every day by the truckload, and you begin to have an idea of the scope of a lodging property's laundry.

Add to the sheer volume of wash the responsibilities of making it look, smell, and feel good and getting it to the right place at the right time. Then consider that linen (sheets, towels, tablecloths, and other items) is a housekeeping department's second-largest expense, and you will understand why good laundry management is essential to the success of a lodging operation.

12.1 Getting to Know the Laundry Attendant

AFTER SUCCESSFULLY COMPLETING THIS SECTION, YOU WILL BE ABLE TO:

♦ Explain the important role laundry attendants play in a lodging property.

♦ Prevent injuries.

♦ Identify linen types.

♦ Explain how to clean and maintain the work area.

♦ Describe the laundry cycle.

What is a Laundry Attendant?

A laundry attendant at a lodging property could be defined as a housekeeping department employee who launders linens and employee uniforms. While this definition is technically correct, it does not describe the effect they have on guests.

Cleanliness is an important factor for guests when they determine whether to return to a property. By cleaning and ironing towels, sheets, tablecloths, and uniforms, laundry attendants make a difference in the success of their property and in the comfort of the guests.

Laundry attendants have a job to be proud of—without them, the property would be empty. No one would check into a room that had torn blankets and dirty towels, and no one would dine at a restaurant whose napkins and tablecloths were soiled.

The laundry attendants make the towels, linens, and uniforms spotless and attractive. They make a difference!

Exhibit 1 lists all the tasks that a typical laundry attendant performs.

Superior Performance Standards

The condition of linens and employee uniforms should enhance each guest's overall experience. Making sure these items are clean and fresh after laundering is the laundry attendant's ultimate goal. The property's superior performance standards help them achieve that goal.

What are some of these standards? Laundry attendants must:

• Carefully examine linens to prevent worn, torn, or permanently stained pieces from remaining in inventory

• Properly use laundry equipment

• Remove spots and stains in the laundry department's spotting station both before and after items have been washed

• Be alert to safety procedures at all times

• Practice teamwork at all times

1. Sort Linens and Uniforms

2. Pretreat and/or Rewash Heavily Soiled Items

3. Load, Use, and Unload Washers

4. Load, Use, and Unload Dryers

5. Iron Linens Using a Mechanical Flatwork Ironer

6. Use Mechanical Linen-Folding Equipment

7. Fold Linens by Hand

8. Iron Laundry by Hand

9. Mend and Sew Linens and/or Uniforms

10. Clean and Maintain Work Areas

11. Fill Banquet and Restaurant Linen Requisitions

12. Deliver Guest Service Supplies to Room

13. Process Contract-Cleaned Linens and Uniforms

14. Issue and Receive Employee Uniforms

15. Restock Housekeeping Closets and Carts

16. Provide Towel Service to Recreation Areas and Carts

- Demonstrate professional behavior at all times

- Wash their hands after taking a break

In addition, they must make sure all finished laundry:

- Is free of wrinkles

- Has a fresh fragrance

- Is pH-balanced so it does not cause skin irritation

Preventing Injuries

To do their job, laundry attendants need to repeat the same actions throughout the day. This kind of movement can cause **repetitive stress injuries** if they are not careful. Muscles can weaken from repeating the same motions.

There are several ways laundry attendants can help protect themselves from injury:

- Before beginning a shift each day, they stretch out all of the muscles that they'll be using:

  - Slowly shrug shoulders several times.

  - Slowly bend down and touch their toes several times.

  - Hold out their arms from their body and slowly make small circles with them. Make each circle slightly bigger than the one before.

- During a shift, they stop for a minute once in a while to stretch their muscles again.

- Laundry attendants can switch tasks with each other about once every hour, if allowed. This gives some of their muscles a rest and lets them use different muscles throughout the day.

Laundry attendants also use special equipment. They must be very careful around these equipment pieces—especially such equipment as rollers and ironers which operate at very high temperatures.

Linen Types

Each property uses many different types and sizes of **linens.** All of them will likely pass through the hands of the laundry attendant. It is important for them to learn the types and sizes of linens their property uses because they are the people who protect linens from excess wear and tear. They are the people who keep them clean. And they are the people who make sure that they go in the right spot after they are clean.

A property may use the following linens:

- Washcloths
- Hand towels
- Bath towels
- Beach towels
- Bath mats
- Blankets
- Sheets
- Pillowcases
- Mattress pads
- Tablecloths
- Napkins
- Cleaning cloths
- Shower curtains and liners

The materials that linens are made of may include:

- Acrylic
- Cotton
- Polycotton
- Nylon
- Polyester
- Wool
- Blends

Maintain Work Areas

Cleaning is an ongoing responsibility of everyone who works in a laundry. Laundry attendants also perform maintenance on a daily basis as part of their laundry duties.

Laundry attendants clean as they work by picking up and throwing away food scraps, trash, and other items that fall from soiled laundry as soon as they finish sorting the laundry. They check floor drains to prevent backups and clean lint, mop strings, and other debris from floor drains.

Separate carts are used for soiled and clean laundry. These carts must be maintained by making sure they have no sharp edges or rusty spots and by oiling cart wheels as necessary.

Keeping work tables clean is another important part of the laundry attendant's job. Soiled linens are not placed on work tables. If the tables become soiled, they are wiped clean with a clean, damp cloth.

If trash chutes on guestroom floors empty into a trash bin in the laundry, then trash that falls outside the bin must be placed back in the bin. The trash is emptied regularly to prevent any buildup.

Before closing the department at the end of the day, everything is stored in its proper place. Clean linen is never stored on the floor.

Lint filters are also cleaned on a regular basis. It is important to reduce the amount of lint in the air as breathing lint is bad for people's health.

While equipment repairs are the responsibility of the maintenance or engineering department, laundry attendants look and listen for unusual equipment noises or operation. If something is leaking, they put in requests for repairs. Also, they report the following problems to their supervisor:

- Chemical dispenser levels that don't move

- Linens that don't look or feel clean

- Washer gauges that are not within acceptable temperatures

Laundry attendants also clean the outside of machines.

The Laundry Cycle

Every laundry uses a basic cycle of operation. This cycle includes the following steps:

- Collecting soiled linens

- Transporting soiled linens to the laundry

- Sorting

- Washing

- Extracting

- Finishing

- Folding

Exhibit 2 diagrams a version of this process.

Apply Your Learning 12.1

Please write all answers on a separate sheet of paper.

1. Why is the job of a laundry attendant important?

2. How can a laundry attendant demonstrate superior performance standards?

3. How can laundry attendants protect themselves from repetitive stress injuries?

4. List three types of linens that a hotel might have.

5. Why is it important to reduce the amount of lint in the air?

6. What are the steps in the laundry cycle?

Exhibit 2
The Flow of Laundry

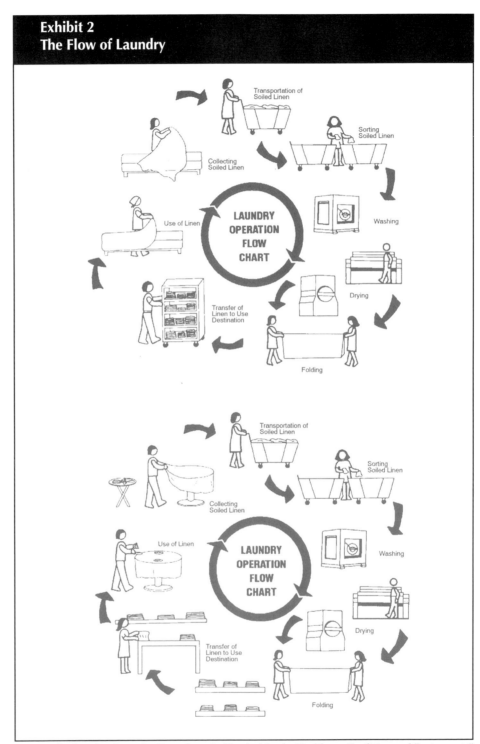

Source: "On Premises Laundry Procedures in Hotels, Motels, Healthcare Facilities, and Restaurants" (pamphlet) (St. Paul, Minn.: Ecolab, Institutional Products Division), undated.

12.2 Washing and Drying Linens

AFTER SUCCESSFULLY COMPLETING THIS SECTION, YOU WILL BE ABLE TO:

♦ Explain how to sort linens and uniforms.

♦ Identify how to pretreat or rewash heavily soiled items.

♦ Describe how to load, use, and unload washers.

♦ Describe how to load, use, and unload dryers.

Sort Linens and Uniforms

Linens are usually collected by guestroom attendants and bus persons and delivered by their departments to the laundry. Laundry attendants typically enter the laundry cycle at the **sorting** stage.

Exhibit 1 gives step-by-step procedures for sorting linens and uniforms.

Pretreat or Rewash Heavily Soiled Items

Heavily soiled laundry is often treated by either rewashing or **pretreating,** though many properties send out or recycle soiled linen. Pretreating takes extra time. If the chemicals in the washer are formulated correctly for the property's water conditions, pretreating may not be necessary.

Laundry attendants wear heavy latex utility gloves and protective goggles to pretreat and transfer items to the washer. This protects them from the chemicals that are being used.

Typically, one of the following methods is used to pretreat soiled items:

• Use a spray bottle filled with an approved spotting solution to spray the stains, spots, and soil. The spray should break up the stain or soil so that the chemicals will remove it in the washer.

• Place the heavily soiled, stained, and spotted linens in a soak tank filled with an approved soaking solution. Leave it in for a set amount of time.

Linens then need to set for a few minutes before they are put in the washer.

When linens are removed from the washer, laundry attendants again check for linens that did not come clean. They are then treated again and rewashed.

Load, Use, and Unload Washers

The next step in the laundry cycle is **washing** linens.

Exhibit 2 gives step-by-step instructions for loading, using, and unloading washing machines.

Load, Use, and Unload Dryers

After washing, linens need to be dried. Most washing machines now have **extracting** capabilities. Extracting removes excess moisture from laundered items through a high-speed spin. This reduces the weight of the laundry and makes it easier for workers to lift the laundry and move it to the dryers. It also reduces drying time.

Linens should be sorted by fabric type before they are dried. Steam cabinets or tunnels are often used to dry blends because they give these fabrics a finished, wrinkle-free look.

Towels, washcloths, and other no-iron items are typically dried in a dryer. Exhibit 3 gives step-by-step instructions for loading, using, and unloading dryers.

Apply Your Learning 12.2

Please write all answers on a separate sheet of paper.

1. How does sorting benefit fabrics?
2. Describe one method for pretreating soiled items.
3. What is a laundry production log?
4. Why should wash start times be staggered?
5. What is the correct temperature for a dryer?
6. What problems are caused by overloading a dryer?

Exhibit 1
Sort Linens and Uniforms

Materials needed: Heavy latex utility gloves and laundry carts for soiled linens and uniforms.

STEPS:	HOW-TO'S:
1. **Follow safety precautions when sorting laundry.**	❏ Wear heavy latex utility gloves. ❏ Be careful to avoid cuts from broken glass in table linens. ❏ Do not handle linens or uniforms containing or stained with bodily fluids. Notify your supervisor.
2. **Look for and remove items from soiled laundry as you sort it.**	❏ Remove pens, pencils, corkscrews, change, paper, etc. from uniform pockets. ❏ Remove employee name tags, employee service pins, promotional buttons, etc. that are attached to the garments. ❏ Remove food scraps, silverware, glasses, china, wine corks, etc. from table linens before washing.
3. **Sort linens according to use and fabric type.**	❏ Sort linens into groups. Sorting helps prevent unnecessary wear and damage to fabrics. Different fibers, weaves, and colors require different wash formulas and methods. Sorting linens by fabric type ensures that the right wash formulas and methods are used. Common groups are: • Sheets • Pillowcases • Bath towels • Hand towels • Beach towels • Washcloths • Bath mats • Shower curtains and liners • Blankets and mattress pads

(continued)

Exhibit 1
Sort Linens and Uniforms *(continued)*

STEPS:	HOW-TO'S:
	• White tablecloths • White linen napkins • Pastel tablecloths • Pastel linen napkins • Dark tablecloths (sorted by color) Always wash red and burgundy linens seperately from other items. • Dark napkins (sorted by color) • Housekeeping cleaning cloths • Buffer pads (wash alone, don't dry) • Kitchen cleaning cloths ❑ Always separate cleaning cloths from guest linens. ❑ Separate greasy cloths, which are fire hazards, from other cleaning cloths. ❑ Sort and wash table linens separately from other linens.
4. Sort uniforms according to department.	❑ Put the same color shirts together, all the same color skirts together, all the same color pants together, all the same color aprons together, etc. ❑ Put heavily soiled uniforms into separate piles for special handling.
5. Place sorted laundry in the correct laundry carts.	

Exhibit 2
Load, Use, and Unload Washers

Materials needed: Laundry scales, a laundry protection log, washers, nylon mesh bags, laundry chemicals, and laundry carts.

STEPS:	HOW-TO'S:
1. Prepare loads of laundry.	❑ Use scales to weigh the soiled items. Some lodging properties determine load size by counting out a specific number of items.
	❑ Do not put too many or too few items in a load. Overloaded washers will not get linens clean. Partially full washers waste water and chemicals.
2. Organize your work.	❑ Follow the laundry production log to determine the order in which to wash loads. The laundry production log is used to track productivity. You may need to record the loads you wash on the log.
	❑ Wash heavily soiled linens first so that stains will not set and ruin the items. Food and beverage linens require a longer wash formula and must be scheduled so overall production won't slow down.
	❑ Stagger the starting times of washers at least two to five minutes apart. Staggering start times:
	• Aids in a smooth and constant work flow
	• Does not use up the water supply
	• Does not cause electrical overloads
	• Prevents flooding and clogged drains from machines draining at the same time
	❑ Schedule loads to meet the production demands of other departments.
	❑ Keep enough flatwork, such as tablecloths and sheets, washed to allow continuous operation of the ironer.
	❑ Wash towels when there is enough clean flatwork on hand to keep the ironer busy.

(continued)

Exhibit 2
Load, Use, and Unload Washers (continued)

STEPS:	HOW-TO'S:
3. **Be aware of special considerations.**	❑ Wash new colored linens separately the first few times to avoid dyeing other fabrics.
	❑ Wash dark-colored fabrics at lower temperatures to prevent fading.
	❑ Do not wash colors with chlorine bleach. Use only approved chemicals in washers. Uniforms will often have more than one color of fabric within a single garment and will require a cold-water wash to prevent fading of darker colors onto lighter colors.
	❑ Place delicate items, items with decorative buttons, and items with strings (such as aprons), in nylon mesh bags to prevent damage or tangling.
4. **Load washers.**	❑ Fill washers from front to back and from side to side. Filling washers this way will allow room for the laundry to fall into the wash solution.
	❑ Leave a three- to four-inch gap at the top of the washer.
	❑ Only put one load in each washer; never over- or underload washers.
5. **Calculate wash formulas.**	❑ Follow your supervisor's instructions or the instructions on the tag in each type of garment. Commercial washing machines may have many choices of wash cycles and a range of detergents, soaps, and fabric conditioners. You will be shown how to work the equipment at your property.
	❑ Find out the following:
	• *Time* – How much time will be needed to wash the laundry you have loaded? Heavily

(continued)

Exhibit 2
Load, Use, and Unload Washers *(continued)*

STEPS:	HOW-TO'S:
	soiled items require more chemicals and a longer wash time. Moderately or lightly soiled linens will be washed with fewer chemicals and in fewer cycles.
	• *Temperature*—What temperature should the water be in order to get the items clean?
	• *Agitation*—How much agitation is needed to loosen the soils in these fabrics?
	• *Chemicals*—What chemicals will do the best job on the particular soil and fabric types? At some lodging properties, the detergent will be automatically added by the machine.
	• A laundry supervisor or an equipment service or chemical representative may preset time, temperature, and mechanical action.
	❏ Certain washers may be set aside for certain fabrics. If so, find out which washers to use for each fabric type and soil condition.
6. Set the controls on the machine according to fabric type.	
7. Unload washers.	❏ Remove wet laundry promptly from washers to prevent wrinkles.
	❏ Don't wrestle with heavy laundry. Remove a few pieces at a time from the top of the load.
	❏ Shake out the linens as you remove them to avoid twisted and wrinkled fabrics.
	❏ Place wet linens in carts for clean laundry until you place the linens in the dryers. If empty dryers are nearby, put the wet laundry directly in the dryers. If laundry is very wet at the end of the cycle, more extraction time may be needed. Otherwise, extra drying time will be needed, which is more costly than extraction.

Exhibit 3
Load, Use, and Unload Dryers

Materials needed: Dryers, laundry scales, laundry carts, hangers, and nylon mesh bags.

STEPS:	HOW-TO'S:
1. Check dryer for correct temperatures. Dryers should work between 165 and 185 degrees Fahrenheit (74 and 85 degrees Celsius) for the greatest efficiency.	
2. Clean lint from filters at least twice a day to prevent fires. Clogged filters are a fire hazard and decrease the efficiency of the equipment.	
3. Load dryers.	❑ Follow your supervisor's or the equipment manufacturer's loading instructions. Loading dryers correctly prevents wasted energy. Overloading increases the drying time and wrinkling. Underloading wastes energy. ❑ Load dryers by weight or piece count.
4. Set time, temperature, and cool-down time.	❑ Know the drying times and temperatures for each fabric. ❑ Always let pillowcases and sheets run through a cool-down cycle of three to five minutes to reduce wrinkles and save the permanent press features of the fabric. The cool-down cycle will reduce the chance of burns. ❑ Run table linens through a three- to five-minute cool-down cycle in the dryer before folding.

(continued)

Exhibit 3
Load, Use, and Unload Dryers *(continued)*

STEPS:	HOW-TO'S:
5. Dry items.	❑ Dry uniforms with polyester fibers on medium heat to prevent damage to the fabric.
	❑ Dry delicate items, items with strings, and items with decorative buttons in nylon mesh bags to prevent damage and tangling.
6. Remove items from dryers.	❑ Avoid burns from hot dryer surfaces.
	❑ To prevent wrinkling, drape linens over the edge of laundry carts as soon as they are removed from the dryer.
	❑ Shake out dry linens and stack them loosely. If time permits, fold linens as you remove them from the dryer.
	❑ Hang uniforms as you remove them from the dryer, even if they will be ironed.
	❑ Avoid dropping clean linens on the floor. If you drop clean linens on the floor, put them with soiled linens to be rewashed.
	❑ Do not let dryers run after the laundry has closed. Running dryers after closing time and leaving linens in dryers are serious fire hazards.
	❑ Do not leave linens in the dryers overnight.

12.3 Ironing and Folding Linens

AFTER SUCCESSFULLY COMPLETING THIS SECTION, YOU WILL BE ABLE TO:

♦ Explain how to iron linens by machine or by hand.

♦ Describe the steps to fold linens by machine or by hand.

Use a Flatwork Ironer

Sheets, pillowcases, tablecloths, and slightly damp napkins go directly to flatwork irons. Ironers vary in size and degree of automation. Uniforms are generally pressed in special ironing equipment. Steam tunnels are being used more often for removing wrinkles from polyester blend uniforms.

Exhibit 1 gives step-by-step instructions for ironing linens using a flatwork ironer.

Iron Laundry by Hand

Uniforms, specialty items, and napkins for VIP functions may be ironed by hand. Laundry attendants set the temperature of the iron to match the type of fabric. If the iron is too cool, it will not produce a smooth finish. If it is too hot, it will scorch the fabric.

The item is spread smoothly on the ironing board. Laundry attendants usually use their hands to smooth out wrinkles.

Ironed-in wrinkles are hard to remove and increase their work.

If the iron sticks to the fabric, the iron is too hot. If the iron drags on the fabric, the iron is too cool. Using an ironing cloth between the iron and the fabric can help protect delicate fabrics and synthetics. This allows the laundry attendant to use a higher temperature without scorching or damaging the fabric.

The iron is moved lightly over the fabric. It cannot rest on one spot for too long as it would scorch the fabric. Laundry attendants move the iron back and forth over the fabric several times until the wrinkles are gone.

Use Mechanical Linen Folding Equipment

Most linen folding is still done by hand, but some pieces of linen may be folded using mechanical equipment. An automatic folder and crossfold equipment can supply a finished folded product for stacking.

Laundry attendants shake out and prepare linens for mechanical folding. Each piece of equipment will have special procedures and specific safety guards.

Folding equipment is set to different speeds depending on the type of linen. In general:

• Fold sheets at the speed of 60 to 120 feet per minute

- Fold pillowcases at the rate of 30 to 75 feet per minute

- Fold table linens at the rate of 30 to 60 feet per minute

Folded linens are then stacked neatly on clean storage shelves.

Fold Linens by Hand

Folding usually sets the pace for the linen room. Washing and drying items faster than they can be folded leads to unnecessary wrinkling and resoiling.

Laundry attendants must inspect linens as they fold, storing those that are to be reused and rejecting stained, torn, or otherwise unsuitable items. This inspection may increase folding time. Folding and storing is done well away from the soiled linen area to avoid resoiling clean laundry.

Exhibit 2 gives step-by-step instructions for folding linens by hand.

Apply Your Learning 12.3

Please write all answers on a separate sheet of paper.

1. Which types of items are ironed by flatwork irons?

2. Which types of items are usually ironed by hand?

3. Which is more common—folding by machine or folding by hand?

4. Why should synthetic items be allowed to cool before folding?

5. What task dictates the pace of the laundry room work?

Exhibit 1
Iron Linens Using a Mechanical Flatwork Ironer

Materials needed: Flatwork ironer, a feed cart or shake-out basket, and clean, dry linens.

STEPS:	HOW-TO'S:
1. **Shake out linens.**	❑ Use a feed cart for moving sheets to the ironer. Allow space to shake out linens. Flatwork refers to any item that must be sent through a mechanical flatwork ironer.
	❑ Shake out the linens over the side of a feed cart or shake-out basket. A feed cart is a long, narrow cart on which linens can be spread out and fed more easily into ironers.
2. **Learn the speed settings for each type of linen.**	❑ In general:
	• Iron sheets at the speed of 90 to 110 feet per minute.
	• Iron pillowcases at the rate of 45 to 75 feet per minute.
	• Iron table linens at the rate of 45 to 75 feet per minute.
	The wide range of speeds are due to many factors, including:
	• The size of the ironer (number of rollers)
	• The heat source and temperature (thermal or steam)
	• The type of material being processed (100 percent cotton versus polyester/cotton blends)
	❑ Iron pillowcases and table linens more slowly than sheets because the additional thickness holds more moisture.
3. **Feed the linens carefully to avoid accidents and injuries.**	❑ Be very careful when working with a mechanical ironer. High temperatures and roller mechanisms can be very hazardous.
	❑ Avoid stretching the fabric while ironing. Stretching may cause an ironed tablecloth or napkin to lose its square shape.

Exhibit 2
Fold Linens by Hand

Materials needed: Clean linens, linen carts, clean work tables, and an "extra hand" sheet folder.

STEPS:	HOW-TO'S:
1. **Allow synthetic or synthetic blend items to cool before removing them from the dryer when possible. Heat causes the synthetic fibers in linens to become brittle. Handling warm linens wears them out faster.**	
2. **Move linens in carts for clean linens to the folding tables.**	
3. **Remove items that are stained, spotted, or damaged.**	❑ Be alert to lipstick stains on pillowcases. ❑ Remove all spotted, stained, or damaged towels for further treatment later. ❑ Pretreat and rewash stained or spotted items.
4. **Fold sheets and banquet tablecloths.**	❑ Use an "extra hand" sheet folder to fold sheets and banquet tablecloths. If your property does not use an "extra hand" sheet folder, ask a co-worker to act as the extra hand. ❑ Do not use your chin or mouth to hold the sheet or tablecloth while folding. ❑ Pull a sheet or tablecloth from the cart by a hemmed edge. Sheets are hemmed on the ends and not on the sides. ❑ Fold the hemmed end in half with the finished side of the hem on the outside. ❑ Step on the foot pedal of the "extra hand" sheet folder to open the clamp.

(continued)

Exhibit 2
Fold Linens by Hand *(continued)*

STEPS:	HOW-TO'S:
	❑ Attach the two corners that are held together to the clamp. Let the folded center of the sheet or tablecloth hang down.
	❑ Starting at the clamp, line up the unhemmed side edges as you move away from the clamp.
	❑ Keep moving away from the clamp until one of your hands has reached the opposite end of the cloth. Straighten the cloth as you walk backward.
	❑ With your right hand, hold the opposite corners of the hemmed edge, and run your left hand back along the top of the unhemmed edges to the center of the cloth.
	❑ Walk toward the clamp. Open the clamp with the foot pedal and attach the corners in your right hand to the corners already held in the clamp.
	❑ Keep holding the center of the folded cloth in your left hand.
	❑ Pull the cloth back gently with your left hand, smoothing wrinkles with your right hand.
	❑ Grasp the clamped corners of the cloth with your right hand near the clamp.
	❑ Open the clamp with your foot and remove the corners.
	❑ Hook the center of the unhemmed edge (halfway between your hands) under the clamp.
	❑ Bring your hands together and transfer the corners held by your left hand to your right hand. You are now holding the sheet (folded to one-fourth its size). Practice should lead to a smooth motion in folding the linens.
	❑ With your left hand, grasp the cloth near the clamp and open the clamp with your foot. Fold the cloth one more time as you place it on a work table or linen rack.

(continued)

Exhibit 2
Fold Linens by Hand *(continued)*

STEPS:	HOW-TO'S:
5. **Fold and stack pillowcases.**	❑ Sort pillowcases by size as you fold them. Some lodging properties will use only standard-size pillowcases and will place three pillows on a king-size bed. ❑ Grasp the closed end of the pillowcase. ❑ Shake or flip it to straighten any wrinkles or folded edges. ❑ Lay the pillowcase flat on a clean work table with the long end of the pillowcase running from left to right and the closed end of the case to your left. ❑ Smooth out wrinkles with your hands. ❑ Pick up the front left and right corners and fold them over to meet the back left and right corners. Then fold the left (closed) end over the right end. By folding this way, you will have seen the entire outer surface of the pillowcase during the folding process. ❑ Smooth out wrinkles with your hands. ❑ Place pillowcases in a stack so that the side that was against the table during folding is on top when stacked for storage.
6. **Fold and stack washcloths.**	❑ Pick up each terry washcloth and lay it flat on the work table. In your property, washcloths may be folded only in half or stacked flat without folding. ❑ Fold the terry washcloth in half and then in quarters, smoothing out wrinkles with your hands at each fold. ❑ Stack the washcloths neatly.

(continued)

Exhibit 2
Fold Linens by Hand *(continued)*

STEPS:	HOW-TO'S:
7. **Fold towels and bath mats to display the property's logo.**	❑ Place towels and bath mats on the folding table with the length of the towel running from left to right and the logo facing down and to your right Even if your towels and mats do not have the property's logo, use the same folding procedure to make sure that you look at all sides of the towel or mat.
	❑ Pick up the front left and right corners and fold over one-third of the way across the length of the towel or bath mat. Pick up the rear corners and bring them toward you to the folded edge.
	❑ Fold the cloth in half from left to right. Turn the cloth over so that the logo is up, and place the folded cloth in the appropriate stack. You may be told to simply fold bath mats in half.
	❑ Stack by size and color as you fold.
8. **Fold terry bathrobes.**	❑ Shake out each bathrobe and place it flat, back-side-down, on a clean folding table.
	❑ Be sure each bathrobe has a sash that is smooth and free from knots.
	❑ Straighten the sash, and make sure that it passes through the sash loops.
	❑ Straighten the lapels of the robe. Overlap one lapel about six inches over the other lapel.
	❑ Loop the ends of the sash neatly on the front of the robe.
	❑ Carefully turn the robe over. Fold the sleeves across the back. Fold the robe lengthwise into thirds.
	❑ Turn the robe over and make sure the sash is neatly arranged.
	❑ Stack the clean robes.
9. **Stack cleaning cloths flat without folding**	
10. **Stack table linens by size and color.**	

12.4 Delivering Linens

AFTER SUCCESSFULLY COMPLETING THIS SECTION, YOU WILL BE ABLE TO:

◆ Explain how to fill banquet and restaurant linen requisitions.

◆ Describe how to issue and receive employee uniforms.

◆ Explain how to restock housekeeping closets and carts.

◆ Identify how to provide towel service to recreation areas.

After folding, laundered items are post-sorted and stacked. **Post-sorting** separates any linen types and sizes that were missed in pre-sorting. There should be enough storage room for at least one par. Finished items should be allowed to "rest" on shelves for 24 hours after laundering because many types of linens are more easily damaged right after washing. Once linens are on shelves, yellowing and fading can be spotted easily.

Linens are usually transferred to their use areas via carts. Use areas include:

• Banquet areas

• Restaurants

• Employee check-in areas

• Housekeeping closets

• Recreation areas

Fill Linen Requisitions

Table linen requisitions are often used to let laundry attendants know how many of each type of linen the food and beverage outlets need for the next day. These requisitions are based on the amount of business those outlets have forecasted for the next day. Laundry attendants carefully count linens to supply the correct quantities, colors, and sizes.

As each type of linen is supplied, laundry attendants enter the number of items issued. If they do not have enough items, they write on the requisition the number they do have and circle it so that the outlet will know the count is short.

The clean linens are then placed on a cart specifically designed for clean linens. The laundry attendant then notifies the food and beverage department that they can come to the laundry to pick up their linens.

Issue and Receive Uniforms

The housekeeping department usually stores the uniforms for the entire property. The human resources department authorizes the issue of uniforms to new employees and sets up guidelines for replacing lost, damaged, ill-fitting or badly worn uniforms.

New employees are often given a **uniform authorization form** by the human resources department. The form lists the employee's size and the type of uniform (by position) to be issued. The forms also show all issued uniforms that have not been turned in. Human resources and the controller will decide if the employee will be charged for missing or purposely damaged items.

The laundry attendants read the uniform authorization form and then give each employee the correct uniform. They check to make sure all items (pants, shirts, ties, etc.) are included.

The laundry attendant also explains the cleaning procedures for issued uniforms and then asks the employee to sign the form to indicate that he or she received the uniform. The laundry attendant then signs his or her initials on the form. A copy is filed in the uniform room and a copy is given to human resources.

When an employee returns a uniform, the laundry attendants pull all copies of outstanding uniform authorization forms for this employee from the uniform room records. On the form, they check off each uniform piece that is turned in. If the employee reports that a uniform is missing or if a garment appears to have been damaged on purpose, the laundry attendant records this on the uniform authorization form.

The laundry attendants then remove any employee identification and either return uniforms to inventory or place it with the uniforms to be laundered.

Restock Housekeeping Closets and Carts

Laundry attendants may be asked to collect soiled laundry from each floor. If a property does not have linen chutes on each guest-room floor, laundry attendants may retrieve soiled linen carts from the housekeeping closet. These closets are kept locked. Laundry attendants unlock the closet and place on the cart the bags of soiled linens in the closet, locking the door behind them. If the property does have linen chutes, laundry attendants dump the soiled linen down these chutes.

The task of running clean linens and guest amenities from the laundry to housekeeping closets is called **"linen running."** Clean linens are stacked neatly on a cart and taken to the housekeeping closets. Linens and amenities are stacked neatly on the shelves following the par stock list in the closet.

Laundry attendants may also be asked to stock housekeeping carts with the appropriate number of towels, washcloths, and bed linens.

Provide Towel Service to Recreation Areas

Towels used in recreation areas are usually a different color than guestroom towels. Laundry attendants take a linen bag and a linen cart stacked with clean recreation-area towels to the pool, health club, or other recreation area.

They collect the soiled towels from the area and place them in the linen bag. They then leave the correct number of clean towels.

Apply Your Learning 12.4

Please write all answers on a separate sheet of paper.

1. List some of a lodging property's linen use areas.

2. What is the name of the form used to determine how many linens are delivered to the restaurant?

3. Who issues uniform authorization forms?

4. Where do laundry attendants find bags of soiled guestroom linen?

5. What does a laundry attendant use to collect soiled linens from recreation areas?

Quick Hits

SECTION 12.1—GETTING TO KNOW THE LAUNDRY ATTENDANT

- Laundry attendants ensure that the property's towels, sheets, tablecloths, and uniforms are in top condition.

- Laundry attendants must make sure that all laundry is free of wrinkles, has a fresh fragrance, and is pH-balanced to avoid skin irritation.

- Laundry attendants should exercise and change tasks to avoid getting repetitive stress injuries.

- The laundry cycle includes collecting linens, transporting, sorting washing, extracting, finishing, folding, storing, and transferring.

SECTION 12.2—WASHING AND DRYING LINENS

- Linens are sorted into groups to help prevent unnecessary wear and damage to fabrics.

- Heavily soiled laundry is often treated by pretreating or rewashing.

- Wash formulas take into account time, temperature, agitation, and chemicals.

- Loading dryers correctly prevents wasted energy.

SECTION 12.3—IRONING AND FOLDING LINENS

- Flatwork irons are usually used to iron sheets, pillowcases, tablecloths, and napkins.

- Uniforms, specialty items, and napkins for VIP functions are ironed by hand.

- Folding equipment can be set to different speeds depending on the type of linen being folded.

- Folding sets the pace for the linen room. Laundry attendants can inspect linen while hand folding it.

SECTION 12.4—DELIVERING LINENS

- Linens need time to rest on the shelves after laundering.

- Laundry use areas include banquet areas, restaurants, employee check-in areas, housekeeping closets, and recreation areas.

- Table linen requisitions communicate how many of each type of linen the food and beverage outlets need for the next day.

- The uniform authorization form is issued by human resources. The laundry department usually issues, receives, and stores property uniforms.

Public Space Cleaner

Sections

Most people—including guests—trust first impressions. In a hotel, a guest's first impression often revolves around what he or she sees and experiences in the property's public areas.

Public areas consist of a property's entrances, lobbies, corridors, elevators, restrooms, and health facilities. Other areas that the guest sees include dining areas, banquet and meeting rooms, spas, and sometimes, administration and sales offices. Nothing can make or break an impression more than the cleanliness and condition of a property's public areas.

The condition of public—or front-of-the-house—areas makes a strong statement about the rest of the property. Spotless and well-kept public areas signal guests to expect the same level of care and attention in their guestrooms. They show, too, that the property most likely maintains the same standards of cleanliness for its "employee-only" areas—or for its room and corridors in the back of the house. To a large extent, the responsibility for cleaning public and other functional areas rests with the public space cleaner.

13.1 Getting to Know the Public Space Cleaner

AFTER SUCCESSFULLY COMPLETING THIS SECTION, YOU WILL BE ABLE TO:

♦ Describe the importance of the public space cleaner to a lodging property.

♦ Identify the superior performance standards that public space cleaners must have.

♦ List ways to respond to unusual guest situations.

♦ Explain what a deep-cleaning assignment is.

What Is a Public Space Cleaner?

A **public space cleaner** is the housekeeping department employee who cleans almost all areas of the property, except guestrooms. It is their work and their commitment to quality that keep the property's "red carpet" stain-free when guests see it. They make sure that guests are greeted with a spotless lobby, clean corridors, beautiful pool areas, and immaculate rest rooms.

The property relies on its public space cleaners to create an elegant impression on everyone who walks through the doors.

Without the public space cleaners, the windows would be smudged and the trash cans would overflow. Without public space cleaners, the floors would look like a herd of elephants just passed through the property. But because of the public space cleaners, the windows sparkle and the trash cans shine. And the floors look like a host of angels just floated through the property.

Public space cleaners make the property beautiful and memorable. Public space cleaners make a difference!

Exhibit 1 lists all the tasks that a typical public space cleaner might be asked to perform.

Superior Performance Standards

The condition of the property entrance, lobby, guestroom corridors, guest contact office areas, and all other public areas should enhance each guest's overall experience. Making sure these areas are attractive, fresh, and well-maintained at all times is the public space cleaner's ultimate goal. The property's superior performance standards help them achieve that goal.

Public space cleaners are hired for their ability to meet superior performance standards. These standards include having the public space cleaner:

Exhibit 1
Task List—Public Space Cleaner

1. Follow the Public Space Daily Assignment Sheet

2. Switch Tasks When Assigned Areas Are in Use

3. Prepare Public Space Cleaning Carts

4. Transport Soiled Linens to the Laundry

5. Clean HVAC Grates and Vents

6. Prepare Trash for Recycling

7. Empty and Clean Public Trash Cans

8. Move Furniture

9. Sweep Hard Floors

10. Mop Hard Floors

11. Use a Buffer Machine

12. Clean and Wax Tile Floors

13. Remove Stains From Tile Floors

14. Clean and Wax Hardwood and Parquet Floors

15. Vacuum Carpets

16. Clean, Seal, and Wax Marble Surfaces

17. Clean and Seal Concrete Floors

18. Steam-Extract Carpets

19. Remove Stains From Carpets or Fabric Upholstery

20. Vacuum Fabric and Upholstered Furniture

21. Steam-Extract Fabric Upholstery

22. Clean Walls and Baseboards

23. Clean Mirrors and Dust Furnishings

24. Clean Doors

25. Clean and Polish Brass

26. Clean Windows, Tracks, Sills, and Screens

27. Clean Blinds

28. Clean, Straighten, Remove, and Rehang Drapes

29. Clean Fireplaces

30. Clean Chandeliers, Light Fixtures, and Ceiling Fans

31. Take Clean Linens to Housekeeping Closets

32. Clean Housekeeping Closets

33. Throw Away Housekeeping Trash

34. Receive, Process, and Store Housekeeping Deliveries

35. Rotate and Flip Mattresses

36. Clean Vending and Ice Machines and Surrounding Areas

37. Empty and Clean Public Ash Urns

38. Clean and Sanitize Public Drinking Fountains

(continued)

Exhibit 1
Task List—Public Space Cleaner *(continued)*

39. Clean Stairwells, Handrails, Fire Corridors, and Ledges

40. Clean Elevators

41. Clean Escalators

42. Clean Public Telephone Areas

43. Clean and Restock Public and Employee Rest Rooms

44. Clean Coat Check Areas

45. Clean the Front Office and Lobby Areas

46. Clean the Guest Library or Business Center

47. Clean Floors and Empty Trash in Shops and Gamerooms

48. Clean Food and Beverage Outlets

49. Clean and Supply Guest Exercise Facilities

50. Clean and Supply the Pool and Changing Rooms

51. Clean Public Space in Unusual Environments or Circumstances

52. Clean Sidewalks and Parking Lot Areas

53. Clean Main Housekeeping Office and Storage Areas

54. Clean Employee Cafeteria and Break Areas

55. Clean Executive and Administration Offices

- Thoroughly vacuum all carpeting, including edges, corners, and behind doors

- Make sure carpets are free of stains and holes

- Make sure walls and baseboards are free of stains, tears, and marks

- Clean air vents and grills

- Clean public rest rooms

- Practice teamwork at all times

- Be alert to safety procedures at all times

- Wash your hands after taking a break

Unusual Guest Situations

While dealing directly with guests is not something public space cleaners do very often, they still need to know how to respond to guests. The job of the public space cleaner takes them into every area of the property. Guests who are lost, looking for information, or trying to find a vending machine may turn to a public space cleaner for help. Public space cleaners respond professionally and courteously to guests. Helping guests can be a rewarding part of their job.

But they may also need to work with guests in awkward or unpleasant situations. For instance, they may see a guest doing something illegal or dangerous. Or a guest may be in trouble and need medical help. Public space cleaners have to be prepared to help guests and the property in these situations.

Here are some suggestions for responding to unusual guest situations:

- *Sick guest.* Ask if the guest wants medical attention. If so, call the PBX operator and explain the situation right away. If you need to clean up vomit, remember to wear gloves, goggles, and aprons, and follow the other bloodborne pathogen safety procedures. Vomit is a body fluid that can carry disease.

- *Intoxicated guest.* If you see a guest who has had too much to drink, call the PBX operator, the manager on duty, or a security staff member and tell him or her what you saw and where the guest is.

- *Suspicious person.* A suspicious person is anyone—an employee, visitor, or guest—who gives you the feeling that something might be wrong. If you think someone is suspicious but are not sure, it is best to check things out.

Deep Cleaning Assignments

Deep cleaning (cleaning tasks other than routine duties) keeps the property fresh and clean. There are many deep-cleaning tasks that help the property shine, including:

- Shampooing carpets

- Removing soil and stains from wall coverings and baseboards

- Washing windows, casements, and shades

- Dusting high and hard-to-reach areas

- Cleaning vents and fans

- Vacuuming under furniture that requires heavy moving

- Cleaning and vacuuming drapes

- Cleaning carpet edges

- Stripping and waxing hard floors

- Removing gum from the underside of chairs and tables

- Polishing brass

- Cleaning fabric on furniture

- Washing lamp shades

Deep-cleaning tasks are often assigned in two ways:

- **Daily Specials.** Every day, public space cleaners could get a different special assignment, which they would find at the bottom of their assignment sheets. The tasks should make their job more interesting and help maintain the property's superior performance standards.

- *Specialist Tasks.* Sometimes tasks will take an entire shift to do. In this case, supervisors may ask public space cleaners to perform only deep-cleaning assignments that day. If so, the person assigned becomes the property's **"specialist"** for the day.

Apply Your Learning 13.1

Please write all answers on a separate sheet of paper.

1. Why is the job of public space cleaner important to a lodging property?

2. What are some of the superior performance standards that public space cleaners must meet?

3. What should a public space cleaner do if he or she sees an intoxicated guest?

4. What is a daily special?

13.2 Getting Organized

AFTER SUCCESSFULLY COMPLETING THIS SECTION, YOU WILL BE ABLE TO:

♦ Describe how to use a public space daily assignment sheet.

♦ Identify ways public space cleaners can work efficiently.

♦ Describe public space cleaning carts and how they are used.

♦ Explain how to transport soiled linens to the laundry.

♦ Describe how to safely move furniture.

Follow the Public Space Daily Assignment Sheet

Public space cleaners are given a **public space daily assignment sheet** each day. It lists all the tasks that they are to perform in the order in which they are to do it. Public space cleaners need to complete each task within the time given on the sheet. They inform their supervisor when they are unable to complete any task by the assigned time. The supervisor then decides whether to assign help or whether the public space cleaner should skip some tasks.

As public space cleaners complete assigned tasks, they check it off the sheet. Some properties require public space cleaners to mark their start and finish time for each task. At the end of the shift, they sign and date it and give it to their supervisor.

Switch Tasks When Assigned Areas Are in Use

If guests or co-workers are using an area that a public space cleaner is assigned to clean, they select another task that will take the same amount of time to complete.

When they have to switch tasks, public space cleaners notify their supervisor to suggest switching. Supervisors need to know about substitutions so that they will know why the scheduled cleaning wasn't completed.

Sometimes a guest or manager will request that public space cleaners clean an area not on their assignment sheets. In those instances, they tell the person that they will make sure it gets taken care of. They then contact the housekeeping office to find out whether they should clean the area or if someone else will clean it instead.

Once the substituted assignment is complete, public space cleaners return to their original task. All changes are recorded on the assignment sheet.

Prepare Public Space Cleaning Carts

Public space cleaning carts are used to stock all of the supplies that public space cleaners need to do their jobs. These may include the following items:

- Vacuum cleaner
- Broom
- Dustpan
- Feather duster
- Mop
- Garbage bags
- Plastic liners
- Cleaning cloths
- Razor blade in a safety holder

Personal items such as purses, snacks, or jackets are stored in employee lockers or other designated areas—not on carts.

Cleaning caddy supplies are containers (usually metal or plastic) that hold the supplies needed for cleaning assigned areas. Public space cleaners pick up stocked cleaning supply caddies in the housekeeping department at the beginning of their shifts. These caddies are placed on the public space cleaning cart.

Public space cleaners are responsible for checking to make sure they have enough cleaning supplies to complete their assigned areas. These cleaning supplies might include:

- Spray bottle of all-purpose cleaner
- Furniture polish
- Other approved cleaning chemicals
- Sponge
- Scrub brush
- Cleaning cloths
- Johnny mop

At the end of the shift, public space cleaners turn the caddy back in for restocking or restock it themselves in the housekeeping department.

Transport Soiled Linens

Transporting linens to the laundry department throughout the day helps laundry attendants stay on schedule and saves space in the housekeeping closet. Laundry bags filled with soiled linens are collected from the housekeeping closets or from room attendants' carts. The bags are emptied onto carts for soiled linens.

Soiled linens are sorted in either the housekeeping closets or in the laundry department. Linens that are badly stained or spotted are sorted from those that are not so that spots can be pretreated.

Public space cleaners bundle dirty linens and place them on carts for soiled linens. They then take carts with soiled linens to the laundry. If there is a linen chute, the soiled linens are dropped down it.

Move Furniture

Public space cleaners are often called upon to move furniture. In guestroom areas, guests sometimes move furniture to another room and do not return it. Furniture from suites and public spaces may be used for a function and may need to be returned to its proper location. Or public space cleaners may need to move furniture to properly vacuum or clean floors.

Two or more public space cleaners are needed to move heavy or awkward furniture.

Apply Your Learning 13.2

Please write all answers on a separate sheet of paper.

1. What do public space cleaners use to find out their assigned tasks?

2. When might a public space cleaner have to switch tasks?

3. What items are stored on a public space cleaning cart?

4. What items are stored on a public space cleaning caddy?

5. Name two places where public space cleaners might pick up soiled linen from.

13.3 Cleaning Floors

AFTER SUCCESSFULLY COMPLETING THIS SECTION, YOU WILL BE ABLE TO:

◆ Explain how to clean hard surface floors.

◆ Describe how to use a buffer machine.

◆ Explain how to clean carpeted surfaces.

There are many types of floors that public space cleaners need to care for. These can include tile floors, hardwood, parquet, marble, and carpet. It is important that public space cleaners are properly trained to use the equipment needed so that they are not injured and the property is not damaged.

Sweep Hard Floors

The first step in sweeping floors is to move all equipment and furniture as necessary to expose all areas of the floor. In any room, public space cleaners begin in the back corner, away from the door. They then use a broom to sweep dirt into a small pile. One way to avoid stirring up dust is to keep the broom's bristles on the floor as much as possible.

Public space cleaners pick up dirt using a dustpan as they go so that they don't leave piles of dirt for guests or others to walk through. They then empty the dirt from the dustpan into the trash can on their cart and continue to sweep until the entire floor is clean.

Mop Hard Floors

While sweeping picks up dirt and dust from the floor, most hard floors also need to be mopped periodically. Never wet-mop wood or marble floors unless they have been treated with a waterproof sealer.

Most of the time, anyone mopping works from the back of the room to the front. Overlapping mopped sections will help them avoid walking on cleaned areas and will ensure that the entire floor area is clean. This method of overlapping is often called "the figure 8."

Exhibit 1 contains step-by-step instructions for mopping a hard floor.

Remove Stains from Tile Floors

Before floors are waxed, stains have to be removed. Public space cleaners always wear protective items such as latex utility gloves and protective goggles when removing stains. It protects them from the strong chemicals and from blood or other body fluid stains. They then test the stain remover by applying it to a small area out of sight. If it damages the floor, they need to report it to their supervisor immediately.

Exhibit 1
Mop Hard Floors

Materials needed: caution signs, floor cleaner, a mop bucket, a spray bottle, and a mop.

STEPS:	HOW-TO'S:
1. **Set up caution signs.**	
2. **Select the appropriate cleaner.**	
3. **Mop the floor.**	❑ Use Method 1 or Method 2 to mop the floor: **Method 1:** • Mix the appropriate cleaner with water in the mop bucket and apply it to the floor. • Dump dirty water and refill the mop bucket with clean rinse water. • Mop the floor with rinse water, changing the water as needed. • Wring the mop and soak up excess water so the floor is just damp. **Method 2:** • Mix the appropriate cleaner and water in a spray bottle. • Fill the mop bucket with clean rinse water. • Spray the floor with the cleaner. • Dip the mop in the rinse bucket, wring the mop, and mop up the cleaning solution. ❑ Begin in the back of the room, away from the door. ❑ Mop from left to right in three-foot sections, working toward the door. Each three-foot section should overlap the previous one.
4. **Let the floor air dry.**	

(continued)

Exhibit 1 Mop Hard Floors *(continued)*	
STEPS:	**HOW-TO'S:**
5. Empty the mop bucket, rinse it with clean water, and hang it to dry.	
6. Rinse the mop in clean water and hang it to dry.	
7. Put away caution signs and other equipment and supplies.	

Certain stains have special procedures:

- *Blood stains.* Cover the area with paper towels. Pour a fresh solution of phenolic liquid detergent or disinfectant and water on the paper towels. Let the solution stand for 15 minutes. Throw away the paper towels in a sealable plastic container. Put the container in a separate trash can for special handling. Wipe the area with dry paper towels. Wash hands immediately after removing gloves.

- *Burns.* Rub with #0 steel wool, if necessary, and a strong all-purpose detergent solution. If the burn has destroyed the tile, the property will probably have to replace it.

- *Candy or chewing gum.* Scrape up gum or candy with a putty knife. Apply an all-purpose detergent solution. If necessary, rub with #0 steel wool dipped in an all-purpose detergent solution. To remove gum from hard or 100 percent vinyl resilient tile, use denatured alcohol. Rinse the spot with a wet cloth or sponge.

- *Heel marks.* Rub with an all-purpose detergent and #0 steel wool.

- *Ink stains.* Clean with a strong all-purpose detergent solution and steel wool. If the stain persists, dampen a cloth with ammonia and place it over the stain for several minutes. Rinse well.

- *Nail polish.* Blot as much of the polish as possible using a dry cloth or sponge. Clean with all-purpose detergent solution. Apply nail-polish remover. Do not use nail polish remover on rubber or asphalt tile.

- *Urine.* If the stain is fresh, use absorbent paper towels to blot it until you can't soak up any more urine. Use #0 steel wool if necessary and a strong bleach solution. Follow with an auto-scrubber or bio-enzyme cleaners. Put in a sealable plastic container any paper towels, steel wool, etc. used to clean urine stains. Put the container into a special trash can. Wash your hands thoroughly as soon as you remove your gloves.

Clean and Wax Tile Floors

Public space cleaners begin this task by placing caution signs warning people that the floors may be wet. They then clear the floor of movable equipment and sweep or dust-mop the area.

Tile floors usually need to be wet mopped daily. Floors in busy public spaces need to be kept dry and wet mopped when traffic is light. Mops are usually labeled or marked to keep wet mops and wax mops separate.

Built-up wax may look yellow or have gray or black patches. Old wax must be stripped before new wax is applied. After the floor has been stripped, it should be completely clean and ready to receive a new wax coat.

Because of the heavy chemicals, public space cleaners wear heavy latex utility gloves and protective goggles when stripping a floor. They then mix water and an approved ammonia-based floor stripper. They apply a heavy coat of this solution with a mop and let it stand for 10 minutes or until a haze appears.

A brush is used to hand-scrub the edges. They then scrape the wax loose from corners with a small putty knife. A hand cloth can be used to pick up residue in corners and along edges. The wax is then scrubbed loose using a buffer machine with a brush or nylon pads. Clean rinse water and a wet vacuum or a wrung-out mop is then used to pick up wax and dirt.

Finally, public space cleaners add one cup of white vinegar to 2.5 gallons of rinse water. This solution is applied as a final rinse to get rid of any film from the wax and stripping solution. The floor is then left to air dry.

Typically, a property will apply one coat of sealer and three coats of wax to floors. In high-traffic areas, they may use two coats of sealer and three coats of wax. The approved liquid wax is applied evenly to the clean, dry tile floor. Public space cleaners make even strokes with little overlap to achieve the best results. The floor is allowed to dry for 30 minutes or longer before public space cleaners go back over missed areas and apply the next coat. Each coat is applied at a right angle to the previous coat to help catch any missed hairlines.

The wax finish is then touched up with a spray bottle mix of half liquid wax and half water. The mix is sprayed lightly on the floor just ahead of the buffer machine. It is then buffed until a glossy finish appears.

Finally, the public space cleaner rinses all mops well and hangs them to dry. They then clean other supplies and equipment and hang them to dry. After the floor and equipment dries, public space cleaners put away the caution signs and other equipment and supplies.

Clean and Wax Hardwood and Parquet Floors

Public space cleaners place caution signs in their work area whenever they are cleaning or waxing hardwood and parquet floors. They begin by sweeping or dust-mopping the floors to remove all loose dirt. This helps prevent dirty wax buildup. Water should not be used to clean hardwood floors.

A buffer machine waxes hardwood floors. Public space cleaners attach a buffer pad and work a small amount of wax into the buffer pad with their fingers or a cloth. They then buff the floor until it shines, working from the far side of the room to the entrance in a slow fanning motion.

Once the wax is dry, a second coat is applied to difficult areas to get an even finish. Then public space cleaners attach a clean, unwaxed buffer pad to the buffer machine and buff the floor again.

Finally, the buffer pads are removed, cleaned and hung to dry. Pads should never be left on the buffer. All equipment—and caution signs—are then put away.

Clean, Seal, and Wax Marble

Public space cleaners use a dry dust cloth or dust mop to remove dust on marble surfaces. A waxing mop can be used to apply a clear, water-resistant sealer.

Sealed marble is usually washed with a clean, soft cloth or mop that has been dipped into a mixture of fresh warm water and a mild detergent. Acids such as lemon juice or white vinegar will scar the surface of the stone and cause permanent damage. Acid-based strippers will damage marble floors. The marble is scrubbed to remove any ingrained residue. It is then wiped dry with a dry cloth. Water can discolor the surface if it soaks into the stone. The climate of the lodging property's region of the country will determine how often the marble must be washed.

Waxing is done with a buffer machine, using an approved non-yellowing floor wax.

Clean Concrete Floors

Storage areas, the receiving dock, and other back-of-the-house areas may have un-finished concrete floors. The floors should be sealed when they are new as spills can cause permanent stains.

Concrete floors are typically cleaned by sweeping and damp mopping. They are sealed the first time with a waxing mop dipped into an approved sealer which is then spread evenly on the floor. When resealing, public space cleaners wear heavy latex utility gloves and protective goggles. They scrub the floor with a mild detergent, using the scrubber attachment on the buffer. They remove any stains with an approved stain remover. They then rinse the floor thoroughly and remove all water and residue with a wet vacuum or mop and wringer. The floor is then air dried and sealer is reapplied.

Use a Buffer Machine

Whenever using large pieces of machinery, public space cleaners must follow safety precautions. These include placing caution signs in the work area, checking the electrical cords for tangles or damage, and making sure the machine is unplugged when switching brushes or pads.

It is also very easy to lose control of a buffer and damage furniture or walls. Anyone using a buffer should practice with it until they are comfortable with keeping control over it.

Scrub brushes or pads are attached by tilting the buffer machine backward until the operating handle rests on the floor. The brush or pad must be clean so that it won't damage the floor. The brush or pad is then twisted on the studs counterclockwise.

After the attachments are in place, public space cleaners plug in the buffer machine and buff the floor by working from the far side of the room to the entrance. They work backward slowly in a fanning motion from left to right. It is best to operate the buffer machine with one hand and use the other hand to move the electrical cord out of the machine's path.

At regular intervals, public space cleaners check the pad or brush and change them when they get dirty. If a film is left on the floor, public space cleaners have to mop it and then buff it again using a clean brush or pad.

When they are done using the machine, public space cleaners remove the buffer pad or brush from the machine, clean it, and hang it to dry. Pads and brushes must never be left on the machine. The buffer machine and caution signs are then put away.

Vacuum Carpets

One of the most common tasks that a public space cleaner will perform is vacuuming carpets. They vacuum carpets in guestroom hallways, lobbies, meeting rooms (though sometimes this task is done by banquet setup employees), and offices.

Exhibit 2 is a step-by-step breakdown of how to vacuum carpets.

Steam-Extract Carpets

While daily vacuuming is the most important step to maintaining carpets, **steam extraction** is the second-line defense against worn carpets. It is the best method for cleaning synthetic carpets. Carpets with natural fibers such as wool, flax, or cotton should not be cleaned with a wet process, or the fibers may fade or shrink.

Steam extractors spray a fine mist of hot water and detergent into the carpet and vacuum it out at the same time. The

pressurized mist loosens the dirt in the carpet fibers. The vacuum pulls out the water and dirt.

Exhibit 3 is a step-by-step breakdown of how to steam-extract carpets.

Remove Stains From Carpets or Upholstery

Like tile floors, there are special procedures for removing stains from carpeting. As always when dealing with chemicals or body fluids, public space cleaners need to wear heavy, latex, utility gloves and goggles. Some special procedures include:

- *Blood.* If a blood stain is fresh, blot with a paper towel, then spray the spot with a solution of ammonia and cold water. Blot with a paper towel to remove extra wetness. Apply a small amount of approved detergent to the spot. Use a blotting motion to work the detergent into the carpet. If it is working, keep adding detergent and blotting until the stain is gone. Rinse with tap water in a spray bottle and dry again with a paper towel. Spray lightly with water again and apply a pad of paper towels and a weight to hold the paper towels down on the spot. Allow the spot to dry. If there is still a stain on the carpet, you may need to use a commercial blood remover or special shampoo. Throw away the paper towels in a sealable plastic container. Put the container in a separate trash can for special handling. Wipe the area with dry paper towels. Wash hands immediately after removing gloves.

- *Burn marks.* Use small, sharp scissors to clip away charred fibers from carpet

Exhibit 2
Vacuum Carpets

Materials needed: Caution signs, a stiff broom, a vacuum cleaner, and a vacuum bag.

STEPS:	HOW-TO'S:
1. Place caution signs if necessary.	
2. Remove dirt from room corners and carpet edges.	❑ Use a small, stiff broom to brush dirt from room corners and carpet edges to a carpeted area that a vacuum can reach. ❑ Push down on the broom and pull it towards you—away from the wall.
3. Plug in the vacuum cleaner.	❑ Try to use an outlet near the door. ❑ Make sure the cord is in an out-of-the-way place so that no one trips over it.
4. Vacuum from one side of the room to the other.	❑ Begin vacuuming in a back corner of the room. Don't stand in wet areas while vacuuming. You might get electrocuted. ❑ Vacuum toward the door so that you vacuum over your footprints. ❑ Carefully vacuum room corners, carpet edges, and high-traffic areas. ❑ Report any rips in the carpet to the engineering department so staff members can repair them.
5. Check and empty the vacuum bag, and clean beater brushes periodically.	
6. Unplug the vacuum, wind the cord correctly, and return the vacuum to your cart.	❑ Pull on the plug, not the cord, when unplugging the vacuum.

Exhibit 3
Steam-Extract Carpets

Materials needed: Caution signs, a steam extractor, carpet pre-spotting solution, an approved detergent, defoamer, and a vacuum cleaner.

STEPS:	HOW-TO'S:
1. **Place caution signs in your work area.**	
2. **Move equipment and furniture.**	❑ Carefully lift and carry all portable equipment to an area approved by your supervisor. ❑ Carefully move furniture to expose all areas of the carpet that need to be cleaned.
3. **Vacuum the carpet.**	
4. **Spray heavily soiled areas or spills with a carpet pre-spotting solution.**	
5. **Remove candle wax.**	❑ Cover the dried wax deposit with absorbent paper towels. ❑ Apply a hot flat iron to the top side of the paper towel. This should make the towel absorb the wax.
6. **Set up the steam extractor.**	
7. **Plug in the extractor and allow the wash tank to heat the water (if the tank has heater coils).**	
8. **Add defoamer to the extraction tank to prevent excess foaming.**	

(continued)

Exhibit 3
Steam-Extract Carpets *(continued)*

STEPS:	HOW-TO'S:
9. Use the extractor according to the instructions with the machine.	❑ Start at the far side of the area and work back to the entrance.
	❑ Inject steam into the carpet.
	❑ Work quickly to prevent overwetting the carpet. Do not soak the carpet. Excess water can shrink the jute backing or carpet lining, bring some stains from the backing or lining to the carpet surface, and put undue strain on carpet seams. Don't stand in excess water while using the extractor. You could get electrocuted.
	❑ Give special attention to pre-spotted areas. If carpets aren't cleaned often, heavily soiled areas will require many passes of the steam extractor. The extra water and detergent could damage the carpet.
10. Empty dirty water in a mop sink or dock area drain, not down guestroom toilets.	
11. Allow the carpet to dry completely.	❑ Working on wet carpets can cause resoiling.
12. Vacuum the carpet again.	
13. Put the room back in order.	❑ Replace equipment and furniture that you moved out of the way or removed from the room.
	❑ Place aluminum foil or cardboard squares under furniture legs to prevent stains on the carpet.
14. Clean the steam extractor.	
15. Store all furniture and supplies in the correct locations.	

surfaces with high piles. Mix carpet cleaner and water according to the manufacturer's instructions. Apply the cleaner to the burn mark with a sponge. Place a thick, folded cleaning cloth over the burn mark and press firmly to remove the water or use a wet vacuum to remove large amounts of water.

- *Candy or chewing gum.* Apply ice to the candy or gum that is stuck to the carpet or furniture. Hold the ice on the candy or gum until it is brittle enough to crumble off. Apply an approved degreaser to the stain. Rinse the spot with a wet cloth or sponge and blot excess water with a sponge or dry cloth.

- *Nail polish.* Blot as much of the polish as possible using a sponge or dry cloth. Public space cleaners must inform their supervisor about the stain as the type of carpet or upholstery will determine the correct way to remove it.

- *Urine stains.* Use absorbent paper towels to blot up any fresh urine. Once it is blotted up, contact a supervisor who can check the fabric type and determine what stain removal method should be used. Any cloths, paper towels, sponges, gloves or other items used to clean urine must be placed in a sealable plastic container and disposed of in a special trash can.

Apply Your Learning 13.3

Please write all answers on a separate sheet of paper.

1. When sweeping, where should a public space cleaner begin?

2. What is one method for mopping a floor?

3. What does a public space cleaner use to scrub wax off a tile floor?

4. How should a public space cleaner remove burns from a tile floor?

5. How can a public space cleaner prevent dirty wax buildup on hardwood floors?

6. What type of chemical can scar the surface of marble?

7. Where should a public space cleaner begin vacuuming a room?

8. What is a steam extractor?

9. How should a public space cleaner remove fresh blood from carpeting?

13.4 Removing Trash and General Cleaning

AFTER SUCCESSFULLY COMPLETING THIS SECTION, YOU WILL BE ABLE TO:

♦ Explain how to empty trash and prepare it for recycling.

♦ Describe how to clean HVAC grates and vents.

♦ Explain how to clean walls, baseboards, mirrors, doors, blinds, housekeeping carts, public drinking fountains, stairwells, handrails, fire corridors, ledges, elevators, and public telephone areas.

♦ Describe how to rotate and flip mattresses.

Prepare Trash for Recycling

Many lodging properties have a recycling policy. It is not necessary for public space cleaners to sort trash in containers when they are emptying them in public areas. It is better to wait until they are at the large trash bin. However, in non-public areas, public space cleaners can separate recyclable items by type into plastic bags on their cart as they collect trash.

When sorting recyclables, public space cleaners wear heavy latex utility gloves. They do not reach into the trash to pull out an object. Rather, they empty the contents onto a newspaper and search it with their eyes. They also never handle trash with their bare hands. They don't want to risk contact with glass, sharp objects, or bloodborne pathogens. These safety practices are followed whenever public space cleaners work with or handle trash.

Recycled items such as aluminum cans, glass, paper, etc. is placed into proper recycling bins to be picked up by a recycling company.

Empty and Clean Public Trash

Public space cleaners empty trash by pulling out the plastic liner and tying a knot in the top of the bag. They then place the entire bag in the trash bag on their cart. They use a spray cleaner and a cleaning cloth to wipe out the trash can as needed. If it is very dirty, they take it to the dock area to wash it.

Throw Away Housekeeping Trash

Public space cleaners will empty trash bags from their cart throughout the shift as needed. They'll empty items to be recycled in the correct recycling bin and empty non-recyclable trash into trash bins or trash compactors. If the property uses reusable bags, the soiled bags will be taken to the laundry department.

Trash cans are washed at the dock area with detergent and a long-handled brush. They are rinsed, drained, and allowed to air dry before being returned to use.

Trash bags should always be held from the top, never from the bottom. Sharp objects such as needles can prick a person through a trash bag.

Empty Public Ash Urns

While many hotels ban smoking in public areas, wherever there are ashtrays, public space cleaners will be responsible for cleaning them. Ash urns need to be emptied often to prevent stale tobacco odors.

The two most common type of ash urns in lodging properties are wall-hanging ash urns and sand-filled ash urns.

Wall-hanging ash urns are cleaned by removing cigarette butts and other trash. The metal liner is then removed and emptied into a trash container. Public space cleaners need to make sure there are no hot ashes that could start a fire in their trash bag. The liner is then washed with soapy water, wiped dry and returned to the ash urn.

Public space cleaners clean sand-filled ash urns by removing debris with a strainer tool. Wet sand is emptied into trash bags and fresh sand poured in to replace it. Usually sand urns are taken to housekeeping once a week to be thoroughly cleaned. Once the debris is removed, the sand is smoothed and some properties use a stamping tool to stamp the sand with the property's logo.

After emptying the urn, public space cleaners will usually vacuum around it to clean up sand or debris that may have spilled and wipe any spots from the wall around the urn with a damp cloth followed by a dry cloth.

Clean HVAC Grates and Vents

Public space cleaners need to wear heavy latex utility gloves when cleaning HVAC grates and vents to prevent cuts from any sharp edges on vents and grates. The steps to cleaning grates and vents are:

- Dust vents and grates
- Vacuum easy-to-reach vents and grates with a portable vacuum cleaner
- Vacuum hard-to-reach vents and grates with a step ladder

Clean Fabric and Upholstered Furniture

Upholstery may be fabric, vinyl, or leather. Different cleaning procedures are needed for each type. In general, public space cleaners remove loose cushions and put them on furniture. They wipe spills from vinyl or leather furniture with a damp cloth. They remove spills from fabric upholstery using the same methods as for carpeting.

A small, stiff brush is used to brush debris from furniture seams, folds, and buttons. Public space cleaners then use a vacuum cleaner with attachments or a portable vacuum cleaner to vacuum the fabric surface of the furniture. Some properties have public space cleaners use a damp cloth rather than a vacuum cleaner to clean vinyl and leather furniture.

Clean Walls and Baseboards

When cleaning walls and baseboards, public space cleaners usually use a cloth on a broom or a long-handled feather duster to dust the walls and wall coverings. These tools help them remove dust and cobwebs from hard-to-reach areas. Other areas can be wiped with a damp cloth. When dusting, public space cleaners work from the top of the room down. If they're right-handed, they usually move clockwise around the area. If they're left-handed, they move counter-clockwise as they clean.

Painted walls and wall coverings are usually washed with a clean, damp cloth without detergent. An approved detergent might be sprayed on spots and stains and rubbed gently with a clean cloth. Abrasive cleaners and abrasive scrub pads can damage walls.

The best solution for stubborn stains or serious damage may be for maintenance to repaint the wall or replace the wall covering. Therefore, public space cleaners need to report to their supervisor:

- When cleaning does not remove stains and dirt
- Tears or punctures in the wall covering
- Areas where the wallpaper paste is not holding
- Other damage

Baseboards should be wiped clean with a damp cloth.

Clean Mirrors and Dust Furnishings

Furnishings, pictures, and signs are dusted with a clean, slightly damp cloth, followed by a dry cloth. Natural finished wood surfaces are dusted with only a dry cloth unless otherwise instructed. No one should use a chemical cleaner, glass cleaner, brass polish, or furniture polish unless told to do so. Some cleaning products may damage some surfaces.

Art objects and sculptures may be very expensive and should get special care. Each property will have its own procedures for cleaning them and public space cleaners will be taught those procedures on the job.

Mirrors need to be cleaned so that they are free from spots and streaks. Water is sprayed onto the mirror and the mirror is then polished to streak-free brilliance with a lint-free cloth. Public space cleaners are especially careful not to spray water on the frame unless it is a polished aluminum or chrome frame.

Clean Doors

Doors quickly collect fingerprints and smudges as guests and employees use them to get from one place to another. Fingerprints can be removed by using a damp, clean cloth and an approved all-purpose liquid detergent in a spray bottle. A small amount is sprayed directly on the door and then is wiped off immediately. A clean, dry cloth is then used to polish the door.

Detergent should not be allowed to streak down the door or to dry as it can permanently stain the finish.

Hardware on doors is cleaned with a damp cloth and then polished to a brilliant finish with a dry cloth. Public space cleaners do not use abrasive detergents to clean door knobs or other hardware because abrasives could permanently damage hardware finish. Some brass doorknobs are coated with lacquer to prevent tarnishing.

Clean Blinds

Public space cleaners wear heavy latex utility gloves to prevent cuts from the sharp edges of blinds. The steps to clean blinds are:

- Use a clean cloth, a small broom, or a brush to wipe the dust from the blinds.

- Use a damp cloth followed by a dry cloth to clean stubborn dirt from each slat.

- Wipe the rods, poles, and cords of the blinds.

- Wipe the area behind the blinds.

- Test blinds to make sure they work correctly.

Clean and Sanitize Public Drinking Fountains

Because guests drink from drinking fountains, public space cleaners need to take special care with ensuring that they get clean. One way to take special care is to use a foodservice sanitizing solution for cleaning drinking fountains. Also, they do not use the same cloths or chemicals that they use for other cleaning. The sanitizing solution used on drinking fountains help to kill germs and make surfaces safe.

Public space cleaners clean drinking fountains by spraying the surface of each drinking fountain with sanitizing solution. They then polish the surfaces with a clean bar towel that is suitable for sanitary cleaning. They then remove lint and dust from the grill with a small brush and wipe down cabinets with a cloth.

Clean Stairwells, Handrails, Fire Corridors, and Ledges

Handrails are cleaned by sweeping away any cobwebs or dirt and then wiping down with a damp cloth and mild detergent.

Stairwells and fire corridors are not storage areas. They must be kept open for traffic in case of emergencies. These areas, along with ledges and balconies are cleaned by:

- Picking up any debris.

- Removing chewing gum or sticky residue with a putty knife.

- Removing floor mats and sweeping thoroughly.

- Taking badly soiled mats to the dock or mop sink area.

- Spraying mats with grease-cutting detergent and then scrubbing.

Sealed floors are mopped. While cleaning, public space cleaners check the conditions of emergency signs and directional tape that may be on the floor in fire corridors or stairwells. They also note maintenance needs or poor conditions on their public space daily assignment sheet.

In snowy or icy weather, public space cleaners may put rock salt on steps or outside corridors. However, as soon as the bad weather has passed, they'll need to clear the salt away.

Clean Elevators

Elevators are taken out of service when they are cleaned. The elevator will then stay on one floor and the door will stay open until it is placed back in service. This means that the public space cleaner must work quickly so that the elevator can be returned to use, slowing down as few guests as possible.

The steps for cleaning elevators are:

- Vacuum carpeted areas.

- Clean hard floors by sweeping, mopping, or waxing.

- Dust all surfaces with a dust cloth or a damp cloth followed by a clean, dry cloth.

- Dust the ceiling and lights.

- Clean the door tracks with a brush or small broom followed by a vacuum cleaner.

- Clean the inside of elevators doors with a dry cloth.

- Put the elevator back in service.

- Close the door and wipe the outside of the door with a dry cloth.

Rotate and Flip Mattresses

The executive housekeeper will set a regular schedule of rotating and flipping mattresses and may assign this task to either public space cleaners or room attendants. Whoever is assigned this job will work with a partner to turn mattresses. The mattress and box springs are too heavy and bulky for one person to safely flip.

First, all linens are taken off the bed and placed on a chair, desk, or table. Then one person stands at one end of the mattress and the other person stands at the other. The mattress is lifted off the box springs and set on the other bed or leaned against the wall. It is then inspected for tears, soil spots, and broken springs.

The box springs are turned so that the right side is on the left. Then the mattress is turned. Usually the mattress corners will be marked with a marker. The mattress is placed on the box springs so that the appropriate number is in the upper corner of the bed. For example, one system might have the number 1 in the upper corner from January to March, 2 from April to June, 3 from July to September, and 4 from October to December.

Apply Your Learning 13.4

Please write all answers on a separate sheet of paper.

1. What type of protective equipment should public space cleaners wear when sorting or handling trash?

2. What is used to clean walls and baseboards?

3. How are blinds cleaned?

4. How many people are needed to rotate and flip mattresses?

13.5 Cleaning Public and Employee Areas

AFTER SUCCESSFULLY COMPLETING THIS SECTION, YOU WILL BE ABLE TO:

♦ List the tasks involved in cleaning employee and public restrooms.

♦ Explain how to clean public telephone areas, coat check areas, the front office, the lobby, shops, game rooms, guest exercise facilities, pool area, the employee cafeteria, employee break areas, and administrative offices.

♦ Explain how to clean sidewalks and parking lot areas.

Public space cleaners find themselves performing their duties in every area of the hotel except guestrooms. This takes them into public areas and employee areas. In all of these areas they'll find themselves vacuuming, mopping, dusting, and emptying trash. However, many areas also have special needs.

Clean Public and Employee Rest Rooms

One of the most important jobs that the public space cleaner will do is to clean the public and employee rest rooms. No guest wants to use a dirty bathroom and employees appreciate the care that a clean bathroom demonstrates.

When the property is especially busy with conventions or conferences, the rest rooms must be checked more often. A daily function sheet helps public space cleaners monitor rest rooms according to the break schedules of guests. Rest rooms also need more attention during bad weather.

Exhibit 1 gives a step-by-step breakdown on how to clean and restock public and employee rest rooms.

Clean Public Telephone Areas

Public phones include pay phones, house phones, and public fax machines. There are often trash cans in these areas that need to be emptied. Phones need to be cleaned with an approved disinfectant and a damp cloth.

Public space cleaners need to look for graffiti around the phones—people will sometimes write phone numbers and other information on the wall. Also, guests sometimes leave credit cards or other personal articles next to the telephone. These items must be turned in immediately to the lost and found department.

Some properties stock notepads, pens, and telephone directories around the phone. These should be replaced as needed.

Exhibit 1
Clean and Restock Public and Employee Rest Rooms

Materials needed: A stocked public space cleaning cart, heavy latex utility gloves, protective goggles, "temporarily out-of-service" signs, a bowl brush or johnny mop, buckets, disinfectant, floor mops, a stiff toothbrush, and bathroom supplies.

STEPS:	HOW-TO'S:
1. **Prepare to clean.**	❑ Park your cleaning cart across the entrance to show that the rest room is out of service. ❑ Place a "temporarily out of service" sign by your cart. ❑ Put on heavy latex utility gloves and protective goggles. ❑ Flush all toilets and urinals. Collect trash and place it in the trash can.
2. **Swab the toilets with bowl cleaner.**	❑ Lower the water in each toilet bowl by pumping a bowl brush or johnny mop in the bowl. ❑ Press the water out of the brush or johnny mop against the inside of the toilet bowl. ❑ Pour toilet bowl cleaner into each toilet. Swab inside the entire bowl, especially under the rim. ❑ Don't flush the toilet.
3. **Swab the urinals with bowl cleaner.**	❑ Remove any trash from the urinal before cleaning. Remove the urinal screen, and place it in a bucket with hot water and disinfectant. ❑ Pour toilet bowl cleaner into each urinal. Swab the inside with a bowl brush or johnny mop. Do not flush the urinal.

(continued)

Exhibit 1
Clean and Restock Public and Employee Rest Rooms *(continued)*

STEPS:	HOW-TO'S:
4. **Empty the trash, including sanitary napkin disposal containers.**	❑ Be careful handling trash. Remove the liner. Tie the liner at the top and place it in the trash bag on your cart. ❑ Check the trash can and clean it as needed. ❑ Put all of the trash into the bag on your cart so you can take out the recyclables later.
5. **Clean and polish walls and stalls.**	❑ Spray an approved cleaner on the walls around the toilets, including the stall walls and ledges and inside the doors. Wipe with a damp mop. Urine that has splattered on walls is unsightly, causes ordors, and will speed the corrosion of metal stalls. ❑ Pay special attention to cleaning any urine splatter in stall areas. ❑ Polish all surfaces with a clean, dry cloth or with a dry mop. ❑ Spray cleaner and wipe the walls around the urinals with a damp cloth, and polish with a dry cloth.
6. **Clean and polish hand dryers and paper towel dispensers.**	❑ Open the paper towel dispensers and wipe all surfaces with a damp cloth. ❑ Polish the hand dryers and paper towel dispensers with a dry cloth.
7. **Clean and empty ashtrays and ash urns.**	❑ Make sure cigarettes are not burning. Empty them into the trash. ❑ Wash ashtrays and liners. ❑ Return clean ashtrays to the correct spot.

(continued)

Exhibit 1
Clean and Restock Public and Employee Rest Rooms (continued)

STEPS:	HOW-TO'S:
8. **Clean and polish mirrors.**	❑ Remove any stickers or other unauthorized materials from mirrors.
	❑ Use water, not glass cleaner, to clean mirrors. There may be hair spray residue on mirrors. Glass cleaner will mix with the hair spray and cause streaking.
9. **Clean wash basins and fixtures.**	❑ Spray an all-purpose cleaner on basins and fixtures.
	❑ Wash, rinse, and wipe dry with a cloth.
	❑ Use a stiff toothbrush to clean the overflow drains.
	❑ Pay special attention to the drain plugs and fixture bottoms. If possible, remove drain plugs, wipe clean, and replace them.
	❑ Polish fixtures with a dry cloth.
	❑ Wipe the outside of soap dispensers and open the lids. Leaving the lids open when you clean saves time when you later refill the dispensers.
10. **Clean the baby-changing table.**	❑ Spray an all-purpose cleaner on the baby-changing table.
	❑ Wipe it carefully with a clean cloth.
11. **Finish cleaning the toilets.**	❑ Swab the inside of the bowl with a bowl brush or johnny mop.
	❑ Press the water out of the brush or mop against the inside of the toilet bowl.
	❑ Flush the toilet.
	❑ Immediately report any toilets that don't flush properly so that the maintenance department can fix them.
	❑ Place "temporarily out of service" signs if necessary.

(continued)

Exhibit 1
Clean and Restock Public and Employee Rest Rooms (continued)

STEPS:	HOW-TO'S:
	❏ Spray the tank or pipes and the seat with all-purpose cleaner.
	❏ Wipe the tank or pipes and the seat with a damp cloth. Polish with a dry cloth.
	❏ Wipe the outside of the bowl to the floor or wall with a damp cloth followed by a dry cloth.
	❏ If floor bolt covers are missing, note it on your assignment sheet.
12. **Finish cleaning the urinals.**	❏ Swab the inside again with a bowl brush or johnny mop.
	❏ Press the water out of the brush or mop against the inside of the urinal.
	❏ Flush two or three times.
	❏ Immediately report any flushing problems to the maintenance department.
	❏ Place "temporarily out of service" signs if necessary.
	❏ Spray the outside of each urinal with all-purpose cleaner. Wipe down the outside with a damp cloth. Polish the chrome with a dry cloth.
	❏ Replace the urinal screen.
13. **Sweep the floor.**	
14. **Mop the floor.**	
15. **Wipe baseboards.**	

(continued)

Exhibit 1
Clean and Restock Public and Employee Rest Rooms *(continued)*

STEPS:	HOW-TO'S:
16. **Restock supplies.**	❏ Replace or refill the following (as needed): • Toilet tissue • Toilet seat liners • Paper towels • Hand-washing soap • Female sanitary products • Disposable diapers • Guest amenities • Fresh flowers
17. **Clean doors.**	
18. **Periodically recheck rest rooms.**	❏ Restock supplies as needed. ❏ Empty trash as needed. ❏ Clean anything that needs attention.

Clean Coat Check Areas

The tasks involved with cleaning coat check areas are:

• Collecting any trash

• Straightening coat hangers on the racks

• Sweeping hard floors

• Mopping hard floors if they are still dirty after sweeping

• Vacuuming carpets

• Dusting the area (especially coat racks and other furniture)

• Securing the area before leaving

Clean the Front Office and Lobby Areas

The front office area includes the front desk, the reservations office, and the PBX office. When cleaning these areas, it is important that public space cleaners not get in the way of front desk employees, night auditors, or guests.

Exhibit 2 is a step-by-step breakdown of how to clean the front office and lobby areas.

Clean Floors and Empty Trash in Shops and Game Rooms

The amount of cleaning that a public space cleaner will do in shops and game rooms will vary among properties. If the shop or game room is contracted out, the public space cleaner may not have any duties in them whatsoever. Usually a technician is responsible for cleaning games and the shop manager for cleaning shelves.

Some general guidelines for what a public space cleaner may be asked to do in retail shops and game rooms include:

- Cleaning the floor
- Vacuuming carpets and upholstered furniture
- Dusting open walls, baseboards, and game machines
- Cleaning the display windows and entry door

Clean and Supply Guest Exercise Facilities

Guest exercise facilities are one of many amenities that lodging properties offer their guests. When exercise facilities are available, guests expect them to be clean and well maintained. Public space cleaners can do this by picking up used towels and emptying trash containers. They need to follow bloodborne pathogen safety procedures when handling towels as towels may have blood or other body fluids on them.

Perspiration can cause a buildup of offensive odors, so it is important that exercise equipment and the carpet is disinfected on a regular basis. This is usually done with a disinfectant spray that is then wiped off with a clean cloth.

The maintenance department is usually responsible for draining and cleaning the whirlpool, but the public space cleaner may clean the sauna or steam room. They'll also clean any lockers or rest rooms connected to the exercise facilities.

Public space cleaners will also vacuum, sweep, and mop the floors in the exercise area and restock towels and other supplies.

Clean and Supply the Pool and Changing Rooms

The maintenance department is usually responsible for cleaning the swimming pool and treating the water, but the public space cleaners will clean the area around the pool, the changing rooms, and the shower areas. They'll also restock towels and other supplies.

There should be no china or glassware near the pool. Public space cleaners need to remove any that they find and watch for any broken glass.

They also need to wipe pool furniture daily with a cloth soaked in warm water and a mild detergent. Afterward, they rinse it thoroughly with a hose or cloth. Pool furniture collects body oils and sunscreen lotions, which will discolor vinyl materials and can rust the aluminum frames.

The pool deck and surrounding areas needs to be kept free of excess water during high-use times to eliminate slips and falls. Large amounts of water can be picked up with a wet vacuum while small areas can be dried with a dry mop or a cleaning cloth.

Exhibit 2
Clean the Front Office and Lobby Areas

Materials needed: A stocked public space cleaning cart, a vacuum cleaner with attachments, and disinfectant spray.

STEPS:	HOW-TO'S:
1. **Pick up trash and empty trash cans.**	❑ Pick up any trash on the floor. ❑ Keep recyclables separate from other trash.
2. **Clean the telephones.**	❑ Spray an approved disinfectant on a damp cloth and clean each telephone receiver and base. ❑ Use a clean, dry cloth to wipe all telephones. ❑ Pay special attention to telephone receivers.
3. **Vacuum carpets and upholstered furniture.**	❑ Vacuum under desks and other areas. Move furniture as necessary. ❑ Use the correct vacuum cleaner attachments to vacuum upholstered furniture. ❑ Be sure to vacuum the arms, seat, in back of the seat, in back of the furniture, and between the seat, back, and sides. ❑ Remove and store the vacuum cleaner attachments.
4. **Dust the area.**	❑ When working around computers, be careful not to disturb ongoing work. Only dust keyboards when the computer is off.
5. **Clean hard floors.**	❑ Mop and wax the hard floors.
6. **Steam-extract carpets when scheduled to do so.**	
7. **If guests approach the area you are cleaning, step out of the way until they leave.**	

Clean Employee Cafeteria and Break Areas

The employee cafeteria and break rooms are very important to employee morale. Consider the overall impression and level of cleanliness that you would appreciate in these areas.

A kitchen steward may be assigned to clean the employee cafeteria. At the very least, they are likely to be assigned the cleaning of foodservice equipment and production equipment.

Other tasks that a public space cleaner might be asked to do include:

- Removing trash and washing trash cans

- Cleaning tables and chairs

- Dusting any other furnishings

- Cleaning self-service stations

- Cleaning floors

- Cleaning walls and baseboards

- Cleaning windows, tracks, sills, and screens

- Cleaning light fixtures and ceiling fans

- Rearranging furnishings in the room

Clean Executive and Administration Offices

It is especially important for public space cleaners to practice professionalism when cleaning executive and administrative offices. Offices contain confidential materials. Public space cleaners must work quickly and quietly, disturbing occupants as little as possible. They also must never discuss anything they see or overhear while cleaning.

Office cleaning tasks include emptying trash, vacuuming the carpet, dusting, disinfecting telephones, straightening furniture, and cleaning the door.

Clean Sidewalks and Parking Lot Areas

The exterior of the property is as important as the interior. It is the exterior of the property that the guest will first see and begin to form an overall impression of the property.

Public space cleaners will often be assigned to clean the sidewalks and parking lot areas. This first involves public space cleaners picking up trash from the area and checking shrubs and landscaping for debris. If there is chewing gum on sidewalks, it should be removed with a putty knife.

An oil-absorbent powder can be sprinkled on oil spots in the parking lot. A wide push-broom or a straw broom is used to sweep sidewalks. After being swept, the property may wash walks with a power sprayer every three to four weeks to cut down on dirt and stains. Weed killer is usually used on sidewalk cracks where there is a grass or weed problem.

Apply Your Learning 13.5

Please write all answers on a separate sheet of paper.

1. How does a public space cleaner clean a baby changing table?
2. What is included in the front office area?
3. Who is usually responsible for cleaning employee cafeterias?
4. Why is it important to keep the parking lot and sidewalks clean?

Quick Hits

SECTION 13.1—GETTING TO KNOW THE PUBLIC SPACE CLEANER

- Public space cleaners clean everything at the property except guestrooms.

- Public space cleaners make sure the property entrance, lobby, guestroom corridors, guest contact office areas, and all other public areas shine.

- Some of the unusual guest situations that public space cleaners may encounter are sick guests, intoxicated guests, and suspicious people.

- Deep cleaning tasks are usually assigned as daily specials or as specialist tasks.

SECTION 13.2—GETTING ORGANIZED

- The public space daily assignment sheet lists all the tasks public space cleaners perform in the order that they are assigned to do it.

- If a public space cleaner is unable to clean an assigned area, he or she needs to switch tasks and let their supervisors know about the substitution.

- Public space cleaning carts carry all of the equipment public space cleaners need while their caddies hold the cleaning supplies.

- Transporting linens to the laundry department is one way public space cleaners can help laundry attendants and guestroom attendants.

- Following safety procedures while moving furniture helps protect public space cleaners from injury.

SECTION 13.3—CLEANING FLOORS

- When sweeping, public space cleaners pick up dirt as they go so that piles aren't left on the floor.

- Hard wood floors need to be mopped periodically.

- There are different procedures for removing different stains from tile floors.

- Tile floors usually need to be wet mopped daily. Every so often, old wax must be stripped and new wax applied.

- Hardwood floors are swept and dust-mopped. Buffer machines are used to wax them.

- Special care must be taken with marble surfaces to prevent damage.

- Concrete floors must be sealed on a periodic basis.

- Buffer machines help public space cleaners wax and buff floors.

- Carpets need to be vacuumed daily.

- Steam-extraction is used to help maintain synthetic carpets.

- Special procedures exist to remove different types of stains from carpeting.

SECTION 13.4—REMOVING TRASH AND GENERAL CLEANING

- If a property has a recycling program, public space cleaners need to sort the trash they have collected.

- Trash bags and trash should be handled carefully to avoid injury.

- Ash urns need to be emptied often to prevent bad odors.

- HVAC grates and vents are usually cleaned with a vacuum cleaner.

- Walls and baseboards are cleaned with a cloth or a long-handled feather duster.

- Most furnishings are dusted with a clean, slightly damp cloth, followed by a dry cloth.

- Fingerprints and smudges need to be removed from doors.

- Public drinking fountains need to be sanitized.

- Elevators must be taken out of service before being cleaned.

- Two people usually work together to rotate and flip mattresses

SECTION 13.5—CLEANING PUBLIC AND EMPLOYEE AREAS

- One of the most important jobs that the public space cleaner will do is clean the public and employee rest rooms.

- Public telephone areas need to be disinfected and graffiti removed.

- Public space cleaners are responsible for the cleanliness of coat check areas, the front office, the lobby, game rooms, guest exercise facilities, the pool area and changing rooms, cafeteria and break areas, and executive and administrative offices.

- Public space cleaners are often called upon to clean sidewalks and parking lot areas.

Unit

3

Food and Beverage Division

Food and Beverage Division

Sections

Food and beverage facilities—no matter what the size—are of paramount importance to the reputation and profitability of the hotel. There is no doubt that in many cases the quality of a hotel's food and beverages powerfully affects a guest's opinion of the hotel and influences his or her willingness to return. In fact, some hotels are as famous for their restaurants as for their guestrooms.

A hotel's food and beverage outlet(s) attract members of the local community, convince hotel guests to dine on the premises, and return a fair profit.

Virtually all lodging properties offer some level of food and beverage service. Large hotels usually have a wide array of facilities, while small properties may have just one dining room that serves breakfast, lunch, and dinner. Even limited-service hotels often offer some sort of continental breakfast.

14.1 Getting to Know the Food and Beverage Division

AFTER SUCCESSFULLY COMPLETING THIS SECTION, YOU WILL BE ABLE TO:

♦ Describe the importance of the food and beverage operation to a hotel's success.

♦ List the primary departments commonly found in the food and beverage division.

♦ List the most common positions found in a food and beverage operation.

♦ Describe proper telephone etiquette practiced by food and beverage employees.

♦ Explain the process by which food and beverage employees take reservations.

♦ Summarize the various tipping policies restaurants use.

The Food and Beverage Division

The food and beverage division is a very important revenue center for a lodging property. In fact, it is typically second only to the rooms division in the amount of revenue that it earns. A good food and beverage operation can help establish the quality of the hotel in the eyes of guests and can provide a competitive advantage over other lodging properties. This can justify higher average room rates and may help keep occupancy levels high.

The primary departments that make up the food and beverage division of most large lodging properties include:

• Banquet and catering—responsible for banquets and special functions

• Culinary operations—responsible for food production

• Stewarding—responsible for ware-washing, clean-up, and purchasing

• Restaurant operations—responsible for food service in all food outlets

Types of Food Service Operations

There are many varieties of hotel food and beverage operations:

• Gourmet and specialty restaurants

• Coffee shops

• Lounges or dining rooms in which live music or shows are performed

• Room service

- Combined banquet and meeting room facilities

Food service in hospitality suites or employee food service may be additional operations.

Food Service Positions

While the number and variety of food and beverage service positions will depend on the size of a property's food and beverage operation, some basic positions include:

- Restaurant server
- Banquet server
- Banquet setup person
- Bus person
- Kitchen steward
- Room service attendant

Restaurant Servers

Restaurant servers take guest orders and then serve food and beverages to guests. The skills that the servers require may differ depending on the type of restaurant and the level of service.

Restaurant servers are responsible for:

- Preparing for service
- Greeting guests
- Taking the order
- Serving the order
- Creating a friendly atmosphere where guests can enjoy themselves
- Closely monitoring guests' alcohol consumption
- Completing service
- Helping co-workers as needed

Banquet Servers

Banquet servers provide food and beverage service to banquet guests. They try to exceed guest expectations whenever possible.

Banquet servers are responsible for:

- Preparing for service
- Inspecting tables for cleanliness and proper setup
- Greeting guests
- Serving food and beverages
- Completing service
- Breaking down function rooms and service areas
- Keeping a count of the number of guests served
- Helping take inventory

Banquet servers rely heavily on **banquet event orders** (BEOs). BEOs tell them what the banquet is and what needs to be done.

Banquet Setup Persons

Banquets are special events at a lodging property. They can be anything from a small meeting room to a large dinner-dance or reception. Banquet setup employees prepare function rooms to meet the needs of banquet guests.

Banquet setup employees are responsible for:

- Setting up function rooms according to banquet event orders and property policies
- Cleaning and maintaining all function rooms
- Using, cleaning, and maintaining department equipment

- Handling audiovisual equipment for functions (at some lodging properties, an outside company handles this)

- Breaking down function rooms and service areas

Like banquet servers, banquet set up employees rely heavily on banquet event orders (BEOs). BEOs tell them what the banquet is and what needs to be done.

Bus Persons

The primary job of a bus person is to set and clear tables and help restaurant servers and guests as much and whenever possible. Bus persons are responsible for:

- Preparing tables for service

- Prepping side stations, condiments, and silverware

- Busing soiled linens, dishes, glasses, and silverware from tables

- Assisting servers and guests to ensure total guest satisfaction

Bus persons may be the earliest arriving employees to the restaurant and, along with servers, may be expected to help set up the restaurant dining area for service.

Room service attendant is discussed in the last section of this chapter.

Telephone Courtesy

Food and beverage employees make frequent use of the telephone while performing their duties. Guests will call restaurants to make reservations, ask questions, or to order food or room service. Food and beverage employees try to make every caller feel important by being friendly, polite, and professional on the telephone.

They use the same phone techniques as rooms division employees as discussed in Chapter 5.

Taking Restaurant Reservations

Successful restaurants at lodging properties can get very busy. During these busy times, the host or hostess may need help taking reservations. It is helpful if all food and beverage workers are familiar with taking reservations. This helps the staff work better as a team and it helps make everyone's job easier and more enjoyable.

When taking a reservation, food and beverage employees:

- Greet the guest warmly. If it's a phone reservation, they answer within three rings, and use proper phone etiquette. If someone is making a reservation in person, they welcome him or her to the restaurant.

- Find out:

  - The name the reservation will be under

  - Whether the guest wants a booth or table, if both are available

  - The date and time of the reservation

  - The number in the party

  - Whether there are any special requests

  - The guest's phone or room number

  - Whether a smoking or non-smoking table is desired (if it is legal to smoke in a public food establishment in the state)

- Repeat the information back to the guest to make sure it is correct. Spell names for the guest to ensure correct pronunciation.

- Thank the guest for calling. They initial the reservation in case someone has questions about it later.

Tipping Policies

Many food and beverage positions, including restaurant server, banquet server, and room service attendant, traditionally receive tips for performing their duties. Sharing tips with other food and beverage employees is one way to recognize that excellent service is impossible without the efforts of all food and beverage employees. All members of the food and beverage operation team depend on each other to help provide excellent service to all guests.

Every lodging property restaurant has its own tipping policies. Below are a few of the more common ways restaurants handle tips:

- Employees are allowed to keep all of their individual tips.

- Employees share their tips with a few specific co-workers, such as the server, bus person, and banquet setup person.

- All employees combine their tips, which are then evenly divided.

Apply Your Learning 14.1

Please write all answers on a separate sheet of paper.

1. What departments can be found in the food and beverage division?

2. List three types of food service operations that may be found on a lodging property.

3. Why is it important that ALL food and beverage employees are familiar with how to take reservations?

4. List the three common tipping policies used in lodging restaurants.

14.2 Menus and POS Equipment

AFTER SUCCESSFULLY COMPLETING THIS SECTION, YOU WILL BE ABLE TO:

◆ Describe the process involved in creating a restaurant menu.

◆ List the factors for creating a restaurant menu.

◆ Explain the importance of being familiar with a restaurant's menu.

◆ Summarize the use of point-of-sale equipment in a food and beverage operation.

Restaurant Menus

A successful food service operation begins with the menu. Much planning and design goes into deciding what food a restaurant will offer to its guests. In fact, the menu is the first and best marketing tool a lodging restaurant can have. It tempts guests with its offerings, and sells guests with its scrumptious descriptions.

The menu dictates what resources are needed and how they must be expended. Typically, the more complex and varied the menu, the more expensive and elaborate the restaurant operation.

When planning a menu, managers consider the following factors:

• What is the target market (i.e., guests) for the restaurant

• What type of food, beverages, and services will be offered

• Location of the property

• Transportation and parking accommodations and facilities

• Competition

When planning a restaurant menu, it is also necessary to determine how the menu will affect the following:

• *Labor*—an adequate number of qualified employees with the appropriate skills are required to produce all menu items.

• *Equipment*—equipment must be available to produce all items required by the menu.

• *Space*—adequate square footage is required for all equipment and for receiving, storing, serving, clean-up, and other needs.

• *Layout and design*—the menu affects space and equipment necessary for efficient production.

• *Ingredients*—recipes, which specify necessary ingredients, are important. All ingredients should be readily available at costs that support anticipated product selling prices.

- *Time*—the menu will affect timing of food production and service.

- *Cost implications*—equipment, space, personnel, and time concerns can all be translated into costs. The menu will also affect expenses for utilities and supplies.

The restaurant menu can be viewed as the directions or the owner's manual for the restaurant staff. They read it and become familiar with it. It is their job to know all of the items on the restaurant's menu. Guests will often ask questions about the food on the menu. All food and beverage employees are able to answer the following questions about any item offered:

- What are the ingredients?

- How is it prepared?

- How large are the portions?

- What goes with it?

- What does it taste like?

- What may guests substitute for this item?

- What cannot be substituted for this item?

Food and beverage employees make a point to sample as many of the items offered on the menu as possible. If they try something and like it, it is easier to suggest that item to a guest. Employees also explain any words on the menu that a guest may not understand.

Successful food and beverage employees ask the chef about any new items or changes in recipes. Guests often are interested in chef and daily specials because they offer an added value. Food and beverage employees tell guests what specials are offered without making them wait. They also know which dishes are considered house specialties. Guests will often try these if they are described well.

Depending on the type of restaurant, the menu may change frequently. For instance, in some restaurants, menus change with every meal period. They may even change on a daily basis. If so, food and beverage employees have an extra challenge of being able to sell everything on these menus.

During busy times, the restaurant may run out of a popular item. Food and beverage employees track what's not available before approaching a table to take an order and are prepared to suggest another item instead.

Point-of-Sale Equipment

A **point-of-sale (POS) system** is made up of a number of POS units, usually found in the property's restaurants, gift shops, room service stations, and front desk area. Point-of-sale units are like cash registers. They add up guest charges and print a bill.

Typically, a POS system will either be manual, electronic, or computerized. The majority of systems at most lodging properties today are computerized. At these properties, the computerized POS system is used for all money activities or transactions in the property's restaurants and lounges.

Electronic and computerized POS units store information in their memory and print the check after all charges have been entered. Most of these units have a roll of paper on which they print guest checks. The paper is often called tape because it is usually three to five inches wide and looks like calculator or adding machine tape. The tape may have two or three layers of paper that will provide copies of the guest check.

Computerized POS units in different food and beverage outlets may be linked to each other, or they may be linked to POS units at the front desk. With these units, a guest's restaurant check can be transferred and automatically added to a guest's folio.

Most properties program the keys on point-of-sale units according to standard prices for all items offered in the restaurants or lounges. This makes food and beverage employees' jobs easier, because they don't have to enter prices.

Most computerized point-of-sale units require employees to sign onto the system at the beginning of a shift. At the end of their shift, they must sign off the system.

Apply Your Learning 14.2

Please write all answers on a separate sheet of paper.

1. List five of the seven areas of a food and beverage operation that will be affected by the restaurant menu.

2. Why should food and beverage employees be familiar with how menu items are prepared?

3. What should food and beverage employees be prepared to do when a particular item on the menu is not currently available?

4. List the three types of POS systems.

5. Describe how programmed keys on POS equipment can make a food and beverage employee's job easier.

14.3 Food Production and Presentation

AFTER SUCCESSFULLY COMPLETING THIS SECTION, YOU WILL BE ABLE TO:

♦ Explain the importance of quality food production to a restaurant's success.

♦ Describe a typical kitchen at a lodging restaurant.

♦ List the most common terms used to describe how food is prepared.

♦ Summarize proper plate presentation.

♦ List common garnishes used in restaurants.

Food Production

Excellent food is a basic requirement for a successful food operation. A lodging restaurant will not continue to operate unless the food served is as good or better than all nearby competing food service operations.

Excellent food requires quality ingredients. To get the best results from the quality ingredients, food is produced as close as possible to the time of service. Proper cooking methods are followed as food is produced. For instance, if a stew is to be simmered for two or three hours, it should be simmered and not boiled violently. Once

food is prepared, it is properly cared for until it is served. Food is kept hot or cold for the shortest possible time before service.

Excellent service depends on correctly timing meals. Guests want meals at the correct temperature, courses brought after a previous one is finished, and all the entrees for the entire party brought at the same time.

Usually, a course order is turned in to the kitchen when the previous course is about one-quarter to one-half finished, or sooner if the restaurant is busy. Food and beverage employees prepare the table for each course before delivering it.

The Kitchen

A complete kitchen in a typical large lodging restaurant may consist of a range section (which includes the stock kettles, ranges, broilers, grills, steamers, fry kettles, and roasting ovens); the garde-manger (cold food) sections; the pantry (salad) area; the butcher shop; the pastry shop and sometimes a bake shop; the scullery (dish and pot washing) areas; an employees' cafeteria kitchen; the banquet kitchen, and the room service kitchen. In smaller lodging restaurants, the kitchen may not contain a butcher, pastry, or bake shop. It is also common to see the garde-manger section combined with the pantry area.

Excellent food is produced and served when the food and beverage staff has the proper tools and equipment with which to work. Therefore, the kitchen and all its contents are kept in proper working condition at all times.

Basic Food Preparation Terms and Timing

One of the best ways to describe the food offered in a restaurant is to describe how it is prepared. Successful food and beverage employees use the following terms accurately when describing menu items:

Baked—Cooked by dry heat in an oven.

Boiled—Cooked in boiling liquid.

Braised—Browned in a small amount of fat, then cooked slowly in a small amount of liquid.

Broiled—Cooked by direct heat from above.

Fried—Cooked in fat.

Deep-fried—Cooked in enough fat to cover the food.

Grilled—Cooked on a grid over direct heat, usually hot coals.

Poached—Cooked in enough simmering liquid to cover the food. A liquid is simmering when it is just below the boiling point.

Roasted—Cooked uncovered without water added, usually in an oven, by dry heat.

Sautéed—Browned or cooked in a small amount of hot fat.

Steamed—Cooked in steam with or without pressure.

Stewed—Simmered slowly in enough liquid to cover the food.

Plate Presentation and Garnishes

Part of food quality comes from appearance. Guests like to see attractive-looking meals. The way a plate or glass is presented and garnished can make the difference between an average experience and an exceptional one.

Plate presentation changes from property to property, but some common rules of plate presentation are:

- The correct plate is used.

- The food looks fresh and appealing.

- There are no drips down the side of the glass or plate.

- The entree portion is placed at the 6 P.M. position.

- An appropriate garnish is used.

Garnishes are often used to accent food on a plate. They add color, form, and texture to the presentation. Some common garnishes are:

- Parsley

- Lemon slices or wedges

- Orange slices or wedges

- Cherries

- Tomato wedges or cherry tomatoes

- Carved or grated carrot

- Chocolate curls

- Endive

- Fresh flowers

Apply Your Learning 14.3

Please write all answers on a separate sheet of paper.

1. Briefly explain the importance of correctly timing meals.

2. Describe the areas found in a typical kitchen at a large lodging restaurant.

3. Define the following food preparation terms: "braised," "deep-fried," "poached."

4. At what clock position should an entrée portion be placed?

5. List five of the most common garnishes used in lodging restaurants.

14.4 Food Health and Safety

AFTER SUCCESSFULLY COMPLETING THIS SECTION, YOU WILL BE ABLE TO:

◆ Identify common safety guidelines to follow in a restaurant's kitchen.

◆ Summarize the steps for performing the Heimlich Maneuver.

◆ Explain the importance of practicing sanitation in a food and beverage operation.

◆ Describe the Temperature Danger Zone for foods.

Kitchen Safety

The kitchen is likely to be the busiest place in a lodging restaurant—and the spot with the highest potential for accidents.

By following some simple guidelines, food and beverage employees can help keep themselves, their co-workers, and guests safe:

• Avoid spilling beverages by watching for sudden movements or gestures made by people nearby.

• Do not put hot ashes into the same trash bin as papers or other flammable objects.

• When walking close behind someone, call out "behind you." This way the person is less likely to make a sudden turn or stop.

• Use the correct door when entering or leaving the kitchen service area.

• Wipe up all spilled liquids or foods at once. Leave the area clean and dry. If it is not possible to completely dry it, cover the area with a chair.

• When glass or china breaks, use a broom and dust pan to sweep up the broken pieces. Then use a damp paper towel to pick up all remaining slivers and small pieces of glass.

• Put broken glass or china into separate trash containers; don't throw it in with other garbage.

• Throw out food if there is any chance that broken glass or china may have gotten into it.

• Move crates, cartons, and other out-of-place items from stairways, aisles, and other walkways.

• Know where to find and how to use all fire extinguishers in the restaurant and kitchen.

• Keep fire doors closed.

• Know the location of all emergency exits in the restaurant and kitchen.

Heimlich Maneuver and First Aid

Emergencies and accidents can happen anywhere, lodging restaurants especially.

Training in proper first-aid procedures helps food and beverage employees give first aid to anyone in the restaurant who needs it and possibly save someone's life.

Choking is one of the most common restaurant accidents that require first aid. When food and beverage employees think a guest may be choking, they follow these steps:

- Find out if the person can breathe, talk, or cough. If he or she can, do not give first aid.

- If the person cannot talk, breathe, or cough, a food and beverage employee should call the property emergency number immediately and ask for help.

- If the guest is conscious and a food and beverage employee has been properly trained, he or she should give the **Heimlich maneuver**, which consists of grasping a person around the waist and thrusting on the person's abdomen to force any blockage out of the airway.

Food and beverage employees who have not been properly trained in first-aid procedures such as the Heimlich maneuver or CPR do not try to give them. Instead, they get help immediately. Trying to perform first-aid procedures without training can do more harm than good. For example, improperly performing the Heimlich maneuver could drive food farther down the airway and damage lungs and ribs.

Sanitation

One of the most important responsibilities of food and beverage employees is to practice good sanitation procedures. Many diseases can be transmitted to guests by unsanitary food handling.

Many properties have specific personal hygiene guidelines which represent a crucial component of sanitation. In general, food and beverage employees:

- Stay home when sick

- Cover cuts, burns, sores, and abrasions with a tight, dry, antiseptic bandage

- Shower or bathe daily

- Keep clothes or uniform clean at work; change apron if it becomes soiled

- Follow the property's policies about jewelry

- Keep hair clean and tied back

- Use soap and plenty of hot water to wash hands frequently, especially after performing activities that might contaminate foods, such as:

  - Touching eyes, mouth, ears, nose, or hair

  - Smoking

  - Eating or drinking

  - Using the rest room

  - Sneezing or coughing

  - Using a tissue or handkerchief

  - Handling raw food, such as unwashed fruits or vegetables or uncooked meat

  - Taking out the trash

  - Touching any dirty surfaces, such as wash rags, money or credit cards, or soiled dishes or linens

If food and beverage employees wear latex utility gloves, they wash their gloved hands as thoroughly as they would wash their bare hands. Gloves can spread germs just as easily as bare hands. In addition, food and beverage employees never wash their hands in sinks used for preparing food.

Food and beverage employees help make sure germs don't get into food by keeping it at the proper temperature. Most germs can only survive and multiply between the temperatures of 40 and 140 degrees Fahrenheit (4 and 60 degrees Celsius)—the **Temperature Danger Zone**. If food and beverage employees are responsible for maintaining soup, bread, or other hot items, they make sure they are held above 140°F (60°C). If they are responsible for maintaining salads, salad dressings, or other cold items, make sure they are held between 32° F and 40° F (0° C and 4° C). By keeping hot foods hot and cold foods cold, food and beverage employees can prevent germs from spreading.

There are many other work habits that food and beverage employees can follow to protect themselves and guests:

- Always use tongs, serving utensils, or scoops when necessary. Always serve ice with a scoop. Never touch ice or prepared food with hands.

- Never touch food-contact surfaces, such as the rims or inside of cups, or the tines of forks.

- If a food item has already been served, reuse it only if it is an individually wrapped item, such as crackers or bread sticks.

- Wipe up spills promptly.

- Never stack plates of food to carry them to the table. Contaminants on the bottom of plates might be transferred to the food on the plate below.

- Wash hands after clearing tables and before touching clean tableware.

- Wash hands twice after using the rest room.

- Cover mouth when coughing or sneezing, and then wash hands.

- Wash all dirty tableware immediately after use.

- Wash all raw fruits and vegetables before preparation.

Health Department Regulations

Every food and beverage operation must follow local health department regulations. These regulations cover everything from making sure can openers are clean to using only health-department-approved cleansers. Health department regulations vary depending on the area.

The health department conducts regular inspections to make sure a lodging restaurant is following regulations. Some food and beverage outlets consider health department regulations only when it's time for an inspection. However, successful lodging restaurants and successful food and beverage employees know that following the regulations is part of everyone's daily responsibilities.

Apply Your Learning 14.4

Please write all answers on a separate sheet of paper.

1. As it relates to kitchen safety, where should broken china or glass be placed?

2. When walking closely behind someone, what should you say?

3. When you think someone may be choking, what is the first thing you should do?

4. List five activities that, once performed, require thorough hand washing.

5. Hot food should be kept above what temperature (both Fahrenheit and Celsius)?

6. Cold food should be kept between what temperatures (both Fahrenheit and Celsius)?

14.5 Room Service Attendant

AFTER SUCCESSFULLY COMPLETING THIS SECTION, YOU WILL BE ABLE TO:

◆ Describe the important role played by room service attendants at a lodging property.

◆ List the tasks commonly performed by room service attendants.

◆ Describe the safety procedures used when delivering food to guestrooms.

◆ Summarize proper elevator courtesy guidelines.

What is a Room Service Attendant?

Room service attendants take guests' orders, place orders with the kitchen, deliver orders to guestrooms, and serve guests in their rooms. At some properties, room service order-takers record guests' orders and room service attendants serve the orders.

Having food delivered to the guestroom is a luxury many guests at a lodging property will want to experience. Room service attendants make guests feel special and pampered by providing this service each day. Room service attendants:

• Help business people stay on schedule by delivering food and beverages that allow them to keep working

• Make a private dinner for two possible

• Help guests host functions for friends, family members, or business associates

Room service attendants are responsible for many tasks, including:

• Selling food and beverages

• Delivering food and beverages

• Presenting food and beverages to guests in guestrooms or hospitality suites

• Removing items when guests are done with them

• Helping co-workers as needed

Exhibit 1 lists the tasks that room service attendants are called upon to perform.

To be excellent team players, room service attendants can:

• Deliver food and beverage orders promptly to the kitchen or bar to prevent last-minute rushing for everyone involved.

• Deliver soiled linens to the laundry department throughout a shift to prevent linen shortages and laundry work back-ups.

• Keep hallways clear of used room service items so that others will not trip over them.

• Conduct inventories according to the schedule to ensure that other room

Exhibit 1
Task List—Room Service Attendant

1. Perform Beginning-of-Shift Duties
2. Preset Room Service Trays and Carts
3. Process Express Breakfast Orders
4. Deliver VIP Amenities
5. Use the Point-of-Sale Equipment
6. Take and Record Room Service Orders
7. Handle Special Room Service Requests
8. Place the Room Service Order
9. Perform Pantry Prep for Room Service Orders
10. Prepare Coffee
11. Prepare Hot Tea
12. Prepare Hot Chocolate
13. Prepare Iced Tea
14. Assemble the Beverage Order and Food Condiments
15. Pick Up the Room Service Order
16. Deliver the Room Service Order
17. Serve the Room Service Order
18. Serve Coffee or Hot Tea
19. Check IDs
20. Present and Settle the Guest Check
21. Retrieve Trays and Carts
22. Close Out the Guest Check
23. Follow Up With Guests
24. Respond to Dissatisfied Guests
25. Clear and Reset Trays and Carts
26. Handle Soiled Room Service Linens
27. Set Up Portable Bars in Suites or Guestrooms
28. Set Up and Serve Small Group Dinners and Receptions
29. Set Up and Serve Small Buffet Banquets
30. Set Up and Serve Coffee Breaks
31. Maintain Room Service Side Stations
32. Pick Up and Restock Room Service Supplies
33. Perform Closing Shift Duties
34. Make Shift Deposit and Collect Due-Backs
35. Use the Room Service Logbook

service attendants won't run out of supplies.

- Report repairs to engineering, and fill out a maintenance request form if necessary.

- Bus soiled dishes often so stewards won't fall behind.

Successful room service attendants strive to meet the following superior performance standards:

- Answer the telephone by the third ring.

- Be familiar with all menu items, including specials and desserts.

- Suggest items such as daily specials, appetizers, desserts, and beverages.

- Tell each guest the approximate time of delivery, and deliver food and beverages by that time.

- Use portable heaters for all hot food.

- Ask permission to enter guestrooms.

- Set tables, remove coverings, and arrange dishes attractively.

- Use only full, capped, and clean condiment containers.

- Politely ask guests to call room service when finished so that he or she may retrieve dirty dishes.

- Remove service trays and dishes promptly so that no trays or dishes remain in the hall from one meal period to the next.

Guestroom Safety for Room Service Attendants

As a function of their duties, room service attendants use carts and trays to deliver food to guestrooms. While restaurant servers are able to make sure their work area (the dining room) is clean, room service attendants can never be sure what the condition of a guestroom will be. There might be water spilled on the floor, clothes hanging from a chair, or smoldering cigarettes and scattered newspapers on the table. That's why room service attendants are careful when they enter and work in a guestroom. The following tips help keep room service attendants, guests, and equipment safe. Room service attendants:

- Watch where they push their cart.

- Look at the floor of the guestroom before they enter.

- Pick up items off the floor before pushing the cart into the room, or politely ask the guest to move his or her belongings.

- Do not confront guests if they see a gun, drugs, controlled substances, pets, or damage to the room. Instead, they deliver the order and then report the problem to their supervisor. If they feel uncomfortable, they excuse themselves right away and tell their supervisor about the problem.

- Make it their goal to always bring room service equipment into the room. However, if a guest does not want them to enter the room, they don't leave until the guest brings all the items into the room. Room service equipment in the hallway can be a safety hazard.

- Take along a doorstop so they can prop open the door while they're in the guestroom. Keeping the door open provides extra security.

Elevator Courtesy

Most properties that offer room service also have service elevators which the room service attendants use to transport food and food service carts. However, since there may be times that room service attendants must use the guest elevators, they are aware of proper elevator courtesy, as described in Chapter 5 of this text.

If it does not appear that the room service cart will fit comfortably on the elevator with the guests, room service attendants will wait for the next elevator.

Apply Your Learning 14.5

Please write all answers on a separate sheet of paper.

1. List at least four tasks that a room service attendant performs.

2. What should a room attendant do if a guest does not wish him or her to enter the room?

3. How can a room service attendant safely move through guestroom corridors?

4. When should a room service attendant not use an elevator?

Quick Hits

SECTION 14.1—GETTING TO KNOW THE FOOD AND BEVERAGE DIVISION

- The food and beverage division of a lodging property is a very important revenue center. Typically, it is second only to the rooms division in the amount of revenue that it earns.

- Departments in the food and beverage division can include banquet and catering, culinary operations, stewarding, and restaurant operations.

- Food and beverage positions can include restaurant server, banquet server, banquet setup person, bus person, kitchen steward, and room service attendant.

- Because they make frequent use of the telephone in the performance of their duties, food and beverage employees always practice proper telephone etiquette—making every caller feel important.

- Most restaurants have common guidelines for taking reservations. All food and beverage employees should be familiar with these guidelines.

- Tipping policies in restaurants include: every employee keeps their own tips; employees share tips with other, specific co-workers; or all employees split tips evenly.

SECTION 14.2—MENUS AND POS EQUIPMENT

- A successful food service operation depends largely on the restaurant menu. The menu is the first and best marketing tool that a lodging restaurant can have.

- Factors considered when creating a menu include: target market, type of food and beverage served, location, and competition.

- Food and beverage employees should be familiar with the items on the menu, be able to describe how items are made and prepared, and know when a menu or menu items have changed.

- Most properties today use computerized POS (point-of-sale) equipment to handle all food and beverage transactions.

- POS equipment is often linked across the property, enabling a guest's restaurant check to be added to his or her room account at the front desk.

SECTION 14.3—FOOD PRODUCTION AND PRESENTATION

- Quality food and quality food production are essential to a successful food and beverage operation. How food is prepared and timed is important to guests' enjoyment of their meals.

- Kitchens in lodging restaurants can include such sections as a bake or pastry shop, or they may be smaller and simply contain range, cold food, salad, and dishwashing sections. Regardless of a kitchen's size, it is necessary that all equipment and components are kept in proper working order.

- There are basic food preparation terms that food and beverage employees are familiar with so that they can explain them to guests. These include such terms as "baked," "fried," "roasted," and "steamed," among others.

- While the quality of the food and how it is prepared is essential, guests also enjoy how food is presented. Guests like attractive looking meals that are presented and garnished properly.

SECTION 14.4—FOOD HEALTH AND SAFETY

- The restaurant kitchen is busy place and has a high potential for accidents. Food and beverage employees can keep themselves, their co-workers, and guests safe by following basic kitchen safety guidelines.

- Food and beverage employees who have been properly trained may be able to assist a guest who is in need by performing the Heimlich maneuver or other first-aid procedures.

- There are many important and necessary sanitation guidelines in a food and beverage operation that are in place to protect guests and employees. It is vital that all food and beverage employees be familiar with and practice these guidelines.

SECTION 14.5—ROOM SERVICE ATTENDANT

- Room service attendants are responsible for taking guests' room service orders, placing the orders to the kitchen, delivering the food to the guestroom, and serving it to the guests.

- When delivering food to guestrooms, room service attendants must practice safety.

Restaurant Server

Sections

In many restaurants, servers perform the bulk of the food and beverage serving duties, assisted by buspersons. Depending on the food service operation, servers may greet and seat guests, take their food and beverage orders, bring the ordered items to the table, check back with guests to make sure every thing is satisfactory, present the guest check for payment, take the check to a cashier, return change to the guest, thank the guest, and clear tables.

Servers may also help with such minor food preparation tasks as adding dressings to salads, portioning soups, and dishing up desserts from service equipment located behind counters or in side stations.

Servers must work quickly yet carefully. They must be able to do several things during one trip through the dining area, such as carry food to one table, present a guest check to another, and remove used dishes from a third.

15.1 Getting to Know the Restaurant Server

AFTER SUCCESSFULLY COMPLETING THIS SECTION, YOU WILL BE ABLE TO:

◆ Describe the job of a restaurant server.

◆ List ways restaurant servers can work as a team.

◆ Identify superior performance standards for restaurant servers.

◆ Explain how to suggestively sell and upsell.

What Is a Restaurant Server?

A restaurant server at a lodging property helps make a guest's stay memorable by providing outstanding food and beverage service.

Restaurant servers are responsible for:

• Preparing for service

• Greeting guests

• Taking the order

• Serving the order

• Creating a friendly atmosphere where guests can enjoy themselves

• Closely monitoring guests' alcohol consumption

• Completing service

• Helping co-workers as needed

Their duties vary based on the type of restaurant. Restaurants in lodging properties range from formal, full-service establishments to fast-food places. At formal restaurants, restaurant servers may prepare some items, such as flaming desserts, at the table. At fast-food or other informal restaurants, they may operate a drive-up window or deliver food off the premises.

Exhibit 1 lists many of the tasks that restaurant servers typically perform.

Working as a Team

Restaurant servers are part of a service delivery system. They give guests *and* co-workers great service.

To be excellent team players, restaurant servers and the serving staff can help:

• The hosts and hostesses by:

  – Greeting and seating guests

  – Answering the phone

  – Letting them know when there are guests who are ready to leave so that they can plan which guests to seat there next

Exhibit 1
Task List—Restaurant Servers

1. Set Up the Restaurant for Service
2. Stock and Maintain Side Stations
3. Fold Napkins
4. Prepare Breads and Bread Baskets or Trays
5. Prepare Service Trays
6. Take Restaurant Reservations
7. Work Efficiently
8. Greet and Seat Guests
9. Approach the Table
10. Provide Appropriate Service for Children
11. Lift and Carry Trays, Bus Tubs, or Dish Racks
12. Serve Water
13. Check IDs of Guests Ordering Alcohol
14. Take Beverage Orders
15. Process Beverage Orders
16. Prepare and Serve Coffee
17. Prepare and Serve Hot Tea
18. Prepare and Serve Iced Tea
19. Prepare and Serve Hot Chocolate
20. Take Food Orders
21. Serve Bread and Butter
22. Prepare Ice Buckets
23. Serve the Meal
24. Check Back to the Table
25. Respond to Dissatisfied Guests
26. Maintain Tables
27. Sell After-Dinner Items
28. Prepare Takeout Items
29. Present the Guest Check
30. Settle Guest Checks and Thank Guests
31. Clear and Reset Tables
32. Handle Soiled Restaurant Linens
33. Inventory, Requisition, and Restock Restaurant Supplies
34. Perform Closing Sidework

- The bus persons by:
  - Immediately removing from tables the items guests do not need anymore
  - Clearing and resetting tables
  - Restocking side stations so that supplies are always available

- The kitchen staff by:
  - Writing orders neatly and completely
  - Asking guests all the necessary questions when they place orders, such as, "How would you like that prepared?"

– Pointing out special or unusual orders to the cook

– Properly sorting and stacking used glasses, china, silverware, etc.

An additional duty they may be asked to take on is helping to train other employees. Many supervisors ask qualified employees to work with new employees or current employees who are having trouble in a certain job area.

Superior Performance Standards

The quality of the food, drinks, and service at a restaurant should enhance each guest's overall experience. Providing excellent service, beverages, and meals at a reasonable price is every restaurant's ultimate goal.

Restaurant servers:

• Demonstrate professional behavior within the property

• Make sure the dining room is properly lit, has a comfortable temperature, and looks neat

• Are familiar with all restaurant menus and food and drink offerings

• Are familiar with all menu items, including specials and desserts

• Know whether the kitchen is out of any menu items, and find out what will be offered in place of sold-out items

• Quickly approach guests and greet them warmly

• Introduce themselves to guests, and use their names whenever possible

• Accommodate special guest requests when appropriate

• Use suggestive selling throughout the guest's visit to make his or her experience more enjoyable

• Make sure food is served at the correct temperature, attractively presented, and pleasing to the senses

• Frequently check back to the table to ensure guest satisfaction

• Be alert to safety procedures at all times

• Wash their hands after taking a break

Suggestive Selling and Upselling

Suggestive selling encourages guests to buy additional food and beverages. An example of suggestive selling is suggesting an appetizer to go with beverage orders. **Upselling** means suggesting more expensive and possibly better quality items.

Suggestive selling and upselling require tact and good judgment. If guests know exactly what they want, servers don't try to change their minds. Instead, they suggest additional items that will improve guests' meals. And they pick up on when guests want suggestions.

Suggestive selling makes some servers nervous. This is probably because selling reminds them of a pushy salesperson they've known. Using suggestive selling and upselling techniques, however, is not being pushy. These techniques are part of providing good service.

The key to effective selling is a good knowledge of the menu. Servers have to know all of the products the restaurant sells. When they are completely familiar with the menu and how each item is prepared, they can suggest dishes confidently and professionally.

Here are some techniques servers use for more effective suggestive selling and upselling:

- Develop a selling attitude.

- Be enthusiastic. It's easier to sell something they're excited about.

- Make food sound appetizing. Use words like "fresh," "popular," and "generous" when describing menu items.

- Ask questions. Find out if guests are really hungry or just want something light; whether they like chicken or beef; or whether they feel like having something hot or cold.

- Suggest specific menu items. Don't simply ask: "Would you like soup with your meal?" Instead, point out: "A cold bowl of borscht would go nicely with your salad on a hot day like this."

- Suggest personal favorites. Try as many menu items as possible, and tell guests they've tried them: "You'll like the Chicken Kiev. It's one of my favorites here." But they are honest—they don't say that something is their favorite when it isn't.

- Offer a choice: "Would you like a slice of our famous cheesecake or our home-made pecan pie for dessert?"

- Suggest the unusual. People dine out to get away from the routine fare they have at home. And most people don't know what they want to order when they arrive.

- Suggest foods and beverages that naturally go together—soups and sandwiches, bacon and eggs, steak and baked potatoes, coffee and dessert.

- Compliment guests' choices. Make guests feel good about their choices even if they don't order what servers suggest.

And finally, they ask for the sale. After they suggest and describe an item, they ask whether the guest would like it. A good way to do this is to describe several items and ask which the guest would prefer.

Apply Your Learning 15.1

Please write all answers on a separate sheet of paper.

1. What is the main task of a restaurant server?

2. How can restaurant servers work as a team with the kitchen staff?

3. What are some of the superior performance standards that restaurant servers strive to achieve?

4. What is upselling?

5. What is suggestive selling?

15.2 Preparing for Service

AFTER SUCCESSFULLY COMPLETING THIS SECTION, YOU WILL BE ABLE TO:

- Describe how to set up a restaurant for service.

- Explain the importance of side stations.

- Identify safe ways to prepare and carry service trays.

- Describe ways to work efficiently while serving.

Set Up the Restaurant for Service

Restaurant servers work with bus persons to set up tables in their area. They make sure that each table in their section is perfect. This includes checking:

- Silverware
- Glasses
- Napkins
- Salt and pepper shakers or grinders
- Sugar bowls or caddies
- Tablecloths
- The evenness of placemats
- Condiments

- Chairs and booths
- Flower arrangements
- Table lamps
- Floor and carpets
- Overall table appearance
- Ice buckets

Exhibit 1 gives a step-by-step breakdown for preparing the restaurant for service.

Side Stations

Side stations are service areas where supplies are stored. They are stocked with such items as glasses, silverware, and dishes. These supplies help servers work more efficiently as they reduce the distance that servers have to go to get the supplies which guests need.

Servers make sure that all items in their side stations are stocked to par levels. They also make sure there is a bucket of sanitizing solution and a clean cloth at their station.

Throughout a server's shift, they maintain their stations. A **sidework checklist** lists sidework and the restaurant server who is assigned to complete each task. Common sidework tasks include folding napkins and wiping service trays.

Sidework tasks are a very important part of keeping a restaurant running well. Servers can't provide high-quality service if they waste time returning to the kitchen for items that should be in the side stations.

Exhibit 1
Set Up the Restaurant for Service

Materials needed: Silverware, glasses, napkins, salt and pepper shakers or grinders, salt and pepper, cleaning cloths, sugar bowls and caddies, sugar, artificial sweetener, tablecloths or place mats, condiments, sanitizing solution, foodservice film, vases, flowers, table lamps, candles or lamp fuel, dessert trays or carts, lemons, cream, creamers, ice buckets, approved detergent, silver polish, an ice scoop, ladles, and an opening duty checklist.

STEPS:	HOW-TO'S:
1. Check the silverware on the tables in your section and in the side station.	❑ Make sure silverware is clean and free from food and water spots. ❑ Replace unacceptable items. ❑ Do not hand-polish silverware. ❑ Check silverplate silverware for tarnish. Return tarnished silverware to the dish room and ask the chief steward to burnish or polish it. ❑ Make sure silverware is in the correct position on the table. Supply missing silverware if necessary. Never touch the eating surface of silverware with your hands. ❑ Make sure the side station silverware trays are fully stocked.
2. Check the glasses on the tables in your section.	❑ Look for cracked, chipped, or spotted glasses. ❑ Throw away cracked or chipped glasses. ❑ Return spotted glasses to the dish room. It is unsanitary to hand-polish glassware. ❑ Replace all glasses removed from service.

(continued)

Exhibit 1
Set Up the Restaurant for Service *(continued)*

STEPS:	HOW-TO'S:
3. Check the napkins on the tables in your section.	❑ Replace wrinkled, spotted, torn, or missing napkins. ❑ Refold napkins that are folded incorrectly.
4. Check salt and pepper shakers or grinders on the tables in your section.	❑ Make sure salt and pepper shakers or grinders are free from food residue, spots, chips, and cracks. ❑ Replace unacceptable shakers or grinders. ❑ Empty and wash shakers and grinders periodically. Make sure they are completely dry before refilling them. Don't use water to clean wooden grinders. Don't use water to clean wooden grinders. ❑ Make sure all shakers and grinders are full at the beginning of service. Fill them if necessary. ❑ Wipe and polish metal lids to remove moisture and dried salt or pepper. Replace lids that are cracked, dented, or chipped.
5. Check sugar bowls or caddies on the tables in your section.	❑ Make sure sugar bowls or caddies are clean. Fill bowls or caddies two-thirds full of sugar packets and one-third full of artificial sweetener packets. Most health departments do not permit the use of loose sugar. ❑ Clean bowls or caddies if necessary and fill them as needed. ❑ Place packets upright and facing the same way so guests can read the printing on them.

(continued)

Exhibit 1
Set Up Restaurant for Service *(continued)*

STEPS:	HOW-TO'S:
6. Check the tablecloths on the tables in your section.	❏ Adjust each tablecloth so that it hangs evenly on all sides with the seams facing down. Some restaurants use two tablecloths or a top cloth (called a "topper") turned over a base cloth. Toppers should be lined up properly.
	❏ Check each cloth for holes, wrinkles, or stains. Replace unacceptable tablecloths.
7. Check the evenness of place mats (if used instead of tablecloths).	❏ Set up place mats neatly and consistently. Make sure they are clean and free from holes, tears, or stains.
	❏ Place the mats right-side-up with the printing facing guests so they can read the printing.
	❏ Line up each mat with the table edge and with the mat on the other side of the table.
	❏ Change paper place mats each time you reset a table.
8. Check the condiments on the tables in your section and in the side station.	❏ Make sure each condiment container is full of fresh condiments, with no spots, spills, or fingerprints on it.
	❏ Replace containers or dispensers that are chipped, cracked, or dented.
	❏ Remove container or dispenser lids. Make sure the rims are clean.
	❏ Make sure syrup and honey dispensers are not sticky. Wipe clean any dispensers or containers as needed.

(continued)

Exhibit 1
Set Up the Restaurant for Service *(continued)*

STEPS:	HOW-TO'S:
	❏ Preset condiments according to your tabletop guidelines for each meal.
	❏ Do not preset condiments that need refrigeration. Deliver these with the meal.
	❏ Make sure chairs and booths are free from food, dust, and fingerprints. Pay special attention to the arms, legs, and spindles of chairs.
9. **Check chairs and booths in your section.**	❏ Make sure chairs and booths are free from food, dust, and fingerprints. Pay special attention to the arms, legs and spindles of chairs.
	❏ If necessary, wipe chairs and booths clean with a damp cloth and sanitizing solution followed by a dry cloth. If possible, pull out seating cushions and wipe up crumbs.
	❏ Check under tables and chairs for gum, and remove any gum you find.
	❏ Report upholstery stains, burns, rips, and tears to your supervisor.
	❏ Place each chair so the edge of the seat is even with the table edge.
	❏ Clean high chairs and booster seats with a damp cloth and sanitizing solution, if necessary. Let them air dry.
	❏ Make sure safety straps on high chairs are clean and in working order. Replace any missing or broken straps.
	❏ Wrap clean high-chair trays with foodservice film to keep them sanitary.

(continued)

Exhibit 1
Set Up the Restaurant for Service *(continued)*

STEPS:	HOW-TO'S:
10. **Check flower arrangements on the tables in your section.**	❑ Check vases for cracks, chips, and fingerprints. Clean or replace vases as needed. Make sure vases are full of fresh water if live flowers are used. ❑ Make sure live flowers are fresh and neatly arranged. Replace wilting flowers. You are responsible for maintaining flower arrangements. ❑ Make sure artificial arrangements are free from dust. ❑ If necessary, use a soft, dry cloth to gently wipe the leaves and petals of artificial arrangements. A wet cloth can damage silk flowers.
11. **Check table lamps in your section for fuel or wax.**	❑ Make sure lamps are clean and free of chips and cracks. Clean or replace lamps as needed. ❑ If lamps have brass or silver trim, make sure the trim is free from spots and tarnish. Polish brass or silver trim if necessary. ❑ Place new candles in each candle lamp as needed, or refill lamps using liquid fuel. Make sure that wicks are in good condition.
12. **Check the floor and carpets in your section.**	❑ Make sure carpets have been vacuumed and that the floor is free of debris and dust. Check for stains and for food that has been ground into the carpet. ❑ Ask the bus person to remove spots. Tell your supervisor about hard-to-remove stains so that carpet cleaning can be scheduled. ❑ Tell your supervisor about burns, stains, or tears in the carpet.

(continued)

Exhibit 1
Set Up the Restaurant for Service *(continued)*

STEPS:	HOW-TO'S:
13. Check the overall appearance of your tables.	❑ Make sure all of your tables are set the same way. ❑ Make sure there is enough room to pass between tables without disturbing guests. Adjust tables as necessary to provide enough aisle space for good service.
14. Prepare display dessert trays or carts when applicable.	
15. Sign out enough guest checks to last throuhout your shift.	❑ Always double-check that you have the correct number of checks. Make sure they are in the correct sequence. ❑ Keep track of every check. ❑ Follow your restaurant's check-control procedure.
16. Cut lemons for hot tea and iced tea.	
17. Prepare cream for coffee and tea.	❑ Make sure creamers are clean. ❑ Keep cream refrigerated until it is ready to be served.
18. Set up bread stations.	
19. Set up salad stations.	❑ Make sure the correct ladle is available for each type of salad dressing. Be able to identify the salad dressing offered at your restaurant.
20. Set up soup stations.	
21. Make coffee and iced tea.	
22. Complete other tasks according to your opening duty checklist.	

Service Trays

Service trays are used to help transport food, dishes, and equipment throughout the restaurant. Servers most commonly use two types of trays:

- A 12-inch to 14-inch beverage tray, which should be used only for serving beverages or serving food for a single guest.

- A large restaurant service tray, usually 27 inches long and oval in shape, to be used for serving food for a party of more than one and clearing tables.

Trays are always used when servers are delivering or clearing items. Trays are usually washed in the kitchen at the end of the meal period and then sprayed with sanitizing solution throughout service. Servers help clean the trays, set them up, and stock their side stations with trays.

Servers lift safely when carrying trays. They bend at the knees so that their shoulder is below the tray. They then pull the tray with one hand onto the palm of the other hand. They balance the tray at shoulder level on their fingertips, not on their forearms. Trays carried on a forearm have a greater likelihood of tipping over. They then keep their back straight as they stand up and steady the tray with their free hand.

Working Efficiently

Servers work smart to keep up their energy and provide better guest service—especially during busy times. They make sure that they never move between the kitchen and the dining room with empty hands. They're always carrying something—food, beverages, condiments, coffee, etc. each time they move between the two. They clear used plates, glasses, and other items from tables before entering the kitchen. They always carry a tray with them so they are prepared to clear items.

One trick that servers use is to think of their entire section as one big table and to look at all guests to see whether they need anything each time they are in the dining room. Whenever they have nothing else to do, they start cleanup duties.

Apply Your Learning 15.2

Please write all answers on a separate sheet of paper.

1. How can a server help set up a restaurant for service?

2. What is sidework?

3. What type of tray is used for serving beverages?

4. What is one way that servers work efficiently?

15.3 Taking Orders and Serving Drinks

AFTER SUCCESSFULLY COMPLETING THIS SECTION, YOU WILL BE ABLE TO:

◆ Explain how to greet and seat guests.

◆ Identify how servers approach tables.

◆ Describe ways to provide appropriate service for children.

◆ Explain how to serve beverages.

Greet and Seat Guests

A host will usually handle seating, but sometimes servers help out. When they do, they smile and give a warm greeting. They then ask whether the restaurant is holding a reservation for them and whether they have any seating preferences.

Some guests may have special needs such as Braille menus, high chairs, booster seats, etc.

Servers usually use a seating chart to decide where to seat a party. Each restaurant will have a different policy for how to balance tables. Overloading one section will make good service difficult. However, if a party requests a certain table and it is available, servers will usually give it to them even if it overloads a section. The dining room manager can often adjust a server's workload.

Servers then pick up enough menus for each guest and ask the party to follow them. They communicate confidence by:

• Holding the menus high on their arm

• Standing up straight and giving their full attention to the party they are seating

• Moving service equipment to one side to clear a path for the guests

• Describing restaurant highlights

Servers then help the guests with seating by pulling high chairs away from the table, helping guests with disabilities as appropriate, and pulling out a chair for a guest. Servers never touch a child or any other guest unless they have permission. They also let the guests decide who will sit in the chair they pull out.

Servers then present the menu, usually closed and right-side-up, to each guest from the guest's right side, using their right hand. They then remove any extra place-settings.

Approach the Table

Greeting guests immediately puts guests at ease and assures them that someone will take care of them. The server's greeting is one of the guests' first impressions of the server and the restaurant. Therefore, servers work at sounding warm and sincere.

Guests don't like to wait, and they hate to be ignored. A brief contact and a sincere apology for any delay will usually overcome any negative feelings that could develop.

Exhibit 1 gives a step-by-step breakdown for how to approach a table.

Provide Appropriate Service for Children

Special attention to children will increase guest satisfaction. Servers ask parents how they can help the children have a good time and also allow the parents to enjoy their meals.

High chairs and booster seats should be cleaned and sanitized after each use. The tray should be wrapped in foodservice film to keep it clean.

Other things servers do to provide appropriate service for children are:

- Ask parents whether children will need a high chair or booster seat

- Seat guests with children away from the center of the room

- Remove knives from the place settings of small children

- Make sure high chairs, trays, bibs, menus, coloring books, and toys are sanitary

- Provide menus, coloring books, toys, bibs, crackers, or other items

- Serve children their meals first

Serve Beverages

The first beverage typically served is water. In some restaurants, servers or bus persons will bring full water glasses to the table. In other restaurants, water may be served only by request or may be delayed until after beverage orders have been taken.

Servers refill water glasses whenever they are less than half-full, usually pouring from a pitcher.

All servers use the same order-taking system to help remember who ordered what. In some restaurants, servers write the orders on the back of a guest check, and the point-of-sale unit prints the order on the front. In those cases, servers don't have to worry about **standard food and drink abbreviations**. However, most restaurant servers do have to find out what food and drink abbreviations are used by the restaurant and use those on the guest check.

Servers typically pre-ring drink orders on the restaurant's point-of-sale equipment.

In most restaurants, bartenders set up drink glasses and ice if needed. In other restaurants, servers will set up the correct glasses in the order that they will call the drinks and then they place the glasses on the kitchen or bartender side of the service bar. When they call orders, they say in a clear voice, "Ordering," and then announce the drink order, including any special instructions. The reason restaurant servers follow a specific **calling order** is that some drinks take more time to prepare than other drinks, or they do not hold up as well as other drinks.

Either the server or the bartender will garnish a drink after it has been prepared. The server then collects one beverage napkin for each drink. They then check the beverage order:

- Is it the correct beverage?

- Is it in the correct glass?

- Is the garnish correct?

Exhibit 1
Approach the Table

Materials needed: Menus, the wine list, and a water pitcher.

STEPS:	HOW-TO'S:
1. Greet guests.	☐ Greet guests within 30 seconds after they are seated. Be relaxed, pleasant, and professional.
	☐ Introduce yourself by name. For example, "Welcome. I'm Carlos, your server."
	☐ If you are unable to greet your guests within 30 seconds, stop by the table and let them know you will be back soon. Apologize for the wait when you return.
	☐ Encourage guests to tell you if they have any special needs or requests.
	☐ Try to "read" guests right away. Be alert to guests who may have been drinking and may become intoxicated quickly.
2. Bring or pour water.	
3. Deliver menus, if	☐ Give a closed menu, right-side-up, to each guest in the following order: • Children (children's menu when available) • Women • Men
	☐ Place the wine list in a neutral location. Or hand it to the guest who asks for it.
	☐ Present each menu from the guest's right side, using your right hand.
4. Remove extra place settings and adjust centerpiece items to balance the table.	

- Have special instructions been followed?

- Has anything spilled over the side?

Servers then line their tray with a linen napkin and center the glasses on the tray so that the tray is well-balanced. If possible, heavy or tall glasses are placed in the center of the tray.

Servers then place a beverage napkin with the logo facing the guest. The glass is then placed on the center of the napkin. Servers handle glasses away from the rim or lip and handle stemmed glasses by the stem or base. Their hands will warm the drink if they touch the outside of the glass, however, sanitation concerns mean that servers never put their fingers inside a glass.

When the guest has finished a drink, servers pick up napkins and empty glasses before replacing them with additional drinks.

Apply Your Learning 15.3

Please write all answers on a separate sheet of paper.

1. What attitude does a server have when greeting guests?

2. Why should servers greet guests immediately?

3. List three things that servers can do to provide appropriate service to children.

4. Why should servers follow a calling order for beverages?

15.4   Serving Food

AFTER SUCCESSFULLY COMPLETING THIS SECTION, YOU WILL BE ABLE TO:

♦ Describe how to take food orders.

♦ Explain how to serve a meal.

♦ Identify ways to respond to dissatisfied guests.

♦ Explain how to maintain tables.

♦ Describe ways to sell after-dinner items.

Take Food Orders

Servers begin taking orders by telling guests about specials. It is their job to always know about the daily specials, the soup of the day, and the vegetable of the day. If the chef does not announce the specials, the servers have to ask. Guests get annoyed if they ask what the soup or vegetable of the day is and they have to wait for the server to go to the kitchen to find out.

Servers take orders in a standard clockwise fashion so that someone else can serve their guests without having to ask who ordered what.

While taking orders, servers will ask questions so that they don't have to later interrupt their guests to find out necessary preparation and service information. They also work at not sounding mechanical when describing choices, but attempt to make every item sound good.

By suggesting additional items, servers can enhance the guests' dining experience, increase revenue for the restaurant, and increase their own tips.

When placing food orders with the kitchen, servers sometimes have to speak with the chef to explain special orders. They make an effort to always be polite and to keep conversations to a minimum.

Exhibit 1 gives a step-by-step breakdown for taking food orders.

Serve the Meal

The timing of food preparation is important to a smooth dining experience. Each guest in a party should be served at the same time. Planning and organization helps servers make it possible to serve all guests quickly.

Good service is so smooth that the guests are hardly aware of the servers. When they are able to serve each course without asking questions, guests are not interrupted. Tray service saves steps and lets servers take care of many guests at once.

Exhibit 2 gives a step-by-step breakdown for serving the meal.

Check Back to the Table

Servers make sure that the guests are satisfied with their meal. They approach guests after the guests have taken a few bites and ask specific questions about the food, such

Exhibit 1
Taking Food Orders

Materials needed: An order pad or guest checks, and a pen.

STEPS:	HOW-TO'S:
1. **Tell guests about specials.**	❑ Know the daily specials. If appropriate at your restaurant, try to taste each one. ❑ Always describe specials and chef's choice items, such as the soup of the day, before guests ask. ❑ Describe the ingredients and the preparation of specials in an appealing way. Always give the price of specials.
2. **Ask for the food order.**	❑ Offer to help guests with menu selections. Answer any questions about the menu. ❑ Ask if they are ready to order.
3. **Follow an order-taking system.**	❑ Know the numbering system for the chairs at each table. Chair #1 at each table is typically the chair closest to the door or some other landmark in your restaurant. ❑ When writing orders on your order pad or guest check, write the order for the guest in chair #1 on the first line of the order form. ❑ Take the orders of children first, then women, and then men. Write their orders in the corresponding place on the order pad. For instance, if the guest in chair #2 is the only woman at the table, take her order first and write it on line #2 on the order pad. ❑ Continue to take food orders in a clockwise pattern around the table.

(continued)

Exhibit 1
Taking Food Orders *(continued)*

STEPS:	HOW-TO'S:
4. **Stand in the correct position to take orders.**	❑ The place where you stand varies among restaurants: 　• In different positions around the table so you can speak one-on-one to each guest 　• In one position to get the attention of the entire table so that everyone can hear your suggestive selling 　• It depends on the table and the guests ❑ Always stand up straight as you take orders. Do not rest the order pad on the table. ❑ Look at each guest when he or she is ordering. Watch for hesitation in making a decision. This provides you an opening to offer a suggestion.
5. **Ask the appropriate questions.**	❑ Pay attention to details and know your menu thoroughly. ❑ Know what questions to ask for each item to determine the guests' choices. For instance, know if a guest must choose soup or salad. ❑ Know when you need to ask for more information, such as how the guest would like an item cooked. ❑ Repeat each completed order to the guest, especially if there are special details or requests regarding preparation or service.
6. **Suggest additional courses.**	❑ Suggest additional courses such as appetizers, soups, and salads when you take the food order. ❑ Think about what the guest has selected and suggest items that will go well with the entree.

(continued)

Exhibit 1
Taking Food Orders *(continued)*

STEPS:	HOW-TO'S:
7. **Try to meet special requests.**	❑ Some guests may request an item to be prepared in a way not listed on the menu.
	❑ Write all special requests on your order pad and tell kitchen employees about the requests when you place the order.
	❑ You may need to check with the chef or your supervisor before making a promise to a guest.
8. **Ask if guests would like another beverage.**	❑ Check on drink levels. Suggest another drink if a beverage is one-half to three-fourths empty.
	❑ Clear empty glasses before serving new beverages.
9. **Collect the menus if you haven't already done so.**	
10. **Change ashtrays as needed, and tidy the table to keep it as fresh as possible.**	
11. **Pre-ring the food order.**	
12. **Place food orders with the kitchen.**	

as, "How is your sirloin?" or "Are you enjoying your salad?"

They also ask whether there is anything else they can bring at that time. Repeat business happens when satisfied guests tell their friends about their positive dining experience, so servers work at making the experience as positive as possible.

If the food or beverage is unsatisfactory, servers apologize to the guest and take care of the problem immediately.

Respond to Dissatisfied Guests

Guests do the restaurant a favor when they complain—they are giving servers a

Exhibit 2
Serve the Meal

Materials needed: An order pad or guest checks, a service tray, condiments, and ashtrays.

STEPS:	HOW-TO'S:

1. **Time the preparation of the food.**	❏ Turn in the order for each course when guests are about three-fourths finished with the previous one. If the kitchen is busy, turn in the orders sooner.
	
	❏ Serve courses in the following order, unless guests request a different order:
	
	    • Appetizers
	    • Soup
	    • Salads
	    • Entrees
	    • Dessert
	    • Cordials
	    • Coffee
	
	❏ Check with the cook or your supervisor if you are concerned that an order is not being prepared in a reasonable amount of time. Don't make guests wait without an explanation from you or your supervisor.
	
	❏ If you are too busy to pick up an order as soon as it is ready, ask another restaurant server for help.

2. **Prepare the table for each course before serving it.**	❏ Clear any empty plates or glasses from the guest's right with your right hand. Always ask guests if they are finished. ❏ Wait to clear glasses or plates until more than one guest at a table is finished, so guests who are still eating or drinking do not feel rushed.

(continued)

Exhibit 2
Serve the Meal (continued)

STEPS:	HOW-TO'S:
	❑ Never stack dirty plates in front of guests. Pick them up separately and stack them away from guests.
	❑ Bring all condiments and accompaniments to the table before serving the order.
	❑ Only bring full—not partially full—condiment bottles to guests.
	❑ If you will be serving an item that guests will share, bring a plate for each guest.
3. **Pick up the food order.**	❑ Check the food before you take it out of the kitchen:
	• Does the food look fresh and appealing?
	• Have all preparation instructions been followed?
	• Is the presentation garnished?
	• Have all special requests been met?
	• Is the plate clean?
	• Is hot food hot and cold food cold?
	❑ Ask the cook to make any corrections necessary to meet the property's high standards.
	❑ Notify your supervisor immediately of any problem in the food preparation so that he or she can speak to the guests and correct the situation.
	❑ If you are having trouble meeting guest needs, ask your supervisor or another server for help until you can catch up.
	❑ Don't let the guests suffer because you're busy.
	❑ Thank the kitchen staff for their cooperation.

(continued)

Exhibit 2
Serve the Meal *(continued)*

STEPS:	HOW-TO'S:
4. **Deliver food.**	Food is delivered either:
	• Using a tray draped with a napkin
	• Using a tray without a napkin
	❑ Use your order pad or guest check to help remember who ordered what. You shouldn't have to ask the guests.
	❑ Serve the children first, women next, then men, and the host last.
	❑ Serve food from the guest's left side with your left hand whenever possible. Don't reach in front of guests.
	❑ Place the plate with the first course on top of the base plate, if a base plate is included in your restaurant's table setting.
	❑ Place the entree plate so that the main item is closest to the guest.
	❑ Place side dishes to the left of the entree plate.
	❑ If a guest asks for something extra, deliver it as quickly as possible so that the meal does not get cold.
	❑ Ask if guests would like you to bring or do anything else for them at this time.
	❑ Remove empty beverage glasses and exchange ashtrays as needed.

chance to fix the problem. A guest with a problem who doesn't complain to the server is probably complaining to other potential guests.

Servers can respond to dissatisfied guests by:

* Listening to the guest

* Apologizing to the guest

* Taking appropriate action

* Thanking the guest

Maintain Tables

Servers maintain tables throughout the meal to keep the guest experience a pleasant one. An important part of maintaining table appearance is to remove items the guest no longer needs throughout the meal. This is called **pre-busing**.

Some restaurants clear items as soon as a guest finishes a course. Others wait until all guests in the party have completed the course. By the end of the meal, before dessert service, only beverages and items that go with them, such as cream, sugar, lemon, etc., should remain on the table.

Exhibit 3 gives a step-by-step breakdown for how to maintain tables.

Sell After-Dinner Items

After-dinner items are great sales builders. Many people will be tempted by a dessert if the server describes it well and as soon as possible after the meal. Once servers have cleared the entire table, they bring out the dessert cart or display tray and describe each dessert using mouth-watering terms.

They also describe in detail one or two of the restaurant's more popular desserts, suggesting their favorites. If guests say they are too full to have dessert, the servers suggest a light item such as ice cream, or suggest that guests share a dessert.

Servers also offer coffee and tea as soon as they take dessert orders. Many guests who have dessert will also have hot coffee or tea.

Apply Your Learning 15.4

Please write all answers on a separate sheet of paper.

1. Why should servers suggest additional items when taking orders?

2. What two things make it possible for servers to serve all of their guests quickly?

3. How should servers respond to dissatisfied guests?

4. What is pre-busing?

5. What should servers suggest if guests say they are too full for dessert?

**Exhibit 3
Maintain Tables**

Materials needed: A large service tray, clean napkins, and clean ashtrays.

STEPS:	HOW-TO'S:
1. **Be aware of guest needs.**	❑ Serve anything the guest needs. Do all that you can to meet guest needs.
	❑ Use good manners with guests.
	❑ Be attentive to children, especially those in high chairs. Pick up items from the floor, and provide extra napkins as needed.
	❑ If a guest requests a service beyond your ability or authority, tell the guest you'll have it taken care of right away. Then tell your manager at once.
2. **Check food and beverage levels.**	❑ Refill water glasses, coffee cups, hot tea pots, and iced-tea glasses whenever they are less than half-full.
	❑ Do not interrupt guests to ask if they want more water, coffee, or tea. But if a guest stops you and says he or she doesn't want a refill, move on to the next guest.
	❑ Refill bread as needed.
3. **Change ashtrays often using the "capping" method.**	❑ Turn a clean ashtray upside-down and place it over the dirty ashtray on the table. Ashtrays should be changed each time they contain one or two cigarette butts.
	❑ Pick up both ashtrays and place the dirty one on your tray. This method will prevent ashes from falling on guests or the table as you remove the ashtray.
	❑ Place the clean ashtray back on the table.

(continued)

Exhibit 3
Maintain Tables *(continued)*

STEPS:	HOW-TO'S:
4. **Pre-bus the table.**	❏ As guests finish their meals and beverages, ask them if you may clear dishes, glasses, silverware, and other items.
	❏ Clear items from the guest's right side with your right hand.
	❏ Always ask if guests are finished before you clear something. Some restaurants clear items as soon as a guest finishes a course. Others wait until all guests in the party have completed the course.
	❏ Remove used napkins and other trash from the table.
	❏ Place used items on your tray.
	❏ Wipe crumbs from the table into a cleaning cloth. Place the crumbs onto your tray.
	❏ Cover the soiled items with a napkin.
	❏ Take trays of soiled items to the dish room.

15.5 Completing Service

AFTER SUCCESSFULLY COMPLETING THIS SECTION, YOU WILL BE ABLE TO:

♦ Identify ways to prepare takeout items.

♦ Explain how to present the guest check.

♦ Describe how to settle guest checks.

♦ Explain how to clear and reset tables.

♦ Describe closing sidework duties.

Prepare Takeout Items

Servers, especially servers at a lodging property, may be asked to prepare foods to-go or to help box leftovers. If room service is open when a to-go order is placed, a room service attendant may assemble the items.

Servers begin preparing takeout items by washing their hands thoroughly. They then put to-go items in sanitary takeout containers according to the guests' requests. They place lids on cups and provide straws for cold beverages. They use serving utensils, not their fingers, to place food in takeout containers.

Servers then add paper napkins and individual packets of appropriate condiments, such as salt, pepper, mustard, ketchup, salad dressing, etc.

For leftover food, servers bring a takeout container on a tray to a tray jack in full view of the guest. They do not prepare the takeout container in the dishroom as the leftover food may be contaminated by other food. They then use serving utensils to neatly transfer the leftover food from the guest's plate to the takeout container.

At some restaurants, servers may prepare artistic figures with aluminum foil to package takeout items. The foil may be made into a swan or other figure in front of the guest.

Present the Guest Check

Finally, servers present the guest check to the guests according to their property's policies. In some restaurants, the check will be printed by the point-of-sale unit.

At the end of the meal, guests may become impatient to leave and will be annoyed by having to wait for the check, so servers work hard to make sure their guests do not have to wait for them.

Guest check folders keep checks clean and provide a place for guests to put their money or credit cards. If the property uses comment cards, they are included in the check folder.

Exhibit 1 gives step-by-step procedures for presenting a guest check.

Settle Guest Checks

Guests may settle their checks with cash, traveler's check, credit card, a charge to

Exhibit 1
Present the Guest Check

Materials needed: A guest check, a guest check folder, and after-dinner mints.

STEPS:	HOW-TO'S:
1. **Prepare guest checks.**	❑ Review the check carefully to be sure it is complete and accurate. ❑ Make sure all drinks and desserts are included on the check.
2. **Decide when to present guest checks.**	❑ The way you present the check is either: • Present the check immediately after you serve the main entrée. 　___ Breakfast 　___ Lunch 　___ Dinner • Present the check after the entire meal. 　___ Breakfast 　___ Lunch 　___ Dinner ❑ Place the check near the center of the table unless a guest specifically asks for the check.
3. **Present guest checks in a check folder with a pen.**	
4. **Serve after-dinner mints with the check, if appropriate.**	
5. **Sincerely thank guests and invite them to return. Use the guests' last names if you know them.**	

their room, a charge to a city account, check, coupon, voucher, or gift certificate.

When a guest pays by cash, the server presents change in the guest check folder. If the guest leaves while the server is settling the check, the change is the server's tip.

Traveler's checks must be signed in the server's presence and is otherwise treated as cash.

When a guest settles a check with a credit card, the server must get an approval code and imprint the card on the back of the guest check and on a credit card voucher. The server then completes the voucher and presents it with a pen to the guest in a guest check folder. The guest then totals the bill and signs the voucher.

Guests who are staying at the property with approved credit accounts may charge restaurant meals and drinks to their room. This is called a **house account.** Some employees, such as sales staff members or managers may also have house accounts. Servers ask guests to print their names and room numbers on the guest checks and sign it.

Some local customers may have charge accounts. This allows them to be directly billed each month. Such local accounts are called **city ledger accounts**. When settling these accounts, servers ask guests to print the company name or group name on the check and provide the city ledger account number. They then ask guests to sign the guest check.

It is extremely important that servers get as much information as possible from guests settling guest checks by personal check. This information helps assure that a personal check is good or can be traced if it is returned for non-sufficient funds.

Servers are taught their restaurant's policies for each type of coupon, voucher,

or gift certificate. For example, many restaurants do not give change for gift certificates and coupons. However, they might receive smaller gift certificates in the place of change. Servers carefully read the document to make sure it is valid and unexpired. If it is, they treat it like cash.

Finally, servers thank the guest when returning change and the receipt and invite the guest to return.

Clear and Reset Tables

It is important that tables are cleared and reset promptly. This makes it possible to seat waiting guests quickly, and it adds to the neat appearance of the dining room.

Servers work with the bus person to clear and reset tables. While it is important to clear and reset tables as quickly as possible, the needs of the servers' other guests always come first.

Servers clear and reset tables by:

- Gathering items needed to reset the table

- Clearing used dishes, silverware, glasses, and linens

- Cleaning the table with a sanitizing solution

- Replacing tablecloths

- Resetting the table

- Cleaning chairs

- Checking tables

- Taking soiled items to the dishroom

- Breaking down the tray of soiled items

- Storing sanitizing solution and the tray jack at the side station

Perform Closing Sidework

Servers typically work from a closing duty checklist at the end of their shift. It usually includes such tasks as:

- Remove soiled linens
- Store condiments
- Store bread and butter
- Restock silverware
- Break down the coffee station
- Break down ice buckets
- Break down water pitchers
- Reset all tables
- Straighten, clean, and restock side stations

Apply Your Learning 15.5

Please write all answers on a separate sheet of paper.

1. What is the first step to preparing take-out items?
2. What do guest check folders do?
3. What is a house account?
4. Why do tables need to be cleared and reset promptly?
5. What tells servers what their closing sidework duties are?

Quick Hits

Section 15.1—Getting to Know the Restaurant Server

- Restaurant servers provide outstanding food and beverage service to guests.

- Restaurant servers help hosts and hostesses, bus persons, and the kitchen staff.

- Suggestive selling encourages guests to buy additional food and beverages.

- Upselling suggests more expensive and possibly better quality items.

Section 15.2—Preparing for Service

- Restaurant servers help bus persons set up the restaurant for service.

- Side stations are service areas where supplies are stored.

- Service trays help transport food, dishes, and equipment throughout the restaurant.

- Working efficiently helps the server provide better guest service and be less tired at the end of a shift.

Section 15.3—Taking Orders and Serving Drinks

- Servers communicate confidence when escorting guests to tables.

- Greeting guests immediately helps put them at ease and assures them that they will be well taken care of.

- Children often have special needs in a restaurant. Attending to those needs make the experience of all guests a better one.

- Servers use an order-taking system to provide excellent beverage service.

Section 15.4—Serving Food

- Servers are prepared to answer questions about the menu and take orders using the restaurant's standard procedures.

- All guests at a table are served their meal at the same time.

- Servers check back to the table after guests have had a few bites.

- Servers respond to dissatisfied guests by listening, apologizing, taking action, and thanking the guest.

- Servers maintain tables throughout the meal.

- After-dinner items make great sales builders.

Section 15.5—Completing Service

- Sanitation procedures are followed when preparing takeout items.

- The guest check must be presented promptly so that guests don't have to wait.

- Guests may settle their check by cash, traveler's check, credit card, a charge to their room, a charge to a city account, check, coupon, voucher, or gift certificate.

- After guests leave, servers and bus persons clear and reset tables.

- The closing duty checklist tells servers what closing sidework they need to perform.

Banquet Setup Employee

Sections

The design and décor of function rooms, like the food and beverages that are served in them, can take many forms. A simple coffee break may be served in an undecorated, themeless room, while an elaborate reception featuring foods from around the world may be served in a function room with complex decorations to fit the theme. The type of function room chosen and how it is decorated are largely dictated by the needs and expectations of the client.

The banquet setup employee is the person who sets up the room and prepares any special equipment that a guest has requested. They do this by following a banquet event order. Once an event is complete, they put away all the equipment and tables, clean the room, and return it to its pre-event state.

16.1 Getting to Know the Banquet Setup Employee

AFTER SUCCESSFULLY COMPLETING THIS SECTION, YOU WILL BE ABLE TO:

◆ Describe the importance of banquet setup employees.

◆ Explain what a banquet event order is.

◆ Identify the different types of function rooms common at a lodging operation.

◆ Explain how banquet setup employees handle guest packages.

◆ Define basic food and beverage equipment terms.

Banquets are special events at a lodging property. They can be anything from a small meeting room to a large dinner-dance or reception. Banquet setup employees prepare function rooms to meet the needs of banquet guests.

A good definition of a banquet setup employee might be: A food and beverage employee who does everything possible, within reason, to make each banquet guest's dining and meeting experience exactly what he or she wants it to be, and who exceeds guest expectations whenever possible.

Banquet setup employees are responsible for:

• Setting up function rooms according to banquet event orders and property policies

• Cleaning and maintaining all function rooms

• Using, cleaning, and maintaining department equipment

• Handling audiovisual equipment for functions (at some lodging properties, an outside company handles this)

• Breaking down function rooms and service areas

Exhibit 1 lists many of the tasks that a banquet setup employee is expected to do.

Banquet setup employees are part of the entire lodging property team. As team members, they help other departments by:

• Following dishroom procedures when dropping off dirty tableware.

• Reporting needed equipment repairs to maintenance using the maintenance request system.

• Taking soiled linens to the laundry department to help them manage their production.

• Taking care of their internal customers (kitchen staff, maintenance staff, laundry staff, banquet servers, etc.) with the same concern they show guests.

Exhibit 1
Task List—Banquet Setup Employee

1. Follow Banquet Event Orders and Change Orders

2. Set Function Room Lighting

3. Vacuum Function Room Carpets

4. Steam-Extract Function Room Carpets

5. Sweep Floors in Function Rooms

6. Mop Floors in Function Rooms

7. Clean and Wax Hardwood and Parquet Floors in Function Rooms

8. Set Up Function Rooms

9. Set Up Support Services for Functions

10. Place Tablecloths on Function Room Tables

11. Skirt and Flounce Function Room Tables

12. Set Up and Break Down a Dance Floor

13. Set Up and Take Down Staging

14. Install and Remove Air Walls

15. Set Up and Take Down Coat Check Areas

16. Hang Banners and Decorations for Functions

17. Handle Audiovisual Equipment for Functions

18. Install Telephones in Banquet or Meeting Areas

19. Receive, Store, and Ship Packages for Guests

20. Break Down and Clear Function Rooms After Events

21. Refresh Meeting Rooms

22. Set Up Portable Bars

23. Set Up Buffets

24. Set Tables for Banquets

25. Set Up Function Rooms for VIP Guests

26. Perform End-of-Shift Duties

Superior Performance Standards

The quality of the food, drinks, and service at a lodging property enhances each guest's overall banquet experience. Providing excellent service, beverages, and meals at a reasonable price is every property's goal. Superior performance standards help it achieve that goal.

Superior performance standards that banquet setup employees help meet are:

- Demonstrating professional behavior within the property

- Setting up meetings, coffee breaks, banquets, and other functions promptly and attractively

- Refreshing function rooms as needed

- Greeting guests warmly as they enter the room

- Being alert to safety procedures at all times

- Knowing how to set up and operate audiovisual equipment

Banquet Event Orders

Banquet setup employees are responsible for preparing for banquets and other functions. Banquets, meetings, and receptions are called functions.

When the catering or sales department arranges a function with a client, the details are written on a **banquet event order** (BEO), which may also be called a function sheet.

A BEO provides all the information needed to prepare for a function. Changes in function arrangements are written on change orders. A BEO gives banquet setup employees the information they need to plan their work efficiently and set up function rooms and other rooms correctly.

Exhibit 2 provides the step-by-step breakdown for following banquet event orders and change orders.

Function Rooms and Storage Rooms

Function rooms are rooms where banquets, meetings, and receptions are held. Banquet setup employees become familiar with their property's function rooms.

Each function room may vary in size, style, and the number of people it will hold. Certain rooms may be used only for certain types of functions.

Guest Packages

One of the services many lodging properties offer is processing packages for function guests. Function guests, especially meeting planners, will often have materials and equipment for their meetings shipped to the property before their function. They may also have the materials and equipment shipped back to them after they leave the property.

Front desk employees may help send items back to guests. The banquet manager usually talks with guests about the fees for this service. Most groups have a master account set up before the function begins. Fees for sending packages will likely be added to this account. Banquet setup employees are expected to offer help in receiving, storing, and shipping these materials.

Typically, a property will keep an incoming mail logbook and banquet setup employees will write when a package arrives, the name of the guest it is addressed to, and where it will be stored. It is then stamped with a date and time of arrival so that guests know how promptly items are delivered.

The property will designate an area in which guest packages are stored before a function. Packages can be protected by storing heavy items below smaller or lighter ones. When the packages are delivered to function guests, they sign for the package in the incoming mail logbook.

After the function, guests may wish to send materials and equipment to their home, office, or next destination. Banquet setup employees may be asked to provide

---

Exhibit 2
Follow Banquet Event Orders and Change Orders

Materials needed: Banquet event order (BEO) and change orders (if any).

STEPS:	HOW-TO'S:
1. Review banquet event orders for functions to be set up during your shift.	❑ Note the following information: • The room the function will be held in • The number of guests expected • Table setup specifications (including the sizes, types, and colors of tablecloths and table skirts) • The menu for the function (including beverages, number of courses, and dessert) • The time guests will arrive • The time food should be plated (put on plates) • The time to serve each course • The type of function • Any special requests
2. Review change orders for changes that will affect room setup.	❑ Make sure the BEOs are in order, with the first function of your work shift at the front.

---

boxes, packing materials, tape, a pen or marker, and labels.

Food and Beverage Terms

The banquet department uses many special pieces of equipment. Many of them are defined below.

Bus tub

A large tub, usually plastic, in which soiled dishware is placed and taken to the dish room.

Chafer

A metal holder that keeps food hot using canned, gel-type fuel. Chafers are usually made of stainless steel, silver, or copper.

China

Items such as plates, cups, saucers, bowls, and other serving pieces. These items are typically earthenware or porcelain.

Condiments

Salt, pepper, and other spices and sauces served with meals.

Decoy system

Bus tubs and dish racks with one dirty dish, glass, etc. in them to show you where to place dirty items.

Drip bucket

A bucket that collects drips of water produced by ice melting in a food and beverage display.

Glass froster

A cold storage unit, like a small refrigerator, that cools glasses so they frost when you take them out.

Glassware

Tumblers, wine glasses, champagne flutes, beer steins, water glasses, etc.

Hot box

An insulated or heated cart used for transporting food and keeping it warm.

Linen roll-up

Silverware rolled up in a linen napkin.

Linens

Tablecloths, napkins, place mats, aprons, and other cloth items needed for service.

Oval tray (service tray)

A large plastic tray, usually lined with rubber or cork, used to carry food and beverages.

Portable bar

A cabinet on rollers used to store and serve beverages, glassware, napkins, stirrers, etc.

Ramekin

A small receptacle used to hold butter and sauces.

Silverware

Eating utensils, including knives, forks, spoons, and serving utensils. Silverware is usually stainless steel.

Table skirt

Pleated or folded linen used to decorate tables. Clips or T-pins are often used to attach table skirts to tablecloths.

Tray jack (tray stand)

A metal or wooden frame that supports oval trays.

Apply Your Learning 16.1

Please write all answers on a separate sheet of paper.

1. What is a banquet?

2. List two superior performance standards for a banquet setup employee.

3. What kind of information is recorded on a banquet event order?

4. Who usually makes shipping and payment arrangements with function guests?

5. What is a tray jack?

16.2 Banquet Equipment and Setups

AFTER SUCCESSFULLY COMPLETING THIS SECTION, YOU WILL BE ABLE TO:

♦ List the types of audiovisual equipment.

♦ Describe standard table setups.

♦ Explain how to prepare a table for a function.

♦ Identify how to install telephones in function areas.

Audiovisual Equipment

Audiovisual equipment is often provided as part of a function room's standard setup. Banquet setup employees are required to know how to set up, operate, and maintain this equipment in order to provide excellent service to function guests.

They handle and maintain the following equipment:

• Liquid Crystal Display (LCD) or Digital Light Processing (DLP) projection equipment

• Laptop computers

• Closed circuit television system

• DVD players

• Videocassette players

• Audiocassette players

• Flat-screen televisions

• Internet and wireless access

• Televisions

• Overhead projectors

• 16mm film projectors

• 35mm slide projectors

• Microphones

• Speakers

• Flip charts and markers

• Whiteboards and markers

• Chalkboards and chalk

• Projector screens

• Extension cords

• Power strips

As audiovisual equipment has grown more elaborate and complex, more properties are hiring consultants to handle all audiovisual equipment. If audiovisual equipment is set up by the guest or an outside contractor, banquet setup employees simply bring in the appropriate support equipment, such as tables, screens, extension cords, etc.

Banquet setup employees may also be asked to check the operation of equipment, turning on each piece of equipment and testing the controls to make sure everything works. If an overhead projector is being used, they provide a replacement bulb in case the bulb burns out during the function.

Electrical surge protectors are used with all computer and video setups. Also, only heavy-duty electrical cords are used to supply a current to audiovisual equipment. Banquet setup employees are often asked to tape down all cords.

If the banquet setup employees set up the audiovisual equipment, they will also review the setup and operation of the equipment with the guest. When the function is over, they'll check to make sure no tapes, slides, disks, or transparencies have been left in or around the equipment before putting everything away.

Standard Table Setups

When tables are set up correctly and set consistently, with evenly lined-up china, straight, crisp tablecloths and napkins, and attractive centerpieces, it shows that banquet setup employees care about providing a quality experience for guests.

Table setup specifications will change with the type of function and type of service provided. Banquet setup employees learn the table setup standards for each type of function held at their properties.

Banquet and meeting tables are available in assorted styles and sizes:

- Rectangular tables are often used as head tables, registration tables, display tables, and meeting tables.

- Round tables with a 5-foot diameter are the most popular size for food functions. They seat eight to ten people.

- Round tables with a 4-foot diameter seat four to six people and are often used for

cocktail receptions and to display wedding or anniversary cakes.

How tables and chairs are arranged plays a very important role in the success or failure of a function. Each setup style has a purpose, and setup instructions should be followed closely.

The following setup styles are often used for functions:

Auditorium or theater style. This arrangement calls for chairs to be set up in rows facing a speaker or stage. A center aisle is provided if possible. Leave a space of one to three inches between each chair. Chairs should never be placed so that they touch each other.

T-shape conference style. Tables are set up in the shape of a "T," in which the base of the "T" is a column of double tables and the top is a column of single tables. Chairs are placed along the top of the "T" and on both sides of the base of the "T."

U-shape conference style. Tables are set up in the shape of a "U." If chairs are placed on both the inside and outside of the tables, use tables that are 30 inches wide.

Round table style. This style is typically used for banquets and receptions. Leave at least four feet between tables and place eight to ten chairs around each table, based upon the instructions on the banquet event order (or function sheet).

Tablecloths, Table Skirts, and Flounces

Most banquet tables are set up with tablecloths. Tables where important people are sitting (such as a head table at a wedding reception) and tables that display items (such as a wedding cake) may be skirted and flounced in addition to having tablecloths. A **"flounce"** is a strip of decorative material attached to the edge of a table. Taffeta is used when the material needs to be pleated. Lace is also used to flounce tables.

If a table is going to be skirted, the tablecloth usually won't hang down over the table edge. Table skirts are pieces of linen that are folded or pleated to hang from the edges of tables to the floor.

Fresh, clean tablecloths, correctly hung table skirts, and crisp flounces are a necessary and important part of professional food presentation. Banquet setup employees always check linens and flounces for rips, stains, and wear. They replace linens and flounces that do not meet their property's standards.

The BEO will usually detail the size, type, and color of tablecloths being used for a function. Banquet setup employees examine the tablecloths to make sure each one is clean and has no spots, wrinkles, or damage. Banquet tablecloths must be starched, pressed, and free of wrinkles.

Round banquet tables are usually set with two tablecloths on each table. Both are placed seam-side down. The bottom cloth is spread over the table with the center crease running one way and the overhang divided evenly over the sides of the table. The top tablecloth is then spread over the bottom cloth with the center crease running in the opposite direction.

Exhibit 1 gives a step-by-step breakdown for how to skirt and flounce function room tables.

Hang Banners and Decorations for Functions

Sometimes guests will provide specific banners or decorations that they want put up in the room. The BEO will provide direction about what needs to be placed.

Whenever possible, banquet setup employees should try to hide the method they use to attach banners and decorations to the wall. Also, it is very important that only approved methods are used. Some tapes, nails, and other attachment devices can damage walls.

Install Telephones

Sometimes—especially for business meetings, telephones need to be set up in the function room. Telephones are installed by either banquet setup employees or the maintenance staff. Usually, the tasks involve pulling telephones out of storage and plugging the phones into the telephone jacks. If portable jacks need to be installed, the maintenance department will handle it.

Banquet setup employees then check to make sure the phones work and place a message pad and pen by each phone.

Exhibit 1
Skirt and Flounce Function Room Tables

Materials needed: A banquet event order (BEO), change orders (if any), tables, tablecloths, table skirts, a bolt of lace or taffeta, and clips or T-pins.

STEPS:	HOW-TO'S:
1. **Use the skirts and flouncing material specified in the banquet event order.**	
2. **Examine the tablecloths and skirts.**	❑ Make sure each tablecloth and skirt is clean and has no spots, wrinkles, or damage. ❑ Return unacceptable linens to the laundry department.
3. **Place tablecloths on tables before attaching table skirts.**	❑ If tables are round, place two tablecloths on each table. ❑ If tables are rectangular, only place one tablecloth on each table.
4. **Attach skirts to the tables.**	❑ Use clips or T-pins to attach skirts to the edge of the table. ❑ Place a clip or T-pin between each fold or pleat of the table skirt. ❑ Be careful not to wrinkle the tablecloth or skirt. ❑ As you attach the table skirt, make sure the bottom just skims the floor.
5. **Flounce tables.**	❑ Use clips or T-pins to attach material to the top of the table skirt on one end of the table. ❑ Slowly unroll the material from the bolt and attach it around the edge of the table.

(continued)

Exhibit 1 Skirt and Flounce Function Room Tables *(continued)*	
STEPS:	**HOW-TO'S:**
	❏ Make sure the material is clean and has no spots, wrinkles, or damage.
	❏ Keep the top edge of the material even with the table edge.
	❏ If you need to pleat the flounce, pleat the material evenly using the full width of your hand to measure the distance between each pleat.
	❏ Compare your work with others to make sure the flounce looks the same on all tables.
6. **Remove skirts and flounces.**	❏ Remove clips or T-pins and place them in the appropriate container. Be sure to remove all clips and T-pins. They can injure laundry attendants if left in the material.
	❏ Send dirty skirts and flounces to the laundry department for cleaning.

Apply Your Learning 16.2

Please write all answers on a separate sheet of paper.

1. List at least three types of audiovisual equipment that is set up in function rooms.
2. What is an auditorium-style arrangement?
3. What is a flounce?
4. Who installs portable jacks in function rooms?

16.3 Function Types

AFTER SUCCESSFULLY COMPLETING THIS SECTION, YOU WILL BE ABLE TO:

♦ Describe how to set function room lighting.

♦ Explain how to set up a function room.

♦ Identify the types of support services needed at functions.

♦ Explain how to set up and take down dance floors, staging, air walls, coat check areas, portable bars, buffets, coffee breaks, and VIP function rooms.

Set Function Room Lighting

Lighting controls at a lodging property can range from simple-to-operate switches and dimmers to complex, computerized, stage lighting control boards. Banquet setup employees have to be taught each room's individual system and practice changing the light settings for each room. They may be asked to learn such things as floodlight controls, spotlight controls, and other special-effect lighting controls.

When cleaning, lights are turned to full brightness to make it easier to see dirt and trash. The banquet event order (BEO) will give instructions for how to set lights for each function. The banquet setup employee may also be responsible for showing the function host how to work the lighting controls, or be available to adjust lights for audiovisual needs.

Set Up Function Rooms

The BEO will explain exactly how many and what type of tables and chairs to set up. It will also explain any special needs that a function might have.

Exhibit 1 gives a step-by-step breakdown of how banquet setup employees set up function rooms.

Set Up Support Services

The BEO will detail exactly what type of support services each function needs. It may be as simple as setting up a registration table or it may involve working with the maintenance department to set up screens, portable booths, curtains, special electrical hookups, etc. for exhibits.

Exhibit 2 gives a step-by-step breakdown of how to set up support services for functions.

Set Up and Break Down a Dance Floor

Banquet setup employees are sometimes asked to set up a portable dance floor. They first clean the floor in the function room by sweeping, vacuuming, or mopping.

Banquet setup employees then use a cart to move the dance floor sections to the

Exhibit 1
Set Up Function Rooms

Materials needed: A vacuum cleaner, cleaning cloths, a banquet event order (BEO), change orders (if any), banquet tables, a putty knife or scraper, an all-purpose cleaner, tablecloths, chairs, additional furniture, staging, table skirts, flounces, audiovsual equipment, standard meeting amenities, water pitchers, glasses, dinner plates, and linen napkins.

STEPS:	HOW-TO'S:
1. **Check the function room.**	❑ Wipe fixtures with a clean, damp cloth followed by a clean, dry cloth. ❑ Report maintenance problems so the problems can be fixed before the function.
2. **Set the room's heating, cooling, and lighting controls.**	❑ Check the room's heating and cooling controls. Adjust them as necessary. ❑ Follow the banquet event order to set the lighting.
3. **Set up tables in the function room.**	❑ Get the number and type of tables specified on the BEO. ❑ Move tables into the room carefully to prevent injury to yourself or damage to the tables. Work with a partner to handle tables. Tables may be rolled on carpeted floors, but not on hard floors. ❑ Report damaged tables to the maintenance department or to your supervisor. Do not use tables with broken legs or jagged edges. ❑ Arrange the tables as specified on the BEO. ❑ Place tables at least four to five feet apart if guests will be seated back to back. ❑ Set up round tables so that all table legs are lined up in the same direction. ❑ Keep tables at least six inches away from walls.

(continued)

Exhibit 1
Set Up Function Rooms (continued)

STEPS:	HOW-TO'S:
4. **Clean tables.**	❑ Remove any chewing gum with a putty knife or scraper.
	❑ Wipe the tops of the tables using the two-cloth procedure.
	❑ Wipe the legs and braces of the tables using the two-cloth procedure described in Step 1.
	❑ Pay special attention to dried-on food, sticky residue, or grease. Spray soiled areas with an all-purpose cleaner, then wipe using the two-cloth procedure.
	❑ Replace any table that you cannot clean. Tell your supervisor about the problem.
5. **Place tablecloths on each table if indicated on the BEO.**	
6. **Set up chairs.**	❑ Follow the BEO for the number of chairs needed. If the BEO doesn't specify how many chairs to place at each table, place one chair for each 24 inches of table length.
	❑ Move chairs on carts when possible to increase efficiency and reduce the chance of injury.
	❑ Stack only ten or fewer chairs per cart.
	❑ Handle chairs with care. Avoid bumping chairs against other objects.
	❑ Make sure chairs are clean and free from tears, stains, or damage. Do not use damaged or broken chairs. Many chairs have metal "feet" for easy sliding. If these are missing, replace them. Broken chairs can injure a guests.

(continued)

Exhibit 1
Set Up Function Rooms *(continued)*

STEPS:	HOW-TO'S:
	❑ Wipe the seats, backs, legs, and braces with the two-cloth procedure.
	❑ Line up chairs evenly along the sides of the tables.
	❑ Place chairs so that the front edge of the seat is even with the edge of the table.
	❑ Stand at one end of the room and check the alignment of the chairs. They should line up perfectly.
7. **Set up additional furniture.**	❑ Follow the BEO to set up other furniture, such as a lectern or bar stool for the speaker, or extra chairs around the outside walls.
	❑ Move furniture carefully to avoid injuries and furniture damage.
8. **Set up a head table.**	❑ Set up the head table at the front of the room, at least 10 feet from the wall unless otherwise specified. Place the head table on staging in large rooms and as requested.
	❑ Cover the table with a tablecloth so that the cloth hangs over three sides of the table. Make sure it hangs over the sides closest to the other tables.
	❑ Skirt and flounce the table on three sides. Leave the side of the table farthest away from the other tables unskirted.
	❑ Put a lectern in the center of the table, if needed.
	❑ Place chairs only on the unskirted side of the table.

(continued)

Exhibit 1
Set Up Function Rooms *(continued)*

STEPS:	HOW-TO'S:
9. **Set up audiovisual or electronic equipment.**	
10. **Place standard meeting amenities on the tables.**	❑ Follow the BEO instructions for placing amenities, decorations, and other items.
	❑ If the BEO doesn't specify how to arrange amenities, ask your supervisor.
	❑ Arrange items with printing and logos so that the logos are lined up as you look down the table.
	❑ Place centerpieces, ashtrays, and matches in the middle of each table, if needed.
11. **Set up a water station or water pitchers on tables.**	❑ Check glasses and pitchers for spots, chips, cracks, and residue.
	❑ Throw away chipped or cracked glasses and pitchers. Return spotted glasses and pitchers to the dish room.
	❑ Line dinner plates with linen napkins folded according to your supervisor's directions. Moisture will form on the outside of the water pitchers. Linen napkins on underliner plates will absorb runoff.
	❑ Fill pitchers with ice and water.
	❑ Place one pitcher on each lined plate.
	❑ If you are placing water glasses at each table:
	• Place one pitcher for every three guests on each table
	• Place one glass upside-down at each plate according to your property's standard table setups.
	OR

(continued)

Exhibit 1 Set Up Function Rooms *(continued)*	
STEPS:	**HOW-TO'S:**

	• Arrange around the water pitcher enough glasses for each guest at the table.
	❑ If you are setting up a separate table as a water station:
	  • Cover it with a tablecloth.
	  • Skirt the table if necessary.
	  • Put glasses and filled water pitchers on the water station.
	  • Place one upside-down glass at each guest's position on the table, or arrange four to six upside-down glasses around each water pitcher.

12. **Perform any other duties assigned by your supervisor.**	❑ Cooperate with other employees in finishing all assigned tasks.
	❑ Tasks may include:
	  • Setting up creamers
	  • Stocking clean linens
	  • Arranging flowers for centerpieces
	  • Stocking ashtrays and matches
	  • Stocking clean glasses
	  • Folding napkins
	  • Filling sugar bowls and caddies
	  • Filling salt and pepper shakers
	  • Setting up plating stations
	  • Setting up trash areas
	  • Setting up soiled dish areas
	  • Setting up beverage stations
	  • Teamwork is essential to delivering excellent service

(continued)

Exhibit 1 Set Up Function Rooms *(continued)*	
STEPS:	**HOW-TO'S:**
13. **Check the details of the function room setup.**	❑ Review the BEO again. Make sure you have not missed any setup details. You should finish the setup at least 15 minutes before the start of the function.
	❑ Check the overall look of the room.
	❑ Recheck the position of chairs, tablecloths, and tables. Adjust them as needed.
	❑ Recheck the lighting of the room as well as the heating or cooling setting.
	❑ Make sure blinds or drapes hang the same way. Blinds and drapes are usually closed if audivisual aids are to be used.
	❑ Remove trash and debris.
14. **Place the group name on the reader board outside the function room.**	
15. **Leave the room and lock the doors if the room will not be used immediately.**	

Exhibit 2
Set Up Support Services for Functions

Materials needed: A banquet event order (BEO), change orders (if any), tableclothes, table skirts, standard meeting amenities, trash cans, an easel, a message corkboard, and tacks or stick pins.

STEPS:	HOW-TO'S:
1. **Set up registration tables.**	❏ Check the banquet event order (BEO) for the number and type of tables to set up.
	❏ Place tables in the lobby or near the entrance to the function room as stated in the BEO.
2. **Cover, skirt, and flounce registration tables according to the BEO.**	
3. **Place amenities on registration tables.**	❏ Place the following itmes on registration tables:
	• Pens or pencils
	• Message pads
	• Ashtrays and matches (if smoking is allowed)
	• Pitcher with water and water glasses
	❏ Arrange other items supplied by guests as indicated on the BEO. Guests may have items sent ahead for the function.
4. **Place a trash can near the tables.**	
5. **Set up a message board.**	❏ Put a message corkboard on an easel near the registration table to hold messages for guests who are at the function.
	❏ Provide tacks or stick pins.
6. **Help set up exhibit booths.**	❏ Place a six- or eight-foot banquet table in the area of each booth, as stated on the BEO.
	❏ Cover, skirt, and flounce tables according to the BEO.
	❏ Place the number and type of chairs specified on the BEO.
	❏ Place a trash can in each booth.

function rooms, making as many trips as is needed to safely transport the floor. A portable dance floor is very expensive and can last a long time if it is treated with care. The sections are placed on the floor according to the instructions that came with the floor. Any broken sections are reported to maintenance.

Dance floor sections are connected with a screwdriver and the installed screw sets. The first row must be perfectly lined up or gaps will form between the sections. A rubber mallet is used to pound sections together if they do not easily mesh. Pounding with a regular hammer will damage the wood. Once the sections are pushed flush against each other, the screws for each row are tightened.

The dance floor is locked in place with the set screws and then an edging is placed around it according to the manufacturer's instructions. Banquet set-up employees then clean and wax the floor.

When it is time to break a dance floor down, banquet setup employees remove the edging and then screw out the set screws from each dance floor section. They use crowbars to separate the sections while being careful to avoid damaging the floor. The floor sections are then stacked upright on a cart and pushed to the storage area.

Set Up and Take Down Staging

Staging (risers) is used to raise part of a room. Staging may be used for the following:

- Head table
- Bandstand
- Speaker's podium at large meetings

When setting up staging, banquet setup employees inspect the stage and report any damage to the maintenance department. Then, after making sure stage sections are in the lock position, they use a cart to move stage sections to the function rooms.

Working in teams of two or more, banquet setup employees unload stage sections as close as possible to their final position. They then pull out the stage legs to unlock the stage from its upright position. They slowly lower each side of the stage to the floor. They then push the stage sections so they are flush against each other and connect the sections with bolts or locking brackets.

Carpet sections are placed on top of the stage to prevent guests from stepping into the cracks between the sections.

When it is time to take apart and store the stage, banquet employees reverse the steps used to set up the stage.

Install and Remove Air Walls

Air walls are usually stored in function rooms, either against a side wall or in a special storage cavity built into the side wall. They slide on overhead tracks.

Air walls are used when the BEO specifies that the function takes place in one section of a larger room. Banquet setup employees extend air walls by pushing gently to allow the walls to move on their overhead tracks. It is important that they don't force the wall along the tracks, as they could hurt their backs or damage the air wall.

Some air walls have locking brackets to hold them open. The ones that do must be locked in place once they are extended. If necessary, banquet setup employees inflate air wall sections once they are secure. They usually use a portable air pump to seal the wall and prevent noise from passing from one section to the next.

When it is time to remove the air walls, the air sections are deflated, any brackets or locks are unlocked, and walls are gently pushed into their storage cavity or other storage locations.

Set Up and Take Down Coat Check Areas

During cold or wet weather, it is common to have a coat check area for each function. The BEO will explain where the coat check area should be set up.

Banquet setup employees bring out clothing racks and hangers from storage areas and place tables and chairs as directed by the BEO. They also place a sign in each coat check area explaining that items are left at the risk of the owner. Most properties accept no liability for the safety or security of checked items.

If a property employee is asked to take guests' coats and issue claim tickets, the banquet setup employees provide these tickets. Coats are returned only in exchange for the matching ticket stub.

When it is time to take down coat check areas, banquet setup employees check the area for any items left behind by guests, following the property's lost and found procedures. They then return clothing racks, hangers, and signs to storage and remove any air walls, tables, or chairs that were set up.

Finally, banquet setup employees clean the area by:

- Folding and stacking chairs
- Removing dirty linens
- Throwing away litter
- Vacuuming the area

Set Up Portable Bars

Most receptions require a bar setup. The bar may be set up by the beverage department or by the banquet setup staff. The BEO will explain how many bars are needed and where they should be placed.

Portable bars must be inspected to be sure they are free from chips, cracks, sharp edges, and other damage. The employees setting up portable bars also make sure that all equipment is working properly.

The setup employees roll portable bars carefully into their proper position. Portable bars are usually placed in the corner of the room, away from the door and near electrical outlets so that soda dispensers and ice wells can be used.

Tables are often set up behind the bar and are covered with tablecloths. Banquet setup employees clean the bars with detergent. They place a clean drip bucket under the ice bin drain hose.

The bartender will place the liquor on the bar, but banquet setup employees may be asked to prepare and stock everything else in the bar. Everything else may include:

- Pitcher of water
- Beverage napkins
- Stirrers
- Straws
- Appropriate glasses
- Bucket of ice
- Drip bucket
- Garnishes
- Mixers
- Nonalcoholic beverages

- Corkscrew and bottle opener

- Bar utensils

Glasses are placed upside down on a plastic mat once they have been checked for chips, cracks, spots, or residue.

Set Up Buffets

The appearance and layout of a banquet buffet can be as important to the guest as the food. The banquet tables are placed according to the BEO in a way that is convenient for the guests and the kitchen.

Banquet tables are covered with clean tablecloths and are usually skirted and flounced. Banquet setup employees then set up buffet service equipment, utensils, and plates. For a double-sided buffet table, they set up the same items on both sides of the table. Double-sided tables allow two lines of guests to serve themselves.

Any cords from heat lamps or other service equipment are taped securely to the floor with duct tape or a walkover guide.

Set Up Coffee Breaks

Setting up an efficient and complete coffee break can be one of the banquet setup employee's most important duties. For many guests, especially busy conference participants, coffee breaks are a necessity. Coffee breaks provide time for guests to relax, get to know others at the meeting, and discuss issues informally. If a meeting is tense, the coffee break allows tempers to cool. No wonder, then, that nothing will annoy guests more than coffee service that has been set up improperly or is delivered late.

In addition, the coffee break may be a guest's first encounter with a property's food service. An attractively presented, well-organized, and complete coffee break will encourage guests to try room service.

Set Up Function Rooms for VIP Guests

VIPs (Very Important Persons) are guests who receive extra-special treatment. A property may call the following guests VIPs:

- Executives of major companies

- Meeting planners who bring many guests to the property

- Other guests selected by the general manager, the sales staff, or other managers

Many properties have special procedures for setting up function rooms for VIP guests. While all guests deserve excellent service, lodging property employees make extra certain that nothing goes wrong for VIP guests.

Lodging properties will often use executive chairs for VIP guests instead of the standard banquet chairs. This will be explained on the BEO. Also, VIP amenities are often placed in the room. These might be centerpieces, items with logos on it, or mints. There may also be a refreshment station set up with sparkling water or special refreshments.

Apply Your Learning 16.3

Please write all answers on a separate sheet of paper.

1. How should lights be set when cleaning a function room?

2. How does a banquet setup employee find out how many tables need to be set up in a function room?

3. What is one type of support service used at functions?

4. What type of tools are needed to set up and take down a dance floor?

5. When is staging used in a function room?

6. What items are needed to set up a coat check area?

7. Why should banquet setup employees inspect portable bars?

8. Who might be a VIP at a property?

16.4 Banquet Cleanup, Maintenance, and Safety

AFTER SUCCESSFULLY COMPLETING THIS SECTION, YOU WILL BE ABLE TO:

♦ Describe how to respond to maintenance needs.

♦ Identify how banquet setup employees contribute to the property's security.

♦ List the general cleaning tasks a banquet setup employee might perform.

♦ Describe how to break down and clear function rooms after an event.

♦ List end-of-shift duties.

Maintenance Needs

Banquet setup employees help keep the property in excellent condition. They see the function rooms and storage rooms up close every day.

There are two types of maintenance needs: urgent and routine. An urgent need is one that requires attention right away, such as a leaking pipe. A routine need is one that can be scheduled for later repair by maintenance or engineering, such as a window that doesn't open easily.

To handle an urgent maintenance need, banquet setup employees:

• Call the maintenance or engineering department.

• Request an immediate response.

To handle a routine maintenance need, they:

• Explain the problem to their supervisors.

• Help their supervisors fill out a maintenance request form, if they ask for help.

Security

Banquet setup employees are a key part of their property's security system. They watch who comes in and out of function rooms and storage rooms, and look for unusual situations or people not authorized to be in back-of-the-house areas. The property counts on them to help prevent theft of tables, chairs, and other items. They report missing items to their supervisors or security employees. If they see someone who does not belong in an area, they immediately notify their supervisors or security personnel.

They are also alert to and report dangerous situations, such as burned-out light bulbs, broken windows and locks, people who seem suspicious or out-of-place, and other problems or possible problems.

General Cleaning Tasks

Like public space cleaners, banquet setup employees must perform a number of cleaning tasks in the rooms that they are setting up. These tasks include:

- Vacuuming function room carpets

- Steam extracting function room carpets

- Sweeping floors in function rooms

- Mopping floors in function rooms

- Cleaning hardwood floors and parquet floors in function rooms

- Wiping tables and dusting as needed

- Break down water pitchers.

Break Down and Clear Function Rooms After Events

The banquet setup staff removes tables, chairs, staging, dance floors, audiovisual and other equipment after an event.

Exhibit 1 is a step-by-step breakdown of how to break down and clear function rooms after events.

Perform End-of-Shift Duties

At the end of each shift or event, there are a number of duties that banquet setup employees are called upon to do. These include:

- Collect soiled linens and take them to the laundry.

- Break down ice buckets.

- Breaking down the coffee station.

- Cleaning tables and chairs.

- Wiping down function room furnishings.

- Vacuuming carpets.

- Cleaning and restocking banquet side stations.

- Setting music, HVAC, and lighting system controls.

Apply Your Learning 16.4

Please write all answers on a separate sheet of paper.

1. How should banquet setup employees handle urgent maintenance needs?

2. How do banquet setup employees contribute to their property's security?

3. What are some general cleaning tasks that public space cleaners perform?

4. What does the banquet setup staff remove after an event?

Exhibit 1
Break Down and Clear Function Rooms After Events

Materials needed: Carts, trash cans, large outdoor trash bins, a vaccuum cleaner, and cleaning cloths.

STEPS:	HOW-TO'S:
1. Clean tables and chairs.	
2. Store chairs.	❑ Stack the chairs. Never stack more than 10 chairs together.
	❑ Place stacked chairs on a cart if possible and move them to the storage area or to another function room to be set up.
3. Store tables.	❑ Fold tables. Place folded tables on a cart if possible.
	❑ Place round tables top to top and back to back.
	❑ Move tables to storage or to another function room for setup. Be careful to protect walls, doorways, carpets, and hard floors when moving furniture.
4. Remove and store audiovisual equipment.	
5. Remove and store dance floors.	❑ Use carts for moving heavy items.
6. Remove and store staging.	❑ Use carts for moving heavy items.
7. Remove all trash and debris.	❑ Put all trash in trash cans.
	❑ Empty full trash bags from the cans into large trash bins. Do not let trash pile up in banquet setup and storage areas.
	❑ Follow your property's recycling procedures when handling aluminum cans, styrofoam cups, and other recyclable items.

(continued)

Exhibit 1
Break Down and Clear Function Rooms After Events *(continued)*

STEPS:	HOW-TO'S:
8. Vacuum floors.	
9. Wipe fixtures in the room with a clean, damp cloth followed by a dry cloth.	
10. Remove air walls.	
11. Report any equipment damage or other problems to your supervisor.	

Quick Hits

Section 16.1—Getting to Know the Banquet Setup Employee

- Banquet setup employees do whatever it takes to make each banquet guest's dining and meeting experience an excellent one.

- Banquet setup employees set up, maintain, and break down function rooms.

- Banquet Event Orders (BEOs) are the banquet maps. They provide all the details of how an event should be set up.

- Function rooms are rooms where banquets, meetings, and receptions are held.

- Many lodging properties process packages for function guests.

Section 16.2—Banquet Equipment and Setups

- Audiovisual equipment has grown increasingly complex and is often handled by an outside contractor.

- There are assorted styles and sizes of tables. There are also many different setup styles, the most common being auditorium, T-shape, U-shape, and round.

- Tablecloths help make a function room look attractive. Often, skirting and flouncing is done on head tables or display tables.

- Banners and decorations must be hung carefully so that walls are not damaged.

- Banquet setup employees sometimes bring phones to meeting areas.

Section 16.3—Function Types

- Lighting controls in a function room can be simple or complex.

- Function rooms will be set up according to the instructions on the BEO.

- Support services include screens, registration tables, portable booths, curtains, and electrical hookups.

- Portable dance floors must be handled carefully so that they can last a long time.

- Staging is often used for head tables, bandstands, or speaker's podiums.

- Air walls are moved along overhead tracks.

- Coat check areas include clothing racks, hangers, signs, and tables. Sometimes properties issue claim checks and have an employee take and issue coats.

- Banquet setup employees sometimes set up portable bars, though bartenders will handle any liquor.

- Buffets and banquets must be attractive.

- Efficient coffee break setup is very important to guests in meetings.

- Properties select certain guests as VIP guests. These might include executives, meeting planners, or other important guests.

Section 16.4—Banquet Cleanup, Maintenance, and Safety

- There are two types of maintenance needs: urgent and routine.

- Banquet setup employees help provide security by watching who comes in and out of function rooms and being alert to suspicious individuals.

- Banquet setup employees perform many general cleaning tasks in function rooms. These include vacuuming, sweeping, mopping, and dusting.

- After events are over, banquet setup employees clear the rooms and break down the equipment.

- At the end of their shifts, banquet setup employees perform a number of duties to prepare for the next shift or the next day.

Banquet Server

Sections

Banquet and catering can enhance the overall image of a food-service organization within the community. For many guests, their first contact with a property occurs when they attend a banquet or catered event. If a guest's experience is positive, he or she may return to the property with family and friends.

If the guests experience a banquet that exceeds their expectations, they may bring groups to the property to experience the same kind of menu and service that delighted them previously.

Service personnel serve food and beverages and might include hosts, captains, food servers, buspersons, and banquet managers. Service is often synchronized, which means the entire service staff will enter the function room through one set of doors to serve each course. They place the courses in front of guests in unison and using precise movements. This requires a great deal of training, rehearsal, skill, and staff.

17.1 Getting to Know the Banquet Server

AFTER SUCCESSFULLY COMPLETING THIS SECTION, YOU WILL BE ABLE TO:

♦ Describe the role banquet servers play in exceeding guest expectations.

♦ List the silverware that a property might use.

♦ Explain how to care for and use glassware and china.

♦ Identify ways to promote restaurants at a property.

Banquet servers provide food and beverage service to banquet guests. Perhaps a better definition, though, would be that banquet servers are food and beverage employees who do everything possible, within reason, to make each guest's dining and meeting experience exactly what he or she wants it to be, and who exceeds guest expectations whenever possible. Banquet servers are responsible for:

• Preparing for service

• Inspecting tables for cleanliness and proper setup

• Greeting guests

• Serving food and beverages

• Completing service

• Breaking down function rooms and service areas

• Keeping a count of the number of guests served

• Helping take inventory

Exhibit 1 lists many of the tasks that banquet servers are expected to perform.

To be excellent team players, banquet servers can:

• Follow dishroom procedures when dropping off dirty tableware.

• Report needed equipment repairs to maintenance using the maintenance request system.

• Take soiled linens to the laundry department to help the laundry manage its production.

• Take care of internal customers (kitchen staff, maintenance staff, laundry staff, etc.) with the same concern that they show guests.

Like banquet setup employees, banquet servers rely heavily on **banquet event orders** (BEOs). BEOs tell servers what the banquet is and what needs to be done.

Superior Performance Standards

The quality of the food, drinks, and service at a lodging property should enhance each

Exhibit 1
Task List—Banquet Server

1. Follow Banquet Event Orders and Change Orders
2. Receive, Store, and Ship Packages for Guests
3. Fold Napkins
4. Place Tablecloths on Tables
5. Skirt and Flounce Tables
6. Prepare Salt and Pepper Shakers and Grinders
7. Prepare Sugar Bowls or Caddies
8. Set Tables for Banquets
9. Prepare Bread
10. Prepare and Serve Coffee
11. Prepare and Serve Hot Tea
12. Prepare and Serve Iced Tea
13. Prepare and Serve Hot Chocolate
14. Prepare, Lift, and Carry Service Trays
15. Serve Water
16. Take and Serve Beverage Orders
17. Serve Bread and Butter
18. Serve Each Course at Sit-Down Banquets
19. Maintain Tables During Service
20. Maintain Buffets
21. Set Up and Maintain Hors d'Oeuvres for Receptions
22. Provide Service for Cocktail Receptions
23. Provide Break or Continental Breakfast Service
24. Refresh Meeting Rooms
25. Provide Appropriate Service for Children
26. Respond to Dissatisfied Guests
27. Settle Individual Guest Checks
28. Settle Group Checks
29. Clear Tables
30. Perform End-of-Shift Duties

guest's overall banquet experience. Providing excellent service, beverages, and meals at a reasonable price is every property's ultimate goal. Superior performance standards help banquet servers achieve that goal.

Banquet servers must:

- Demonstrate professional behavior within the property.

- Refresh function rooms as needed.

- Greet guests warmly as they enter the room.

- Serve food and beverages according to high-quality service standards appropriate for the type of function.

- Anticipate and quickly respond to guests' needs.

- Be alert to safety procedures at all times.

- Make sure food is served at the correct temperature, attractively presented, and pleasing to the senses.

Silverware

Think of silverware as the tools guests need to eat their meals comfortably. At home, the basic "tools"—a knife, teaspoon, and dinner fork—may be enough. But there are more than 40 additional types of silverware. Types of silverware can include:

- Dinner fork
- Cocktail fork
- Salad fork
- Dessert fork
- Dinner spoon
- Soup spoon
- Iced tea spoon
- Dinner knife
- Steak knife
- Butter knife

Washable silverware, such as forks, knives, and spoons, is typically made of stainless steel. True silverware, which is made of silver, is extremely expensive and rarely used.

Glassware Types

Banquet servers show guests that they are service professionals by following these steps when serving beverages:

1. Use the right glass for the beverage.

2. Pour beverages only into sparkling clean glasses without cracks, chips, or spots. Throw away glasses with cracks or chips, and return spotted glasses to the dishroom.

3. When pouring at a table, leave the glasses on the table. Never pick up a glass to pour unless there is no other way to pour without spilling.

4. Pour from the right side with their right hands.

5. Never add ice to a hot glass.

6. Always use an ice scoop or tongs—not their hands or a glass—to pick up ice.

China

When you go to a banquet or a meeting, the china—plates, bowls, cups and saucers, and serving pieces—tells you a lot about the type of establishment you're in. China tells you whether an establishment is casual, formal, trendy, or traditional. Lodging properties choose their china very carefully to present a certain image to guests. Banquet servers can enhance that image by doing the following before delivering meal orders:

1. Inspect all china to make sure it is spotless and free of cracks and chips. Throw away cracked or chipped china, and tell their supervisor about it. Return spotted china to the dishroom.

2. Use the correct items for the food they are serving.

Promote Restaurants

Banquet servers have many opportunities to promote the other restaurants and services of the property. They are prepared to tell guests the following about each restaurant at the property:

- Hours of service
- Type of food served and price range
- Specialties
- Reservations policy
- Dress code (if any)

Banquet servers can suggest the property's restaurants by mentioning specific items served. For example, they can say, "If you're still here tomorrow, try the café. It has excellent eggs Florentine."

They can also suggest the property's facilities to guests who show an interest in recreation. Features such as pools, spas, and gyms contribute to repeat business.

Apply Your Learning 17.1

Please write all answers on a separate sheet of paper.

1. How can a banquet server be an excellent team player?
2. What is washable silverware typically made of?
3. From what side of a guest should a beverage be poured?
4. What does a banquet server need to know about the property's restaurant?

17.2 Preparing for Service

AFTER SUCCESSFULLY COMPLETING THIS SECTION, YOU WILL BE ABLE TO:

◆ Describe how to fold napkins.

◆ Explain how place-settings should be arranged.

◆ Describe how to prepare condiments and bread.

◆ Identify ways to prepare beverages such as coffee, hot tea, iced tea, and hot chocolate.

Linens and Napkin Folding

Fresh, clean linens and crisply folded napkins are a necessary and important part of professional food presentation, whether guests are having coffee and a snack or a seven-course banquet.

Banquet servers always check linens for rips, stains, and wear, and replace linens that do not meet the property's standards. The supervisor will inform the laundry department about problems with the napkins and determine which napkins to rewash and which to throw away.

Banquet servers always wash their hands before folding napkins as guests will wipe their mouth with napkins. Napkins get the same sanitary care as food.

There are many napkin folds that can be used to enhance the appearance of tables. The way banquet servers fold napkins will vary with the type of function, the season, and the time of day. Silverware wrapped in linen napkins are called **linen roll-ups**.

Once folded, napkins are stored in a clean area of the side station, away from splatters and spills.

Standard Place-Setting Arrangements

All tables in a function room should look the same, even if different banquet servers set them. When tables are set consistently, with evenly lined-up dishes, attractive centerpieces, and straight, crisp tablecloths, it shows guests that employees care about providing a quality dining experience.

Place-setting arrangements will change with the type of function and type of service provided. It is important to know the standard place-setting arrangement for each type of function held at a property.

All functions must be set and ready 15 minutes before the scheduled start time. A supervisor or banquet captain may check all tables. Once table setup has been approved, banquet servers should be in the room, ready to welcome guests.

Exhibit 1 provides a step-by-step breakdown of how to set tables for banquets.

Prepare Condiment Containers

Before a banquet begins, banquet servers prepare and clean such items as salt shakers, pepper shakers, pepper grinders, and sugar bowls or caddies.

If shakers and grinders are cleaned and refilled regularly and stored in a warm, dry place between meal periods, they work with few problems. If shakers or grinders are not completely dry before being filled, the contents will clump together and not come out.

Salt and pepper shakers are filled with a small kitchen funnel up to the threads. They are placed on a service tray to catch any spills while filling.

Pepper grinders are also called pepper mills. Guests often like fresh ground pepper on salads, pasta, and red meat entrees. To fill grinders, servers must unscrew the retainer nuts from the tops of the grinders and remove the tops. The grinders are then filled with whole peppercorns or rock salt. They are filled only three-quarters full as overfilling can interfere with the grinding action.

Sugar bowls and caddies are cleaned with a cleaning cloth to wipe dust and crumbs away. Sugar packets are then placed neatly in one side of each bowl or caddy and artificial sweetener in the other side. If a property serves unrefined sugar, bowls are filled with an equal number of packets of unrefined sugar, white sugar, and artificial sweetener.

Sugar and sweetener packages from previous meals can be re-used if they are free from stains and damage. Packets are placed upright and facing the same direction.

Prepare Bread

Banquet servers often put bread onto trays or into baskets to serve at each table. Pre-prepared breads may be delivered by or picked up at the storeroom. Breads prepared in the bakery are picked up in the bakery or delivered by the baker. The amount of bread needed will be on a food requisition.

Breads are never heated in a microwave oven. Microwaves cause bread to lose its moisture and quickly become tough and hard. Instead, properties use bread warmers for any bread they wish to serve warm. Many bread warmers have a water tank to keep the bread from drying out. Bread is placed in the warming units until it is time to serve it. Banquet servers have to avoid warming more bread than is needed for each table as pre-warmed bread cannot be served at a later time.

Banquet servers remove all crumbs and food residue from bread baskets before setting them up for service. Bread trays are cleaned and polished. Generally speaking, servers set up one bread basket or tray for every 10 people or for every table of fewer than 10 people. A folded linen napkin is placed in each basket or on each tray and then stored in the pantry or side station until needed. Just before serving time, the bread is placed in the baskets or on the trays.

Prepare Beverages

Banquet servers prepare several types of beverages for any given banquet. The most commonly prepared beverages are:

- Coffee
- Hot tea

Exhibit 1
Set Tables for Banquets

Materials needed: Banquet event order (BEO), change orders (if any), tables, tablecloths, place settings as specified in the BEO, serviceware, and napkins.

STEPS:	HOW-TO'S:
1. Place tablecloths on the tables as directed by the banquet event order (BEO).	
2. Check the BEO to find out how many place settings you need to set.	
3. Collect the serviceware needed.	❑ Make sure all china, glasses, and silverware are clean and have no spots, cracks, or chips.
	❑ Throw away chipped or cracked glass or china. Return stained or spotted items to the dishroom.
	❑ Handle china, glasses, and silverware by the edges, and do not touch anywhere food or a guest's mouth will touch.
	❑ Collect the following serviceware for each breakfast place setting:
	• 1 dinner fork
	• 1 dinner knife
	• 1 teaspoon
	• 1 water glass
	• 1 mug or cup and saucer
	❑ Collect the following serviceware for each lunch and dinner place setting:
	• 2 dinner forks or 1 dinner and 1 salad or dessert fork (lunch tables may be set with only one dinner fork, depending on the menu)
	• 1 dinner knife
	• 2 teaspoons
	• 1 bread and butter plate
	• 1 water glass
	• 1 mug or cup and saucer

(continued)

Exhibit 1	
Set Tables for Banquets *(continued)*	
STEPS:	**HOW-TO'S:**
	❑ Gather any specialized silverware or wine glasses as indicated on the BEO.
	❑ Get one set of salt and pepper shakers for every 10 people or for every table of fewer than 10 people.
	❑ Get one sugar bowl or caddy for every 10 people or for every table of fewer than 10 people.
	❑ If smoking is permitted, get one ashtray and one pack of matches for every five guests.
4. **Arrange silverware on the table.**	❑ Unless otherwise requested in the BEO, set eight places at a 5-foot round table and ten places at a 6-foot round table. Your supervisor may arrange one place setting as an example.
	❑ Leave a 12-inch space on the table directly in front of each chair. A dinner plate will be replaced in the 12-inch space.
	❑ Place the dinner fork to the left of the plate space. Place the salad fork or second dinner fork to the left of the first fork.
	❑ Place a dinner knife to the right of the plate space with the sharp edge toward the plate space.
	❑ Place the spoons to the right of the knife.
	❑ Make sure the handles of the silverware line up evenly about two inches from the table edge.
	❑ Do not touch the eating surfaces of the silverware.
5. **Preset specialized silverware (if appropriate).**	❑ Set a fish fork or an appetizer fork horizontally across the top of the 12-inch plate space, with the handle to the right.
	❑ If there is an appetizer and a fish course, place an appetizer fork above the fish fork with the handle to the left.

(continued)

Exhibit 1
Set Tables for Banquets *(continued)*

STEPS:	HOW-TO'S:
	❑ Place a steak knife between the dinner knife and the spoons, with the sharp edge turned toward the plate space. ❑ Do not touch the eating surfaces of the silverware.
6. **Arrange glasses.**	❑ Place the water glass one-half inch above the tip of the dinner knife. ❑ Place a mug or cup and saucer to the right of and slightly below the water glass. Turn the handle to the right and angle it toward the table.
7. **Put the bread and butter plate slightly above and to the left of the forks.**	
8. **Put napkins where instructed by the BEO or your supervisor.**	
9. **Prepare and place salt and pepper shakers.**	❑ Place one set of salt and pepper shakers near the center of each table of ten people or fewer. ❑ If tables are set for more than ten people, place a set near the center of the table after every 10th place setting.
10. **Prepare and place salt and pepper shakers.**	❑ Place one sugar bowl or caddy near the center of each table of ten people or fewer. ❑ If tables are set for more than ten people, place a bowl or caddy near the center of the table after every 10th place setting.
11. **Follow the BEO or your supervisor's instructions to place decorations and other items on the tables.**	

(continued)

Exhibit 1
Set Tables for Banquets *(continued)*

STEPS:	HOW-TO'S:
12. **Check the table carefully.**	❑ Line up all place settings carefully from one end of the table to the other and across the table. All functions must be set and ready 15 minutes before the scheduled start time.
	❑ Make sure place settings directly line up across from each other.
	❑ Replace any missing items.
	❑ Light all table lamps.
	❑ Your supervisor or a banquet captain may check all tables. Once table setup has been approved, you should be in the room, ready to welcome guests.

- Iced tea

- Hot chocolate

Other beverages such as carbonated drinks or water are also served, but they require very little advance preparation.

Coffee. Coffee pots have to be checked for cleanliness. If a coffee pot was left on the burner too long, it may have coffee residue in the bottom. At the end of the night, pots are returned to the dish room and washed in the dish machine.

Banquet servers make coffee either by the pot in a drip coffee maker or by the urn.

Many lodging properties use filter packs that are premeasured to meet the tastes of most guests. To make coffee by the pot, banquet servers empty these filter packs onto the filter in the grounds holder. The grounds holder is then returned to the coffee maker. A clean pot is then placed under the grounds holder. Water is poured from a measured pitcher or a clean coffee pot into the coffee maker.

Coffee strength **layers** as water passes through the ground coffee. The first third of the pot is too weak, the second third is too strong, and the final third is too weak. To get the right flavor, banquet servers let the full pot drip to blend the layers and arrive at the desired strength.

The full pot of fresh coffee is then moved to a reserve burner and the grounds are thrown away and the holder rinsed. Coffee begins to go bad immediately after it is brewed. The oils in the coffee break down and a foul odor and taste develop.

Some coffee urns have two compartments. One is for heating water and the other is for brewing coffee. Other urns have three compartments—one for hot water and two for coffee. In this case, the right compartment is always used for decaffeinated coffee. To make coffee in urns, banquet servers:

1. Check to make sure it is clean.

2. Add water to the urn.

3. Heat the water until it boils.

4. Place a cloth or paper filter in the brew basket.

5. Measure the correct amount of ground coffee into the filter and spread it evenly.

6. Place the brew basket in the coffee urn.

7. Put the water arm over the brew basket, replace the lid, and press start.

Coffee is prepared as close to service time as possible. Water should never be run through the grounds twice.

Hot Tea. Hot tea is brewed either by the two-cup pot or by the individual cup. If a property uses ceramic tea pots, the banquet servers preheat them by filling them with hot water from the drip coffee maker. Serving items (including sugar, artificial sweetener, and spoons) are placed on a service tray. Since banquet servers often serve the same items to many people, they will typically use a service tray, not a beverage tray, for service items, mugs, and tea cups. They also place a tea bag and a lemon wedge on side dishes or bread-and-butter plates and put them on the service tray. Most guests prefer to place their tea bags into the hot water. While tea usually takes eight to ten minutes to brew, some guests may prefer more or less time. Finally, hot water from the coffee maker is run into the clean tea pots and the teapots are placed on the tray.

Iced Tea. To make iced tea in a drip coffee maker, banquet servers place the correct number of tea bags in a clean, empty coffee pot. The pot is placed on a drip-coffee-maker burner and a clean, empty grounds holder is placed on the coffee maker to funnel the water. The tea is then brewed and allowed to steep in the hot water for eight to ten minutes. Banquet servers then fill clean plastic pitchers with ice and—after removing the tea bags—pour the brewed tea into the pitchers. They then stir the tea with a clean iced-tea spoon to help cool the tea. Warm tea will melt the ice in a guest's glass and make the tea too watery. If a property garnishes its iced-tea glasses, the banquet servers will garnish the glasses during setup and place them (along with lemon wedges, sugar, spoons, and beverage napkins) on a service tray.

Hot Chocolate. Hot chocolate is usually made with a hot chocolate machine. As each machine is different, banquet servers learn on-the-job how to use it and make hot chocolate.

Apply Your Learning 17.2

Please write all answers on a separate sheet of paper.

1. What should banquet servers check linens for?

2. When should a function be set up and ready by?

3. What is another name for pepper grinders?

4. How are breads prepared when they are served warm?

5. What items are needed to make a fresh pot of coffee?

17.3 Serving the Banquet

AFTER SUCCESSFULLY COMPLETING THIS SECTION, YOU WILL BE ABLE TO:

◆ Describe ways to anticipate guest needs.

◆ Explain how to prepare, lift, and carry service trays.

◆ Explain how to serve beverages and bread.

◆ Identify how each course is served in a banquet.

◆ Describe how to maintain tables during service and clear them at the end of service.

◆ Explain how to settle individual guest checks.

◆ List end-of-shift duties.

Anticipating Guest Needs

Has a server at a banquet or reception ever offered you something you wanted or needed before you asked for it? If so, how did you feel about that dining experience? Probably pretty good.

That's the type of service every banquet server should provide guests. Whenever appropriate, servers take the necessary steps to make sure each guest has a positive experience. For instance, they:

- Offer to help guests find their seats, whether they are assigned ahead of time or not.

- Ask guests with young children whether they would like child seats or high chairs.

- Provide extra attention to senior citizens, if appropriate.

- Refill water glasses and bread baskets as soon as they are half full or less.

- Whenever guests leave the table, refold their napkins and straighten their place settings.

- Remove all silver, glass, and china that guests have finished using.

- Provide additional supplies, such as note paper or pens, as needed.

- Work quietly so they won't disturb guests during meetings, receptions, presentations, etc.

By anticipating guests' needs, you will exceed guests' expectations and help make each guest's banquet experience an enjoyable one.

Prepare, Lift, and Carry Service Trays

Service trays are large trays that banquet servers use to transport everything the guest needs. They are especially important to banquet servers as banquet servers need to be able to serve all guests at one table at the same time.

Exhibit 1 provides a step-by-step break down on how to prepare, lift, and carry service trays.

Serve Beverages

The host of each function will have selected the beverages when booking the function. The beverage choices will be listed on the banquet event order. When first arriving at the table, the banquet server tells guests which beverages are available and asks them what they would like to order. If a guest asks for a beverage not included on the BEO, banquet servers tell the guest whether there is an extra charge and what that charge is.

Beverage orders are written on the guest check according to how the guests are seated. Each property will provide banquet servers with a system to write checks, usually using the same reference point in a function room. Banquet servers also use standard drink abbreviations so that anyone can deliver orders.

Beverages are carried out to guests on a service tray and the tray is placed in a tray jack in the function room. Whenever beverages are poured from a pitcher (such as water, carbonated beverages, iced tea, coffee), they are poured from the guest's right, using the server's right hand. He or she pours without picking the glass up from the table. The server also holds a clean linen napkin in the left hand under the base of the pitcher to catch drips from any moisture on the pitcher.

Glasses are placed in front of guests from the guest's right with the banquet server's right hand. A beverage napkin is placed on the table in front of each guest with the property's logo facing the guest. Glasses are handled by their stem, base, or handle and placed in the center of each beverage napkin.

Water may be poured a few minutes before the guests arrive or as soon as guests arrive. Water glasses are refilled whenever they are less than half-full unless the guest declines a refill.

The only coffee served is coffee that is less than 30 minutes old. Coffee drinkers instantly know the difference between fresh and stale coffee. Also, old, stale coffee gives off an offensive odor that will spread throughout the room. If coffee is made in an urn, guests will probably serve themselves. The banquet servers only need to make sure there is enough cream, sugar, artificial sweetener, and mugs or cups and saucers.

Coffee cools quickly. Guests expect banquet servers to keep their coffee hot and fresh. Therefore, banquet servers refill coffee cups or mugs as soon as they are less than half-full or until the guests signal that they have had enough.

Serve Bread and Butter

Bread and butter service varies slightly from function to function. Generally speaking, prepared butter ramekins or dishes are pulled from a service refrigerator and placed on a tray. Butter dishes and knives are placed on small plates. Bread is placed in a napkin-lined basket or bread tray.

At a formal, sit-down banquet, bread is served with the first course. If a basket of crackers, bread sticks, or other specialty breads was served with the appetizers, this basket is removed from the table before serving breads for the main course.

The basket or tray of bread is placed in the center of the table so guests can serve themselves. Butter dishes are placed near the bread basket. Banquet servers check

Exhibit 1
Prepare, Lift, and Carry Service Trays

Materials needed: Service trays.

STEPS:	HOW-TO'S:
1. **Get items needed to serve banquet guests.**	
2. **Put items on service trays.**	❑ If plates are hot, use a clean linen napkin to handle them.
	❑ Check each plate to make sure the food has been correctly prepared and garnished.
	❑ Work with the chef to correct any problems.
	❑ Spread the weight of items evenly across the tray.
	❑ Place heavy items in the center and lighter items around the edges.
	❑ Do not overload. Ask a co-worker to carry a second tray of plates if necessary.
	❑ Serve all guests at one table at the same time.
3. **Lift and carry loaded trays.**	❑ Bend at the knees so your shoulder is below the tray.
	❑ Pull the tray with one hand onto the palm of your other hand.
	❑ Balance the tray at shoulder level on your palm or fingertips.
	❑ Keep your back straight and use your legs to stand up.
	❑ Steady the tray with your free hand.
4. **Be safety-conscious at all times.**	❑ Avoid tipping or spilling the tray.
	❑ Watch for opening doors and wet spots on floors.
	❑ Do not try to pass people in the aisle. If possible, step aside and let others pass.
	❑ Say "behind you" to let others know when you are behind them.

baskets and trays throughout the meal and bring fresh bread and butter when the original bread is gone.

Serve Each Course

The banquet manager or captain will signal when to serve each course. Courses are typically served in the following order:

- Appetizers
- Soup
- Salads
- Entrées
- Dessert
- Cordials
- Coffee

The table has to be prepared for each course before it is served. This is done by clearing away empty plates or glasses and bringing all condiments and accompaniments to the table before serving the order.

As each order is brought out of the kitchen, banquet servers check it by asking the following questions of themselves:

- Does the food look fresh and appealing?
- Have all preparation instructions been followed?
- Is the presentation garnished?
- Have all special requests been met?
- Is the plate clean?
- Is hot food hot and cold food cold?

If there is a problem with any of the plates, they ask the cook to fix it—always thanking the kitchen staff.

Courses are delivered on service trays and placed on tray jacks in the function rooms. Generally speaking, plates are delivered to guests in this order:

1. Children
2. Women
3. Men
4. Host

Whenever possible, food is served from the guest's left side with the server's left hand. The plate with the first course is placed on top of the base plate if a base plate is included in the table setting. The entrée plate is placed so that the main item is closest to the guest. Side dishes are placed to the left of the entrée plate.

Banquet servers also ask guests whether they would like the server to bring or do anything else for them. They then deliver those extra items as quickly as possible so that the meal does not get cold.

Maintain Tables During Service

Keeping tables clear and attractive during a function makes guests feel more comfortable. By the end of the meal, before dessert service, only beverages, the items that go with them (cream, sugar, etc.) and silverware needed for dessert should remain on the table.

Exhibit 2 gives step-by-step instructions for maintaining tables during service.

Clear Tables

All banquet servers work together as a team to clear tables. It is usually very important to clear tables quickly as servers need to be out of a function room by the time a speaker begins or other events start.

Exhibit 2
Maintain Tables During Service

Materials needed: A service tray, a cleaning cloth, beverages, bread, and clean ashtrays.

STEPS:	HOW-TO'S:
1. **Clear items from the table.**	❏ Ask guests if they are done before removing anything.
	❏ Remove dirty tableware and any other items not being used.
	❏ Clear dishes, glasses, and silverware from the guest's right side with your right hand.
	❏ Scrape and stack dishes quietly—out of the guests' sight.
	❏ Place items on a service tray.
	❏ Wipe crumbs from the table into a cleaning cloth. Brush the crumbs onto your tray.
	❏ Take the tray of soiled items to the dish room. By the end of the meal, before dessert service, only beverages, the items that go with them (cream, sugar, etc.), and silverware needed for dessert should remain on the table.
2. **Refill beverages and bread.**	❏ Do not interrupt guests to ask if they want more water, coffee, or tea. Refill glasses unless a guest tells you that he or she doesn't want more.

Typically, stewards will set up a decoy system for dirty items that consists of racks with one dirty dish, glass, etc. in them to show servers where to place dirty items.

Exhibit 3 gives a step-by-step breakdown on how to clear tables.

Settle Individual Guest Checks

The banquet captain or food and beverage manager typically handles the banquet bill. However, if a guest orders an item that was not on the banquet event order, it will be necessary to process an individual guest check.

The bartender will usually prepare a check for beverages. If the guest ordered something from the restaurant, the cashier will prepare the check.

Many properties use guest check folders as they keep the checks clean and provide a place for guests to put their money or credit cards.

Guests who are staying at the property with approved credit accounts at the front desk may charge meals to their room. This is called a "house account." Other guests have approval to charge their meals to their company or to a group account. These are called "city ledger accounts."

If a guest is paying by check, it is extremely important to get as much information as possible to ensure that a personal check is good or can be traced if it is returned for non-sufficient funds.

Exhibit 4 gives a step-by-step breakdown for settling individual guest checks.

Perform End-of-Shift Duties

At the end of the shift, banquet servers help return everything to its place. While the exact tasks will vary according to the functions that were worked, some general tasks include:

- Break down ice buckets.

- Break down water pitchers.

- Break down the coffee station.

- Clean and restock banquet side stations.

Apply Your Learning 17.3

Please write all answers on a separate sheet of paper.

1. Name at least two things that a banquet server can do to help guests have positive experiences.

2. What is a service tray?

3. How are beverage orders written on the guest check?

4. When is bread served at a formal, sit-down banquet?

5. Which usually comes first: the salad course or the soup course?

6. What is a decoy system?

7. When will a banquet server have to settle an individual guest check?

Exhibit 3
Clear Tables

Materials needed: Cleaning cloths, a service tray, and a tray jack.

STEPS:	HOW-TO'S:
1. Carry a service tray to a tray jack near the tables you need to clear.	
2. Clear dishes, glasses, silverware, and napkins.	❏ Scrape food and debris from all dishes onto one dish. ❏ Stack the same kinds of dishes together in small piles. Place the dish with the food and debris on top of the stack. ❏ Place glasses on the tray in several spots so that one area is not heavier than other areas. ❏ Pile silverware in one area of the tray. ❏ Place beverage napkins in one area of the tray. ❏ Remove objects such as silverware from linen napkins, and place them in the correct place on your tray. Silverware and other items can tear linens in the washer or dryer. They can also hurt laundry attendants. ❏ Place linen napkins in one area of the tray.
3. Carry the loaded tray to the dish room.	
4. Unload items.	❏ Sort the items according to the decoy system set up by the stewards. ❏ Put broken glass in the proper trash can. ❏ Place glasses upside-down in the correct racks. ❏ Place silverware in the silverware-soaking solution. ❏ Place soiled linens in the appropriate bags or racks.

(continued)

Exhibit 3
Clear Tables *(continued)*

STEPS:	HOW-TO'S:
5. Wipe the tray with a clean, damp cloth.	
6. Place a clean, damp cloth on a service tray and return to the function room.	
7. Remove condiments and centerpieces from the tables and place them on your tray.	
8. Remove tablecloths.	❑ Fold the ends into the middle so crumbs don't fall on the floor. ❑ Place the tablecloths on your tray.
9. Clean chairs.	❑ Remove soiled items from chairs and place them on your tray. ❑ Wipe crumbs from chairs into your cleaning cloth. ❑ Brush the crumbs from your cloth onto the tray.
10. Unload the tray.	❑ Carry the tray to the side station or pantry and return condiments and centerpieces to the correct locations. ❑ Take soiled tablecloths to the dish room or laundry area and place them in the correct bags or racks.
11. Wipe the tray with a clean, damp cloth and store it in the correct location.	

Exhibit 4
Settle Individual Guest Checks

Materials needed: Guest checks, guest check folders, a hand-held calculator, comment cards, and pens.

STEPS:	HOW-TO'S:
1. Ask your supervisor when to present checks to banquet guests, if necessary.	
2. Review guest checks before you present them to guests to be sure they are complete and accurate.	
3. Present guest checks in a check folder with a pen.	❑ If your property uses comment cards, include one in the folder. ❑ Present the check directly to the person who ordered the item or items. ❑ Draw the guest's attention to the check by saying something such as: "Sir, this is the check for the wine. I can take care of it when you're ready."
4. Settle guest checks paid by cash.	❑ Present change in the guest check folder. ❑ Always provide a receipt with the change. ❑ Do not claim a tip until guests leave. If the guest leaves while you are settling the check, the change is your tip.
5. Settle guest checks paid by traveler's check.	❑ Ask the guest to sign the traveler's check in your presence. ❑ If the check is already signed, ask to see a driver's license. ❑ If the signatures do not match, calmly report the problem to your supervisor. ❑ If the signatures match, record the state and license number on the back of the check and return the driver's license to the guest before making change. ❑ Return any change and the receipt to the guest in the guest check folder.

(continued)

Exhibit 4
Settle Individual Guest Checks *(continued)*

STEPS:	HOW-TO'S:
6. **Settle guest checks paid by credit card.**	❑ Make sure the card is valid and unexpired. If it is expired or invalid, return it and ask for another form of payment. ❑ If the card is valid, tell the guest you will return in a few minutes with the credit card. ❑ Take the credit card and guest check to the lounge or property cashier for processing. ❑ Present the completed credit card voucher and a pen to the guest in a guest check folder. ❑ Ask the guest to total and sign the voucher. ❑ Make sure the voucher is totaled and signed. Give the credit card and the guest's copy of the voucher to the guest. ❑ Give the guest a receipt. ❑ If a credit card is declined, politely ask the guest for another card or form of payment. If necessary, ask the guest to step away from the group so that he or she will not be embarrassed.
7. **Settle guest checks charged to house and city ledger accounts.**	❑ If a guest wishes to charge a check to his or her room, ask the guest to: • Print his or her name and room number on the check. • Sign the check. • Present a room key to show that he or she is a guest. ❑ If a guest wants to charge a guest check to a company or group master bill account, ask the guest to: • Print the company name or group name on the guest check. • Provide the city ledger account number. • Sign the guest check. ❑ If the guest does not know the company or group account number, ask the cashier to call the front desk to make sure that the guest is authorized to charge to the account. ❑ Give the guest a receipt showing the charge.

(continued)

Exhibit 4
Settle Individual Guest Checks *(continued)*

STEPS:	HOW-TO'S:
8. Settle guest checks paid by personal card	❑ Provide a receipt in the guest check folder.
9. Thank the guests when you return their change or receipt, and invite them to return.	
10. Settle guest checks paid by credit card.	

17.4 Types of Banquets

AFTER SUCCESSFULLY COMPLETING THIS SECTION, YOU WILL BE ABLE TO:

◆ Define a function room.

◆ Explain how to setup and maintain a buffet.

◆ Describe reception service.

◆ Identify the tasks involved with serving continental breakfast.

◆ Explain how to refresh a meeting room.

Function Rooms

Function rooms are rooms where banquets, meetings, and receptions are held. Each function room may vary in size, style, and the number of people it will hold. Certain rooms may be used only for certain types of functions.

Banquet departments will often keep diagrams of standard function room setups. These are helpful aids to both banquet setup employees and banquet servers.

Buffets

During a **buffet**, guests serve themselves the food that banquet servers put on a buffet table. The server keeps the food on the buffet table full and looking attractive.

Many buffets have items that must be kept hot, cold, or at room temperature during the buffet. Hot food can be kept hot with **chafing dishes**. Banquet servers monitor the amount of water in the liners of the hot chafing dish and make sure that the heating element stays on. When guests are not in the serving line, servers replace the lids to help keep foods hot.

Cold food is kept cold by ice on the buffet. Servers replace ice as needed and remove any ice that gets into food containers.

When a container of food is less than one-quarter full, they get a full container from the kitchen and replace the old container. Food from the old container is not combined with the new container. Instead, the old food is taken to the kitchen and given to the appropriate person.

Dishes are restocked when there are fewer than ten in a stack. A stack should never get below five dishes. Each food container needs an appropriate serving utensil and any that falls on the floor is replaced with a clean one from the kitchen.

Banquet servers also wipe up any spills on the buffet table.

Receptions

Receptions can be a function for anything from a small business gathering to a large wedding. Hors d'oeuvres and snack foods are served as finger foods at most receptions. Tables are often decorated with food or flower displays.

Banquet servers bring out the equipment for hot and cold food. They set up ice beds for cold items and chafing dishes or electric warmers for hot items. If a chafing dish is heated by canned, gel-type fuel, servers place one can on a bread-and-butter plate under a half-size chafer and two cans under a full-size chafer. Cans of fuel are lit 10 minutes before putting the food in the chafing dishes.

Servers arrange stacks of beverage napkins on the service table and then place cocktail forks or picks, knives, and small plates on the table. About 10 to 15 minutes before guests are expected, servers bring out the food and place it in the beds of ice or chafing dishes.

Continental Breakfast Service

Many lodging properties of all sizes offer continental breakfast to their guests. Banquet servers usually collect food, beverages, and service items and take them to the function room. Service items may include:

- Small plates
- Linen or paper napkins

- Forks, spoons, and knives
- Glasses
- Mugs or cups and saucers

Ice beds are set up for cold items—including sodas, juices, and bottled waters. Chafing dishes or electric warmers are set up for hot food. Decaffeinated coffee dispensers are placed to the right of regular coffee dispensers and labeled.

Meeting Rooms

When guests reserve a function room to hold a meeting, they often order beverage service or snack service. The banquet event order will indicate when guests plan to take breaks in their meeting and what should be served.

During the meeting breaks, banquet servers:

- Pick up any trash in the room.
- Replace dirty tablecloths.
- Refill food and beverages.
- Replace dull pencils (if they belong to the property) and restock notepads.
- Make sure the tables are fresh and neat.

When a room for a function continues beyond one day, the banquet setup employees will typically refresh the rooms.

Apply Your Learning 17.4

Please write all answers on a separate sheet of paper.

1. How can hot food be kept hot on a buffet?

2. What service items might be set for a continental breakfast?

3. What sort of services do meeting room guests often order?

Quick Hits

SECTION 17.1—GETTING TO KNOW THE BANQUET SERVER

- Banquet servers provide food and beverage to banquet guests.

- Banquet servers help a property provide excellent service, beverages, and meals at a reasonable price.

- There are more than 40 types of silverware that a banquet guest might use.

- Banquet servers always use the right type of glassware for each beverage.

- China is carefully inspected to present the right image to guests.

- Banquet servers need to know about the property's restaurants and services.

SECTION 17.2—PREPARING FOR SERVICE

- Clean linens and crisply folded napkins present a professional image.

- All place-setting arrangements should look exactly the same and be set up and ready 15 minutes before a function is scheduled to start.

- Banquet servers clean and fill salt shakers, pepper shakers and grinders, sugar bowls, and sugar caddies.

- Banquet servers prepare bread baskets and bread before a function.

- Before a banquet begins, servers prepare coffee, hot tea, iced tea, and hot chocolate.

SECTION 17.3—SERVING THE BANQUET

- Servers exceed guest expectations when they anticipate guest needs.

- Service trays are essential tools for banquet servers.

- Beverages are served to guests from the guest's right on a beverage napkin.

- Servers bring out baskets of bread and plates of butter for each table.

- Typically, courses are served in this order: appetizers, soup, salads, entrees, dessert, cordials, and coffee.

- Banquet servers keep tables looking clear and attractive to help make the guests feel more comfortable.

- When guests order something that is not on the BEO, the banquet server must bring out an individual check.

- At the end of a shift, banquet servers clean up the area and break down equipment and beverage stations.

SECTION 17.4—TYPES OF BANQUETS

- Function rooms are rooms where banquets, meetings, and receptions are held.

- Servers keep food on buffet tables full and looking attractive.

- Hors d'oeuvres and snack foods are usually served at receptions.

- Banquet servers deliver food and beverages to the room where continental breakfasts are served.

- Banquet servers refresh a meeting room and deliver food and beverages during breaks.

Bus Person

Sections

Buspersons are key service employees who help keep a food-service operation running smoothly. They help the servers by clearing plates, resetting tables, pouring water, and delivering some food to tables. They also often help out with sidework such as cleaning side stations, cleaning coffee urns, refilling supplies, and folding napkins.

When guests come into a food and beverage operation and see glistening tables, clean floors, and well-set tables, it is because of the work of the buspersons. They help create a first impression for guests by doing their jobs with excellence.

18.1 Getting to Know the Bus Person

AFTER SUCCESSFULLY COMPLETING THIS SECTION, YOU WILL BE ABLE TO:

◆ Explain the important role bus persons play in a lodging restaurant's operation.

◆ Describe the tasks and performance standards expected of bus persons.

◆ Summarize the use of china and silverware in a restaurant operation.

◆ List ways in which bus persons can anticipate guests' needs.

What Is a Bus Person?

A bus person at a lodging property could be defined as someone who sets and clears tables and helps restaurant servers. While this definition is technically correct, it leaves out the heart of a bus person's job. A better definition might be: A food and beverage employee who does everything possible, within reason, to make each guest's dining experience exactly what he or she wants it to be, and who exceeds guest expectations whenever possible.

Bus persons are responsible for:

• Preparing for service

• Setting tables

• Helping restaurant servers provide high-quality guest service

• Maintaining tables

• Clearing tables

• Creating a friendly atmosphere where guests can enjoy themselves

Bus persons make a difference!

Working as a Team

Bus persons must give guests *and* co-workers great service.

To be excellent team players, bus persons can help:

• Hosts and hostesses by:

– Greeting and seating guests

– Answering the phone

– Taking reservations when hosts and hostesses are busy

• Restaurant servers by:

– Setting tables according to restaurant policy

– Providing beverage service for guests when servers are busy

– Clearing and resetting tables promptly after guests leave

– Checking side stations periodically to make sure they are stocked

Superior Performance Standards

The quality of the food, drinks, and service at a restaurant should enhance each guest's overall experience. Providing excellent service, beverages, and meals at a reasonable price is every restaurant's ultimate goal.

To display superior performance standards, bus persons must:

- Be familiar with all restaurant menus and food and drink offerings.

- Demonstrate professional behavior.

- Make sure the dining room is a comfortable temperature, is properly lit, and looks neat.

- Quickly approach guests and greet them warmly if restaurant servers and hosts or hostesses are busy.

- Be alert to safety procedures.

- Keep tabletop items clean and attractively arranged.

- Keep coffee, tea, water, and other non alcoholic beverages filled at each table.

- Clear and reset tables promptly after guests leave.

- Keep dining room floors neat and clean.

China

When people eat at a restaurant, the **china**—plates, bowls, cups and saucers, and serving pieces—tells them a lot about the type of restaurant they are in. China tells people whether an establishment is casual, formal, trendy, or traditional. Typically, restaurants chose their china very carefully to present a certain image to guests. Bus persons can enhance that image by doing the following simple things:

- Inspect all china carefully to make sure it is spotless and free of cracks or chips. Report any cracked or chipped china to a supervisor. Return spotted china to the dishwasher.

- Stock enough of each type of china in the side and other stations so guests receive food on the correct china.

Silverware

Think of **silverware** as the tools that guests need to eat their meals comfortably. At home, the basic "tools"—a knife, teaspoon, and dinner fork—may be enough. But there are more than 40 additional types of silverware, and guests expect bus persons to provide the right silverware at their tables.

Washable silverware, such as forks, knives, and spoons, is typically made of stainless steel. True silverware, which is made of silver, is extremely expensive and rarely used.

Anticipating Guests' Needs

Many people might remember an experience in a restaurant when the server or bus person kept their table exactly the way they wanted it by bringing food and beverages just when they wanted them or by clearing items as soon as they were through with them. These kinds of dining experiences make us feel pretty good.

It is this type of service that bus persons provide for guests. Whenever appropriate, they take the necessary steps to make sure each guest has a positive experience. As bus persons do their job, they can also help restaurant servers by watching guests and determining their needs. For instance, bus persons can:

- Ask guests arriving with young children if they would like child seats or high chairs.

- Refill water glasses as soon as they are half full or less.

- Remove unwanted items from tables.

- Notice when guests are looking around and stop at their table and tell them their server will be right with them. Then tell the restaurant server that his or her guests need to see him or her.

By anticipating guest needs, bus persons will exceed guest expectations and help make each guest's dining experience an enjoyable one.

Bus Person Duties

The primary job of a bus person is to set and clear tables and help restaurant servers. In general, bus persons are responsible for:

- Preparing tables for service

- Prepping side stations, condiments, and silverware

- **Busing** soiled linens, dishes, glasses, and silverware from tables

- Assisting servers and guests to ensure total guest satisfaction

Bus persons may be the earliest arriving employees to the restaurant and, along with servers, may be expected to help set up the restaurant dining area for service. These duties may include:

- Polishing brass

- Adjusting drapes and blinds

- Adjusting environmental controls in the restaurant

- Setting up serving trays

Exhibit 1 lists the most common tasks that bus persons are expected to be able to perform and perform well.

Apply Your Learning 18.1

Please write all answers on a separate sheet of paper.

1. What is the primary responsibility of a bus person?

2. List three things that bus persons are responsible for.

3. List four superior performance standards that bus persons can display.

4. Why is it important for bus persons to be aware of and anticipate guests' needs?

Exhibit 1
Task List—Bus Person

1. Set Up the Restaurant for Service

2. Prepare Flower Arrangements for the Dining Room

3. Prepare Butter for Side Stations

4. Prepare Breads and Bread Baskets or Trays

5. Prepare Condiments and Crackers

6. Prepare Sugar Bowls or Caddies

7. Prepare Salt and Pepper Shakers and Grinders

8. Fold Napkins

9. Stock Silverware

10. Prepare Service Trays for Servers

11. Lift and Carry Loaded Trays, Bus Tubs, and Dish Racks

12. Prepare Chilled Forks and Plates

13. Stock Ashtrays and Matches

14. Prepare Table-Side Service Carts

15. Prepare Ice Bins in Service Stations

16. Set Up the Water Station and Water Pitchers

17. Prepare Ice Buckets and Ice Bucket Stands

18. Prepare and Serve Coffee

19. Prepare and Serve Hot Tea

20. Prepare and Serve Iced Tea

21. Prepare and Serve Hot Chocolate

22. Set Up, Maintain, and Take Down the Salad Bar

23. Prepare Tables for Service

24. Take Reservations

25. Greet and Seat Guests

26. Serve Water

27. Serve Bread and Butter

28. Maintain Tables

29. Assist Servers to Ensure Total Guest Satisfaction

30. Respond to Dissatisfied Guests

31. Clear and Reset Tables

32. Bus Soiled Dishes to the Dishroom

33. Handle Soiled Restaurant Linens

34. Maintain Side Stations

35. Pick Up and Restock Restaurant Supplies

36. Prepare Takeout Items

37. Perform Closing Sidework and Cleaning Duties

18.2 Prepare Tables for Service

AFTER SUCCESSFULLY COMPLETING THIS SECTION, YOU WILL BE ABLE TO:

♦ Describe the procedures for preparing tables for service.

♦ Explain the importance of napkin folding.

♦ Summarize the procedures for stocking silverware.

♦ Describe how to prepare chilled forks and plates.

♦ Explain how to prepare a table-side cart for service.

Prepare Tables for Service

No guest likes to wait for a table. That's why one of the most important jobs bus persons do is to quickly and correctly set tables to the restaurant's standards.

The guest's first impression of the table is important in setting the tone for a pleasing dining experience. Every table in the restaurant should look the same, whether it is set before the restaurant opened, or five minutes ago, when the last group of guests left the table. When tables are kept clean and set consistently, with evenly lined-up dishes; straight, crisp tablecloths; and attractive centerpieces; it shows guests that the bus persons care about providing a quality dining experience.

Table setup specifications may change with each restaurant and with each meal period. Exhibit 1 provides an example of the step-by-step procedures for preparing tables for service.

Fold Napkins

Fresh, clean linens and crisply folded napkins are a necessary and important part of professional food presentation, whether guests are having coffee and a snack or an entire meal.

One of the many duties bus persons are responsible for is to fold clean napkins in preparation for serving meals. At many restaurants, the same number of napkins are folded before the start of each shift. On busier days, more napkins are folded.

Stock Silverware

Regular silverware used in most restaurants includes knives, forks, and spoons. Special silverware—depending on the food served—may include fish forks, snail tongs, demitasse spoons, and other silverware required for the service of specialty items.

Bus persons may be responsible for stocking the silverware trays that are usually located at the side stations. Silverware

Exhibit 1
Preparing for Table Service

Materials needed: Tablecloths or place mats, cleaning cloths, sanitizing solution, foodservice film, packets of crackers, broom, dustpan, service tray, tray jack, dish dolly or cart, napkins, cream, butter and flowers.

STEPS:	HOW-TO'S:
1. **Clean tables and chairs.**	❑ Clean all tables and chairs before setting up the side station, even if they were cleaned at the end of the previous meal period.
	❑ Wipe tabletops with a damp cloth and sanitizing solution followed by a dry cloth. Clean tabletops before wiping table legs and chairs.
	❑ Wipe the legs, rungs, and bases of the tables. Rinse the cloth as needed.
	❑ Wipe chair seats, backs, legs, and rungs. Wipe booths, banquettes, and any other seats. If possible, pull out seating cushions and wipe up crumbs.
	❑ Check under tables and chairs for gum, and remove any gum you find.
2. **Clean children's seating.**	❑ Wipe high-chair trays with a damp cloth and sanitizing solution and let them air dry.
	❑ After trays have dried, place two packets of crackers on each tray and wrap each tray with foodservice film.
	❑ Wipe the seats, backs, and legs of high chairs and all children's booster chairs.
	❑ Check that the safety straps on high chairs are clean and in working order. Replace any missing or broken straps.

(continued)

| Exhibit 1 |
| Preparing for Table Service *(continued)* |

STEPS:	HOW-TO'S:
3. **Check floors.**	❑ Check under tables for crumbs, food spills, or stains. Sweep up crumbs.
	❑ Use a damp cloth followed by a dry cloth to wipe up spills.
	❑ Report stubborn stains to your supervisor before setting up the station for service.
4. **Place tablecloths or place mats.**	❑ Check each new tablecloth or place mat for:
	• Correct size
	• Stains
	• Tears or holes
	• Unsightly wrinkles
	❑ If place mats are used, make sure the pattern is right-side-up and facing the guest so words on the place mat can be read.
	❑ Line up place mats with the table edge and with the place mats on the opposite side of the table.
	❑ Place the tablecloths on the tables. Make sure they are right-side-up and centered on the tables.
5. **Position tabletop items.**	❑ Pick up tabletop items from your side station. Get enough of each of the following items to set all tables:
	• Centerpieces
	• Salt and pepper shakers and grinders
	• Sugar bowls
	• Condiments and cracker baskets
	• Ashtrays and matches

(continued)

Exhibit 1
Preparing for Table Service *(continued)*

STEPS:	HOW-TO'S:
	❏ Check the condition and appearance of each item. Clean or replace any items if necessary.
	❏ Place the items on a service tray. Do not overload the tray. Make as many trips as necessary to safely carry items.
	❏ Carry the tray to the dining room and place it on a tray jack.
	❏ Place each item neatly in the center of the table according to standard table setup specifications.
	❏ If you are setting booths or tables that are against the wall, place the items at the end of the tabletop, near the wall.
6. Place base plates (if called for by the meal).	❏ Get a rack of clean plates from your side station or the dish room.
	❏ Carry the rack into the dining room. At some restaurants, you will need to empy items from the rack onto a service tray lined with linen napkins before carrying items into the dining room.
	❏ Place the rack on a tray jack. Most dish racks will fit on a tray jack.
	❏ Only use a dish dolly or cart to transport dishes when the restaurant is closed.
	❏ Check each base plate to be sure it is clean and free of water spots, chips, and cracks.
	❏ Return soiled or spotted plates to the dish room. Give chipped or cracked plates to your supervisor.
	❏ Place a base plate directly in front of each chair, about two inches from the table edge.
	❏ If the plate has a logo, place the plate so that the guest can read the logo.
	❏ Return empty dish racks, dollies, or carts to the dish room.

(continued)

Exhibit 1
Preparing for Table Service *(continued)*

STEPS:	HOW-TO'S:
7. Place silverware.	❑ Get a rack of clean silverware from your side station or the dish room.
	❑ Carry the rack to the dining room and set it on a tray jack.
	❑ Check each knife, fork, and spoon for cleanliness.
	❑ Return spotted or soiled silverware to the dish room.
	❑ Use a linen napkin to place silverware on the table. Touch the silverware only by the handle.
	❑ If no base plates are called for by the meal, leave a 12-inch space directly in front of each seat.
	❑ Place forks to the left of the base plate or space.
	❑ Place knives to the right of the base plate or space with the cutting edge of the knife toward the plate or space.
	❑ Place spoons to the right of the knives.
	❑ Leave a small space between each piece of silverware.
	❑ Line up all silverware handles about two inches from the table edge.
8. Place bread and butter plates.	❑ Get a rack of clean bread and butter plates from your side station or the dish room.
	❑ Carry the rack to the dining room and place it on a tray jack.
	❑ Check each bread and butter plate to be sure it is clean and free of chips or cracks. Return soiled plates to the dish room. Throw away chipped or cracked plates.
	❑ Place bread and butter plates to the left of or above the forks at each place setting.
	❑ Return the empty rack to the dish room.

(continued)

Exhibit 1	
Preparing for Table Service *(continued)*	
STEPS:	**HOW-TO'S:**
9. Place glassware.	❑ Get racks of clean glasses from your side station or the dish room.
	❑ Carry one rack at a time to the dining room.
	❑ Place the glassware rack on a tray jack.
	❑ Make sure glasses are clean and free of water spots, lipstick, food residue, chips, or cracks.
	❑ Return soiled glasses to the dish room. Throw away chipped or cracked glasses.
	❑ Place a water glass one-half inch above the tip of the knife blade at each place setting.
	❑ Place wine glasses (if appropriate) to the right of and slightly below the water glass.
	❑ Return empty racks to the dish room.
10. Fold and place napkins at each place setting.	
11. Place cream, butter, flowers, and other perishable items.	
12. Check the overall appearance of the table.	❑ Place each chair so the edge of the seat is even with the table edge.
	❑ Step away from the table and view the results.
	❑ Make sure place settings are lined up.
	❑ Adjust tables and chairs as needed.

is stocked facing the same direction, with the handle-side facing out. Bus persons never touch the eating surfaces of the silverware.

While stocking the silverware, bus persons check each item to make sure that it is clean and without any water spots or food residue. Any soiled silverware is returned to the kitchen for further washing.

Chill Forks and Plates

Restaurants that serve salads, appetizers, or other similar items, provide chilled forks and/or plates to guests who order these items. Bus persons may be responsible for making sure these forks and plates are chilled in advance. Plates and forks may be chilled in a freezer, refrigerator, or a **special chiller** designed for the purpose.

When using a refrigerator, bus persons line a stainless steel pan with a clean linen napkin and place the forks on the pan. They then place a second clean linen napkin over the forks to prevent contamination. Plates are stacked on a similar tray, upside-down on the linen napkin. Bus persons make sure that the stacks do not slide. The pans are then carefully placed in the refrigerator in an area where food will not be spilled on them.

Bus persons always check that the forks and plates are clean before chilling them.

Prepare Table-Side Carts

Restaurants featuring higher-priced items are more likely to have this kind of special service. **Table-side cart service** turns a routine dining experience into a special form of entertainment. Table-side carts may include dessert carts, salad carts, and table-side cooking carts. These carts will vary in style and setup based on the menu items.

Bus persons may be responsible for cleaning and preparing these carts for service. A clean, wet cloth, along with soapy water, is used to wash the shelves, pedestals, legs, and wheels of the cart, in that order. The cart is then wiped down with a new, clean cloth, and finally, polished with yet another new, clean cloth.

The necessary condiments, equipment, linens, and silverware are then placed on the cart. If the cart is a cooking cart, the cooking burner will need the appropriate fuel supply.

Once the cart is loaded, bus persons check the overall appearance of the cart, look for any chips, cracks, etc., and check that the wheels do not squeak.

Apply Your Learning 18.2

Answer TRUE or FALSE to the following questions. Please write all answers on a separate sheet of paper.

1. Table setup specifications are always the same, regardless of restaurant or meal period.

2. Because they are not food items, napkins do not require the same sanitary procedures as food.

3. Some restaurants use special chillers designed to chill forks and plates.

4. Restaurants do not use table-side carts to cook food at guests' tables.

18.3 Prepare Side Stations, Food, and Condiments for Service

AFTER SUCCESSFULLY COMPLETING THIS SECTION, YOU WILL BE ABLE TO:

♦ Explain the purpose of the sidework checklist.

♦ Describe the procedures for preparing condiments, sugar, butter, and salt and pepper shakers and grinders.

♦ Summarize the process of preparing ice and water for service.

♦ Identify the tasks involved in setting up, maintaining, and taking down a salad bar.

The responsibilities of bus persons include setting up and stocking the restaurant's side stations. **Side stations** store extra supplies, which means that bus persons and restaurant servers can eliminate trips to the kitchen by going to side stations instead. This means more efficient service for guests.

The sidework checklist lists sidework tasks and the bus persons who are assigned to complete each task. Some sidework tasks are shared with servers. These tasks are important to the smooth operation of the dining room; successful bus persons review the checklist before their shifts to see what they are responsible for.

By following the sidework checklist and fully stocking the side stations, bus persons can help servers save steps and serve guests more efficiently during rush periods, without running out of supplies.

Bus persons know that before they do any food preparation of any kind, they must thoroughly wash their hands—both sides—with warm water and soap for at least 20 seconds.

Prepare Butter

Butter is typically prepared in one of four ways:

• Butter chips

• Curls

• Rosettes

• Molds

The butter is then stored on a butter dish or ramekin, covered with foodservice film, and placed on a bed of ice.

Prepare Condiments and Crackers

Condiments that most restaurants typically provide include ketchup, mustard, steak sauce, jelly, jam, honey, and syrup. They are usually served in their original containers or in specialty dispensers.

Bus persons make sure that these containers are kept clean. This includes removing the condiment lids, wiping the tops of the containers or dispensers with a paper towel, washing the condiment lids at the sink to remove any food residue, rinsing the lids and spraying them with an approved sanitizing solution, and wiping the outside of containers and dispensers with a paper towel to remove dried residue. It is important to let the lids completely dry before refilling because the contents will clump and block the opening if there is any dampness.

Containers or dispensers that are chipped, cracked, or dented are not used.

Bus persons may also refill and restock condiments. It is common practice to combine contents of partially full containers or dispensers using a small kitchen funnel. However, local health laws may not permit this. Generally, small individual-use bottles are not reused or combined. They are simply thrown away when the tables are cleared.

Some restaurants may use single-service packets of mustard, ketchup, or steak sauce.

In addition to condiments, many restaurants provide individually packaged crackers in baskets on the dining tables. Bus persons may be responsible for ensuring that these baskets stay full. In addition, bus persons routinely remove cracker crumbs, broken crackers, or open or empty wrappers from the baskets.

Prepare Sugar

Bus persons routinely check the sugar bowls to make sure they are full, clean, and free from chips or cracks. Damaged containers are discarded. Bus persons use a clean, damp cloth to wipe away dust or crumbs from the sugar containers. Containers that are excessively dirty are sent to the kitchen for washing.

At many restaurants, sugar is not served in a bowl but in individual packets that are placed in a **caddie**. Non-sugar artificial sweeteners are often served in the same manner. Bus persons place the proper number of sugar packets on one side of the caddie and the artificial sweetener packets on the other. A common ratio is two sugar packets to every artificial sweetener packet. Packets are placed upright and facing the same directions so that guests can plainly see the printing or logo on them.

Packets that were not used during a meal can be reused unless they are stained, damaged, or partially opened. Bus persons also make sure that the side stations have extra sugar caddies.

Prepare Ice Bins and Ice Buckets

A typical restaurant will have ice bins at each side station. These bins need to be kept full throughout each shift. Bus persons and restaurant servers often share this duty.

Because guests consume ice, it is treated like food. A sanitary container is always used to transfer ice from the ice maker to each ice bin. In addition, each ice bin is kept covered when it is not in use, and an ice scoop is used to dispense the ice. Scoops are always left near each ice bin but never inside the ice bins.

At the end of each shift or meal period, bus persons empty and clean the ice bins. They wipe down the inside walls of the bins with a clean cloth and an approved detergent. They then rinse and drain the bins completely and allow them to air dry before adding ice.

Restaurants that offer wine, champagne, sparkling water or other chilled, bottled beverages, may serve them in an **ice bucket** on a stand. Bus persons may be responsible for preparing these buckets and stands for service.

Buckets are filled one-half to two-thirds full with ice. Crushed ice is preferable to cubed ice as this makes it easier to nest bottles in the bucket. Water is then added, filling the bucket up so that the shoulder of the bottle is covered. Once the bucket is filled, it is placed on the bucket stand, with a clean linen cloth draped over the top. Bus persons then place the stands in the proper location at the side stations.

Set Up Water Pitchers

Most restaurants have designated locations for water pitchers, usually at the side stations. These areas should be cleaned or wiped with a cloth before and after each shift or meal period. Clean water glasses are stored at the same station as the water pitchers. Because racks of glass are heavy, bus persons always use proper lifting techniques when carrying them to and from the side stations to prevent breakage or injury. Bus persons make sure to check that all glasses and pitchers are clean before they are stocked or filled.

A clean linen cloth is usually placed on the counter at the side station to serve as a drip base for the water pitchers. This will prevent the side station from becoming messy from moisture or drips.

Bus persons fill the water pitchers by first filling them with ice, using an ice scoop. Bus persons never use the pitcher itself to scoop ice. Pitchers are always filled with more ice than water so that the pitchers stay cold longer. The filled pitchers are then placed back on the drip base.

Set Up, Maintain, and Take Down the Salad Bar

At certain restaurants, bus persons may be responsible for setting up, maintaining, and taking down the salad bar. When setting up the salad bar, bus persons always check that the food meets the restaurant's standards.

The first step in this task is to gather the needed supplies onto a cart. These supplies may include the following:

- Linen skirts for the salad bar, table decorations, a sneeze guard, a soup tureen, and crocks of food and salad dressing

- Salad plates, soup cups, saucers, soup spoons, bread and butter plates, and serving utensils

- Condiments, salt and pepper shakers and grinders, and oil and vinegar cruets

Bus persons must check the salad bar and make sure that it is clean. The sneeze guard is cleaned using glass cleaner and paper towels. The edges of the soup tureen are wiped with a clean, damp cloth.

A linen skirt is placed on the salad bar using a T-pin and then fluffed. Bus persons check linen skirts to make sure they do not have any rips, tears, or stains.

Additional tasks include:

- Placing table decorations on the salad bar

- Adding ice to the salad bar
- Placing the crocks of food and salad dressing onto the salad bar
- Plugging in and turning on the soup tureen
- Stocking the salad bar with salad plates
- Routinely checking the salad bar and surrounding floor area for crumbs or food particles
- Keeping all food and dressing crocks filled
- Restocking salad plates, as needed

At the end of the meal period, bus persons take down the salad bar by:

- Placing all food containers back onto the cart

- Storing food that can be reused in the kitchen
- Discarding food that cannot be reused
- Taking salad plates to the kitchen for washing
- Storing condiments in their proper place
- Removing linen skirts and taking them to the laundry
- Draining the melted ice from the salad bar
- Cleaning the sneeze guard with paper towels and glass cleaner
- Wiping down the salad bar with a clean, damp cloth and a sanitizing solution

Apply Your Learning 18.3

Please write all answers on a separate sheet of paper.

1. Before doing food preparation, how should bus persons wash their hands?

2. List five condiments typically provided by restaurants.

3. What is the common ratio of sugar packets to artificial sweetener packets in a sugar caddy?

4. List six of the tasks performed while taking down a salad bar.

18.4 Perform Busing Duties During and After Service

AFTER SUCCESSFULLY COMPLETING THIS SECTION, YOU WILL BE ABLE TO:

♦ Describe the steps for clearing and resetting tables.

♦ Summarize the steps for busing soiled dining items.

♦ Explain the procedures for handling soiled restaurant linens.

♦ List the steps for maintaining side stations.

♦ Describe the ways that bus persons can assist servers.

♦ Explain the closing sidework and cleaning duties of bus persons.

Clear and Reset Tables

Clearing and resetting tables promptly makes it possible to seat waiting guests quickly, and it adds to the neat appearance of the restaurant. When bus persons keep up with this process, there are only a few tables to reset as part of the closing duties later.

Exhibit 1 shows the step-by-step procedures for clearing and resetting dining tables.

Bus Soiled Dishes

Busing occurs throughout meal service as new courses are served and old courses are cleared, when clearing and resetting tables, or whenever a server requests it. In addition, bus persons bus the side stations as needed. Once the dining table has been cleared and reset, bus persons take the filled **bus tubs** back to the kitchen or dish room for washing.

Because this task of carrying soiled dining items back to the kitchen is performed so frequently, bus persons take care that they are properly loading and lifting the trays, tubs, or racks to prevent spills or injury to themselves or others.

The weight of the items placed in the tray, tub, or rack should be spread evenly to allow for better balance with lifting. Heavier items are placed in the center; lighter items are placed around the edges. Successful bus persons also know that making two trips is better than overloading a cart, tub, or tray in order to make one.

Bus persons lift loaded tubs or racks so that the long end is next to their bodies, use their arms to carry them, and keep them close to their bodies when moving throughout the restaurant.

Once bus persons have carried the soiled items to the kitchen or dishroom, they

Exhibit 1
Clearing and Resetting Tables

Materials needed: A bus tub, a service tray, a tray jack, clean tablecloths and napkins, clean serviceware, cleaning cloths, sanitizing solution, candles or lamp fuel, clean ashtrays, and matches.

STEPS:	HOW-TO'S:
1. **Gather items needed to reset the table.**	❏ Place the correct number of place settings, napkins, etc. needed to reset the table on a service tray. Get a clean tablecloth if necessary.
	❏ Carry the tray to the table and place it on a nearby tray jack.
	❏ Always carry a clean, damp cloth when clearing and resetting tables.
	❏ Get an empty bus tub.
2. **Clear used dishes, silverware, glasses, and linens after guests leave the table.**	❏ Clear tables within five minutes of guest departure.
	❏ Scrape food and debris from dishes into a bus tub.
	❏ Do not scrape plates in view of guests. Work with your back to nearby guests to shield them from seeing the clearing process.
	❏ Place soiled dishes in the bus tub.
	❏ Stack like items together.
	❏ Clear tables as quietly as possible.
	❏ Sort used linens. Place the soiled linens in the bus tub.
3. **Clean the table.**	❏ If tables don't have tablecloths, clean and sanitize the tabletop.
	❏ Wipe under condiment containers and the centerpiece.
	❏ Wipe the condiment containers that will be left on the table.

(continued)

Exhibit 1
Clear and Reset Tables *(continued)*

STEPS:	HOW-TO'S:
4. Replace tablecloths if necessary.	❑ Remove the top cloth from a double-clothed table. Replace only the top cloth if the base cloth is not soiled.
	❑ If there are stains on the base cloth that will show, change both cloths, and clean and sanitize the table.
	❑ To change tablecloths, move flowers, condiments, etc., to the edge of the table away from the side where you are standing.
	❑ On your side of the table, fold the edge of the soiled cloth to the top of the table.
	❑ As you fold the soiled tablecloth up, unfold the new tablecloth on the part of the table you are uncovering. Do not shake out or completely unfold the clean cloth before spreading it onto the table.
	❑ Check to make sure the new tablecloth's seam is facing down.
	❑ Spread the new cloth halfway across the tabletop, moving the dirty cloth out of the way as you spread the new cloth. Arrange the new cloth on your side of the table so it is centered and hangs evenly.
	❑ Move to the opposite side of the table. Move flowers, condiments, etc. to the clean cloth to keep it in place.
	❑ As you pull the new cloth toward you, remove the soiled cloth in the same motion.

(continued)

Exhibit 1
Clear and Reset Tables *(continued)*

STEPS:	HOW-TO'S:
	❑ Roll up the soiled cloth so crumbs are caught in the middle of the cloth. Do not dump crumbs onto the chairs or floor.
	❑ Place rolled-up soiled linens on a chair until you have completely reset the table Do not place soiled linens on the floor.
	❑ Make sure the new cloth is centered and hangs evenly with no wrinkles.
	❑ Wipe the condiment containers and centerpieces with a clean, damp cloth and move them back to the correct spot on the table.
5. Reset the table.	❑ Make sure all glassware, silverware, and dishes are clean, polished (if appropriate), and free from spots, chips, and cracks.
	❑ Place the serviceware on the table. Set all tables the same way to give the restaurant a neat and appealing appearance.
	❑ Handle glassware by the base—never near the lip. Never put your fingers inside glasses.
	❑ Handle plates by the edges. Never place your fingers on the food surface of the plates.
	❑ Handle silverware by the handles.
	❑ Place a clean ashtray and a fresh pack of matches on the table, if appropriate. Leave the matches closed.
	❑ Relight table lamps that have gone out. Replace candles or fuel as needed.
	❑ Wipe clean and replace promotional table tents as needed.

(continued)

Exhibit 1
Clear and Reset Table *(continued)*

STEPS:	HOW-TO'S:
6. **Clean chairs.**	❏ Remove soiled linens from the chair and place them in a bus tub. ❏ Wipe crumbs from chairs into your cleaning cloth. ❏ Brush crumbs into the bus tub, and not onto the floor. ❏ Push chairs to the table so the front edge of the seat is even with the edge of the table.
7. **Check tables.**	❏ Adjust anything that is not lined up properly. ❏ Check the centerpiece to make sure it is still attractive.
8. **Take soiled dishes and linens to the correct area.**	

sort the items according to a decoy system. Most restaurants have decoy systems that consist of bus tubs and dish racks with one dirty dish, glass, etc. to show where each item should be placed. Often these tubs are filled with water and a soaking solution. This sorting makes the dishwashing work easier. Bus persons finish by rinsing the empty bus tub and wiping it dry with a clean cloth.

Handle Restaurant Linens

In restaurants that use linen napkins and tablecloths, bus persons may be required to gather these used linens and take them to the laundry department for cleaning. Bus persons use a linen bag or a rack to gather and transport the soiled linens. This may be done periodically throughout a shift as well as at the end of each shift. This helps keep the dining area clean and it also eases the burden on the laundry department.

Bus persons check each linen item to make sure that it doesn't contain silverware, plates, glasses, condiment containers, etc. These items are costly to replace. In addition, they could tear the linens in the washer or dryer. They could also potentially cause injury to laundry attendants.

The tablecloths and linen napkins are always sorted separately. Other linens may include cleaning towels, uniforms, and aprons. The laundry department may have a specific sorting and counting process. Bus persons follow this process to make the laundry department's job easier.

Maintain Side Stations

Throughout each dining shift, bus persons must maintain the side stations to ensure that the servers and bus persons have the items needed to ensure guest satisfaction. Many restaurants provide bus persons with a **sidework checklist** which lists sidework tasks such as maintaining side stations. By following the sidework checklist and maintaining and fully stocking the side stations, bus persons allow servers to save steps and serve guests more efficiently during rush periods, without running out of supplies.

Exhibit 2 provides a step-by-step breakdown of the procedures involved with maintaining side stations.

Assist Servers

A very important responsibility that bus persons have is to assist servers in providing service to restaurant guests. One way that bus persons help restaurant servers is by providing beverage service to guests when servers are busy. This shows guests that bus persons are service professionals. When helping servers by serving beverages, bus persons follow these basic steps:

- Have the right glass for the beverage.

- Pour beverages only into sparkling clean glasses without cracks, chips, or spots. Report cracked or chipped glasses to a supervisor. Return spotted glasses to the dishwasher.

- When pouring at a table, leave the glasses on the table. Never pick up a glass to pour unless there is no other way to pour without spilling.

- Pour from the right side with the right hand.

- Never add ice to a hot glass. Always use an ice scoop or tongs—not hands or a glass—to pick up ice.

Exhibit 2
Maintain Side Stations

Materials needed: Cleaning cloths, sanitizing solution, clean serviceware, clean ashtrays, salt and pepper shakers and grinders, napkins, condiments, and a sidework checklist.

STEPS:	HOW-TO'S:
1. **Clean side stations.**	❏ Take soiled items to the dishroom. Wipe the shelves and countertop with a clean, damp cloth and a sanitizing solution.
	❏ Throughout service, clean side stations as needed and as your time permits.
	❏ Do not overlook the needs of guests while maintaining your side stations.
	❏ Keep the cleaning cloth in the sanitizing solution when you're not using it.
	❏ Change the sanitizing solution periodically throughout your shift.
	❏ Wipe up spills, bread crumbs, etc. as soon as possible.
	❏ Pick up broken glass with a linen napkin or gloves to prevent cuts. Throw away broken glass in the proper container.
	❏ Throw away wilted or discolored garnishes. Wash and dry the garnish container. Refill the container with fresh garnishes as needed.
	❏ Empty used ice buckets and wipe them out with a bar towel. Store them until they are needed.
	❏ Empty full trash cans.

(continued)

Exhibit 2
Maintain Side Stations *(continued)*

STEPS:	HOW-TO'S:
2. **Stock side stations.**	❏ Check the sidework checklist to see which tasks you are responsible for.
	❏ Perform your assigned sidework duties throughout your shift.
	❏ Bring clean glasses, silverware, dishes, and ashtrays from the dish room to replace used ones.
	❏ Fold extra napkins.
	❏ Replace nearly empty or empty salt and pepper shakers and grinders as needed. Empty salt or pepper from shakers and grinders that are nearly empty into the trash and take them to the dish room for washing.
	❏ Make sure there is always a fresh supply of condiments at the side station.
	❏ Make sure there is a bucket of sanitizing solution and a clean cloth at each side station.
	❏ Keep side-station supplies and equipment orderly.
	❏ Check the side stations throughout the meal period. Stock each side station as needed.
3. **Make fresh coffee when the pot is nearly empty or if the coffee becomes stale.**	

In general, successful bus persons always are aware of guests needs. When guests request something from bus persons, the bus persons either help the guests themselves or quickly alert a server. Bus persons always use good manners when interacting with guests. They are attentive to children, pick up items on the floor, and provide extra napkins as needed.

When bus persons remove items from dining tables while guests are still eating—this is called **pre-busing**—they first ask the guests if they are done with the item. Items are cleared from the right side of guests. Cleared items are placed in the bus tub or tray as are any crumbs, food particles, or soiled linens. Bus persons leave drinks and condiments on the table until the end of the meal. Full bus tubs or trays are then taken into the kitchen.

Perform Closing Sidework and Cleaning Duties

Once the dining period is over, or when a shift ends, the bus persons perform their closing sidework and cleaning duties. Typically, bus persons will have a checklist that they use to determine that they have completed all of their end-of-shift tasks.

Exhibit 3 provides an example of the tasks that may be required of bus persons at the end of their shifts.

Apply Your Learning 18.4

Please write all answers on a separate sheet of paper.

1. Why is it important to clear and reset tables promptly?

2. Where should heavier items be placed in the bus tub? Why?

3. What does the "decoy system" refer to?

4. How does maintaining side stations help servers?

5. List three ways that bus persons can assist servers in helping guests.

Exhibit 3
Performing Closing Sidework and Cleaning Duties

Materials needed: Closing duty checklist, a kitchen funnel, a bar towel, pitchers, a putty knife, a condiment requisition, serviceware, cleaning cloths, a broom, a dustpan, caution signs, and a vacuum cleaner.

STEPS:	HOW-TO'S:
1. **Consult your closing duty checklist.**	
2. **Remove soiled linens.**	❑ Check side stations and the entire dining room for scattered soiled linens.
3. **Store condiments.**	❑ Remove condiments from the side stations and return them to the kitchen pantry.
	❑ Use a clean kitchen funnel to combine each type of condiment. Wipe the containers with a damp cleaning cloth before storing them.
	❑ Complete a condiment requisition for the next day. Order enough condiments to bring stock back to par levels.
4. **Store bread and butter.**	❑ Return unused butter and unserved rolls or bread to the kitchen.
	❑ Follow sanitation rules in judging what to save and what to throw out.
	❑ Place unserved butter in the proper kitchen cooler.
5. **Restock silverware.**	❑ Take soiled silverware to the dish room. Follow dish room procedures for unloading soiled silverware.
	❑ Pick up clean silverware from the dish room and restock the side station.

(continued)

Exhibit 3
Performing Closing Sidework and Cleaning Duties *(continued)*

STEPS:	HOW-TO'S:
6. **Break down the coffee station.**	❑ Empty all coffee pots into an approved sink.
	❑ Throw away coffee grounds. Rinse the grounds holder and return it to the coffee maker.
	❑ Take coffee pots to the dish room for washing.
	❑ Throw away open cream or cream that has been out of the refrigerator too long.
	❑ Return all other cream to the correct kitchen cooler.
	❑ Store unused coffee filter packs.
	❑ Wipe the coffee maker and surrounding area with a clean, damp cloth.
	❑ Clean the nozzle head on the grounds holder, and clean the area around the nozzle head.
7. **Break down ice buckets.**	❑ Remove corks, foil scraps, labels, and other debris from buckets to avoid plugging drains.
	❑ Empty ice and water into the appropriate sink.
	❑ Return empty wine and champagne bottles to the bar for inventory.
	❑ Dry the ice buckets with a bar towel.
	❑ Store buckets in the designated side station.
8. **Break down water pitchers.**	❑ Empty ice and water into the appropriate sink.
	❑ Take pitchers to the dish room for washing. Pitchers should be washed and sanitized between meal periods.
	❑ Restock the side stations with clean pitchers.

(continued)

Exhibit 3
Performing Closing Sidework and Cleaning Duties *(continued)*

STEPS:	HOW-TO'S:
9. **Clean the dining room chairs and tables.**	❑ Wipe tabletops and edges with a damp cloth, followed by a dry cloth.
	❑ Use a damp cloth followed by a dry cloth to wipe table legs and bases, and the seats, backs, and legs of chairs.
	❑ If necessary, use a putty knife to scrape gum from the undersides of tables.
	❑ Wipe the seats and backs of booths and banquettes, along with the table legs or bases.
10. **Wipe all furnishings, displays, railings, etc. in the dining room with a damp cloth, followed by a dry cloth.**	
11. **Vacuum carpeted areas.**	❑ Place caution signs.
	❑ Empty the vacuum cleaner bag if necessary.
	❑ Clean up spills with a damp cloth followed by a dry cloth. Report stained or damaged upholstery or carpeting to your supervisor.
	❑ Unwind the cord and plug the vacuum cleaner into an outlet near the door. Make sure the cord is out of the way so that no one trips.
	❑ Begin vacuuming at the far side of the room, and work toward the main entrance.
	❑ Move chairs and tables as needed.
	❑ Pay special attention to corners, carpet edges, high-traffic areas, and under booths or banquettes.
	❑ Vacuum booth seats and upholstered chairs if necessary.

(continued)

Exhibit 3
Performing Closing Sidework and Cleaning Duties *(continued)*

STEPS:	HOW-TO'S:
	❑ Vacuum booth seats and upholstered chairs if necessary.
	❑ Unplug the vacuum and carefully wind the cord. Empty the vacuum cleaner bag if needed.
	❑ Store the vacuum cleaner as soon as you finish vacuuming to prevent accidents.
	❑ Report carpet or equipment problems to your supervisor.
12. Sweep floors.	❑ Remove trash, boxes, and portable equipment from the area.
	❑ Start in a back corner of the area, away from the door.
	❑ Sweep dirt into a small pile. Use a dust mop in areas where there is no greasy residue on the floor.
	❑ Pick up the dirt using a dustpan before sweeping further.
	❑ Keep the broom bristles on the floor at all times to avoid stirring up dust.
	❑ Be sure to sweep around, behind, and under equipment and in aisles and open areas.
	❑ Empty dirt from the dustpan into the trash.
	❑ Continue to sweep and pick up dirt until the entire floor is clean.
13. Reset all tables.	❑ Follow table setup policies for the next meal period.
	❑ In a restaurant with tablecloth dinner service and place mat breakfast service, do not strip and reset tables for breakfast while guests are still seated in the area.

(continued)

Exhibit 3
Performing Closing Sidework and Cleaning Duties *(continued)*

STEPS:	HOW-TO'S:
	❑ Clear the table down to the tablecloth and centerpiece, and wait to reset the table until the guests leave.
	❑ Turn glasses upside-down so they will not collect dust.
	❑ Check the appearance of each table to be sure it is complete.
14. **Straighten, clean, and restock all side stations.**	❑ Take all soiled equipment to the dish room. Wipe the station as needed.
	❑ Wipe the cabinets, counters, and shelves.
	❑ Restock clean dishes, glasses, silverware, and linens at side stations so that they will be fully stocked for the next meal period.
15. **Set music, HVAC, and light system controls, as appropriate.**	❑ Report burned-out light bulbs, equipment malfunctions, etc. to your supervisor so they can be corrected before the next meal period.

Quick Hits

SECTION 18.1—GETTING TO KNOW THE BUS PERSON

- A bus person is a food and beverage employee who does everything possible, within reason, to make each guest's dining experience exactly what he or she wants it to be, and who exceeds guest expectations whenever possible.

- Superior performance standards displayed by bus persons include: being familiar with restaurant menus, greeting guests, clearing and resetting tables promptly, and keeping dining room floors clean.

- The type of china and silverware served in a restaurant helps define its character and image to guests.

- Bus person duties include preparing tables for service, prepping side stations and condiments, busing soiled linens and dining items, and assisting servers whenever possible.

SECTION 18.2—PREPARE TABLES FOR SERVICE

- Preparing tables for service in a prompt, consistent way is important for setting the tone for a pleasing dining experience.

- Fresh, clean linens and folded napkins are a necessary and important part of food presentation. Most restaurants have specific standards for folding their napkins.

- Bus persons are responsible for stocking silverware in an orderly matter and making sure that silverware is clean and sanitary prior to serving.

- Chilled forks and plates are provided with certain menu items and are prepared in a freezer, refrigerator, or a specially designed chiller.

- Some restaurants offer table-side cart service for their guests. Bus persons are responsible for cleaning and preparing these carts for service.

SECTION 18.3—PREPARE SIDE STATIONS, FOOD, AND CONDIMENTS FOR SERVICE

- Restaurants often provide bus persons with a sidework checklist that details the tasks and duties they should perform in addition to their busing duties.

- Bus persons are responsible for preparing butter, condiments, crackers, and sugar for service using proper sanitary procedures.

- When preparing ice or water for service, bus persons use the same sanitary procedures that they would for preparing food. After all, guests consume ice and water.

- Bus persons follow the proper health and sanitation procedures when they set up, maintain, and take down the salad bar after service.

Section 18.4—Perform Busing Duties During and After Service

- Tables must be cleared and reset promptly so that waiting guests can be seated quickly. This also reduces the number of tables that must be reset during closing duties.

- One of the more common tasks performed by bus persons is carrying soiled linens, dishes, silverware, and glasses from the dining area into the kitchen. Bus persons practice proper safety and sanitary procedures when performing this duty.

- Bus persons ease the burden on the laundry department by sorting, counting, and then transporting soiled linens from the dining area to the laundry area.

- When bus persons properly maintain side stations, they help servers save steps and therefore serve guests more efficiently.

- Bus persons can assist servers in helping guests in a number of ways, including: serving beverages, pre-busing soiled dining items, being aware of guests' needs, and responding to dissatisfied guests.

- Bus persons have a number of closing sidework and cleaning duties that they perform to prepare the restaurant for the next day's food service.

Glossary

access control—Steps a property takes to watch or control the property's entrances, especially those that lead to guestrooms or guestroom areas. Access control helps protect the property, its guests, and employees.

accounting division—The hotel division responsible for keeping track of the many business transactions that occur in the hotel and managing the hotel's finances.

activity report—A daily log that gives detailed descriptions of what happened on a particular day and at a particular time during a shift.

airport hotel—A hotel located near a public airport. Although airport hotels vary widely in size and service levels, they are generally full-service.

amenity caddies—Containers on housekeeping carts that hold guest amenities such as stationery, menus, comment cards, soap, shampoo, trash bags, etc.

Americans with Disabilities Act (ADA)—Legislation passed by the U.S. Congress that requires commercial operations both to remove barriers to the disabled in the workplace and to provide facilities for customers with disabilities.

arrivals list—A list of the guests expected to arrive on a given day; used to facilitate the guest registration process.

assets—Items such as money, equipment, supplies, and the personal valuables that have material value.

athletic club—A club may include lodging and dining facilities, as well as recreational facilities such as gymnasiums, swimming pools, and courts for squash, handball, and racquetball; may also include lodging and dining facilities.

attitudinal complaints—Complaints from guests who feel rude or tactless employees have insulted them.

banquets—Special events at a property that can be anything from a small meeting room to a large dinner-dance or reception.

banquet event order (BEO)—A work order for the catering department that confirms final banquet arrangements such as time and place of function, room setup, menu, service notes, gratuity, payment, and guarantee clauses. Also called a function sheet.

banquet servers—Employees that serve food and beverage to banquet guests.

bloodborne pathogens—Viruses, bacteria, and other microorganisms that are carried in a person's bloodstream and other body fluids and can cause the Hepatitis B Virus (HBV), the Human Immunodeficiency Virus (HIV), and other infections.

buffer machine—Floor care equipment that accommodates both brushes and pads to perform some carpet and hard floor cleaning tasks. On hard floors, these machines can be used to buff, burnish, scrub, strip, and refinish.

buffet—An assortment of hot and/or cold foods attractively arranged on platters and offered on a table in a self-service fashion.

bus tub—A container for carrying soiled dishes to the kitchen or dish room for washing.

busing—Clearing soiled linens, dishes, glasses, silverware, and other items from tables.

caddie—A small container used for holding individual packets of sugar and artificial sweeteners.

call accounting system (CAS)—Telephone equipment that enables hotels to place and price local and long distance telephone calls without assistance from phone company operators or hotel staff.

calling order—Sequence in which drinks are made to maximize efficiency, since some, such as frozen drinks, take longer to make while others don't hold up as well once they are poured.

captain—The person on a cruise ship who is responsible for its operation and the safety of all those onboard. The captain sees that all company policies and rules, as well as national and international laws, are followed.

cardiopulmonary resuscitation (CPR)—An emergency procedure in which cardiac massage and artificial respiration are used to maintain circulation of oxygenated blood to the brain in individuals who have no pulse and are not breathing.

career path/ladder—A series of positions an individual may take on the way to his or her ultimate career goal.

cash bank—An amount of money given to a cashier at the start of each workshift so that he or she can handle the various transactions that occur; the cashier is responsible for this cash bank and for all cash, checks, and other negotiable items received during the workshift.

categories—Classifications of hotels according to their size, ownership, price, location, the guests they serve, and other factors.

caution signs—Safety signs that are yellow and black in color; used to warn against a possible hazard, such as a wet floor.

central reservation system—A network for communicating reservations in which each participating property is represented in a computer system database and is required to provide room availability data to the central reservations center on a timely basis.

chafing dish—A metal dish or pan mounted above a heating device and used to cook food or keep it warm at the table.

chain restaurant—A restaurant that is part of a multi-unit organization. Chain restaurants often share the same menu, purchase supplies and equipment cooperatively, and follow operating procedures that have been standardized for every restaurant in the chain.

city club—An urban recreational and social facility that can be categorized as athletic, dining, professional, social, or university.

city ledger accounts—Charge accounts for guests who are not currently staying at the property, such as local customers; usually directly billed each month. Also used for posting charges to guests who have already checked out.

cleaning supply caddies—Containers on housekeeping carts that hold cleaning supplies such as sponges, cleaning cloths, spray cleaners, furniture polish, and other approved cleaning chemicals.

clique—An informal work group that forms within a formal work group when two or more members of the formal group set their own goals and consider those goals to be more important than the goals of the formal group.

close-to-arrival—A yield management availability strategy that allows reservations to be taken for a certain date as long as the guest arrives before that date; for example, a hotel may accept a reservation for a Wednesday night if the guest's actual stay begins Tuesday night.

closed-circuit television—Video surveillance equipment with cameras installed at various property locations and monitors at a central screening station; allows security officers to check many areas of a property from one location.

club manager—The hired professional responsible for guiding all of the elements of a private club's operation. Often referred to as the club's general manager or chief operating officer (COO).

club spa—A spa focused on fitness which offers a variety of professional services on a day-use basis.

combustible—A substance that ignites and burns easily.

condiments—A preparation to enhance the flavor or enjoyment of food. Common condiments include ketchup, mustard, steak sauce, jelly, jam, honey, and syrup.

contract food company—An independent food management service hired by organizations whose primary purpose is not food.

convention—Usually, general sessions and committee meetings convened for a common purpose; the traditional form of annual meeting.

convention and visitors bureau (CVB)—A non-profit service organization that promotes a destination and sometimes offers personnel, housing control, and other services for meetings and conventions.

corporate club—A for-profit private club owned by an individual or a company that sells memberships in the club. Also called a develop or proprietary club.

cost center—Division or department within a hotel that does not directly generate income; cost centers provide support for revenue centers.

country club—A private recreational and social facility for individuals and families who live in the surrounding area.

country code—Telephone code needed to dial phone numbers for a specific country.

credit check—A routine assessment of guest charges and payment methods prior to checkout to make sure each guest's charges are within his or her credit limit.

cruise director—Oversees a staff responsible for managing a ship's entertainers, children's counselors, and guest activities, including selling and coordinating shore excursions.

cruise ship spa—A spa aboard a cruise ship that offers professional services, fitness and wellness activities, and spa cuisine menu choices.

culture—A complex set of beliefs, customs, skills, habits, traditions, and knowledge shared by a group of people; a person's culture teaches him or her what is important and how to act in various situations.

daily specials—A deep cleaning assignment technique where public space cleaners get a different special deep cleaning assignment every day in addition to their regular cleaning duties.

danger signs—Safety signs that are red, black, and white in color; used only in areas where there is an immediate hazard, such as where a caustic cleaning liquid has been spilled.

day spa—A spa that offers professional services on a day-use basis.

decoy system—Bus tubs and dish racks with one dirty dish, glass, etc. in them to show employees where to place dirty dishes.

deep cleaning—Intensive or specialized cleaning undertaken in guestrooms or public areas; often conducted according to a special schedule or on a special project basis.

destination spa—A spa that provides guests with lifestyle improvement and health enhancement through professional services, physical fitness, educational programming, and on-site accommodations. Spa cuisine is served exclusively.

dining club—A private club generally found in office buildings and usually only open for lunch.

disturbance—Anything that interrupts normal activities at the property or upsets the comfort of guests.

diversity—The variety among people relative to age, race, gender, ethnicity, religion, physical ability, sexual orientation, marital status, work experience, income, thinking style, personality, personal appearance, job level, interests, etc., that forms the basis for bringing unique perspectives and creative contributions to the task at hand.

downtown hotel—A full-service hotel that is located in a downtown or business district and caters to business travelers; downtown hotels often have restaurants, a coffee shop, a cocktail lounge, room service, laundry and valet services, a business center, a newsstand and gift shop, and a health club.

drip bucket—A bucket that collects drips of water produced by ice melting in a food and beverage display.

emergency codes—Numbers that identify the type of emergency a property is facing.

emergency hotline—A direct telephone link to the PBX operator that guests can use to report emergencies.

emergency key—A key that opens all guestroom doors, even when they are double-locked.

employee areas—Areas in which only employees on duty are allowed.

energy management—Modifications to existing equipment and employee programs and practices to reduce energy usage; may include improvements in efficiency of equipment or systems, reduction of operating load or operating time, recovery of waste energy, and use of cheaper energy sources.

engineering division—The hotel division responsible for taking care of the hotel's physical plant and controlling energy costs.

equity club—A nonprofit private club whose members buy shares in the club and, after expenses have been paid, invest any revenues left over into improving the club's facilities and services.

exemplary—Worthy of imitation; a model of behavior.

exemplary guest service—Providing guests with not only the service they expect but exceeding their expectations.

express check-out packets—Packages which include a guests' charge statement, instructions for express check-out, and a blank guest comment card; often slipped under guestroom doors of expected check-outs in the early morning.

extracting—The removal of excess moisture from laundered items through a high-speed spin.

first-class/luxury hotels—Hotels with high room rates and exceptional service and amenities.

first-in, first out (FIFO)—A rotational stock system in which products held in inventory the longest are the first to be issued to production areas; when newly received products enter storage areas, they are placed under or behind products already in storage.

flounce—A strip of decorative material attached to the edge of a table.

food and beverage division—The hotel division responsible for preparing and serving food and beverages within the hotel; also includes catering and room service.

food service—Commercial and non-commercial operations that sell food and beverage products for immediate consumption. Examples of commercial food service operations include freestanding restaurants, hotel dining rooms, coffee shops, quick-service restaurants, and ice cream stands. Examples of non-commercial food service operations include schools, health care facilities, businesses, prisons, and military installations.

formal work groups—Teams that are established by an organization to accomplish a task or tasks; formal work groups may consist of division, departments, and work sections and normally have a formal manager or supervisor who coordinates, directs, and controls the work of the group.

franchise—Refers to (1) the authorization given by one company to another to sell its unique produce and service, or (2) the name of the business format or product that is being franchised.

franchisee—The person or company that purchases from a franchisor the right to use a franchise concept; the franchisee must usually agree to maintain the franchisor's business and quality standards.

franchisor—A company that owns a trademark, product, or business-format franchise concept and sells the right to use it.

front desk computer system—Computerized system that includes functions for reservations, check-in, room assignment, point-of-sale, check-out, and many other common front desk tasks.

front office logbook—A record of important events and decisions—such as unusual events, guest complaints or requests, and other relevant information—that occurred during previous shifts.

front sheets—Pages within a logbook in which duties and services performed by bell services staff during a shift, as well as other important information for bell staff, are recorded.

function rooms—Rooms where banquets, meetings, and receptions are held.

functional areas—Divisions within a hotel that are organized based on the services they provide. Common functional areas include the rooms division, food and beverage division, marketing division, engineering division, accounting division, human resources division, and security division.

garnishes—Decorative edible items used to enhance the visual appeal of another food item;

common garnishes include parsley, lemon or orange slices or wedges, cherries, tomato wedges or cherry tomatoes, carved or grated carrot, chocolate curls, and endive.

glass froster—A cold storage unit, like a small refrigerator, that cools glasses so they frost when you take them out.

group reservation master—A reservation record for group business; includes information such as group name, name and number of group contact, rates, number of rooms, cut-off date, and master billing instructions.

guaranteed reservation—A reservation that assures the guest that a room will be held until check-out time of the day following the day of arrival; the guest guarantees payment for the room, even if it is not used, unless the reservation is properly canceled.

guest areas—Places such as guestroom hallways where only guests, their visitors, and on-duty employees are allowed.

guest call sheet—A list of guest wake-up calls that includes each guest's name and room number and day, date, and time the call should be made.

guest cycle—The stages of a guest's interactions with a property: pre-arrival, arrival, occupancy, and departure.

guest history file—A record of personal and financial information about a guest that can help the hotel serve the guest on return visits.

guest history system—A collection of guest history files, often in an electronic database.

guest information directory—A set of file folders or a three-ring binder with tabs that details local restaurants, attractions, recreation options, and other services that may be requested by guests.

guest mix—The variety and percentage distribution of hotel guests—individual, group, business, leisure, and so on—who stay at a hotel or patronize a restaurant.

guest service—Meeting any and all guest needs in the way that guests want and expect them to be met.

guest service-related complaints—Guest complaints related to service problems such as long waiting times, a lack of help with luggage, untidy rooms, telephone difficulties, wake-up call errors, food or beverage quality problems, or ignored requests for additional supplies or amenities.

guests—The consumers who stay at hotels.

Hazard Communication Standard—The Occupational Safety and Health Administration's regulation requiring employers to inform employees about possible hazards related to the chemicals they use on the job.

Heimlich maneuver—A generally accepted technique for saving a choking victim by squeezing the trapped air out of the victim's lungs, forcing the obstruction out.

highway hotel—A hotel built next to a highway. These hotels typically feature large property signs, an entrance where travelers can leave their cars as they check in, and a swimming pool. Parking space is plentiful and the atmosphere is informal.

hospitality industry—Lodging and food service businesses that provide short-term and transitional lodging and/or food; sometimes entertainment and travel are also included as part of the hospitality industry.

hot box—An insulated or heated cart used for transporting food and keeping it warm.

hotel chain—A group of affiliated hotels that usually share a common name.

house account—A guest account that allows guests with approved credit to charge restaurant meals and drinks to their rooms.

human resources division—The hotel division responsible for recruiting, hiring, orienting, training, evaluating, motivating, rewarding, disciplining, developing, promoting, and communicating with hotel employees.

image—How others perceive hospitality employees based on appearance, personality, and posture.

incident report—A report that specifically focuses on one unusual event that happened during a shift and that directly affected security, such as crimes, conflicts between people, accidents, fires, weather or natural disasters, and other emergencies.

incoming mail logbook—A logbook in which employees record the time a package arrives, the name of the guest it is addressed to, and where it will be stored. Guests sign the logbook when they pick up their mail.

independent hotel—A hotel with no chain or franchise affiliation; it may be owned by an individual proprietor or a group of investors.

independent restaurant—A food service operation owned by an owner or group of owners with one or more properties having no chain relationship. Menus, food purchase specification, operating procedures, etc. may differ among the owned properties.

informal work groups—Voluntary alliances that are formed by friendships or common interests, rather than dictated by the organization; depending on the situation, informal groups might support or oppose management actions.

institutional food service—A food service operation that provides food service in closed, non-commercial environments, such as hospitals, schools, or correctional institutions.

international access code—A code needed to access an international telephone line for making calls to foreign countries.

international guests—Guests from outside the United States; international guests may need special services such as language services and currency exchange.

interview—A formal face-to-face meeting to evaluate a job candidate.

key-return box— A locked box with an opening for people to return room keys.

layers—The change of strength as water passes through ground coffee; the first third of the pot is too weak, the second third is too strong, and the final third is too weak.

least cost route (LCR)—The component of a call accounting system that routes a dialed call to the type of lines that can carry the call at the lowest cost to the hotel.

limited service hotels—Hotels that do not offer the full range of services customarily associated with hotels. For example, they do not have restaurants or bars.

linen roll-ups—Silverware wrapped in linen napkins.

linen running—Transporting clean linens and guest amenities from the laundry to housekeeping closets.

linens—Cloth articles such as sheets, towels, tablecloths, and napkins.

lockout/tagout—The placement of a lock and tag on an energy isolating device to disable the machinery or equipment, thereby preventing the release of hazardous energy while employees perform repair and maintenance activities.

log book—A record of important activities that take place during a shift.

luggage cart—A wheeled cart used by bell staff for transporting guest luggage safely and securely.

luggage claim ticket—A two-part ticket used to locate and match stored luggage; one portion of the ticket is attached to the luggage and the other portion is given to the guest.

maintenance request form—A form used by maintenance employees to identify items that require repair.

maintenance request log—A log book to document calls or requests from guests requiring maintenance-related assistance; usually kept at the front desk.

maintenance tool log—A log book used by maintenance employees to sign out and check in tools.

management company—A company that manages hotels for owners, typically for a combination of fees and a share of revenues. A management company may or may not have any of its own funds invested in a hotel it manages.

market—Groups of guests with similar characteristics. Some markets for the hotel industry include corporate individuals, corporate groups, convention and association groups, leisure travelers, long-term stay/relocation guests, airline-related guests, government and military travelers, and regional getaway guests.

marketing division—The hotel division responsible for identifying prospective guests for the hotel, conforming the products and services of the hotel as much as possible to meet the needs of those prospects, and persuading prospects to become guests.

master key—A key that can open all guest-room doors that are not double-locked.

Material Safety Data Sheet (MSDS)—A form mandated by the Occupational Safety and Health Administration (OSHA) that informs employees about potentially hazardous materials used in the workplace. The product information from the manufacturer should include chemical identity, hazardous ingredients, physical and chemical characteristics, fire and explosion hazard data, reactivity data, health hazards, precautions for safe handling and use, control measures, and manufacturer's name, address, and telephone number. Vendors and suppliers of hazardous materials must provide an MSDS for each product. The property must make these forms available to employees at all times.

mechanical complaints—Guest complaints concerning problems such as temperature control, lighting, electricity, room furnishings, vending machines, door keys, plumbing, television sets, elevators, and so forth.

medical spa—A business that provides health and wellness care in an environment which combines spa services and conventional and complementary therapies and treatments.

meeting—A planned event in which a group of people gather together to accomplish something.

meeting planner—Someone who plans meetings for an association, a corporation, or some other group.

membership dues—The cost to a private club member for the exclusivity provided by the club's limited membership. Membership dues subsidize the club's operating costs and fixed charges.

mid-price hotels—Hotels that offer facilities and services similar to those at first-class/luxury hotels, but at average rates. They have restaurants and bars, and many have meeting space. Average prices vary by market.

mineral springs spa—A spa offering a source of natural mineral water, thermal springs, or seawater used in hydrotherapy treatments.

minimum stay—A yield management availability strategy requiring that a reservation must be for at least a specified number of nights to be accepted.

miter—A method for contouring a sheet or blanket to fit the corner of a mattress in a smooth and neat manner; the results are sometimes referred to as "square corners" or "hospital corners."

mouth-to-mouth resuscitation—An emergency procedure used to restore breathing when the victim is not choking.

non-guaranteed reservation—A reservation agreement in which the hotel agrees to hold a room for the guest until a stated reservation cancellation hour on the day of arrival; the property is not guaranteed payment in the case of a no-show.

Occupational Safety and Health Administration (OSHA)—An independent federal regulatory agency that develops and enforces mandatory workplace safety and health standards, sets up regulations, conducts inspections, issues citations, and proposes penalties for noncompliance; helps keep employees safe by regulating sanitation, safety, and first aid in the workplace.

package pass—A form that must accompany items or packages removed from the property by employees.

par—The standard quantity of a particular inventory item that must be on hand to support daily operations.

patrols—Regular checks of a property's building and grounds.

personal protective equipment—Equipment designed to protect employees from serious workplace injuries or illnesses resulting from contact with chemical, radiological, physical, electrical, mechanical, or other workplace hazards; examples include face shields, safety glasses, hard hats, gloves, earplugs, respirators, coveralls, vests, and goggles.

personality—Distinctive character, temperament, and behavioral traits of a person; a pleasing, professional personality is desirable in hospitality employees.

point-of-sale (POS) system—An electronic cash register system that transfers a guest's charges from hotel sales outlets—such as restaurants, gift shops, and room service—to the guest's folio at the front desk.

posting system—System in which bell attendants are staged or assigned so they can quickly help guests on a rotating basis.

post-sorting—Separating linen types and sizes that were missed in pre-sorting.

power failure—A loss of electrical power, usually triggered by an emergency such as sever weather, vandalism, or acts of terrorism.

pre-busing—Removing items from dining tables that guests no longer need, in order to keep the dining experience a pleasant one throughout the meal.

preregistration—A process by which sections of a registration card or its equivalent are completed for guests arriving with reservations. Room and rate assignment, creation of a guest folio, and other functions may also be part of preregistration activity.

pre-treating—Treating heavily soiled laundry with a spotting solution or in a soak tank before washing.

preventive maintenance—Inspecting, servicing, adjusting, or performing minor repairs to machinery, equipment, and areas of a lodging property before major damage or malfunction occurs.

preventive maintenance checklist—A checklist used by maintenance employees when performing preventive maintenance inspections.

professionalism—Professional image, attitude, character, standards, and conduct.

property management system (PMS)—A computerized system that helps hotel managers and other personnel carry out a number of front-of-the-house and back-of-the-house functions. A PMS can support a variety of applications software—such as reservations, rooms management, guest accounting, and internal control functions—that help managers in their data-gathering and reporting responsibilities.

public areas—Place that are open to all people, such as hotel lobbies.

public space cleaner—A housekeeping department employee who cleans almost all areas of the property, except guestrooms.

public space daily assignment sheet—A list of all the tasks that public space cleaners must perform for the day in the order in which they are assigned to do it.

purser—The second in command within the hotel department of a cruise ship and the ship's banker, information officer, human resources director, and complaint handler.

ramekin—A small receptacle used to hold butter and sauces.

rate controls—Restrictions on available rate categories to control a hotel's average rate during high-demand periods.

reception—A social event with food and beverages.

registration record—A guest record created upon check-in; includes guest name and address, payment and billing information, planned length of stay, special needs, and guest signature.

repetitive stress injuries—Motion injuries to muscles and joints caused when the same actions are repeated throughout the day.

reservation call conversion form—A form used by reservationists to document all calls received during their shift; usually includes space for documenting inquiries converted into room bookings as well as a space for non-converted calls.

reservation confirmation form—A document provided to guests upon request that confirms the important points of a guest reservation, such as dates, rates, and number of guests.

reservation record—A collection of data that identifies a guest and his or her anticipated occupancy needs before arrival at the property; enables the hotel to personalize guest service and accurately schedule staff.

resort hotel—A hotel, usually located in a desirable vacation spot, that offers fine dining, exceptional service, activities unavailable at most other properties, and many amenities.

resort/hotel spa—A spa that is within a resort or hotel. It provides professional spa services, fitness and wellness activities, and spa cuisine menu choices.

résumé—A formal, written presentation of an individual's work experience, skills, and education. Job applicants use résumés to obtain job interviews.

revenue center—A division or department within a hotel that directly generates income through sales of products or services to guests.

revenue management—The process of using forecasted sales information to determine pricing or room rate strategies in order to maximize room revenue.

room assignment sheet—A list of all rooms that each guestroom attendant needs to clean during his or her shift; typically includes room status codes and terms that can help a guestroom attendant decide which rooms to clean first.

room forecasting—Making an educated guess about future trends, events, sales levels, etc., based on data collected both within and outside an operation.

room rack—A system, either computerized or manual, for organizing rooms according to their current availability or status.

rooming—The process of assigning a guest room and escorting guests and their luggage to that room.

rooms division—The largest, and usually most profitable, division in a hotel. It typically consists of four departments: front office, reservations, housekeeping, and uniformed service.

safe-deposit box—Boxes at or near the front desk made available to all guests for storing valuable items for safekeeping during their stay.

safety instruction signs—Signs that are green and white or black and white; used to give general instructions, such as to tell employees not to eat in storage areas.

scripts—Standard texts that walk reservationists through a sale in the order that is most efficient for them and the caller.

security division—The hotel division responsible for the protection of guests and their property, employees and their property, and the hotel itself.

service trays—Trays used by servers to help transport food, beverages, dishes, and equipment throughout the restaurant or banquet facility.

side station—A service stand that holds supplies, such as tableware, ice, condiments, dairy products, and some beverages, for easy access; helps servers work more efficiently by reducing the distance they have to go to get the supplies guests need.

sidework checklist—A list of routine setup and cleanup work—such as restocking server supply stations, wiping service trays, folding napkins, and filling salt and pepper shakers—that must be done before and after dining shifts.

social catering—An independent catering service that hires food servers as needed.

social club—A private club whose members have no affiliation except that they enjoy being in each other's company.

sorting—Separating linens and uniforms according to use, fabric type, color, and department.

spa director—The employee in charge of the spa who manages all other employees.

spa industry—The hospitality segment that specializes in wellness. Most modern spas offer a wide variety of services to help people lose weight, get in shape, relax, or be pampered.

specialist tasks—A deep cleaning assignment technique. A public space cleaner is assigned to perform a lengthy deep cleaning assignment instead of his or her regular cleaning duties; the public space cleaner becomes a "specialist" in that task for the day.

spirit—A lodging employee's positive attitude, feeling of pride and belonging, and desire to please and satisfy guests.

standard food and drink abbreviations—Common abbreviations used in a restaurant to speed the process of taking and communicating food and beverage orders.

standards of conduct—Performance standards which serve as a foundation for behavior that is or is not acceptable in the workplace; prohibited conduct generally includes behaviors that are disruptive, unprofessional, illegal, or otherwise in violation of workplace policies.

stay controls—Restrictions on reservations based upon how long a guest plans to stay.

steam extraction—A carpet and upholstery cleaning technique that uses a combination of detergent, hot water, and steam to remove dirt from the base of the fibers as well as from the surface.

suburban hotel—A hotel located in a suburban area. Suburban hotels typically belong to a major hotel chain and have 250 to 500 rooms as well as restaurants, bars, and other amenities found at most downtown hotels.

suggestive selling—Techniques used to encourage guests to buy certain menu items with the objectives of increasing sales of the most profitable items and increasing the check average.

suspicious person—Anyone—an employee, visitor, or guests—who gives others the feeling that something might be wrong; the way people look or the way they act might make them appear suspicious.

table linen requisition—A written order that identifies the type and amount of linens needed by food and beverage outlets for the next day.

table-side cart service—A table-service style in which specially trained staff members prepare menu items beside the guests' tables using a cart; the food is prepared and plated on the cart, then served to the guest. Also called French service.

table skirt—Pleated or folded linen used to decorate tables. Clips or T-pins are often used to attach table skirts to tablecloths.

target markets—Market segments—such as business travelers or families—that a property identifies as having good potential, and at which marketing activities are aimed.

taxi line—A staging area outside larger hotels where taxis can wait for guests who need a ride.

temperature danger zone—The temperature range of 40° to 140° F (4° to 60° C), where food spoilage is most likely to occur.

tip pooling—A policy which requires that all tips earned by tipped employees during a shift be pooled and then redistributed evenly so that everyone receives an equal amount.

trade show—An event at which goods and services in a specific industry are exhibited and demonstrated.

travel agent no-show/cancellation form—A document used for recording cancelled and no-show reservations that were booked through a travel agency; completed forms are mailed to the travel agent and a copy is kept for the property's records.

turnaround day—The day when a cruise ship finishes one cruise and starts another one.

turn-down service—A special service provided by the housekeeping department in which a room attendant enters the guestroom in the early evening to restock supplies, tidy the room, and turn down the guest bed.

uniform authorization form—Request for an employee uniform that lists employee's size and type of uniform to be issued.

university club—A private club for university graduates.

unusual complaints—Guest complaints that lodging employees may not have control over, such as lack of a swimming pool, lack of transportation, early lounge or restaurant closing times, bad weather, and so on.

upselling—A sales technique whereby a guest is offered a more expensive alternative than what he or she originally requested and then persuaded to select the upgrade based on its features and benefits, as well as the guest's needs.

VIP (Very Important Person)—Guest who receives special treatment; usually offered the very finest services and accommodations a property has to offer.

washing—Cleaning linens in washing machines with the correct time, temperature, agitation, and chemicals.

waste management—Management and disposal of solid wastes, including aggressive recycling programs for solid wastes such as paper, aluminum, and plastics.

water management—Management of the cleanliness, quantity, and quality of water; includes reducing the amount of fresh water used on a lodging property and properly treating and disposing of wastewater.

white tablecloth restaurant—A luxury restaurant that features fine dining and employs well-trained, creative chefs and skilled food servers; generally small and independently operated.

yield management—The process of using forecasted sales information to determine pricing or room rate strategies in order to maximize room revenue.

Index